Witnesses to the End of the Cold War

Witnesses to the End of the Cold War

∴

EDITED BY

William C. Wohlforth

The Johns Hopkins University Press

BALTIMORE AND LONDON

© 1996 The Johns Hopkins University Press
All rights reserved. Published 1996
Printed in the United States of America on acid-free paper

05   04   03   02   01   00   99   98   97   96   5   4   3   2   1

The Johns Hopkins University Press
2715 North Charles Street
Baltimore, Maryland 21218-4319
The Johns Hopkins Press Ltd., London

Library of Congress Cataloging-in-Publication Data
Witnesses to the end of the Cold War / edited by William C. Wohlforth.
    p.   cm.
    Includes bibliographical references and index.
    ISBN 0-8018-5382-6 (alk. paper)
    1. Cold War.   2. World politics—1945–   3. United States—Foreign
relations—Soviet Union. [1. Soviet Union—Foreign relations—
United States.]   I. Wohlforth, William Curti, 1959–
D843.W524   1996
327.73047—dc20   96-13719

A catalog record for this book is available from the British Library.

Contents •

This book is a contribution to understanding the most consequential international event of the past half-century: the ending of the Cold War between the United States and the Soviet Union. Chapters 1 through 6 contain the transcripts of the 1993 conference of former U.S. and Soviet decision makers described in Don Oberdorfer's "Introduction: The Princeton Conference." They are followed by four chapters in which scholars grapple with key issues raised by the discussants and the events they considered: the role of personality and leadership, the causes and consequences of changing perceptions, and the implications for contending theories of international relations.

As the decision makers' testimony and the scholars' analyses attest, the end of the Cold War was an intricate and complex result of diplomatic and military action and social and political upheaval in the Soviet world. In hindsight, the Eastern European revolutions of 1989 and the dissolution of the Soviet Union itself in December 1991 stand out. But the focus in this volume is on the intricate diplomacy that preceded those upheavals and that facilitated a transformation of superpower relations from the Cold War depths of 1983 to the emergence of deep détente by 1989.

The transformation of superpower relations in the period that this volume covers is only part of the end of the Cold War, but it is an important part that is too often ignored because of knowledge of what followed. The improvement in U.S.-Soviet relations that was achieved by 1989 was unprecedented in the post–World War II era. And the diplomatic achievements of that period set the stage for what followed. It is impossible to understand the events of 1989 and 1991 without reference to the diplomacy that preceded them.

The period highlighted in this book also commands attention because it occurred within the Cold War context of bipolarity, nuclear deterrence, the division of Europe, and the continued existence of clashing political ideologies on the two sides of the East-West divide. After all, the basic question during the Cold War was not "What will we do if Communism collapses?" Rather, the perennial questions posited continuing conflict: "How do we improve matters *given* the ideological and geopolitical circumstances? Should we contain and deter or engage and reassure the Soviet Union?" And in international politics more generally, the maxim "Wait until your rival's socioeconomic system collapses" hardly constitutes helpful advice in most circumstances. Rather, the question is, "Are there strategies for overcoming long-standing rivalries, and which type of strategy is appropriate to which circumstances?" The superpowers' experience between 1983 and 1989 may contain vital lessons for the heated debates over what the proper strategy for the Cold War was, and for the more general question of when different strategies might work to attenuate international tension.

The political debate in both the United States and Russia over the policies that Reagan and Gorbachev pursued during these years illustrates the importance of the period discussed here. Few are the Russians who argue that force should have been used to arrest the revolutions in East-Central Europe in 1989. Instead, the focus of criticism usually is Gorbachev's strategy up to that point. Critics contend that the Gorbachev team should have foreseen the disintegration that its policies would cause and should therefore have moderated those policies. Further, they argue, Gorbachev and his advisors should have bargained harder with the West earlier in the game and thus received more in return for Soviet concessions.[1]

Similarly, the Bush administration's handling of Communism's collapse is comparatively noncontroversial in the United States. But debates rage over whether the Reagan administration's combination of tough talk, big defense increases, and eventual willingness to negotiate with Moscow speeded or delayed the end of the Cold War. Did the U.S. military buildup and tough negotiating posture simply make things needlessly difficult for a Gorbachev bent on bringing the Cold War to an end for his own domestic purposes? Or was the Reagan combination of containment and engagement the perfect balance of incentives to nudge Moscow toward détente on Western terms? Or were arms control and the diplomacy of détente essentially irrelevant to an outcome that was foreordained by the decline and fall of Communism?[2] All of these arguments are simply post–Cold War versions of longstanding debates going back to the origins of U.S. containment policy in the 1940s. Not surprisingly, the discussions reprinted below in chapter 2 fed immediately into a revived debate on the role of the Reagan-era arms buildup.

Oral history is an indispensable but limited source. Historical accounts can neither ignore the recollections of participants nor rely on them exclusively or uncritically. Memories are imperfect, and they are influenced by knowledge of the outcomes of key events. Participants in epochal events possess unique insights but also have a stake in particular interpretations. The transcripts reprinted here reflect two additional considerations. The decision makers who participated in the Princeton Conference came from the wings of their respective governments which favored engagement between the superpowers and cooperation on arms control and regional issues. Soviet and American hard-liners were heard at the conference only indirectly, through the arguments and assessments of their bureaucratic opponents. Such an account leads to more agreement and coherence about what was going on than would have been the case had hard-liners been present. But this circumstance is the unavoidable result of bringing together actual participants in the negotiations, for as a rule, hard-line opponents to negotiations do not involve themselves directly in them. And the focus on participants (who represented a line that eventually prevailed in domestic debates on both sides) also facilitated dialogue *between* rather than *within* the Russian and American teams.

In addition, the conference was open. The participants were not interviewed by panels of scholars armed with documents, ready to contest each and every judgment. They were not secluded from the public and asked to speak off the record. Instead, they were encouraged to respond and relate to each other in a public forum, guided by the questions of Don Oberdorfer, a veteran diplomatic correspondent with an encyclopedic knowledge of the events in question. And, as Oberdorfer notes in his introduction to the conference transcripts, the intellectual rewards of this approach proved to be extraordinary. The transcripts show that these were reflective people who took the time to think through the meaning of the epochal events they had helped to shape. During the conference, they began to recreate the intellectual atmosphere they had experienced when negotiating for their respective countries. For anyone who believes that historical explanation requires understanding the thoughts that guide those whose actions make events, this will be an indispensable source.

Final Technical Note

Chapters 1 through 6 consist of transcripts, only cosmetically edited, of two days of fascinating give-and-take discussion. Emendations were made only to enhance clarity and stylistic consistency. Some minor editorial changes and clarifications are indicated by brackets; larger clarifications are made in endnotes. Ellipses indicate pauses in speech or interruptions caused by audio difficulties or minor distractions. In no instance was the meaning of the original text altered, and there were no additions of text after the fact.

My procedure for editing was as follows. First, I checked the stenographic transcript against audio and video tapes of the conference to catch any speech missed or misunderstood by the stenographers. I resolved conflicts of dates or names by checking the historical record and, in some cases, checking with participants. Second, I edited the text, omitting some material in instances where the discourse was repetitive, speech was unclear, or references were made to goings-on in the conference hall. In a very few instances, I removed text containing digressions unrelated to the subject at hand or invalidated by subsequent discussion.[3] I made the minor grammatical and syntactical corrections that are inevitably necessary to render spoken English more easily readable. I then sent the transcripts to the participants for their review, in order to ensure that my editing had not altered their intended meaning in any instance. In all cases, their suggestions concerned stylistic changes for purposes of greater clarity, or corrections of fact or spelling that had slipped through my initial editing.

The only more complete original source is the videotape produced by C-SPAN, which covered the conference and broadcast some sessions. The full videotape is on file in the C-SPAN archive at Purdue University.

Acknowledgments •

This book is organized around the transcripts of the Princeton Conference on the End of the Cold War, which was held under the auspices of the John Foster Dulles Program for the Study of Leadership in International Affairs at the Woodrow Wilson School of Public and International Affairs, Princeton University. I am grateful to Henry S. Bienen, dean of the Woodrow Wilson School, for his help in making the conference possible. I thank Fred Greenstein for involving me in the project and providing wise counsel along the way. Fred Greenstein and Don Oberdorfer were the key organizers of the conference, and they both were immensely helpful to me in preparing this book. I am also indebted to Robert English for his research assistance and to Boris Makarenko for his crucial help in comparing and rectifying the audio and written records of the conference proceedings.

The Diplomats

Alexander Aleksandrovich Bessmertnykh was Deputy Foreign Minister of the Soviet Union in 1986–87, First Deputy Foreign Minister in 1988–89, Soviet Ambassador to the United States in 1990, and Foreign Minister of the Soviet Union in 1991. He regularly attended meetings between Foreign Minister Eduard Shevardnadze and Secretary of State George Shultz, and attended four of the five Reagan-Gorbachev summits. Previously he had served in the Soviet Embassy in Washington and had been in charge of the United States and Canada Department of the Soviet Ministry of Foreign Affairs. He is currently President of the Foreign Policy Association, Moscow.

Frank C. Carlucci III was National Security Advisor to President Reagan in 1987–88, and Secretary of Defense in 1988–89. After many years as a foreign service officer, serving in Africa and Latin America, Carlucci was U.S. Ambassador to Portugal (1975–78), Deputy Secretary of Central Intelligence (1978–81), and Deputy Secretary of Defense (1981–82). He is now Chairman of the Carlyle Group, an investment banking firm.

Anatoly Sergeevich Chernyaev was personal advisor on foreign affairs to General Secretary Mikhail S. Gorbachev in 1986–91, and a member of the International Policy Commission of the Central Committee (CC) of the Communist Party of the Soviet Union (CPSU) in 1988–91. Previously, he had served for more than three decades in the International Department of the CC-CPSU, specializing in Western European and U.S. affairs. He published a memoir of his "six years with Gorbachev," *Shest' let s Gorbachevym*, in 1993. Chernyaev is currently associated with the International Foundation for Social and Political Studies (the Gorbachev Foundation) in Moscow.

Jack F. Matlock Jr. was Director of Soviet Affairs on the National Security Council staff in 1983–87, and U.S. Ambassador to the Soviet Union in 1987–91. He had previously been Ambassador to Czechoslovakia in 1981–83. A career foreign service officer until his recent retirement, Matlock is fluent in Russian and has written widely on Soviet and Russian affairs. He published a memoir of his years as Ambassador to the Soviet Union, *Autopsy of an Empire*, in 1995 and is currently George F. Kennan Professor at the School of History at the Institute for Advanced Study in Princeton.

Paul H. Nitze was Ambassador-at-Large and Special Advisor to President Reagan and Secretary Shultz on arms control in 1985–89. His career in government spanned the entire Cold War, beginning in the Roosevelt administration. In 1950 he headed the State Department's Policy Planning Staff, and during that period he wrote NSC-68, the document that set forth the basic U.S. strategy of containment. Nitze has published two books of reflections on his four decades of involvement in U.S. national security policy: *From Hiroshima to Glasnost* (1989) and *Tension between Opposites* (1993).

Pavel Palazchenko was special assistant and interpreter for Mikhail Gorbachev in 1985–91. Previously he had been a career diplomat in the Soviet Ministry of Foreign Affairs. He is currently associated with the International Foundation for Social and Political Studies (the Gorbachev Foundation) in Moscow.

Rozanne L. Ridgway was Assistant Secretary for European and Canadian Affairs in 1985–89. A career diplomat with the U.S. Foreign Service, she had previously served as U.S. Ambassador to Finland (1975–80) and the German Democratic Republic (1982–85). She is currently co-chair of the Atlantic Council of the United States.

George P. Shultz was Secretary of State from 1982 to 1989. He had previously served in three other cabinet positions: Secretary of Labor, Director of the Office of Management and Budget, and Secretary of the Treasury. He is an economist by training, and his career combines government, scholarship, and business. He was a professor at MIT; dean of the Graduate School of Business at the University of Chicago; professor at Stanford's Business School; and president of the Bechtel Corporation. Now a Distinguished Fellow at the Hoover Institution, Shultz published his memoir of his years as Secretary of State, *Turmoil and Triumph*, in 1993.

Sergei Tarasenko was principal Policy Assistant to Foreign Minister Eduard Shevardnadze in 1985–91. He was Director of the USSR Ministry of Foreign Affairs Estimate and Planning Administration, and Deputy Chief of the Ministry's United States and Canada Department. He is currently associated with the Foreign Policy Association, Moscow.

Invited Guests

Lawrence Gershwin was National Intelligence Officer for Strategic Programs in the Central Intelligence Agency in 1982 when he wrote National Intelligence Estimate 11-3/8-82, "Soviet Capabilities for Strategic Nuclear Conflict, 1982–92." He currently holds the same position in the CIA.

Harold Saunders is a retired career foreign service officer involved in Middle Eastern affairs in general and the Arab-Israeli peace process in particular. He was Assistant Secretary of State for Near Eastern Affairs during the Carter administration.

Moderators

Fred I. Greenstein is Professor of Politics and Director of the John Foster Dulles Program for the Study of Leadership in International Affairs at Princeton University.

Don Oberdorfer Jr. was Chief Diplomatic Correspondent for the *Washington Post* until his retirement in 1993. As a *Post* correspondent, he covered the events that led to the end of the Cold

War. In addition, Oberdorfer is the author of *The Turn: From the Cold War to a New Era* (1991), a detailed account of these events for which he interviewed most of the key players, including the Princeton Conference participants.

Daniel Schorr is Senior News Analyst for National Public Radio (NPR).

Part I

Witnesses' Testimony

∴

The Princeton Conference   ∴

DON OBERDORFER

In late February 1993, Princeton University played host to a group of men and women who had participated in some of the most important diplomacy of the twentieth century. Led by former U.S. secretary of state George P. Shultz and former Soviet foreign minister Alexander Bessmertnykh, two teams of former high-ranking officials spent two and a half days reliving and analyzing the diplomatic and political episodes of the mid-1980s which eased the global bipolar conflict known as the Cold War.

In a stimulating academic setting, the participants in this extraordinary gathering of former adversaries reflected on the experiences they had shared on opposite sides of the U.S.-Soviet bargaining tables. Their aim was to obtain a clearer understanding of what had happened in those dramatic episodes, and of how they and the established political leaders of the two most important nations had coped with the problems before them.

This "retrospective on the end of the Cold War" grew out of conversations between myself and Prof. Fred Greenstein, director of the John Foster Dulles Program for the Study of Leadership in International Affairs of Princeton's Woodrow Wilson School of Public and International Affairs, as I was researching and writing my book on the negotiations that ended the Cold War.[1] Interviews with nearly all the senior participants in the U.S.-Soviet negotiations provided the core of my contemporary history on the historic developments between the two powers. How enlightening it might be, Fred and I mused, if we could arrange for key participants to sit down with one another to compare notes and deepen their—and our—knowledge.

After much discussion among ourselves and with Dean Donald Stokes of the Woodrow Wilson School, Greenstein and I met in Princeton in June 1992 with former Secretary of State Shultz, who agreed to head the American delegation. Shultz was in Princeton to participate in the fiftieth reunion of his Princeton class of 1942. His willingness to participate, as Greenstein noted at one point in the conference, was a decisive factor in recruiting other former officials on both sides.

As the participants from Washington and Moscow traveled to the small New Jersey town for the conference, which was scheduled for February 25–27, those of us who had designed the meetings wondered how they would get along in a very different setting—in truth, in a different world—from the one they had known. We wondered too if the meetings would add significantly to the store of documentation and knowledge which had already accumulated about the final episodes of the Cold War.

As it turned out, we need not have wondered.

On a human level, the participants quickly warmed to one another, reliving experiences that for each of them had been among the most intense—and memorable—of their careers. An opening dinner hosted by Princeton's president, Harold Shapiro, broke the ice, and the increasingly candid discussions seemed to reduce lingering inhibitions. As the conference proceeded, the Americans and Russians clustered in small groups at meals and breaks, often surrounded by Princeton students, faculty members, and other invited guests. Seeing former diplomatic competitors with their heads together in intimate conversation over coffee or tea was a commonplace sight. The participants seemed to become progressively more relaxed, inside as well as outside the main discussions, which were witnessed by an audience of several hundred persons and taped by C-SPAN, the U.S. cable television network. By the end of the meetings, many of the participants, having shared a new set of intense experiences, parted as friends.

On the substantive side we learned, especially from the Russians, many things that were new, even to those of us who had closely followed the negotiations of the 1980s, and other things that cast new light on developments we had thought we understood.

For example, Sergei Tarasenko, the former personal assistant to Foreign Minister Eduard Shevardnadze, provided the first strong confirmation of the fascinating account, provided by a defector (Oleg Gordievsky, former deputy KGB chief in London) in the pre-Gorbachev early 1980s, that claimed that the KGB had warned Moscow's leaders of an impending U.S. surprise nuclear attack against the Soviet Union. Tarasenko, at the time an official of the Foreign Ministry's United States and Canada Department, recalled being shown a top secret KGB paper warning of a potential U.S. "first strike" against Soviet command centers, and being asked for suggestions on how to counter such a U.S. threat.

Gorbachev had personally concluded by 1986, his second year in office, that "there was no real threat of an attack from the United States against the Soviet Union," despite Reagan's bellicose rhetoric and the U.S. military buildup, according to Anatoly Chernyaev, who was Gorbachev's national security assistant. It was this fundamental change in the Soviet strategic viewpoint, a "deep inner conviction," Chernyaev called it, that was at the heart of Gorbachev's determination to reduce the massive pileup of nuclear arms on both sides through dramatic strides in negotiations.

Chernyaev shed new light on the origins of the famous October 1986 Reagan-Gorbachev summit in Reykjavik, Iceland—one of the most spectacular U.S.-Soviet meetings of all time—at which the two leaders seriously negotiated about the elimination of most or all of their ballistic missiles and discussed elimination of all U.S. and Soviet nuclear arms. The former Soviet national security assistant said that Gorbachev, while vacationing in the Crimea two months earlier, had spontaneously come up with the idea of offering Reagan massive arms reductions at an early summit to be held in London or Reykjavik. The Soviet leader ordered his government secretly to prepare a proposal to slash by half ballistic missiles, nuclear-armed submarines, and heavy bombers. In the process of preparing the proposal, the Soviet military insisted that curbs on the U.S. Strategic Defense Initiative (SDI) be part of the package deal.

Gorbachev's insistence that Reagan's cherished SDI program be confined to the laboratory eventually caused the collapse of the spectacular summit on its final day. The Princeton Conference heard for the first time that the breakup of the summit might have been averted if Marshal Sergei Akhromeev, chief of staff of the Soviet armed forces and a man who was much praised in other respects by conference participants on both sides, had permitted Gorbachev to present a compromise proposal. According to Tarasenko, Shevardnadze had angrily charged in the immediate aftermath of the summit that Akhromeev had "ruined the meeting" by failing to propose the compromise.[2]

The issue of SDI as a U.S. point of leverage on the Soviet Union was discussed by participants on both sides and was the subject of much of the U.S. press coverage of the conference. Shultz told the conference that, in his opinion, SDI's impact on the Soviet Union was a secondary question for Reagan, who was principally motivated by a determination to advance the defense of the United States. Nevertheless, said the former secretary of state, SDI "did turn into a terrific bargaining chip." Bessmertnykh, in comments that were extensively quoted in the U.S. press, said that the beginning of the SDI program was "one of the major moments when the strategists in the Soviet Union started maybe even to reconsider their positions." SDI, he went on to say, "had a long-lasting impact on us." This impact was complex, according to Bessmertnykh, providing some Soviet officials with arguments for speeding the production of strategic offensive arms to counteract the U.S. program, even while bringing other officials "closer to solutions in arms control, because we realized that we were really approaching a very dangerous situation in the strategic counterbalance that we had been living in."

The Soviet decision making leading to the 1979 invasion of Afghanistan came in for harsh criticism by Moscow's former officials and provided the most revealing—and frightening—look at Soviet decision making in the pre-Gorbachev era. The decision to go to war, which jolted the West and cast a long shadow over Soviet domestic and foreign policy for nearly a decade, was described by Bessmertnykh as "the complete breakdown of the policy-making standard" and by Chernyaev as "a totally arbitrary and irresponsible approach to policy making that was typical of the Soviet leadership at that time." Bessmertnykh told the conference that some details of the decisions were kept so secret even within high ranks in Moscow that he had only learned of them after becoming foreign minister in 1991, by examining a thick set of documents left untouched for posterity in the foreign minister's safe.

Leonid Brezhnev, who was general secretary of the Communist

Party at the time of the invasion and theoretically the supreme Soviet leader, was described as so infirm that he had little part in the fateful move. The secret papers ascribed the decision to four top subordinates: KGB chief Yuri Andropov, Defense Minister Dmitry Ustinov, Foreign Minister Andrei Gromyko, and Boris Ponomarev, chief of the International Department of the Communist Party Central Committee. The Princeton Conference was told that the professional military were from the start strongly opposed to moving troops into Afghanistan, and that Soviet scholars specializing in the area had reported secretly to the Foreign Ministry within a week after the invasion that it was "a reckless adventure that will end very badly." Rather than being based on rational calculations or even miscalculations, the decision was described by Tarasenko as a "cynical" exercise in political positioning within the leadership of the Politburo, which was at the time preoccupied with jockeying over the succession to Brezhnev as general secretary.

On the U.S. side, Paul Nitze, who was a consultant to the Joint Chiefs of Staff at the time of the invasion, recounted the belief in the Pentagon that Soviet control of Afghanistan would lead to Moscow's domination of the vital Persian Gulf. U.S. military officials therefore concluded that the Afghan struggle was a strategic question of first importance. Shultz told the conference how he had argued, in an unusual alliance with CIA director William Casey, for placing heat-seeking Stinger missiles into the hands of the mujaheddin, an action that proved devastating to Soviet close air support and hastened Moscow's withdrawal.

Conference participants provided important details of how Moscow and Washington had dealt with the issue of Soviet withdrawal from Afghanistan in the mid-1980s. In a gripping account, Chernyaev recounted Gorbachev's early decision to liquidate the war and his extensive, highly confidential efforts to educate the other members of the Politburo on the Afghan disaster and the need for withdrawal.

Time and again throughout the conference, participants returned to the personal factors that had affected the relations between the two nations, whether these tended to deepen and extend the conflict, as did the decision to invade Afghanistan, or tended to mediate, moderate, and eventually end the conflict. As described by the diplomats and other officials who were involved, the increasing personal con-

tact and growing respect between Reagan and Gorbachev, and between their leading diplomats, Shultz and Shevardnadze, were of
great importance in dissipating the fear and mistrust at the heart of
the Cold War.

Pavel Palazchenko, Gorbachev's interpreter and personal aide, recalled standing with the Soviet leader and a group of his subordinates
at the 1985 Geneva Summit, where Gorbachev and Reagan met for
the first time. When one of the officials launched into a harsh criticism of Reagan and his policies, Gorbachev interrupted, saying,
"This is the president of the United States, elected by the American
people." This kind of respect, said Palazchenko, had a significant effect. Two years later, after the Washington Summit of 1987, Gorbachev reported to the Politburo, according to notes read to the
conference by Chernyaev, that "in Washington, perhaps for the first
time, we understood so clearly how important the human factor is in
international politics." Gorbachev went on to say in a remarkable
report to the Politburo,

For us, Reagan appeared as a representative . . . of and a spokesman for the
most conservative part of the most conservative segment of American capitalism and the military-industrial complex. But it turned out that on top
of all that, it is also important that policy makers, including the leaders
of states, of governments, if they really are responsible people, they also
represent purely human qualities, the interests and the aspirations of common people, and that they can be guided by purely normal human feelings
and aspirations. And in our day and age, this turns out to be of enormous
importance.

Several American participants made the point that Reagan, despite his disdain for the Soviet system, took his opposite number seriously and was deeply impressed with Gorbachev's sincerity. Shultz,
who had observed the human interaction at close hand, told the conference that "the Reagan-Gorbachev relationship was not based on
these two leaders going out of their way to accommodate each other.
On the contrary, I felt that Gorbachev laid it on the line and so did
Reagan. And that one reason they respected each other was that both
could see that the other guy was saying what he thought . . . It was
real." Bessmertnykh said much the same thing in a different way,
remarking that between Reagan and Gorbachev "the ideals were not
similar, but the dedication to those ideals was similar . . . They both
believed in something. They were not just men who could change

their sails and go any way the wind blows . . . This is what they immediately sensed in each other, and this is why they made good partners."

In the final minutes of the Princeton Conference, Bessmertnykh summed up by saying that, for him, the end of the Cold War was deeply affected by great trends that may not yet be completely comprehended. "But," said the former senior Soviet official, the Cold War "was ended by human beings, by people who were dedicated to eradicating this part of history." The revelation of the vital importance of the human element, an incalculable and unexpected interplay of personalities and aspirations, provided the most memorable moments and the most lasting impressions of the Princeton Conference.

Chapter One

∴ Beginning the Transition

The transcripts contained in this chapter and the five chapters that follow are nicely framed by an interview that National Public Radio's Daniel Schorr conducted with George Shultz and Alexander Bessmertnykh on February 26, 1993, during the Princeton Conference. The two former foreign ministers recall the state of superpower relations in the "new Cold War" years of the mid-1980s and the improvement in relations after 1985. In response to Schorr's pointed questioning, Shultz and Bessmertnykh raise what would become a recurrent theme in the conference discussions: the role of developing personal relationships in the diplomatic breakthrough from confrontation to cooperation. The interview is followed by the transcript of the first conference session, held on the evening of February 25, 1993. Participants focused on the initial meetings between the Americans and the new Soviet team under Gorbachev. In the years between 1985 and 1987, Western scholars and pundits carried on a vigorous debate about how much change the new Soviet leader represented. But in the discussions reported here, former high-level U.S. officials remember sensing early on that significant change was afoot, and Gorbachev's close associates confirm that their chief was determined from the outset to bring the Cold War to an end.

Interview with George Shultz and Alexander Bessmertnykh by Daniel Schorr, February 26, 1993*

Announcer: This weekend Princeton University's Woodrow Wilson School is hosting a retrospective on the end of the Cold War. Heading the delegation from the former Soviet Union is Alexander Bessmertnykh, who was foreign minister under Mikhail Gorbachev. The U.S. side is led by former secretary of state George Shultz. NPR senior news analyst Dan Schorr is at the conference and got a chance to sit and talk with the two men who shaped foreign policy under Reagan and Gorbachev. Alexander Bessmertnykh told Dan that the early Reagan years were a nerve-racking time.

Bessmertnykh: The first part of the 1980s [was] the most dangerous period because the two sides mistrusted each other again as they did in the 1950s, but this time with much larger arsenals and weapons, so it took two or three more years to break that vicious circle.

Shultz: Certainly there was a major buildup. And as I saw it, the buildup in the United States was in response to the Soviet buildup. The clearest example of that was the response on our part, on behalf of NATO in Europe, to the deployment of SS-20 intermediate-range ballistic nuclear-tipped weapons by the Soviet Union.

Schorr: Mr. Minister, at what point would you say you began to see light at the end of that terrible tunnel?

Bessmertnykh: I can name a very precise time when we started to hope that the arms control would work—that the new kind of relationship would slowly establish itself between the two countries, and that was 1985.

Schorr: Nineteen eighty-five?

Bessmertnykh: In 1985, with the Geneva meeting of the U.S. president and the Soviet general secretary. Because at that meeting, although it was not very successful in all respects, for the very first time the two leaders said, "We shall not seek superiority over each other." Now it looks like a simple thing, but at that time it was a breakthrough.

Shultz: It was the beginning of something, and we had a characteristic period where further things that amounted to what I call a mini-thaw took place during that year. And then, as often happens, some event tended to set it back. In this case the shooting down of the Korean airliner set everything back.[1]

Schorr: Was that a bad moment?

Bessmertnykh: It was terrible; it was an absolutely terrible moment in the relationship. It looked like everything was just coming down again. And that's one of those typical things in the Soviet-American relationship. We would be planning something, some policies. We would devise some negotiating patterns and suddenly something happens, someone is arrested, someone is shot down, and things would get beyond control. That was the story of the Soviet-American relationship, and I think what was good about it, what was a plus, [was that] we still managed to go through those critical moments and try to keep the safety net of the relationship, which were the working arrangements, working talks, and diplomatic contacts at the working levels between the two diplomatic services. I think that was something new in the history of Soviet-American relations.

Schorr: In this long relationship between the Soviet Union and the United States there were leaders that replaced leaders, but for a long part of that time it was conducted rather at arm's length. There came a point at which personal chemistry began to play an important part: on the presidential level, Reagan-Gorbachev, and on the ministerial level [Shultz-Shevardnadze]. Suddenly they began to trust each other and deal with each other as persons. Tell me about that.

Bessmertnykh: That was one of the great achievements of this time, when the people started to react to each other emotionally, not like who figures [on] whose side, but [like] people. And sometimes 15 to 20 percent of the talks would be just personal. They would sometimes go away from the programs prepared for them by the ministers so they could talk about families and about life in their countries, etcetera.

Gorbachev told me personally many times that he instantly liked and respected the man—a man with an interesting biography—who made it to the presidency of the United States. So he [Reagan] was not that simple, as some people presented [him] to the public opinion of the Soviet Union. Gorbachev was the first to recognize that. Gorbachev was definitely stronger in presentations of positions, because he was younger and he was fresh and he probably studied more, but somehow they managed. It was one of the interesting psychological elements and [part of the] chemistry that helped solidify the American relationship.

Schorr: Mr. Secretary, as we look back on these ten years was there ever a time when you got up in the middle of the night and said: "By God, we could really be heading for a nuclear holocaust?"

Shultz: I never felt it would happen because it was too horrible to imagine, and it was obvious that was the case. So it seemed to me very unlikely that any such thing would take place. But you have to have in your mind, as Mr. Bessmertnykh said earlier, that there were huge stockpiles of nuclear armaments there, so you had to worry about them . . .

Bessmertnykh: Sometimes there was a feeling of great concern that an incident may occur, somewhere, somehow, because there were so many weapons on each side. That kind of fear was always there, but not to the point that you would have some nightmares . . .

Schorr: Thank you, Mr. Bessmertnykh. Thank you, George Shultz. To which I have very little to add, except to say as we go back over mutual perceptions and misperceptions and finally the dawn of the right perception that went through this age, you sometimes wonder: if there were different persons involved and different conditions involved, where would we be today? This is Daniel Schorr at Princeton.

The First Session: Beginning a New Relationship

Mr. Oberdorfer: I thought it would be interesting to begin with the meeting with Soviet ambassador Anatoly Dobrynin in the White House in early 1983, which took place at almost the same time President Reagan denounced the Soviet Union as an "evil empire" and announced the start of the "Star Wars" program. What did you *[indicating Russian panelists]* think of Reagan saying he wanted to improve relations at the very time when he was denouncing the Soviet Union and starting the SDI program? How did you reconcile, for example, his hard-line rhetoric with his request for exit visas for the Russian Pentecostals holed up in the U.S. Embassy? What was your sense of his degree of sincerity?

Mr. Bessmertnykh: I remember those days well. The atmosphere in Moscow was very tense for the first few years of the Reagan administration especially because of the SDI program: it frightened us very much. And of course, we were studying what was true about it and what was not. So when the request for the Pentecostals came it was received by our professionals as a kind of step to get out of the situation. It was seen as an invitation to do something critical that could lead to something else. That's why our response was so fast. There were no great discussions on the subject in Moscow: we just thought that it would be good to reciprocate quickly in order to give the U.S. president something and then see how he responds.

Mr. Oberdorfer: And on the American side, how can a guy have these two seemingly opposite things in mind at the same time, wanting to open relations to negotiate and yet at the same time denouncing the potential negotiating partner as an "evil empire" and all the rest? How can you explain this paradox of Ronald Reagan?

Mr. Nitze: I was testifying before the Senate on the day the president made that remark, and I was asked by Senator Levin of Ohio how I could justify this remark of the president's. And I said I thought there was a prior question: was the accusation true or false? Senator Levin was left bewildered. He couldn't accept either alternative. If he said it was false, then he would play into the hands of the president. If he said it was true, he was playing into the hands of the president. So he dropped the whole issue.

Mr. Oberdorfer: What did Gorbachev think prior to 1985? Did he have any of the views that he later came out with after he became general secretary?

Mr. Chernyaev: You may be a bit surprised when I say that after the summit in Geneva, Gorbachev had basically the same attitude toward Reagan as a person that he had before Geneva.[2] After Geneva, Gorbachev still saw Reagan as a representative of imperialism and a foe, but also saw him as the head of a government with which we had to deal.

Mr. Bessmertnykh referred in his opening remarks to Gorbachev's conviction that it was impossible to implement perestroika without ending the Cold War.[3]

Until a certain point in time, Gorbachev continued to believe that scaling down the Cold War meant basically scaling down the arms race. That was essentially his idea of what to do about the Cold War. Speaking in very rough terms, you can summarize that idea as: "Let Andrei Sakharov continue to sit there in exile in Gorky and we'll work out the settlement with the Americans." But it was an imperative for Gorbachev that we had to put an end to the Cold War, reduce our military budget significantly, and limit our military-industrial complex. So it was absolutely clear to him that he would have to negotiate with President Reagan and indeed that he would have to go very far in negotiating very significant reductions with President Reagan.

In the conference program, there are some questions proposed for· discussion, specifically about Reykjavik. And one of those questions basically is whether Gorbachev was serious in offering his nuclear disarmament program in Reykjavik. I was present in the summer of 1986 when Gorbachev was developing the idea of what he would propose in Reykjavik. I recall when that concept developed in his mind and when he discussed it with me in a one-on-one talk in the Crimea during his summer vacation. And I was present on October 21, 1986, at the Politburo meeting that discussed Secretary Shultz's letter which indicated that the U.S. side would agree to a meeting in Reykjavik. Based on that firsthand knowledge, I can say very definitely that Gorbachev was serious. As a result of Gorbachev's very serious conviction, specific instructions were drawn for the Foreign Ministry and the Ministry of Defense to prepare a Soviet position. It was a political decision. There was no objection to that political decision from anyone in the highest levels of Soviet political leadership. Gorbachev was not a demagogue. This was not a proposal of a demagogue.

Mr. Oberdorfer: I wonder, on the American side, what your impressions of the Geneva Summit were and whether you thought Gorbachev was a person who was really changing. What did you think about this curious new Soviet leader and the way he handled himself and what he was going to do? Did you see then what he was going to become, or was it, as it seems to have been on the Soviet side, much more of a test?

Mr. Shultz: I will tell one story that showed us something about the Soviet side. This was during Gorbachev's big anti-alcohol campaign. Nobody could drink vodka in the Soviet Union. The first night of the Geneva Summit, Mr. Gorbachev gave a dinner. We all went over to the Soviet Embassy for the dinner, and when the first course was served, a man came around with a great big dish of caviar, and we all helped ourselves, and then vodka was poured into the shot-glasses. And Shevardnadze, with a great smile on his face, raised up his vodka glass, and he said to President Reagan, "Mr. President, I had to come all the way to Geneva to get a drink of vodka." I said to myself, "There is some chemistry there between Shevardnadze and Gorbachev and a willingness to kid around a little bit."

I certainly felt, at that Geneva Summit, that there was an ability to talk back and forth very frankly. And the simultaneous translation helped, because both Reagan and Gorbachev are very expressive people. If you just read what they say, you don't begin to get the impact of it as if you are there and you are hearing at the same time as you are watching. I felt that a certain personal contact was made. I think that President Reagan found Gorbachev a person that he felt he could talk to, so he didn't go away with the same opinion that he came with. He thought the situation was open to change.

Soviet experts on our side always had this analysis that somehow there was an underlying Russian sense of inferiority that you had to be careful of. After reading one of these analyses, I said to Reagan before he went to Geneva, "Mr. President, I can assure you that the man you are going to meet does not have an inferiority complex." And he liked Gorbachev, because he was real and could talk frankly. It always seemed to me that one of the reasons Reagan was effective was that he could be very blunt and basically said what he thought. The "evil empire" phrase came in a speech, which I don't think was meant to be a major policy speech, but there it was. He did think it was an "evil empire." On the other hand, he also thought that he should try to deal with these people. When he met Gorbachev and he began to get engaged personally, that had an impact on his attitude. So the exchange in Geneva was very, very important, even though it took a long time before there was another summit.

Mr. Oberdorfer: Ambassador Ridgway, do you have a comment?

Ms. Ridgway: I came to that scene well after the 1983 exchanges and not from a background in Soviet affairs, so much of this was new to me. I had to rely very much on the months and weeks that were spent preparing for the Geneva Summit to become familiar with many of the attitudes on both sides, which were loaded with mythology. It went all the way back to the beginning of the Cold War, sort of a "who struck John" litany of compilations of violations and errors both theological and military. And both sides, I think, were carrying this baggage, much of it legitimate, but nonetheless carrying this collection from decades preceding, as this new opportunity presented itself.

No one has mentioned yet the importance on the U.S. side of what I would call the external validation of Gorbachev by Mrs. Thatcher. It was very much a part of what made it possible for those who wanted to work the relationship in a positive way to go forward. When we got to Geneva, we arrived with a very productive record of bilateral exchanges at the ministerial level, which had developed an agenda that identified the directions in which progress might be made. And it was not burdened by the previous task of developing communiqués loaded with language we later came to say represented the use of two dictionaries, in which phrases such as "détente" and "peaceful coexistence" had come to be part of the problem. In fact, such language was consciously removed, by decision on the U.S. side, and in discussion with the Soviet side. It doesn't count for much, perhaps, in the grand picture of diplomacy, but it was very important that the communiqué became a statement and that it contained, short of the opening paragraphs on "nuclear war cannot be won, must never be fought," a very dry listing of identified areas in which work would be pursued by the two sides. It bears no resemblance in my mind to any document that preceded it.

Sitting there without the background, not knowing of the stormy Madrid meeting between Secretary Shultz and Foreign Minister Gromyko in the aftermath of the KAL shootdown, not

knowing of details, say, of Khrushchev and Kennedy,[4] I watched a
meeting that I think if you were not practiced and not prepared
would have scared a lot of people. These, I found, were two men
who believed everything they said. I don't really think on the basis
of my background that President Reagan suffered from any contradictions in his own view of what he was doing. He believed what
he said and saw no contradiction in it. Mr. Gorbachev was also a
very strong man of very strong views. And there must surely be
gaps in the record of Geneva where the note takers dropped their
pens, where with the give-and-take made possible by simultaneous translation, two men who believed deeply that they had to
convince the other that they were in command of their brief, that
they believed what they were saying, that they had a sense of direction, got onto the subject of the Strategic Defense Initiative.
They began to talk in animated fashion, interrupting each other.
Voices rose. The examples of how each really believed he couldn't
trust the other became somewhat more lurid, and the pens had to
write faster. And as I say, I think jaws dropped, and in some cases
the pens stopped, as we all wanted to keep track of this.

It was a very successful encounter in introducing two very
strong personalities to each other. But if that had been the whole
of the meeting, I think we would have had trouble. What was important was, that having been said and done, when it came time
to instruct delegations on how to proceed with the final documents and how to chart the future, the two men stepped away
from that table, and it was two very practical, directed people
who told us what they wanted done before they left Geneva. So I
think if you looked at the surface, you could say that almost nothing was accomplished there, and if you looked at the documents,
you might say, "How boring," but if you looked at the whole context, you would find that something very special happened on that
occasion.

Mr. Oberdorfer: Pavel, did you drop your pencil?

Mr. Palazchenko: Well, no, I didn't. And actually I recall something
that might contradict a little bit what Mr. Chernyaev said about
Gorbachev coming out of Geneva without changing much the
way he viewed Reagan. That might be true, but the way he saw
Reagan was, even at that time, more complex, not just as the other

side and the potential foe. In Geneva a group of Soviet officials was standing with Mr. Gorbachev and someone was very critical of President Reagan—of the positions that he defended and also of him as a person. Gorbachev interrupted and said, "This is the president of the United States, elected by the American people." This kind of respect was something that was present in Gorbachev's mind from the very outset, and I believe it played a role.

Mr. Oberdorfer: We have talked about two of the four central participants in this, Reagan and Gorbachev. And we have a third central participant right here. The fourth one, unfortunately, because he is president of Georgia, in the former Soviet Union, cannot be here, but Sergei Tarasenko was the closest man to him. What is your sense of when Shevardnadze began to shift his views about Reagan and the American team, and so on, if there was a shift?

Mr. Tarasenko: Well, if I have any trouble with your book it is its emphasis on the meetings between Gorbachev and Reagan and Bush. A lot of the real work was done on the ministerial level. What was brought to the bosses was a digested and refined product, so you can't just say that these two guys met and they decided everything. It took a lot of these ministerial-level discussions beforehand to set the stage. And not only would I certainly credit Secretary Shultz with the simultaneous translation, which certainly put us on a completely new road, but I would say that there were other elements to this story.[5] For the first time, it was not just formal negotiations, but thanks to Secretary Shultz a kind of human element was introduced into these discussions. It was not just one side setting out its position, and the other side responding with its position. For the first time, it was a dialogue between human beings, a process not just between sides, Soviet and U.S., but between personalities—and that mattered.

Shevardnadze was new to the job. He was just an understudy, you know, when he first met with Secretary Shultz in Helsinki. But what I think the secretary did, very wisely, was introduce a kind of thinking aloud about the relationship. I recall once when they talked about human rights early in their relationship and the secretary addressed the issue on a philosophical level: "You will be better off if you will solve this problem; just look what gains the Soviet Union will achieve if you will just ease up on this issue." It was a kind of delicate lecture, a friendly talk. And as the relationship proceeded, this informal side became more and more important, because, to a larger and larger extent, they didn't talk about, say, numbers of armaments and all these arrests and protests and other practical issues, but they talked about what kind of countries we were, what we were hoping to achieve, what we thought could be achieved, what was good for the world, and how we could manage our relationship. That was extremely important.

Going back to this issue of the "evil empire," certainly I am not the best judge of this issue, because the U.S. desk worked in a damage control mode: whatever the president of the United States or any official would say, we would try to present a milder picture of that; or we would try to diminish the damage on the other side if the Soviet general secretary said something damaging. There were always people in the military, the KGB, and the security structures who would use any opportunity to make trouble, to heat up the atmosphere. The task of the Foreign Ministry was to balance it, to counter this threat. That was what both the secretary and the minister were engaged in, trying to put aside this flack, this negative element of the relationship, and trying to get to the core, to the real things, how to solve the problem, how to improve it. I would say that at the Foreign Ministry we didn't take Reagan's speech seriously. Maybe we knew that we were evil. So, what else is new? So the president said, "It is an evil empire!" Okay. Well, we are an evil empire. How could he know? So, okay, let's deal with that. You know, it was not a problem with us.

Mr. Oberdorfer: Frank Carlucci came to this a little later. His dialogue was essentially with the Soviet military, being defense secretary, having been previously deputy secretary of defense, deputy director of the CIA, and more other jobs than you could possibly think of. Frank, as you talked to the people that you met in the military establishment of the Soviet Union, did you find them any different than what you expected to find?

Mr. Carlucci: Yes, I think I found them to be a little different than I expected. Initially it was a bit stiff. I went into these discussions with the full blessing of George and Roz, but a little later on they told me I was going too fast. But we had to get over the Major Nicholson thing, and that cast a pall on the military discussions until Soviet defense minister Dmitry Yazov and I managed to work out a form of an apology. The fact is that I wrote it in Yazov's office, and we managed to get something that was acceptable to both sides.[6]

We laid out a very specific agenda. Initially, they wanted to talk about arms control, and I said, "No, that is not my bailiwick. We can put that last on the agenda, but let's talk about avoiding dangerous incidents. Let's talk about military doctrine. And let's talk about military-to-military relationships." Gradually, particularly with avoiding dangerous incidents and military-to-military relationships, they became quite comfortable. They really wanted to try and explain Soviet military doctrine to us. They came to see it as an opportunity, and for many of us it was an educational process. As we went through one, two, and three meetings, the atmosphere improved considerably. The military-to-military contacts that we established—and I defer to our Russian friends on this—I think had a very substantial impact on Soviet military attitudes. They came to realize that we weren't really the enemy that they had been taught, that many of the things they had been told were not correct, and that they had some work to do in their own system before they could get their house in order. Maybe I am exaggerating here, Sasha, but these contacts, as they extended down the full length of the [Soviet] military, may have had something to do with the reluctance of a lot of the military to participate in the coup attempt.[7]

Mr. Oberdorfer: Ambassador Matlock has been a scholar of U.S.-Soviet relations throughout his career in the foreign service. He is one of the foreign service officers who speaks fluent Russian, who has been involved in Russian affairs as a desk officer, [a member of] the National Security Council, and the U.S. ambassador [to the Soviet Union]. I would like to ask his thoughts about this process.

Mr. Matlock: Well, I would like to go back to the question about the impact of Geneva. It was my definite impression that whatever President Reagan's impact may have been on Gorbachev, Gorbachev made a deep impression on Reagan. I certainly recall that when we got back, he ordered special studies on a number of the questions that Gorbachev had brought up in Geneva. He called us in and he said, "You know, Gorbachev had a lot to say about how

SDI could provide offensive weapons in space. My understanding is that you can't use these offensively, you know, but the man must believe this. Can you tell me what the basis is?" We went back and found that the physical principles were such that you really couldn't use these weapons in any useful way offensively. He said, "Well, in this case, we have got to get the word to him." I know that he used quite a bit of time in his correspondence trying to explain. The next time I saw Academician Yevgeny Velikhov, who was vice president of the Academy of Sciences, a physicist advising Gorbachev on a lot of these scientific matters, I told him: "You advise Gorbachev on these matters. Would you please explain to him that that particular fear has no basis?" After all, Velikhov knew this very well. I don't know what he was telling Gorbachev, but at least he readily said, "Well, of course, you know, this isn't something we should be worried about."

I think that Reagan did take what Gorbachev said seriously. If he [Reagan] thought that he [Gorbachev] was wrong, he wanted to set him straight, because he had a strong confidence in his ability to convince. And this confidence in his ability to communicate and convince was one of the sources of his strength. In the final analysis, I don't know to what degree he was convincing, but his confidence did lead him to take chances because he felt that the Soviet system could change. He did think that it was an "evil empire," but he also thought that it was one that could change, and that we could influence that change. Though there were disagreements at Geneva, and they both argued their briefs very vigorously, the fact is that Reagan came out not convinced by Gorbachev's beliefs, but respecting them. And he came out seeing Gorbachev as a person, as a fellow politician. This appreciation was important when we wanted to convince Reagan that he really should move one way or the other. If you explained to him that Gorbachev probably had a political problem at home limiting his ability to do certain things, and that if we could move just this way, we might be able to help him overcome that problem, he would often find this very convincing. (We usually had to do this with speculation in the early times because our Soviet counterparts weren't leveling with us about what the domestic problems were.) Reagan saw that Gorbachev was a fellow politician who had constraints just as he had, and if we could do it, he was willing to try to find a way around [those constraints]. So I think the impact of the personal contact on Reagan was very substantial.

Mr. Oberdorfer: I don't want to leave this without giving Secretary Shultz the opportunity to tell us about one of the more spectacular efforts to persuade his counterpart, Mr. Shevardnadze, who was from Georgia, that Shultz was serious in wanting to have a real relationship with him. I don't know if you are willing to tell that story in these exalted halls. Do you know the one I mean?

Mr. Shultz: Yes, I do. It was a trip that I took to Moscow under great duress in April of '87. There was a great furor in the United States about two Marines defecting and allowing the KGB the run of our embassy. It was just a wild situation in the United States. Seventy senators, including practically all the senators in the Republican Party, voted that I shouldn't go to Moscow. This was again "linkage." Anyway, I went. It turned into the most productive meeting I think I had. And of course, in the end, it turned out that the Marine spy story was all wrong and there had been nothing much to it. Trying to figure out how to get this meeting going right in the very tense atmosphere and knowing that the Shevardnadzes, both he and his wife, are very proud of their Georgian roots, I decided to do something different for my toast at the opening luncheon.

At these meetings, the Soviet side would always take us to a nice building that they had, where we would have our meetings, and then there would be a semisocial luncheon at which the wives were invited and a fairly large number of people, and we each would give toasts. I did something different. I got the tape recording of a sexy, throaty torch singer singing "Georgia on My Mind." And I got the sheet music of it, and I got the words translated into Russian. Then I got Matlock and a couple of our other Russian-speaking people trained to sing it in Russian. And I started out by singing it myself—"Georgia, Georgia . . ." At the end, it did sort of break the ice and everybody enjoyed it. When everyone settled down, Shevardnadze said to me, "Thank you, George, that shows respect." I thought it was a kind of profound insight on his part, that if you can show that a relationship has a little humor and a little something different to it, you must have some respect for your opposite member or you wouldn't have done that.

Chapter Two

∴ *Arms Buildups and Arms Reductions*

What was the role of military power in explaining the shift from confrontation in 1983 to cooperation after 1986? In tackling this basic question, the panelists discuss American perceptions of Soviet military power, as presented in a National Intelligence Estimate; the U.S. buildup seen from the Soviet side, including Moscow's assessment of the Strategic Defense Initiative; and the origins and impact of Gorbachev's "new political thinking" and of the unilateral arms reduction announced in December 1988. The panelists recall a political reality far more complex than the simple hawk-versus-dove debates of the 1980s. The U.S. buildup is portrayed as a reflection of perceived American weakness in the face of an implacably powerful Soviet Union. In 1983 the CIA saw the Soviet buildup as unlikely to be constrained by economic worries, but by 1986 the Soviet leadership had concluded that arms reductions were virtually a prerequisite for domestic revitalization.

Media coverage of this conference session dramatically demonstrated that the role of Reagan's military policy in the Cold War's end remains politically charged. The exchanges below concerning the Strategic Defense Initiative were rapidly and widely diffused in the media. Most reports, particularly in the conservative press, highlighted Bessmertnykh's comment that SDI had pushed Moscow toward arms control. But dovish accounts zeroed in on Chernyaev's insistence that Gorbachev had been bent on ending the Cold War for his own domestic purposes, and noted Bessmertnykh's statement that SDI had fed the arguments of the Soviet military-industrial complex for more weapons.[1] In truth, the exchanges below seem to support a more complex interpretation: various interests within the Soviet Union used SDI to support conflicting positions. Two things, however, are made abundantly clear in comments by the American participants: SDI was Ronald Reagan's brainchild and baby. Without him, the program would not have been conceived or sustained. And SDI was easily as controversial within the Reagan administration as it was outside it.

Mr. Oberdorfer: This morning we explore the relationship between the changes in ideas and changes in the arms competition. Some Americans credit the Reagan arms buildup with forcing change in Moscow. However, some see the ideological shift by Mikhail Gorbachev as the essential factor, suggesting that this came more from within than from some external factor.

To explore the relationships between the arms issues and political attitudes, we need to remind ourselves about how things looked in the early 1980s as the period under discussion begins. Ten years ago, in February 1983, the Central Intelligence Agency issued an analysis called "The National Intelligence Estimate and Forecast for the Soviet Arms Buildup of 1982 to 1992." Under a policy of glasnost, which it has perhaps copied from the Russians, the CIA agreed to declassify this estimate as of the end of last week and to provide it to us today for the purpose of this conference. Lawrence Gershwin, who as the national intelligence officer for strategic programs of the Central Intelligence Agency was essentially the author of this report, is here to outline its conclusions for us. Mr. Gershwin—

Mr. Gershwin: Thank you, Don. I will focus on the U.S. perception of the Soviet strategic forces buildup as seen in our National Intelligence Estimate. I will also include some material from testimony that [deputy CIA director] Bob Gates and I gave to Congress in 1985. I shall talk about strategic offensive forces, including the SS-20s, and our estimates of future deployments; strategic defensive forces, particularly related to the Anti–Ballistic Missile Treaty; and our perception of Soviet views of nuclear conflict.

Let me start with strategic offensive forces. Despite serious economic problems since the mid-1970s, the Soviets had been procuring large quantities of new strategic weapons. They fielded a new land-based missile force, their ICBM [intercontinental ballistic missile] force, with multiple warheads, so-called MIRVs [multiple, independently targetable reentry vehicles], and then improved that force. They deployed multiple-warhead submarine-launched missiles on new submarines in a rapidly building program. And they deployed the extensive mobile SS-20 system.

While Soviet economic problems in the early to mid '80s were severe, we saw no signs that the Soviets were cutting back on their strategic programs or that they were prepared to make substantial concessions in arms control in order to relieve economic pressures. We saw the Soviets as determined to prevent any erosion of the military gains that they had made in the 1970s and early 1980s. Throughout the 1980s, we saw an extensive modernization and deployment effort for all elements of Soviet strategic forces with the land-based ICBMs, the intermediate-range SS-20s, submarine-launched ballistic missiles, strategic bombers, and long-range cruise missiles. We were aware of all of these efforts in 1983.

In 1983, continued deployments were taking place of accurate ICBMs, the SS-18s and SS-19s, with multiple, independently targetable launch vehicles. New submarines with more accurate missiles were being deployed, mobile SS-20s were being deployed opposite Europe and the Far East, and many major flight test programs for new weapons were under way. Let me just tick off what some of these were: A new self-propelled ICBM, the SS-24, with multiple warheads, was being prepared for deployment in silos and—as we thought possible, even in 1983—on mobile rail cars. A new, small ICBM was being flight tested, which we forecast for both road mobile and silo deployments. This missile was later identified as the SS-25. The SS-N-20, a submarine-launched missile for the Typhoon submarines, [was being tested]. The Blackjack bomber was in flight testing. New Bear aircraft to carry long-range cruise missiles were in testing. And they were also testing ground-, air-, and sea-launched long-range cruise missiles.

We forecast additional ICBMs and SLBMs, the submarine-launched missiles, to begin flight testing in 1983. As it turned out, the flight testing of some of these (the SS-N-23 missile for the Delta-4 submarine, and the new SS-18) actually occurred in the middle of the decade. There was a very vigorous offensive force development and deployment program which caused us serious concern about the Soviets' capability not only to modernize their existing force but also to expand well beyond their current forces.

We noted that if deployments proceeded without arms control constraints, we saw the Soviets as having the potential to increase the number of their deployed ICBMs and SLBMs from about 2,300 up some 10 to 15 percent by the early 1990s. If the Soviets were to have proceeded according to their own proposal in START [the Strategic Arms Reduction Talks], we saw a decrease. And if the

U.S. proposal were followed—which the Soviets indicated no interest in at that time—we saw a dramatic reduction in the size of their long-range missile force.

The number of warheads, which is perhaps a more important measure of the strategic effort, could have been increased at that time from about 7,300 up to 13,000 to 21,000. So we were looking at the potential for a Soviet increase of rather significant proportions, because the new missiles being tested had many warheads and we saw the possibility then of a much, much greater buildup of strategic warheads. The Soviets' own proposal we saw as leading to an increase in warheads, up to about 10,000, whereas the U.S. proposal at that time would [have] come down to about 5,000, which is interesting because that's exactly where START, in fact, ended up: with a proposal, agreed to on both sides, of 4,900 ballistic missile warheads.

We also predicted long-range cruise missiles in all basing modes at about 1,500 to 2,000. I should point out that in early 1983 we did not see very much prospect for an arms control agreement, but both the United States and the Soviet Union, as I have noted, had already presented proposals at START.

What we did not adequately anticipate at the time was that the arms control negotiations process would result in both sides remaining essentially within SALT II limits for a long period of time.[2] I would say that in 1983 there was no particular reason to believe that would be true. Thus, the Soviet force did increase during the 1980s to over 10,000 warheads, but obviously not to the high levels we thought possible in the total absence of an arms control process.

The picture we portrayed in the early to mid 1980s was of a vigorous strategic offensive force effort with the potential for a significant increase in the size and capability of the forces. We did not judge at that time that political or economic factors were playing much of a role in restraining these efforts. We judged that strategic forces would continue to command the highest resource priorities and would be affected less by economic problems than would any other element of the Soviet military. By 1985, as economic problems worsened, however, we expected that even some strategic programs would be slowed down or stretched out.

Let me now talk about strategic defenses. We noted that despite these impressive offensive force developments, the Soviets' potential future developments in strategic defenses could be of even greater significance. This view was formulated before President Reagan announced the SDI program. It was particularly motivated by our observation of a growing Soviet potential for widespread deployment of defenses against ballistic missiles beyond the limits of the ABM [Anti–Ballistic Missile] treaties. It was our belief that if the Soviets moved out with ABM deployments, they would have large nationwide defenses in place by the late 1980s or early 1990s. And we felt that it would give the USSR an important initial advantage.

Views differed throughout the intelligence community on the likelihood of such prospects. We were uncertain of how capable such a system would be, but we did believe that the Soviets would see it as having considerable value in reducing the impact of a U.S. retaliatory strike if the Soviets succeeded in carrying out a well-coordinated, effective initial strike.

We did not note two other observations about Soviet strategic defense in our February 19, 1983, estimate. First was the Krasnoyarsk radar, a blatant violation of the ABM Treaty, which appeared on the scene in the summer of 1983. For some of those who were worried about the possibility of a Soviet ABM breakout, this added fuel to the fire. Later in the decade, the United States publicized, in the Defense Department's document *Soviet Military Power,* the second observation: that the Soviet Union had an enormous secret program for deep underground facilities for wartime protection of its leadership and command and control from nuclear attack. These combined to create the impression that the Soviet Union was very serious about strategic defense and about developing the capability to be able to fight and survive a nuclear war, preserving the key leaders and capabilities needed to carry such a war to its successful military conclusion.

Let me now talk about Soviet views of nuclear war. While not regarding nuclear war as inevitable, we believed that the Soviets regarded it as a continuing possibility and that they rejected mutual vulnerability, which had been the de facto basis for the strategic relationship up to that time. We felt that they sought superior capabilities to fight and win a nuclear war; that they had been working to improve their chances of prevailing; and that a key aspect of their strategic thinking was that the better prepared the USSR was to fight a nuclear war, the more likely that its adversaries would be unwilling to initiate an attack on the Soviet Union and would be hesitant to counter Soviet political and military actions. This has often been referred to as a war-fighting doctrine, as opposed to a purely deterrent posture involving annihilation.

We presented to U.S. policy makers a rather comprehensive assessment of how we believed the Soviet Union evaluated the factors that could lead to the initiation of nuclear war and how the Soviets were prepared to fight a nuclear war. It was a Soviet view of the nature of a U.S.-Soviet confrontation that proceeds through large-scale nuclear conflict, and [it examined] how Soviet forces would operate. This material has never previously been released, and I will commend it to you for your study.

We observed that the Soviets saw little prospect [that there would be] a surprise U.S. attack from a peacetime posture—a so-called bolt out of the blue—or that they would mount such an attack themselves. This was important because a great deal of U.S. planning had focused on the unlikely scenario of such a Soviet surprise attack. Rather, we saw the Soviets believing that a nuclear war, if it occurred, would arise from a NATO–Warsaw Pact conventional conflict preceded by weeks of political crisis.

Their planning was extensive on how to integrate nuclear warfare operations with such a theater conflict. We saw them as believing that it was to their advantage to keep the conflict at the conventional force level where they, in fact, had a military advantage. They did not necessarily believe that nuclear war would escalate beyond battlefield use, but they were prepared for such escalation and they did believe that large-scale use of nuclear weapons in Europe meant the likely and imminent escalation to intercontinental nuclear war. Thus, they saw any use of the Pershing II missiles or the ground-launch cruise missiles being introduced into Europe as an integral part of a U.S. intercontinental attack.

We really could not assess how the Soviets evaluated their own chances for prevailing in such a nuclear conflict. Sizable forces on both sides would survive massive nuclear strikes. Neither side had strategic defenses that could prevent massive damage, even with the improvements taking place. We did see the Soviets as emphasizing the destruction of the U.S. command and control system to prevent or impair the U.S. capability to retaliate. And on their side, we saw the Soviets as working very hard to improve the surviv- ability of their own command and control. And we thought the hardness and redundancy of their system was impressive. We felt they were working hard on the problems of conducting military operations in a nuclear war, improving their abilities and raising the probability of outcomes favorable to the USSR. I would note that the State Department intelligence organization disagreed with that assessment. The Soviet goal for a successful outcome was neutralization of the ability of U.S. intercontinental and the- ater nuclear forces to interfere with Soviet capabilities to prevail in a conflict in Eurasia.

That's a short summary of what is in my 1983 National Intelli- gence Estimate. It goes into considerably more detail, but those are what I believe were the salient points that I wanted to bring to your attention this morning.

Mr. Daniel Schorr [in audience]: Could I ask a factual question be- fore Mr. Gershwin leaves?

Mr. Oberdorfer: Sure.

Mr. Schorr: In the light of subsequent knowledge, how close was your estimate to the truth?

Mr. Gershwin: Well, within the estimate there are many estimates. As I tried to note in my commentary, the potential Soviet buildup without any kind of an arms control process never happened, one reason being that there was an arms control process. So it is a little hard to evaluate what the potential would have been in the ab- sence of that, because, in fact, the way the events ensued, there was such a process.

I think we had a rather accurate portrayal of the programs and when they would be deployed, in light of the fact that the buildup was not as high as it could have been. We obviously, in some sense, overestimated the potential, but again, it was in a somewhat dif- ferent setting.

Mr. Schorr: But what you estimated was happening then, you now know was happening?

Mr. Gershwin: Yes, certainly the picture of what 1983 was like in terms of programs, military efforts, and so on, holds up very well.

Mr. Schorr: Thank you.

Mr. Oberdorfer: Thanks, Larry. Just because we have heard an American view, I want to start by turning over here *[indicates Russian panelists]* and asking Foreign Minister Bessmertnykh to tell us what your own sense was about the things that Mr. Gershwin has told about the Soviet military buildup and the American view of it. How did you see it at that time?

Mr. Bessmertnykh: At that time, I was not aware of all the details of defense planning in the Soviet Union. Only later, when I became a member of the National Security Council and one of the five members of the Defense Council of the country, did I know more about it, but that was already when we were very successful in arms control.

Going back to the period we are discussing, in a certain way I was happy to hear the CIA's appraisal of our efforts, because almost the same story was reported to the Soviet government by our own intelligence services. The figures, of course, were different, but the thrust of the reports that were coming to the political leadership was that after a certain period of accommodation, the United States had suddenly, with the new president who had come to Washington, President Reagan, decided to change the course of defense policy and start an enormous buildup. All the leaks and all the reports that we were getting from our own intelligence in the United States indicated that the United States was serious about overwhelming the Soviet Union in one basic strategic effort.

Our intelligence was doing exactly the same as yours. It was always alarmist. It was always saying that United States had the most malign intentions, and we should do everything to counteract it.

I don't want to deny that much of what you have said was true, especially concerning the programs in the ICBM area. The ICBM was always the heart of the Russian strategic forces. We thought that the only way we could respond to the threat of SDI, especially, was to develop the ICBM program as much as possible. It was with that in mind, and you have got it correctly, that we started to develop two modern ICBMs, which were the SS-24 and SS-25, both intended to be in a mobile mode. As for the other types of strategic forces, such as heavy bombers, the Soviet Union was very much behind, and we understood that we did not have a chance of catching up with the United States.

As for the antisatellite ABM system, I think the CIA's appraisal was definitely exaggerated. We didn't have a chance to enlarge our ABM ability. The Krasnoyarsk Radar Station was actually not so much intended to be part of a future all-territorial ABM system, as the Americans suspected, but rather was an attempt to close the gap in the radar warning system, because we were completely unprotected with radars in the northeastern part of the country. And when the military engineers were looking for a spot to build the radar, they thought that Krasnoyarsk would be a better place because it had a transportation system close by, solid ground, and so forth; but, of course, they had violated the treaty.

I remember that we went and talked with Chief of Staff Marshal Sergei Akhromeev. I asked him, personally, "How could you do it? Because, you know, that was an absolute violation of the treaty." He said that when the plans were presented to the government, the same question was asked, but the designers said, "Well, when it is built, and the Americans start crying out, we will find an answer somehow." So it was one of the stupid things that were done, and it cost us billions of rubles just to build it and then maybe the same amount of money to dismantle it.

Mr. Oberdorfer: Did Akhromeev say at what level this question was asked, about how you were going to deal with the violation?

Mr. Bessmertnykh: I think it was asked in the Defense Council. As for prevailing in a nuclear war, which the United States suspected the Soviet Union believed it might do, I think that in the minds of the Soviet leaders it was completely an opposite picture. Reagan's government formally accepted the proposition of prevailing in a future war, and so our suspicions were strengthened by public statements to that effect. We thought the American idea of "prevailing" in the Cold War might include the possibility of a first strike. So you can see the two mirrors, the two reflective situations, which were caused by tremendous suspicion of each other. And on the basis of that suspicion, we maximized the threat and maximized the figures of the armaments on each side.

I would say that one of the major moments when the strategists in the Soviet Union started maybe even to reconsider their positions was when the SDI program was announced in March 1983. For the first weeks, that announcement seemed a little bit fantastic. But then it started to come to the minds of the leaders that there might be something very, very dangerous in that. We had asked our scientists and strategists, including [Academician Yevgeny P.] Velikhov, to check what it was all about.[3] The SDI program had a long-lasting impact on us. Maybe if it had not been for the SDI, then the programs would have gone more slowly and not so intensively. So in a certain way, the SDI pronouncement might have brought us closer to solutions in arms control, because we realized that we were really approaching a very dangerous situation in the strategic counterbalance that we had been living in.

The second factor that had a great impact was the Chernobyl catastrophe. [After returning from a visit to the United States just weeks after the catastrophe] I reported to Gorbachev one personal remark that George Shultz had made. He said, "After Chernobyl, we all now realize the real danger of everything nuclear," because Chernobyl [according] to U.S. calculations was something like one-third of the smallest nuclear explosive. And if it caused such great damage to almost half of Europe, what will happen if we shall use all those arsenals we now have in our hands?

There is one interesting thing that the American people should understand. The military in the Soviet Union were not all against arms control. I would rather say that the military-industrial complex, with the emphasis on industrial part of the complex, was the major opponent of arms control. The people in the General Staff, such as Marshal Sergei Akhromeev, for example, would be more flexible in understanding the necessity to go forward with arms control as a way to avoid the danger of a conflict. But the people who were designing missiles and designing space and other kinds of weapons were the strongest opponents.

I remember Shevardnadze and I—and I think Sergei Tarasenko was there—had invited some of the inventors of the antisatellite weapons to our Foreign Ministry to discuss whether it was really something we could rely upon, or whether we should go further in pressing the United States into canceling the antisatellite program. The designers who came to our ministry insisted on the beauty of the antisatellite weapon, and they said that what they had created was really a remarkable way of killing the U.S. satellites very, very effectively. But when we started to ask them about how they would do it, how much time it would take for them to start that weapon, how much it would take to put it into orbit, whether it could maneuver in orbit, or something like that, even we—nonscientists, who were not so well read in the technical specifics—realized that it was just something they would like to [use to] impress their leader to get more funds; but it was actually an obsolete and ineffective new weapon.

Mr. Oberdorfer: I would like to ask Foreign Minister Bessmertnykh to clarify one thing: You said early in your response here that the SDI program, as much as anything, caused governmental leaders in Moscow to reconsider. At the same time, I heard you to say that it caused them to increase the offensive effort in order to be able to overwhelm this system if it worked.

Mr. Bessmertnykh: There were different parts of the government which thought differently. The foreign policy part of the Soviet administration believed that because of the SDI program, we now had a good opportunity to work with the military and with the defense sectors of the economy to go further with arms control. But the people who dealt with defense used SDI as an argument for increasing the production of their offensive weapons.

Also, the SDI transformed itself into several options. "SDI I" was too fantastic, so the fear of it evaporated pretty soon. Very quickly we realized that it was impractical and could not be built the way President Reagan thought—a dome over the nation protecting the territory of the United States from anything. It only took us several months to calculate that that was a fantasy.

But then, of course, your people also realized that was a fantasy, and they started working on an SDI II option, and then there was an SDI III option. And when those options were developed, they looked more and more feasible. As soon as the military part of the government realized that, they said we should find a countermeasure against it. Gorbachev mentioned several times, even in the intimate talks with U.S. presidents and, I think, with the secretary of state, "We are working on a countermeasure and we do already have something." He never revealed what he meant by that, because we had really been working on some actions in space using some new discoveries in physics. But basically, the main thrust of the countermeasures was modernization of the ICBM program.

So SDI's impact went both ways. That's why an outside observer might have seen some contradictions; there were different people in the government feeling differently about it. We in the Foreign Ministry—Shevardnadze, myself, all of us, including Gorbachev—believed that we should use this situation to go further with arms control.

Mr. Oberdorfer: Could I ask the American side: what was your perception of this SDI question? Was part of the intention of SDI to affect Soviet behavior? What was your impression of the degree to which the onset or the continuation of the SDI program had an impact on what they were doing or not?

Mr. Shultz: I think that the SDI program was very much driven by Ronald Reagan. It was personal.

An experience he had made a huge impact on him: his visit to the big defense installation at Cheyenne Mountain. It is a big place inside the mountain where there are all sorts of consoles keeping track of everything all over the place. He went there as a presidential candidate, having also been briefed on the heavy Soviet intercontinental ballistic missiles. After being tremendously impressed with all of the things that could be done in this mountain, Marty [presidential aide Martin Anderson] asked the general in charge, "What would happen if an SS-18 hit somewhere near the mountain?" The general said, "It would blow us away." And the future president concluded that this was a hell of a state of affairs: we were absolutely defenseless and we didn't even try to learn how to defend ourselves.

I think this penetrated very deep. He was conditioned in his mind to seize on a report that strategic defense was possible. That proceeded—with a lot of encouragement from the joint chiefs in late 1982 and early 1983—to lead him to make his proposal. The actual proposal in March certainly came as a surprise to me. Although the president did voice his concerns about strategic defense on that snowy evening we talked about, it didn't penetrate to me that this had an immediate operational significance.[4]

Mr. Oberdorfer: In these discussions, then or later, to what extent was there thought about what the Soviets' reaction to it would be, or was that not really a factor?

Mr. Shultz: The president's concern was the defense of the United States. In the intensive arguments just before his speech, the impact on allies, the Soviet response, and the relationship to the ABM Treaty and so on were all thrust at him, and some penetrated and got into the speech and some didn't. The defense of the country remained his main concern. He kept saying—and nobody would believe him—that, as far as he was concerned, if a successful system were developed, he would be ready to share it. Early on, he went further in saying, "If you are worried about this creating the ability of a first strike, I am ready to eliminate ballistic missiles so there can't be any first strike."

I think that the inability of the United States to find a satisfactory way of basing our big land-based ballistic missiles was a tremendous concern. In a way, SDI was sort of a substitute for it. While it never was a bargaining chip in the sense of bargaining about the research program, as such, it did turn into a terrific bargaining chip. I was interested in your [Bessmertnykh's] comments in that regard.

Mr. Oberdorfer: Mr. Chernyaev wanted to say something.

Mr. Chernyaev: On the question of whether Gorbachev was afraid of SDI and what kind of impact it had on his thinking on the settlement, I recall the situation as of March or April 1986. Gorbachev was going to the city of Togliatti to speak on international issues. In his prepared speech, there was a paragraph on SDI. There was one little phrase there that he afterwards repeated several times: "We have to stop being afraid of SDI." Before that, there had been a wide-ranging discussion of this subject in the Politburo, in which it was said that the fact that the Americans think that we are afraid of SDI only encourages them to proceed with SDI. But that was one aspect only; the other aspect was that our science and technology had been able to come up with a response to SDI. I personally never believed that we had an efficient response to SDI. But when I said so to Mr. Gorbachev, he dismissed it, saying, "You just don't understand that subject."

Another thing is even more important. It was at that time, in the spring of 1986, that Gorbachev insisted on the need for a meeting with President Reagan, because there had already been some backsliding following the Geneva Summit. This is when Gorbachev sent a letter to Reagan. The Politburo discussed what we ought to bring to that summit [Reykjavik]. Different options were suggested. I recall one rather sharp remark by Gorbachev in answer to one of those options. He said: "If you will be suggesting to me here any proposals or any scenarios that would proceed from the assumption that we will one day fight a war with America, then I will not accept such a proposal. Until now, during the period of stagnation, we had assumed in our planning that a war is possible, but now, while I am general secretary, don't even put such plans on my desk."

So this, I think, contains an answer to the question of whether Mr. Gorbachev was afraid of SDI or of any other U.S. programs. Since there was no real threat of an attack from the United States against the Soviet Union, and Gorbachev felt so, he assumed the need for an arms reduction process, and this was what underlay his thinking from the start. This is his view, which he proved correct afterwards.

Of course, sometimes he responded to certain U.S. actions and U.S. statements in rather dramatic tones because he felt that he had to do so from the standpoint of the prestige of the country, but that did not change his deep inner conviction that there will be no nuclear war, there will be no nuclear attack. That was what underlay his position.

That phrase, "Don't put on my desk any war-fighting program," was uttered before Chernobyl [April–May 1986], but I would like very much to endorse what Alexander Bessmertnykh said. Chernobyl had a very significant effect, and it even strengthened Gorbachev's conviction.

Mr. Oberdorfer: I would like to ask one of the Americans, what was your reaction to the U.S. SDI program, a new factor in this whole negotiating mix?

Mr. Nitze: Well, my reaction was one of confusion about it. I had no doubt that it was clearly very much on the president's mind. He really always believed deeply that one should have some kind of a defense, or at least get rid of these damn ballistic missiles. I thought he was right about that judgment, but the question was a practical one: would this program help you do that? I doubted the practicality of the program. It seemed to me that those working on the SDI program had underestimated the technical difficulties involved in working out a program that would produce any useful results. It might be very expensive and get nowhere. So the question then was, how do you conduct the negotiations in the light of these confusing indications? I thought the president was fully dedicated to the idea of getting rid of ballistic missiles or having an effective defense. I doubted that an effective defense was possible.

Mr. Oberdorfer: Did you feel that this program had a big effect on the people you were negotiating with, or on the Soviet position in general?

Mr. Nitze: I thought it had a fairly large effect upon the Soviet position, particularly upon Mr. Gorbachev. He took it very seriously. It became kind of a contest of wills between President Reagan and Mr. Gorbachev. Both of them were convinced that they were right about it and locked in battle on this issue.

Mr. Shultz: There was a very dramatic moment at the Geneva Summit. The second day of the summit started out a little bit more tensely than the first day, because President Reagan had a hard private discussion with Gorbachev about human rights problems. They came into a plenary session and we started in on strategic matters, and it drifted into a discussion of SDI.

    The general secretary attacked the SDI program. President Reagan responded at some point in a very forceful and strong way. He carried on for, I don't know, ten or fifteen minutes, talking about why SDI was important and why it was important to be able to defend yourself. It was a very impassioned statement, and with the simultaneous translation you could connect the words with the man and the way he expressed himself. When he finished, there was an absolute dead silence in the room. And if there is a dead silence in a room like that for, say, thirty seconds, it seems like an eternity, but there was total silence. It was obvious that it was up to Mr. Gorbachev to say something. Finally he said, "Mr. President, I don't agree with you, but I can see that you really mean it." And I thought to myself, "Clang, like a coin dropping, Ronald Reagan has nailed into place an element of the U.S. position as something on which, at least as far as he is concerned, he is not going to compromise."

Mr. Oberdorfer: Did Gorbachev understand before Reykjavik the depth of Reagan's commitment? Did he really know that he was not going to be able to shake Reagan out of this idea?

Mr. Chernyaev: I think he did understand the emotional commitment of the president to SDI and that there was also prestige at stake for the U.S. president in this. But before Reykjavik, he did not think that this problem could scuttle the idea that he had for the Reykjavik Summit. He did not think that the emotional commitment of President Reagan to SDI was so totally integrated into U.S. policy. He thought that there was a dividing line between those two things.

Also, when Gorbachev was trying to persuade President Reagan, often speaking very passionately to him, [urging him] to abandon SDI, he did it because he was thinking about trust and he wanted to create a situation of trust. He felt that the deployment of SDI would create a very difficult situation for him because he would have to do something. There would certainly be a backlash in the Soviet Union. He wanted to avoid the kind of atmosphere that would create that backlash.

Mr. Oberdorfer: On that point, to what extent did Gorbachev have a free hand on this subject? Was it necessary for him to take the position that he could defend with other leaders in the Politburo, or could he decide anything he wanted to decide and get away with it?

Mr. Chernyaev: At that time, Gorbachev was, so to speak, playing at full strength, and the decisions that he proposed to the Politburo were accepted by the Politburo, so there would have been no doubt at that time, in 1986, that whatever he proposed would have been accepted by the entire Soviet leadership.

Mr. Oberdorfer: When did his power become attenuated to the point that he was not able to make these decisions by himself?

Mr. Chernyaev: That is a different subject for discussion. I think sometime in 1988.

Mr. Oberdorfer: Yes, Paul.

Mr. Nitze: I think there was one other complicating factor, and that was that some of us on the U.S. side, particularly Bud McFarlane and I, backed by the Joint Chiefs of Staff, felt that there might be a possibility of working out a deal with the Soviet side under which we would delay for at least ten years any movement toward deployment of an SDI system provided the Soviets would agree with us on radical reductions of offensive systems on both sides. Bud was the one of the two of us who took the responsibility of clearing it with Reagan. And I don't believe that Bud ever really did it. He talked to Reagan about it, but he never made it clear to him what we had in mind. All the Joint Chiefs of Staff were wholly in agreement, so that it was really just Reagan against most of the rest of the administration on this. We thought that if we could, it would be perfectly worthwhile to delay any deployment of SDI for ten years provided we got what we wanted in the reduction of, particularly, the land-based big offensive missiles.

Mr. Oberdorfer: I think you wanted to say something, Mr. Secretary.

Mr. Shultz: I did want to say that the president signed a letter to General Secretary Gorbachev in July 1986, before Reykjavik, in which in a rather convoluted formulation he proposed a delay in deployment of seven and a half years, dependent upon certain things. And then, of course, at Reykjavik, this formulation that you mentioned was put on the table by the president. In his view, that was a use of the SDI in the bargaining that didn't compromise the essential aspect of it, namely, the effort to find out through research what could be done.

Ms. Ridgway: I think it is important to ensure that this issue of the SDI and offense/defense isn't seen just as a broad discussion among leaders. There were other things going on that were an important part of the picture. I have always been convinced that President Reagan himself was a true believer in the importance of defense. There is a consistent straight line in the arms control field from SDI through Reykjavik. And if you reject that, then you get confused explanations of Reykjavik. But if you understand that the man really believed this, then you can understand what was happening there.

Beneath the president's own conviction, the SDI proposal was used in a different way by different factions to achieve different things. So you have got some very complex American proposals with respect to SDI reflecting battles on the U.S. side between people who wanted to initiate and pursue with the Soviet Union an offense/defense discussion, who wanted to talk about a new era in which offense came down [and] defense went up[, and those people who wanted to use SDI to stop all arms control talks with Moscow].

As Ambassador Matlock was saying, we wanted to pursue for the president some of the questions that came out of Geneva when the president found that his conviction that he could convince anybody was certainly jarred a little bit by the fact that he hadn't convinced Gorbachev. But below that, there were people who really did want to use SDI, and its implications for the ABM Treaty, to stop the arms control process, who did not see in it [arms control] anything that they believed had value. The impulse from that then added another complication. Some of our allies in NATO were not sure they understood what the purpose of the SDI proposal was, since they hadn't been briefed ahead of time; no one had talked to them about offense/defense. There was a rush of allies to Washington to try to understand. Those who did understand supported it. But throughout this period, as various proposals were put forward, there was considerable doubt in the Alliance as to how, at the end of the day, the SDI notion would be used by the United States.

The Soviet side was not, in my view, unaware of the opportunities that confusion among the allies gave the Soviet side to play a propaganda game with SDI, external to the government-to-government bilateral dialogue. I always thought that on some occasions the Soviets thought that if they kept saying that SDI was an obstacle, they hoped that they could get Alliance pressure back onto the United States to make other kinds of concessions in the offensive part of the talks.

So this is not a single notion that one can understand just by saying, "Well, what did it do to the Soviets?" because certainly, on the U.S. side, it did a lot to muddy up the U.S. analysis of where it was going and what it thought it was doing.

Mr. Oberdorfer: I wanted to ask Frank Carlucci to give his appraisal of how this perception of what Mr. Gershwin described this morning of the Soviet force buildup played on our thinking about what we had to do, and how that cycle was finally broken in the late 1980s.

Mr. Carlucci: You have to bear in mind when you take into account my perspective that I did come out of the CIA in the Carter administration, so I tended to share the views that Larry Gershwin laid before you. Indeed, the DIA [Defense Intelligence Agency] was if anything more hawkish on the estimates. My principal responsibility when I became deputy secretary of defense was to put together the budget revisions. We saw ourselves as behind quantitatively and slipping behind qualitatively.

As we looked at the Soviet force structure and [military] doctrine, they seemed to us to be totally offensive in nature, with heavy emphasis on Spetsnaz divisions,[5] forward-based engineering equipment, ICBMs, tanks; whereas NATO doctrine was clearly defensive in nature. This was a subject that we got into in some detail in our later meetings between the respective defense ministers.

Our first priority was to rebuild our strategic forces, with the highest emphasis being given to command, control, and communications. We set aside a sum of money for this whole undertaking. If my memory serves me correctly, it was somewhere in the neighborhood of $5 billion. Then we went ahead with the B-1, the B-2, and the MX missile, which was very hard to get through politically. Indeed, we were never fully successful.

The second priority was to restore readiness and sustainability. A lot of our divisions simply weren't ready. Our mission-capable rates were far below the acceptable levels because, in the words of the army chief of staff in the Carter administration, we had "hollowed out" our armed forces. Third was to bring into production some of the platforms that had been developed by prior administrations, including the M-1 tank, which took something like twenty years to get into production, the Bradley armored fighting vehicle, and aircraft, such as the F-18.

This was not being done with any view to achieving military superiority. It was being done because we felt that we were behind and we needed to have an adequate deterrent, and that if the trends continued, as Larry described them, by the mid-1990s our deterrent would have completely eroded. And as you all know, there is a substantial lead time for rebuilding military forces.

On SDI, I agree with George that it was very much Ronald Reagan's program. I was not in government when the speech was made, but when I came back as national security advisor I had quite a bit to do with SDI. I can't tell you whether Ronald Reagan ever believed that we would have some kind of an impenetrable shield. I went back and researched his speeches and could only find one fairly obscure speech in which he really said something close to that. Obviously, as everybody knows, he was not a person who wanted to get into the technicalities. He did, as best I could tell, sincerely believe that he could give it [SDI] to the Russians and everything would be fine. I and others would try to explain to him that, technically, that just was not feasible. The only thing that finally convinced him, I remember, was one day when I said to him, "Mr. President, you have just got to stop saying that, because, you know, Gorbachev, among others, doesn't believe you." And he said, "Well, I guess you are right. He really doesn't believe me."

Mr. Matlock: I would say that President Reagan was not only a true believer in SDI, he was definitely a true believer in sharing. This was something that virtually the entire bureaucracy that dealt with these things said we couldn't do. I recall just one incident when we were drafting a letter, and it may have been the one that you mentioned, Mr. Secretary, in July '86. He wanted a section on sharing. We sent a draft in, and he changed it and made a very strong commitment to sharing. I checked this out, and all the experts said, "We can't do that." So I changed it back, and sent it to him. It went back to him four times. Finally, he called me in and said, "Jack, is this my letter?" I said, "Yes, sir, Mr. President." He said, "This is what I want to say." And I said, "Look, Mr. President, everybody tells me we can't do that." He said, "Damn it, it is my letter, that's what I am going to do." And that's the letter he sent.

So he was very sincere in this. Whether he could have carried it out, I don't know, but he certainly would have tried. He did recognize, eventually, that Gorbachev wasn't believing him and then he sort of eased off. But he continued to believe in sharing throughout.

Mr. Shultz: I remember Gorbachev saying to him once, "You won't even sell us milk machines! How can I accept that you are going to do that?"

Mr. Carlucci: Yes, but it took a number of years to get him to that realization.

Mr. Oberdorfer: Well, quite apart from the technicalities, Frank—politically, could the United States have given this to someone? Would Congress have allowed it?

Mr. Carlucci: It depends on what you are talking about, Don. It now appears that you can create a space-based system—but Congress doesn't like space-based systems, so this may never happen—but you could certainly create a space-based system that would cover other parts of the world than just the United States. Indeed, Margaret Thatcher was intrigued with this idea.

The cost of doing that is quite another thing. When I first went to DOD, it was the cost that concerned me. Phase II architecture was estimated to cost $150 billion. First, I had an independent study done to see if the whole thing was technically feasible, because I had my doubts. The word came back, "Yes, it is." It was technically feasible, but at an enormous cost. I called in the program manager, Jim Abramson, and I said, "You are no longer a salesman, you are program manager. I want the costs down." And by the time I left, they began to move toward something called "Brilliant Pebbles"—I am sorry for the jargon—but the cost was down in the neighborhood of $50 billion. If you get it down a little bit more it competes on a cost-effectiveness basis with offensive missiles.

The point is, and I testified to this effect at my confirmation hearing, that some of us saw SDI as adding to deterrence. There is only one aspect of what George said that I mildly disagree with. I didn't see the joint chiefs, George, as enthusiastic about SDI. In fact, they had a lot of reservations about SDI when it was first announced.

Mr. Shultz: Well, they were the ones that told him—

Mr. Carlucci: I know.

Mr. Shultz: —That it was feasible, and that's what triggered the speech.

Mr. Carlucci: But they didn't expect to happen what happened, so . . .

Mr. Shultz: They should be more careful.

Mr. Carlucci: They learned their lesson, because the next thing they knew—

Mr. Shultz: Their problem was that they didn't realize that anybody took them seriously.

Mr. Carlucci: The next thing they knew, a whole organizational structure had been set up outside the procurement mechanism, outside the control of the JCS. They saw that as a real drain on their resources, so they became greatly alarmed. When I went over there [to the DOD], I put it back in the procurement system. And then the joint chiefs began to look at it seriously in terms of adding to our deterrent capability—what would be the attrition rate on incoming missiles, what would be the residual capability. And after some studies, they became satisfied that it would add to our deterrent capability.

The trick was to provide some reassurance to our Soviet friends that they could keep track of this program. A lot of it was complicated a little later on by moving to the broad interpretation of the [ABM] treaty, and the backlash that produced in the Congress. Speaking very candidly, I am certain that a lot of the statements by my predecessor [Caspar Weinberger] about early deployment greatly alarmed Gorbachev. He was talking about deploying in one or two years, which was just not feasible. So we had to tone some of those things down and get it into a framework where it was a little less threatening. However, I am convinced that from day one, as has been said by our Soviet colleagues, they recognized that it had no offensive capability. Leaving that aside, if SDI worked it did have the capability to nullify their principal strategic weapon, which was the land-based ICBMs. The economic costs to the Soviet Union of deploying SDI would have been enormous. So, on that ground alone, it could be justified on a deterrent basis.

The experts are here on how it was linked in the early stages to the arms control negotiations: START, INF. Gradually, through the efforts of George, Paul, Roz, and others, it was delinked from INF, and we began to take an approach which dealt with some of the offensive arms on [their own] merits. That's when progress began to be made.

Mr. Oberdorfer: What do you think fundamentally broke the cycle? Here both countries are ratcheting up their arms. You were saying that the administration felt the United States was behind. The Soviets, I think, did not feel that they were ahead, particularly, but they saw us building up. We saw them building up. Finally, something broke this cycle. What was it?

Mr. Carlucci: I think the realization on the part of both sides that this kind of trend couldn't continue, that we had to enter into a dialogue.

You asked last night how Ronald Reagan could call the Soviet Union an "evil empire" on the one hand and be a forthcoming negotiator on the other. In his mind, that was very simple. I think either Roz or Jack said that, you know, he was convinced that he could change the "evil empire" to a "good empire" through force of persuasion. I remember that he once said to me, and I think he probably said it many times to you, George, "If I could just get Gorbachev over here and fly him over the United States and let him see the neighborhoods and the grocery stores . . ." I regard that as naive, but he believed it. He thought that through this negotiating process, he could change the Soviet Union. I guess I would have to say, in retrospect, he was certainly more right than I was.

Then there were the personal bonds that began to develop between the president and Gorbachev, between George and Shevardnadze; the gradual building of trust. I would like to think military-to-military dialogue played some role in this. Indeed, Sasha [Bessmertnykh], at one point you mentioned to me that it was very helpful in taking some of the pressure off Gorbachev. Certainly, [former Soviet defense minister Dmitry] Yazov had said to me on several occasions that it was helpful. I think there was a whole confluence of things that brought about a realization that we were heading in a crazy direction, that there was a possibility to get out of this dilemma, and that it had to be done on the basis of building mutual trust and continuing existing negotiations.

Mr. Shultz: Let me just insert a comment on the question of how the cycle was broken. Remember that Ronald Reagan's initial proposals for strategic arms talks and for the intermediate-range INF talks were for massive reductions. That is where he started. And at Reykjavik, in a sense, that's what Gorbachev put on the table. So if you want to look at the lineage, I think that's a handy place to start.

Prof. Greenstein: I would like to ask our former Soviet panelists two questions. First, would you tell us a little more about how the awareness of the proportion of Soviet resources that was being drained into military developments developed as the successive post-Brezhnev leadership groups came in? And second, how did the perception not just of SDI but of the entire Reagan administration arms buildup play into your awareness of what could or couldn't continue?

Mr. Bessmertnykh: I think that the rationale of looking at the economic side of the arms race was very much on Gorbachev's mind. When Gorbachev came to power in Moscow in 1985, the economic statistics already indicated that the economy was not doing so well. It is surprising that his coming to power and the slowdown in the economy coincided. It was just a coincidence, but Gorbachev was very much aware of that immediately after becoming the head of the country.

So when you were talking about SDI and arms control, the economic element of the necessity to go down with the reductions was sometimes, in my view, the number one preoccupation of Gorbachev, especially when we were preparing ourselves for Reykjavik. That was a very drastic proposal. It was Gorbachev's personal instruction that we should really try once and for all to be very serious about arms control. Let's go very, very deep down. And again, the economic part of it was very, very strong.

When we were talking about SDI, just the thought of getting involved in this SDI arms race, of trying to do something like [what] the United States was going to do with space-based weapons programs, looked like a horror to Gorbachev. So he was trying to avoid that alternative by going for reductions, while trying to persuade the U.S. side not to do it.

I would like to just comment on some things about the SDI. Frank just mentioned for the first time the connection between the SDI and the ABM Treaty. Of course, we never thought that SDI was an offensive strategic program. But in our strategic analysis the danger lay not in the fact that it was offensive but in the fact that it was defensive, because by creating this strong defense you have denied the Soviet Union the possibility for retaliatory response if we are attacked. That was very strongly felt by everyone. We thought that if the United States feels secure from a second strike, then it may be prompted to make the first strike. That strategic element was very clearly felt by our strategists, and they were trying to persuade Gorbachev of it.

The ABM Treaty was extremely important. Even now it is important to us, because we can't explain the deep and drastic reductions to our own strategists, our experts who watch the process, or the people generally, if we ruin the ABM Treaty. We believe that the ABM Treaty is a kind of safeguard against different kinds of possibilities, especially when you go so deeply down with the arms reductions. This is something I just wanted to be the part of the story, which would explain a certain urgency in our responses to SDI.

Mr. Chernyaev: I would like to add a couple of points in answer to your question about what really led to the breakthrough out of that vicious circle.

On March 1, 1986, Gorbachev proposed to untie the INF missiles from the other arms control issues, untying the package that had played a very negative role in Reykjavik. That put on a realistic footing the negotiations on INF missiles, [weapons] that really were a nightmare for Europe. The SS-20s were a nightmare for Europe, and the Pershing IIs were, of course, a nightmare for us, because they were a gun that was pointed right at our head. As a result of that decision, by the end of that year, 1987, the first treaty of real disarmament that actually reduced the number of nuclear weapons was concluded in Washington in December.

And Secretary Shultz probably remembers that when he visited Moscow in April 1988, General Secretary Gorbachev characterized the INF Treaty as the watershed in our entire relationship. The INF Treaty was not just important in and of itself; working on that treaty created the network of person-to-person links that was mentioned yesterday by Sergei Tarasenko.

But the INF Treaty was signed in an atmosphere that I would still describe as a rather high level of mutual mistrust. It was right after the INF Treaty was signed that the character of our relations changed. And of course, in changing the character of our relations, the personal rapport between Shultz and Shevardnadze and between Gorbachev and Reagan was of great importance.

Let me just once again emphasize that it was after the INF Treaty that our relationship began to evolve in the framework of trust. On December 17, 1987, Gorbachev reported to the Politburo *[Chernyaev reads the notes of Politburo meeting]:*

In Washington, perhaps for the first time, we understood so clearly how important the human factor is in international politics. Before that, we were content with a rather banal formula. We said that in foreign policy, of course, contacts between the leaders of states and governments are important. That goes without saying. But behind that formula, we felt that it is, indeed, personal contacts, but essentially these are contacts between the representatives of two irreconcilable systems that have irreconcilable class differences.

And he emphasized rather sarcastically: "between representatives."

For us, Reagan appeared as a representative of and a spokesman for the most conservative part of the most conservative segment of American capitalism and the military-industrial complex. But it turned out that on top of all that, it is also important that policy makers, including the leaders of states, of governments, if they really are responsible people, they also represent purely human qualities, the interests and the aspirations of common people, and that they can be guided by purely normal human feelings and aspirations. And in our day and age, this turns out to be of enormous importance. That is to say, literally, to incorporate the human factor in international politics. And this has also produced specific results. This is an important aspect of the new international thinking, and it has now produced results. And in Washington, we, perhaps for the first time, felt that in a very, very clear way.

This is what Gorbachev said to the Politburo on December 17, 1987. And both during that meeting of the Politburo and later, after Secretary Shultz's visit to Moscow in February 1988, Gorbachev in his discussions with his colleagues emphasized also the importance of middle-level contacts between people from various U.S. and Soviet government agencies. And he mentioned the specific names of the people whose personal contacts were, he believed, very important in building the relationship.

And I recall how Shevardnadze came to report to Gorbachev the progress in the discussions at working levels between Mr. Bessmertnykh and Ambassador Ridgway, between [Colin] Powell, [Sergei] Tarasenko, and his American counterparts. The conclusion was that it is no longer just bureaucratic officials working and simply defending their locked-in positions. It is people working on something big, something important to both sides. He specifically mentioned Ambassador Ridgway, and he asked me, "Have you noted this really extremely intelligent lady that is in a policy-making position in the United States?" And I said to him, "Yes, I noted her, and it is good that you are noting her, that you are noting the specific people, the specific faces involved in this work."

He said many times afterwards, and mentioned it to Mr. Shultz, that it is very good that we now have this mechanism—he was not even comfortable with the word *mechanism* to describe this group of people from both sides—of serious, intelligent, responsible people on both sides working on something big and important not only for their countries, but for the world.

Mr. Oberdorfer: What Mr. Chernyaev has just told us about Gorbachev's thinking after the Washington Summit emphasizes something very, very essential in this whole process. You have mechanisms, systems, governments, irreconcilable class differences, and then you have people on the other side, and you have individual human beings trying to grapple with these two machines hurtling down into history in their own ways. And somehow, in some mysterious way that I guess historians are going to be talking about for a long, long time, these people, people like the ones at these two tables, were able to connect with each other and talk to each other, and dispel some of the fears that lay at the root of the kinds of military buildups that were discussed this morning, and somehow break this cycle.

I see several people who want to comment—Roz? and I think Paul also wanted to say something.

Ms. Ridgway: Mr. Chernyaev has taken us ahead to 1987, but I think it is important to fill in something here that relates to what he said about people and mechanisms.

When we left Geneva in 1985, we had a work program. We had identified issues on which we wanted to proceed. We had identified some new areas of prospective cooperation, such as research on fusion technologies and the like. We had a commitment to a cycle of summits: Washington, Moscow. And yet, there set in almost immediately a set of obstacles to developing that work program. While I think Jack may remember some of the details in the relationship and the concentration that we understood to be taking place on the Soviet side on some internal party and personnel issues, we found it impossible to get together. The work program commissioned in Geneva did not, in fact, become fully engaged until the summer of 1986, for a whole lot of external reasons. Part of the effort in the spring of 1986 was to find a way to get people back to work around some other issues that had occurred.

It was the Bessmertnykh mission to Washington in July 1986 that attempted to break through this period of stagnation and disappointment that was setting in about our ability to begin working on this program that was intended to ensure that, as we came to a halt for a good reason in arms control, we might make progress on a regional issue, or we could continue to work the human rights and bilateral programs. But there was a period, I think, in which that whole set of relationships and the program that was intended to be the vehicle for keeping us engaged were at risk. It wasn't until the summer of '86, with this private conversation, that we tried to find a way to get around it.

Mr. Oberdorfer: To what extent was it at risk because of disagreement within the U.S. government, rather than disagreement between Moscow and Washington?

Ms. Ridgway: I am not aware of any disagreement between Moscow and Washington. There was almost silence in that period. But we re-engaged in July '86. Paul led a team to Moscow with a very important offense/defense paper in August '86, and we re-engaged the other areas of the bilateral relationship shortly thereafter.

Mr. Oberdorfer: In March 1986, just a day after the end of the Twenty-seventh Party Congress, the United States ordered the Soviet Union to reduce sharply its diplomatic mission to the United Nations in New York from about 270 diplomats to 170. This is something that had been pending for a while, and it had been decided to put this off until after the Party congress, so as not to get involved in Soviet domestic politics. Then, less than a week later, on March 13, two U.S. warships loaded with sophisticated electronic gear sailed six miles inside the Soviet Union's twelve-mile territorial limit in the Black Sea. Although the United States felt that it had a perfect right to do this under so-called innocent passage, Moscow did not particularly like that. In April, the United States bombed Libya in retaliation for a terrorist attack in Berlin, and a planned trip by Shevardnadze was postponed, if you remember, right after that action. Then the Soviet Union was distracted on April 26 by the Chernobyl nuclear disaster, which, of course, captured the attention of the Soviet leadership for quite a time.

This whole period I characterize [in *The Turn*] as "a case of the blahs." Things were kind of bogging down. And I think it was in this context that Mr. Gorbachev decided to propose a working-level meeting of the two top leaders, which turned out to be the Reykjavik Summit.

Ms. Ridgway: But you have got phases and subphases. After Geneva, there was a period of heavy propagandizing on both sides as to who was at fault for failure to make progress on INF, and was it SDI or was it this or was it that. Then there was a consideration of internal domestic political issues that were already on the calendar. Then the Libya thing, together with the decision to go ahead on previously made decisions on the phase-down of the Soviet missions, scuttled a scheduled ministerial meeting.[6] All this came together, and the dialogue never started after Geneva. We spent a lot of time on the search to get that dialogue started. When it did get started, it lasted a month to six weeks when that Zakharov-Daniloff thing landed and ended that part of it, as well.

Mr. Shultz: Actually, because we were not imprisoned by the doctrine of "linkage," the Zakharov-Daniloff affair did not bring the whole thing to a halt, and we did have plenary sessions in which we did make some progress. As soon as the Zakharov-Daniloff affair was settled, we held the Reykjavik Summit—it was delayed somewhat, but it wasn't derailed.

Mr. Oberdorfer: It might have been in other circumstances. Mr. Nitze wanted to say something.

Mr. Nitze: Underlying all of this from the "working-stiffs" level on both sides, there was an entirely different operation going on. We wanted to de-link our negotiations from everything else. We wanted to get on with trying to work out a deal that was acceptable to both sides. The important point from the U.S. side was verification. The president had a phrase: "Trust, but verify." We wanted to be sure that all these agreements that we worked out were, in fact, verifiable and could be implemented; and that both sides knew what the provisions meant and what we and the Soviet side were supposed to do. The question of working out a verifiable agreement was, I think, the most complicated part of the entire negotiations.

Mr. Oberdorfer: Ambassador Matlock—

Mr. Matlock: Yes, there was another very important part of the agenda, which did affect our thinking on the other issues ultimately, and that was the attempt to establish contacts in a broad sense, not just by leaders, but by the societies; to open up Soviet society, to open up the media, and particularly, to encourage better respect for human rights.

Now, we didn't link these. I think that Secretary Shultz is quite right that we didn't stop talking because there was a problem in one area. At the same time, we did feel that politically and in reality, though not as a policy matter, these things were linked, because it was very clear that if you came to even a good arms control agreement and—say—the Soviet Union then invaded another country, the Senate was probably not going to ratify even a good treaty. One could argue as to whether the SALT II [Treaty] was good or not, but the fact is that after Afghanistan, no treaty would have been ratified. There was a political relationship, though not a formal linkage. During this period, the Soviet leadership itself became committed to doing something about human rights, and that did have an effect on President Reagan and his thinking about the system. One of the things that really got him started on trying to establish communication was the Pentecostals. I mean, he really cared about these issues. Finally, by '86—and certainly by '87, when, particularly, Shevardnadze was able to say, "We are doing this in our own interests," and began to work cooperatively to deal with some of these issues—this had a payback effect.

Mr. Oberdorfer: Secretary Shultz wanted to make some comments.

Mr. Shultz: As one policy maker, I became increasingly skeptical of the economic and political analysis of the CIA, though when it came to making estimates of things that you could quantify, like ballistic missiles, it seemed to me that their material was very solid. So I took the estimates that were mentioned this morning very seriously and felt that they did give an accurate picture of the problem, as Frank confirmed. It also seemed to me that it was unlikely that the Soviets would be constrained by economics in the strategic ballistic missile area, because—as a former secretary of defense, Charley Wilson, once said—you get more bang for the buck [from strategic nuclear forces than from conventional forces].

On the other hand, the United States had a terrible problem with deploying land-based intercontinental ballistic missiles. Basically, we couldn't do it. This was an area of very strong Soviet comparative advantage over us. It isn't that we didn't know how to do the engineering and so on, but we simply couldn't find a way to base those missiles in the United States. This was a period when a method called "Dense Pack" was proposed, in which the idea was that you put the missiles close together, and when they are attacked, fratricide [among incoming Soviet warheads] will save some of them. I remember being briefed on this before it was announced and scratching my head about it. I didn't have any way to evaluate it independently, but what astonished me was that when the proposal was made by the president on the advice of the secretary of defense, the Joint Chiefs of Staff immediately disagreed with it and shot it down. I was brought up in the Mel Laird Defense Department days, and I couldn't imagine that happening, but it did disclose the inability to find a basing mode for our intercontinental ballistic missiles. So, to me, that always argued very strongly for a hard push on the START negotiations. It was one of my major disappointments that because of all the pulling and hauling [that took place] to a very considerable extent in the U.S. government, we were not able to push forward on that, and we missed the boat badly.

I would like to make a comment about Chernobyl, following up on Mr. Bessmertnykh's comment. I remember making that calculation—I think you are the one that made it for me, Paul—on the relationship of the Chernobyl explosion to a nuclear weapons explosion. I am sure lots of people did it, and I am sure Gorbachev did it. It is very dramatic—it makes quite a statement to you. I did have some discussions later with Mr. Gorbachev about that.

Another aspect of it also struck me. Periodically, I talked to Gorbachev and to Shevardnadze about the emerging information and knowledge age and the impact that would have. I could see that Gorbachev was very interested in all of this. But the Chernobyl accident really drove the point home, because the first news of it did not come from the Soviet Union. It came from observations from the Swedes and others, who then asked questions of the Soviet Union. The Soviet Union reluctantly acknowledged that there had been an accident and then said it had been taken care of. Then pictures of what was happening were published from a private satellite. More information kept coming out, and the people in the Warsaw Pact countries that were downwind heard about this not from the Soviet Union, but from the West. I think it is fair to say that many Soviet citizens themselves heard about it first over the Voice of America rather than from their own government. You had here a visible example of the power of the information age.

Following up on Jack's bringing up the human rights subject, I recall many conversations with Mr. Shevardnadze in which he kept saying, "We are not going to do this to please you. We have to find out why this is a good thing for the Soviet Union. And we will do it for our own purposes." I recall, and he has told me that he remembers it distinctly, a very careful presentation, which I worked out in my mind and I wrote down, which in effect said: "If people are going to be able to operate successfully in the coming age, then there has to be more openness, they have to be able to communicate. They can't be compartmentalized. There has to be more freedom of movement." I said to him, "To achieve the kind of human rights that you are talking about—economic advance and welfare—you are going to have to address the kind of human rights that we are talking about. It is going to be a precondition. So it is in your interest to do this."

Mr. Carlucci: George mentioned our difficulty in deploying the MX. He describes accurately how that tended to drive the arms control process. In the later years, about '87 and '88, the same difficulty arose with regard to SDI, which brought some of us to realize that SDI's value, at least as a bargaining chip (and I know that the president never saw it as a bargaining chip) was diminishing. As a result of the flap over the broad interpretation [of the ABM Treaty], the Congress passed a provision locking us in effect into the narrow interpretation. That made almost any developmental work impossible and, indeed, impacted some of our existing early warning systems. So even the most diehard SDI supporter began to realize that it was going to be very, very difficult to get this kind of program through. As you have seen in subsequent years, the Congress has forced the shifting of the focus of the program from the space-based systems to the ground-based systems, which from a military point of view, at least, is much less effective, but, I guess, is much less of a threat to the ABM Treaty.

Mr. Oberdorfer: Secretary Shultz said earlier that he didn't know much about this announcement of SDI before it took place. And I would say, as a reporter who was covering it, he was more or less a good soldier on the subject, advancing administration policy without any particular expression of concern about it. But then I am tempted to ask him to repeat the story about his wonderful briefing on SDI that he was given by the head of the SDI organization, General Abramson, when he wanted to find out what it was. Do you remember that?

Mr. Shultz: I certainly do. Paul Nitze was also present. I always thought that the basic idea of trying to figure out how to defend yourself was very appealing. So I thought the president was on the right track, although it was hard for me to evaluate just what SDI amounted to. I was offered a briefing by General Abramson. Paul Nitze had visited the laboratories that were doing SDI work and had given me a fair amount of information. We sat down at this briefing. I have spent a good portion of my life around scientists and engineers at MIT and then at the Bechtel Corporation, so I have had a certain exposure to salesmanship. After a while, I said to General Abramson, "You are telling me the things that I can read in the newspaper." Then I started to raise some questions that I had in my mind as a result of Paul's comments. General Abramson turned to the man who was with him and said, "Gee, I don't know whether the secretary is cleared for this information." And I said, "General, why don't you leave? When you are ready to answer my questions, let me know, and I will invite you back." We never had another session.

Of course, this did not cause me to lose faith in the importance of SDI. But whenever I heard these extravagant claims, and when I heard that the president was getting these private briefings from the general, boy, it really bothered me a lot. Frank, you were involved in some of those in your role as NSC advisor.

Mr. Carlucci: After each of those briefings, I would go in to the president, George, and try to put it in perspective. Mainly, I would tell him, "Look, this thing cannot be deployed in the time frame that the Defense Department was telling you." And that was the central issue. They had it ready to pull off the shelf and be deployed, I think, at one point in a two-year time frame, wasn't it, Paul?

Mr. Nitze: That's right.

Mr. Carlucci: Which was just unimaginable from a technical point of view.

Mr. Nitze: It wouldn't have been worth anything.

Mr. Carlucci: No.

Mr. Matlock: Let me just add a couple of points here on that. And since neither Bud McFarlane nor John Poindexter is here to speak for himself, my impression in working for them was that, although they were certainly in favor of a research program to look at the possibilities, they very much saw the SDI program as an effort to give the Soviet Union an incentive to reduce its heavy

ICBMs. And I know later, when he was no longer in office, McFarlane told me that he was appalled that the president had turned down the offer at Reykjavik. He said, "What Gorbachev offered at Reykjavik was exactly what I was aiming for. Once we had an agreement on reductions, ten years [of delay on SDI testing] was fine. It was crazy to turn that down."

Mr. Shultz: It would take forever in laboratories.

Mr. Matlock: But in any event, I think, for both of them the main incentive in backing it was to provide the Soviets with an incentive on the heavies [ICBMs], because, for the very reasons you pointed out, Mr. Secretary, they felt that there was very little incentive for the Soviet Union to reduce its heavy ICBMs drastically if there was not something like SDI pressing them to do so.

Mr. Carlucci: But surely our Soviet friends realized that it couldn't be deployed within the time frame that we were talking about. You had to have that technical capability. Even though the president of the United States was being told it could be deployed in two years, I am sure you knew it would take eight to ten years to deploy it.

Mr. Bessmertnykh: Well, yes, of course. There was no doubt in our minds. Slowly, we came to understand that the SDI issue was used as pressure in the SALT and START talks. The more you talked about it, especially in the formal talks, the more we realized this, especially in the Foreign Ministry. We made a report to the president about it. We said that we suspected that the insistence with which the United States was now talking about this was probably designed to pressure us into some concessions in the talks. At the same time, of course, the military were talking to Gorbachev and warning him. But very soon after that program was announced there was a realization that it was impossible to implement within that short period of time.

Mr. Carlucci: May I follow up? One of the things that I always thought had possibilities but that got absolutely nowhere with the Soviets, and I would be interested in why, is the idea of CBMs, confidence-building measures, with SDI, letting you see the development of the program—not giving it to you, as the president was talking about, but sharing some of the information as we went along, even allowing your space station to look at some of our satellites—but Gorbachev consistently rejected all those out of hand. Why was that?

Mr. Bessmertnykh: We didn't trust it at all. And all our specialists said that it was absolutely impossible that the Americans would really let us see those things developing in their laboratories. So there was no trust at all about it. It was considered as a ploy, basically.

Mr. Oberdorfer: Pavel, you wanted to say something.

Mr. Palazchenko: Yes. I just wanted to say that I recall that in 1986 or 1987 I and other people in the Foreign Ministry at working levels were writing all kinds of papers about how we should de-emphasize SDI in our positions, that it was counterproductive to emphasize SDI. And then, once we felt that it was beginning, perhaps, to be felt by the leadership that we should de-emphasize SDI, there would be something like a spy scandal or Secretary Weinberger's idea of early deployment or something else, and that would, of course, undermine the position of those like Shevardnadze, who was already convinced in '86 that de-emphasizing SDI would be good for both us and the U.S. side and for the process of arms control. Always, something would happen that would create an atmosphere in which the military and the military-industrial complex—who also, of course, were talking to Gorbachev—could continue to push their line that this was something that we should emphasize.

Mr. Oberdorfer: That is a wonderful lead-in, really, for this afternoon's discussion, in which we will concentrate on these things that happened out of the blue—the shooting down of Korean Airlines flight 007, the killing of Major Nicholson, a number of other unexpected crises that came up that jarred things out of their normal place.

Chapter Three

∴ Managing Crisis Flashpoints

The major superpower crises of the 1983–86 period are the subjects of discussion here: the downing of Korean Air Lines flight 007 in September 1983; the Soviets' reaction to NATO exercise "Able Archer" and subsequent U.S. deployment of intermediate-range nuclear missiles to Europe later that year; the killing of the American liaison officer Colonel Arthur Nicholson in East Germany in March 1985; and the arrest of *U.S. News and World Report* correspondent Nicholas Daniloff in August 1986. The discussion ranges over subjects including the nuts-and-bolts issues of crisis management, civil-military relations in the former Soviet Union, and the difficulties that each side experienced in reading the intentions of the other.

Mr. Oberdorfer: I'd like to start by asking Sergei Tarasenko, who worked in the American section of the Soviet Foreign Ministry in '83, just to tell us, in his own way, what happened that day after the Korean Air Lines flight was shot down. Sergei—

Mr. Tarasenko: On that day I came to my office early, as I had a habit of listening to a BBC broadcast at eight o'clock just to hear the world news. Nobody was in the office at that time. The first item on the news was a report that a plane was lost somewhere near Sakhalin, with the implication that it might have been shot down. I immediately guessed that it was actually the case. I ran across the hall to our chief office, where the governmental telephones were, and I phoned to the headquarters of the border guards. I said to the watch officer, "I listened to this report that a plane might have been shot down over our territory." And he said, "Look, it's not an airliner. This is an American reconnaissance plane which intruded into our air space, so it was shot down. Don't believe these reports that it was a passenger plane." He advised me to phone the Air Defense Command. So I phoned the Air Defense Command, and a watch officer there confirmed the news that a military reconnaissance plane had been shot down over there and he referred me to the Defense Ministry. I was on the phone to the Defense Ministry and the watch officer was starting to give me the same story when suddenly there was a pause, and in a couple of minutes he came back and said, "I cannot continue to talk to you. Please phone another time or try another officer, but not me." And I guessed that somebody had come in at that moment, since it was the time for a change in shifts, so he had been ordered not to talk about this matter.

To me it was hopeless from the beginning. We were in a mess. We had a nasty problem on our hands. So I started to think, what shall we do? At that time Komplektov, who was a deputy foreign minister, came to our office. We discussed the situation and agreed that the best way to proceed was, simply, to tell the truth and to say that it was human error: a pilot error complicated by circumstances, bad weather, and tension in the area, some misunderstanding and military confusion in this particular place. We knew that there would be a Politburo meeting at ten o'clock, so we quickly wrote down a special note to the Politburo, stating the fact and suggesting the line of behavior and the content of the governmental statement on this incident. Komplektov went to [First Deputy Foreign Minister Georgiy M.] Kornienko, and he agreed that this was the best line of behavior. Kornienko then went to Foreign Minister Gromyko. As far as we know, Kornienko's story is that Gromyko agreed in principle that this would be the wise course of action but he virtually said to Kornienko that [he should do] it alone. That [he, Gromyko, would] not go against [Defense Minister Dmitry] Ustinov or the KGB if they should present another view.

Kornienko went to this meeting. I had a chance conversation with a guy from our department who was in the military-political section. I said, "Look, we took the right position, the right approach." And he said to me, "There is no way for the Politburo to buy this story. Believe me, they will announce that this is an imperialist provocation against the Soviet Union. Deliberately done. They will not compromise the Air Defense Forces. They will side with the military, not with you." So indeed, a couple of hours later Kornienko came back, and that story went on the air: you know, the official line.

Mr. Bessmertnykh: I will just add a little bit to that. It so happened that I came to my office early, not because it was my habit—I usually don't come to my office early—but because someone called me and said, "There is an urgent cable from Washington." I came to my office, and the cable was from our chargé d'affaires in Washington. I thought it was the secretary of state who had informed him, but now I know it was the assistant secretary of state who had informed Sokolov [Oleg Sokolov, chargé d'affaires of the Soviet Embassy in Washington] that the passenger plane had just disappeared. The cable said that the American side would like to know whether we knew anything about it. It was the first request from the U.S. side.

When I read the cable I knew nothing about the situation, but I did just exactly what Sergei did. I phoned the General Staff on the government telephone, and something very peculiar happened. I didn't think they would reveal the story to me because I was from the Foreign Ministry, but somehow the man I talked with thought that I was someone from the Defense Department. He said, "Yes, Comrade General, this is the situation. The plane was shot down." I was shocked. I said, "How did it happen?" He said, "Now there's a group sitting in the next room. They're working on the circumstances. We shall report to you later." A couple of years later I found out that there is a man carrying on with the same name as mine; my name is Bessmertnykh and the name of the General Staff general was Bessmertnoi.

I immediately called Gromyko. I had the feeling that Gromyko at that moment didn't know the specifics. Then events started to develop. The only mystery is who prepared that first stupid announcement that was read on the TV. Everybody denies the authorship of that. I couldn't find anyone in the government, so I suspect it might have been in the International Department of the Central Committee, but it was definitely not me. It was definitely not the Foreign Ministry, because Kornienko denied participation in working on the first message. He worked on the second, which was much more intelligent.

Mr. Oberdorfer: When I interviewed Kornienko for my book several years ago, he told me his part of the story. He had learned that the airliner had been shot down. He and others felt that it was a human error, but he felt that the only way for the Soviet Union to handle this was to come out forthrightly and say that it had shot the plane down: admit that it was a mistake; express regret; and then explain something about the circumstances. He then talked to Foreign Minister Gromyko. Gromyko said that he agreed but he did not wish to take this up into the Politburo—sensing, I believe, that there was a controversy about it within the Politburo. And Gromyko, according to Kornienko—and you gentlemen can clarify it—never wanted to get in an argument that involved the political leaders. He did not consider himself at their level, capable of having an argument about some key matter, but he said to his deputy, Kornienko, "You can take it up if you wish to."

Kornienko told me he then telephoned General Secretary Yuri Andropov, explained to him the circumstances and what he felt the Soviet Union should say. And Andropov said, "Just a minute," and he picked up another telephone and called Defense Minister Ustinov. With Kornienko listening on his end, Ustinov, as best Kornienko could get it from the conversation, said to Andropov, "We should not admit any such thing. No one will ever know that we shot it down. And we should just say that this plane came into our air space and we knew nothing about it." And—Kornienko said—that is what Andropov decided to do. The statement was issued within a few hours saying that "an unidentified plane had been warned by Soviet fighters and had flown away in the direction of the Sea of Japan."

So I said to Mr. Kornienko, "How could a person who is the general secretary, the leader of the Soviet Union, who had been the chief of the KGB, who is a sophisticated person, have believed that no one would ever know? He must have known that the United States and its allies have listening posts and devices around the world to listen in to international air travel communications, and other ways to find out what had happened." And Kornienko said to me, "You have to remember, he was really not in very good shape in those days."[1]

In the meantime, even while they were issuing that first statement, Secretary Shultz in Washington was receiving a tremendous amount of information that had been picked up by the listening-post stations in Japan, which not only heard the transmissions from the Korean airliner but listened to the communication between the Soviet fighter pilot who shot down the plane and his ground controlling stations in Soviet Union telling him what to do, and his statement finally that "the target has been destroyed." That was the crucial line in the statement. If I recall correctly, one of the reasons that Secretary Shultz made the immediate statement he did was that he hoped that the Soviet Union, knowing that the United States knew what happened, would not put out a phony story, would not get itself in the position of misleading the world, but would tell the truth about what happened. But I ask you for your recollection.

Mr. Shultz: That's exactly right. I first was told about the plane on the phone early in the morning, around six or six-thirty, and came into the State Department. Information gradually accumulated and we had this transcript, and then we had quite a back-and-forth with the intelligence agencies about the use of the transcript. It seemed to me it would be important to use it, but it is a difficult problem for them because when you release information you compromise how you got it. But they decided under the circumstances that I could use it. The president was in California, but he was agreeable to that. So in the press conference that I held, there was, on the one hand, an expression of rage at what had taken place, but on the other hand the very deliberate effort, by reading it out from the transcript, to say to the Soviets that we had this information, so we knew that the plane had been shot down and they would be well advised not to say otherwise because it was incontrovertible. It was an effort to get them to take the kind of tack Kornienko and you were recommending. But it didn't turn out that way.

Mr. Oberdorfer: We now have the transcript of the Politburo meeting which followed two days later, on September 2, 1983.[2] In the chair was Konstantin Chernenko. Mr. Andropov was either still in the hospital or, I believe, had left for vacation and rest. In this transcript there was a briefing of the Politburo by Defense Minister Ustinov.

Gromyko says, "It's a civilian airliner." He says it right out in his statement. And then Ustinov says, "I can assure the Politburo our airman acted in full accordance with the requirements of military duty. Our actions were absolutely correct. Since the U.S.-made South Korean plane penetrated five hundred kilometers into our territory, it would be extremely difficult to distinguish this plane from a reconnaissance plane by its outline." This is totally untrue. This was a 747—not anything that looks like a reconnaissance plane. Then Mikhail Gorbachev—this was his first crisis, so to speak—said, "The plane was over our territory for a long time." Ustinov says, "Our airmen gave them numerous warnings over Kamchatka and Sakhalin. The plane was traveling without warning lights." As we know now from [the Russian newspaper] *Izvestiia's* interviews with the airmen who shot it down, that is not true either. It was not traveling without lights.

"There was no light showing through the plane's windows," says Ustinov. That was also untrue. He claims, "Warning shots were fired with tracer shells, as is stipulated in international rules." That also is untrue. According to the airman, he did not have any tracer shells, so he fired some other kind of shells which do not show up at all. Ustinov said, "And then our pilot reported to the ground that it was a combat plane and should be shot down." And from the transcripts, that isn't true either. At the end of this meeting, they end up saying that they should take a strong position that what the Soviet Union did was right. Ustinov said, "We must adhere to a firm line. Make an additional announcement without mentioning any warning shots." Chernenko says, "It's gratifying that we hold a single view here. We must take an offensive, not a defensive, line. We must be circumspect and cautious and think about the future but at the same time adopt a resolute and calm stance." And then several years later, as late as 1988, when Defense Secretary Frank Carlucci was in the Soviet Union, the then–defense minister of the Soviet Union had an amazing conversation about this.

Mr. Carlucci: This was Defense Minister Yazov, who, as you know, is now pacing a jail cell. We were riding in the back seat of a car in the Crimea, and we'd been traveling some—I'd say—hour and a half, two hours, and there was a period of silence and all of a sudden he turned to me out of the blue and said, "Why did you use that Korean airliner as a spy plane?" I was startled because we never had any discussions about this. I said, "Don't be silly. We don't use civilian airliners as spy planes. We have all the satellites we need if we want to get information on you." He said, "Yes, that's why I wonder why you used the Korean airliner as a spy plane." So I obviously got nowhere with that conversation. But it reflects the military mind set, which you've described so accurately.

Mr. Oberdorfer: But first, do you [the Russian discussants] think that the people in authority in the Soviet Union really believed and continued to believe that this was a spy plane, or was this something they said in order to justify their position?

Mr. Palazchenko: Certainly many people in the Soviet Union believed that it was a spy plane. About the leaders, I have no way of knowing. The whole thing was exacerbated by the overall Cold War atmosphere. Also, so far as I recall, in some U.S. statements there was an implication that the plane had been shot down knowingly, that they knew that it was a passenger plane. Not just deliberately, but knowingly. I don't think that there was enough information for the United States to make that statement or even a statement with that implication. That further aggravated the overall mutual suspicion. But generally, of course, had the first line that was suggested by the people in the Foreign Ministry been followed, I think we could have avoided a lot.

Mr. Bessmertnykh: There were many more technical details published in the Soviet Union about [the Americans'] intrigue surrounding that plane. There were a lot of stories and maps showing that there had been another plane flying right alongside. There was a certain spy satellite of the United States doing something there. It was so mixed up technically that people got a very strong impression that this was part of a plan by the U.S. military to check the defense systems of the Soviet Union's Far East. It's one of those things which we faced as people who deal with foreign policy. There are issues on which you depend on experts, such as, for example, the issue of verifying the telemetric information coming from the missiles in flight. I'm sure neither George or myself or James Baker would be able to understand what we're talking about [on such issues], although we discussed it for hundreds of hours. We depend on the experts.

In this case we also thought that the experts were giving us correct information. It's another story that they probably were duping us, I don't know, but the impression was that there was something wrong with the plane: it was not just a clear-cut mistake. Yes, we had made a mistake, but there was something wrong with that plane. The sense was that the Americans must have had something to do with it. That was the predominant feeling for the first couple of years at least. Even as late as 1991.

Mr. Oberdorfer: Well, Mr. Carlucci's discussion with General Yazov would have been 1988. But in 1987, when Secretary Shultz met in a very tough meeting, the first meeting with Mr. Gorbachev, Gorbachev said, right out of the blue, in the middle of an argument, "How much did you pay this pilot to put this spy operation on that Korean Air Lines flight?" And Secretary Shultz said, "We didn't pay him."

Mr. Shultz: No. I said, "I won't dignify that question by responding."

Mr. Oberdorfer: At any rate, we somehow got over it in part by Secretary Shultz and Foreign Minister Gromyko having a meeting in a very tense atmosphere in Madrid only a few weeks after this episode had happened. And maybe you could tell about your impression of what happened.

Mr. Shultz: First of all, we felt that the Soviet side should have known what it was doing, whether it did or not. Let me just remind you that the Boeing 747 has the most distinctive profile of any plane in the air. It's very recognizable. And it was a civilian airliner, so its lights indicated its distinctive profile. The RC 136 [a U.S. reconnaissance aircraft] which took off from Alaska somewhere near the same time—with notification because there was some test involved—had been on the ground back in Alaska for over an hour when the Korean Air Lines plane was shot down. So it shouldn't have been a source of confusion as far as we could see.

Our effort, first of all, was to let the Soviet side know that we knew that they had shot it down, hoping that they would not deny that they shot it down, and that we could get on track toward handling this in a sensible way. They didn't do that. Shortly thereafter they finally did say they shot it down. That little back-and-forth didn't do their credibility any good. The Madrid conference was coming up, which was supposed to be a celebration of a successful conclusion of a long meeting having to do with human rights matters. Max Kampleman, who was our chairman and was working with the Soviet side, did a rather remarkable job of bringing this to a conclusion. All of the foreign ministers were to go. Again we had a big argument within the U.S. government about whether I should meet with Gromyko. The predictable people argued that I shouldn't meet with him. I said that I should meet with him; that if you have a problem with somebody, you should meet with them and tell them what your problem is. The president agreed with me.

We set up the meeting and I was determined that what we should talk about in this meeting was the Korean airliner and human rights. Gromyko came to the meeting with a different perspective. So we had something of a contest. There was a very high sense of tension over this. When he came, I invited him to come into our little side room with me and our interpreters, and my intention was to talk to him as another human being and say, "Now let's see if we can't get this on a better track," but I got absolutely nowhere. Then we went into the plenary session. Since it was in the U.S. quarters he spoke first, as a guest, and he filled the air with arms control matters of one kind or another. When it came to my turn, I filled the air with Korean airliner and human rights matters. It was very stormy, and at one point he slammed his book down and he got up and picked up like he was ready to go, and I think he was expecting me to urge him to stay but instead I picked up my papers and said, "Go ahead. Walk out." At which point he sat down, and we continued for a little while.

It was a very tough meeting, and the interpreter—Bill Krimer, I think his name was—told me that in all of his seventeen years of interpreting he'd never seen a meeting like that. But at any rate, Gromyko then went before the assembled foreign ministers and made a chilling speech and basically said, "We did it and we'd do it again. Just don't have any of your airliners fly over our territory." Why he did that is beyond me, but he could not have said anything that would have created a worse reaction. It made it much easier to rally people on a worldwide basis to react. Gromyko was the skunk at the picnic.

Then what happened—and this shows you the way politics works—shortly thereafter was the opening of the UN General Assembly to which all foreign ministers come and Gromyko always came, whether he was invited to Washington subsequently or not. He was scheduled to come, and he must have been apprehensive because he had a very hard time in Madrid. In all of the furor, the governor of New York and the governor of New Jersey decided to show how strong they were, so they denied him landing rights. We immediately said, "Oh, here's a military airfield; you can land there," but they had given him his opening and he canceled out his coming to the United Nations at all. So the two governors thumped their chests, but what they had done was give him an excuse not to come and catch hell from his colleagues in the General Assembly.

I was very interested in a phrase that Gromyko used later. This was the year of deployments of the INF missiles, after which the Soviets walked out of the various negotiations. We had the start of another CSCE [Conference on Security and Cooperation in Europe] meeting in Stockholm in January, and again we had a big argument in the U.S. about whether I should meet with Gromyko on that occasion. And again the president agreed that I should, and we had the meeting. It turned out to be one of our best meetings in the sense that we had a real argument. I told Gromyko that I had listened to his speech and his comments were completely unacceptable. He said, "I'm glad to hear what you say because if you had liked my speech, it would have put me on my guard." I said, "I'm glad you're not on your guard." We went back and forth like that, and it dawned on me, I said, "Finally we're having a conversation." And we did finally get into other things. At the end, as we always did in these meetings, we had a little discussion on how we would characterize this meeting. And Gromyko chose an interesting word, I thought: he said, "It was necessary," as we reemerged from this very hard, intense period.

Mr. Oberdorfer: It's so interesting that Gromyko evidently agreed in the first instance that the Soviet Union should own up to what had happened, but then when the Politburo had decided otherwise, he became the spear carrier going to these meetings and making these thundering statements.

Mr. Tarasenko: That was the rule. That's how things were done in the Soviet Union. The Politburo means you should obey it to the last letter, there's no way you can dissent from a Politburo decision. You have to stick to this version whether you like it or not.

Mr. Bessmertnykh: This is the universal rule. It was the Politburo [in this case]. In another country it would be the president. I mean, when it's considered a top-level decision, you've got to [obey].

Mr. Oberdorfer: Well, we do have cabinet officers who have disagreed with decisions taken by the presidents, and made their positions known—sometimes taking a lot of heat for it. We had the case of Shevardnadze. In the United States, Secretary Vance resigned because he could not agree with something that was decided by President Carter. Secretary Shultz attempted to resign a number of times on other grounds, and made his dissent from some decisions that were made by President Reagan known when the subject came up. Of course, we had obviously two very different political systems.

Mr. Bessmertnykh: Gromyko would not think about resigning, definitely. Gromyko was not that type of man.

Mr. Oberdorfer: Not too long after KAL 007, in early November, a NATO test of a nuclear release system took place. The question was what you would do if you actually decided to use nuclear weapons in war. They felt they should test the weapons and control systems from time to time, not by dropping any missile or anything of the sort, but by sending forth communications of the kind that would be sent if there was an actual nuclear weapons decision. Now let's not forget the circumstances of the fall of 1983. In addition to the Korean airliner case, you had the first deployments of the American medium-range missiles in Europe—the culmination of a battle that had gone on for several years. And you had the U.S. invasion of Grenada as well. It was, perhaps except for the Cuban missile crisis, the point of highest tension between the United States and the Soviet Union since the Second World War.

Oleg Gordievsky, who was at this time the deputy chief of the KGB station in London, and who was then a double agent and later defected, has written a number of times that many in the KGB in

Moscow believed that the United States was just about to attack the Soviet Union. They sent out orders all over the world asking for special information: how many lights are burning in the windows of the State Department, Defense Department. They wanted whatever they could find out to possibly show whether there was going to be a U.S. nuclear attack on the Soviet Union.[3] In his memoir, President Reagan—without referring to this particular incident, but it's clear to me this is the sort of thing he had in mind—wrote that he had learned by late 1983, to his surprise, that "many people at the top of the Soviet hierarchy were genuinely afraid of America and Americans" and that "many Soviet officials feared us not only as adversaries but as potential aggressors who might hurl nuclear weapons at them in a first strike." He said this made him more determined than ever to try to have a conversation with the Soviet leader to dispel such ideas. I'd like to ask our former Soviet officials here, how real do you think the apprehension was—either in ministries where you were or in the military or the KGB—that the United States might actually be preparing or prepared to mount a nuclear attack on the Soviet Union? Is this something that was real, or in your opinion is this just an inflated story?

Mr. Tarasenko: Around this time, Kornienko summoned me and showed me a top secret KGB paper. It was under Andropov. Kornienko said to me, "You haven't seen this paper. Forget about it." It was top secret. In the paper, the KGB reported that they had information that the United States had prepared everything for a first strike; that they might resort to a surgical strike against command centers in the Soviet Union; and that they had the capability to destroy the system by incapacitating the command center. We were given the task of preparing a paper for the Politburo and putting forward some suggestions on how to counter this threat not physically but politically. So we prepared a paper [suggesting] that we should leak some information that we know about these capabilities and contingency plans, and that we are not afraid of these plans because we have taken the necessary measures. Then we proposed that we had better have some staff maneuvers, you know, just to show Western intelligence that we were preparing for this sudden attack on the Soviet Union. [We suggested] some other propaganda, things which would appear in the press. I never knew what was the fate of this, whether they acted on this or not.

Mr. Oberdorfer: As a matter of fact, it was shortly after this NATO test that the Soviet Union placed on higher alert status about a dozen nuclear-capable Soviet fighter aircraft stationed in forward bases in East Germany and Poland, evidently in response to what it perceived as a heightened threat arising from what it could detect of the NATO exercise. Or at least that's what U.S. intelligence reported back to the political leadership in Washington.

Mr. Chernyaev: The most important thing in the context of the subject that we are discussing today is that, unlike the rest of the world, the Soviet society of that time was not horrified by the downing of KAL 007. I think it just shows how far our societies were from each other just two or three years before the process of rapprochement started. At that time, the Soviet leadership did not even have to worry that it would be condemned or even criticized by any influential section of Soviet society for what happened. There was that ironclad law of pre-perestroika socialist morality that the Soviet borders are inviolate and whoever violates those borders would be shot.

Now as to the question of whether the Soviet leadership was afraid that as a result of this situation something might happen and a surprise attack might actually take place: At that time I was very far from the real centers of decision making, even though I worked in the International Department of the Central Committee of the Communist Party of the Soviet Union as a deputy chief of that department. In the West, the role of the International Department of the Central Committee has been exaggerated way out of proportion. I saw remarks even in serious Western publications [stating] that even the KGB stood to attention when the International Department said something; and that is totally and absolutely untrue. Other than policy toward the socialist countries, the International Department was really not involved in real policy making.

But we, the International Department of the Central Committee, were very well informed, we really knew the situation quite well, we had information available to us about everything, and here I come to answer your question. So far as I remember that situation, in the highest echelon of Soviet government there really was no serious fear that this situation might really provoke a nuclear conflict or a large-scale international conflict. Perhaps in individual military districts certain steps were taken, but so far as the political level, I think we can rule out that there was real fear of a nuclear attack.

Mr. Oberdorfer: Secretary Shultz wanted to add something.

Mr. Shultz: I'm reassured, by that comment, of the good sense that prevails on these things. But let me add a comment about what was taking place and where the battle was. This was, again, 1983, the year we deployed those missiles. It was really a very tense struggle for Europe. The Soviet side was trying to scare our allies and cause their publics to prevent them from deploying the missiles. So the idea that this could cause conflict in a way served their propaganda purposes. We were determined all the way through that year that we would have a two-track approach as NATO had declared. If negotiations don't work, deployment. But in order for the European publics to be convinced to go along with the deployment, they had to feel that there was an honest-to-God negotiation going on, a real and honest one. So, we conducted ourselves that way. We constantly wanted to be in the posture of being reasonable people. Tough, determined to defend our interests, but nevertheless reasonable, ready to strike a bargain if one could be reached that was reasonable.

There was a certain clearing of the air through all of this. It was a period of tension, certainly, but it was also a period when the Soviets tested us and our alliance to the ultimate, and what they discovered was that we managed to hold together and deploy the missiles. It was a major event. It must have registered on the Soviet side that the propaganda effort had not worked and there was a new reality created by the fact of deployment of those missiles. I saw that in Gromyko's speech in Stockholm. He was still very much on the aggressive, rough side, but we wound up finally really having a very good, substantive meeting. Of course, he didn't want it to be known that we had such a good meeting. And I was perfectly happy to go along with that, feeling that the substance was of some significance. For instance, we agreed to restart the MBFR talks.[4] That was a major event, because the [Soviet] propaganda was that arms control talks had been shut down and that there was a total deep freeze in the relationship. Gromyko said, "Well, let's not announce that right away." I said, "Fine." But I knew it was bound to be announced in a week or two and therefore would tend to take the edge off the chill.

So, in addition to the substantive things that you listed that tended to create tension, there was also an imagery battle going on, in which the Soviets were trying to increase a sense of tension and we were trying to diminish it.

Mr. Oberdorfer: Before I turn to the next crisis that we are going to mention, I'd like to ask Foreign Minister Bessmertnykh: Secretary Shultz wonders what the impact was in Moscow of the fact that the missiles were so successfully deployed by NATO. What was the sense there?

Mr. Bessmertnykh: There was a lot of concern before the deployment. We were trying to prevent that. I don't remember when we [had ever] raised this kind of campaign. We used all methods possible: pressure, persuasion, . . . everything. It was one of the most intensive campaigns that the two sides ever carried over just one issue. So the decision was definitely a great disappointment. There was a certain mood suddenly cast on Moscow that we had failed. Of course, it wasn't said so much publicly, but the feeling of failure was there. So the next task was [to decide] what to do next, because the situation had tremendously deteriorated as far as Soviet interests were concerned. But looking back from today's position, I think that the fact itself has helped to strongly concentrate on and facilitate the solutions. If it were not for that deployment, which was negative to us, maybe the developments would have been slower and taken many more years, and much more internal and external deliberations. It kind of pushed the whole process into much higher speed and finally brought us to a solution.

Mr. Shultz: Everybody reflects their own experience and looks on things to a certain extent that way. I have spent a lot of time in labor-management relations, and it is often the case in labor-management relations that it takes a strike to clear the air. That is, people have to do their best to stop the deployments, do their best to make the deployments, and it's a battle and it has to go on—and once it's gone on and there is an outcome, there is a certain clearing of the air. So, tension is not necessarily without its constructive elements.

Mr. Oberdorfer: Mr. Nitze has something to add.

Mr. Nitze: The thing that strikes my memory is the intensity of the debate in Germany and in England about the deployment of INF missiles. There were many in both countries who were violently opposed to this deployment. As I remember, in the spring of 1983 they mobilized a series of protest marches in Germany in which they had as many as five hundred thousand people marching at one time in protest against the deployment of the INF missiles. That was the high point of danger as I saw it for us. But the next spring, I remember, they tried again to march, but at that time a tenth the number of people showed up. It was the change from the spring of '83 to the spring of '84 which I think drove home the point that the campaign to get Germany and England to refuse to deploy not only had failed but [had backfired]. By that time I thought we were on solid ground again.

Prof. Greenstein: Let me ask a question of Secretary Shultz. Prompted by your reference to your background, in a sense the theme of this afternoon is navigating the shoals. Did you have a sense at any level that you were consciously drawing on your own equipment during this period? If it doesn't seem self-serving, I wonder if you could say a little bit about whether you were conscious of how you were operating as this period went along?

Mr. Shultz: I wasn't saying, "Gee, this is the way we did it back in—" But we are all products of our experience, and as you go through things of this kind it tends to give you a point of view, an outlook. There are people who think that any strong argument or any conflict is terrible. You should avoid it at all costs. I never felt that way. I think sometimes a good argument and a good fight over something gives people an idea of where your bottom line really is, and they test out what they are able to do and we test out what we're able to do, and as I said, it can clear the air for something more constructive. And I think in many ways that's exactly what took place here.

Mr. Oberdorfer: What started to clear the air was a speech in January 1984 by President Reagan. Of course it was the beginning of an election year, so those skeptics in the press, maybe including me, wondered if it wasn't more election than anything else, but in fact he sort of laid down an olive branch after all this high tension. Ambassador Matlock, who was then in the National Security Council, worked on the speech, which was most famous for its portrayal of a Russian and an American couple. Ivan and Anya were meeting Jim and Sally at a supermarket or someplace or other.

Mr. Matlock: That, President Reagan drafted himself. It was the only part anybody remembers, but it was his. The origins may go back to the secretary's meeting with the Reagans that snowy night. I was asked to come back and join the National Security Council staff in May 1983. I didn't particularly want to. I liked Prague, and I could get my work done in forty or fifty hours a week and have a good time, and I didn't particularly want to leave. I did not like the Washington bureaucracy, and I knew what it means to try to work within the Washington bureaucracy. So I resisted. Actually, when [former NSC aide for Soviet affairs Richard] Pipes had left the National Security Council staff the fall before, Bill Clark had asked me if I was interested, and I thanked him but said, no, I really wasn't. He called me in May to say, "Well, we're reorganizing the position; it will have responsibility for all of Europe as well as the Soviet Union. We really want you back." I agreed to come for an interview, and in the meantime Roz's predecessor Rick Burt called me and said, the secretary really wants you to take this, to come back and salute. But I went in and—

Mr. Shultz: How unlike you.

Mr. Matlock: I'm sorry. In fact, they said, "Look, we want you back because the president's decided it's time to negotiate with the Soviets and he doesn't have anybody on the staff here with any experience doing it." That's the background of my joining the NSC staff. Obviously, this was an offer that under those circumstances I felt I couldn't and shouldn't refuse.

There was a serious concern, beginning with President Reagan, about the lack of communication following KAL. In addition, there was the Andropov statement in late September which, in effect, said, "We can't deal with the Reagan administration. If we'd ever had illusions we could, they have now been dispelled." I think it was decided—it may have been started by a memo from you

[Shultz] or a conversation you had—that the president should make a major speech on U.S.-Soviet relations. We started kicking around various drafts, but not much really fused. Finally, in early December, I had an invitation to go out to dinner with some close friends in Washington with my wife, and I decided, look, this has just got to get drafted. I called, canceled the dinner, and I worked in my office until about three in the morning, getting the heart of a speech together. Then I sent it over to the State Department where the Bureau of European Affairs, Rick Burt and Mark Palmer, finished working on it. They sent it back and I sent it in.

It went to the president, and it came back with a note that it was dull and had nothing new. I thought it had a lot of new things in it, and I believe it was Richard Darman who said, "Gee, if the president thinks there's nothing new in this, I have to wonder, because this turns our policy around. It says things that he's never said before." But in any event, it had to be spiced up and so on, including the story at the end. The speech was essentially ready before the end of the year, but for reasons which we didn't understand, the word came down it wouldn't be given that year. Then it kept being put off until January 16. Since, I have surmised—I don't know for a fact—that Mrs. Reagan's astrologer may have had something to do with it. In any event, whatever the reason was, it did get put off to the sixteenth. That's where the president did lay out the four-part agenda, and we did draft it with an eye for things that would be acceptable to the Soviet Union if the Soviet Union was interested in a peaceful relationship. So we tried to make the proposals in these four areas as accommodating as possible.

Mr. Shultz: In the discussions I had with the president and you [Matlock], we thought about a kind of double speech. I went and said, "I'm going to go to the Stockholm meeting. Then there will be a meeting with Gromyko. You should make a speech setting out the tone and philosophy that we want to use. Then I will have a follow-on speech at the CSCE meeting that has more nuts and bolts and addresses the issues that the conference will address, but in the line of the background of your speech. If you can make it early enough, then that's a message to the Soviets. They will read your speech before they get to Stockholm, and it may have some impact." But the first speech didn't get made until later. There was a tandem there that probably didn't work as intended because Gromyko didn't see the president's speech until he was about ready to leave for Stockholm anyway.

Mr. Oberdorfer: We are in '85 now. Gorbachev has become general secretary after the death of Konstantin Chernenko. And on March 24 an American liaison officer in East Germany, Major Arthur Nicholson, was killed. As I recall it, he was doing an inspection, authorized under the terms of the agreements between the two sides that went back to the end of World War II, when he was shot down and killed.

Mr. Shultz: It was worse than that.

Mr. Oberdorfer: Secretary Shultz remembers it better than I, so go ahead.

Mr. Shultz: He was shot and wounded badly, and then the Soviet side prevented the proper first aid from getting to him, and so he died as a result. So it was a double tragedy.

Mr. Oberdorfer: The then–secretary of defense, Caspar Weinberger, insisted that before any further discussions take place between the United States and Soviet Union, there should be an apology given for Nicholson's death. The question of an apology or something like an apology—at least a recognition of wrongdoing on the part of the Soviet Union—persisted for several years as a block not to the political discussions but to military contacts. The person who discussed this with the Soviet military leadership and tried to get over this hump was Frank Carlucci. Maybe Frank could tell us a little bit about how that worked.

Mr. Carlucci: This, of course, was some years after the incident. The incident occurred, as you pointed out, in 1985. In 1988 I started, as I mentioned last night, a series of meetings with my then–Soviet counterpart Marshal Yazov. We got into the usual hassle that one gets into: where do you meet? We decided to have the first meeting in Bern as a neutral ground. And there was a lot of sparring at the first meeting. I can remember that my first question to him was, "Why don't you publish the military budget?" And the reply I got back was, "I can't." And I said, "Why not?" He said, "Because I don't know what it is." I laughed at first, but then I began to think about it. Indeed, it is scattered through the different departments; and more importantly, how do you price a budget in a nonmarket economy?

After we got over some of those hurdles, we went on to discuss dangerous incidents as part of a somewhat broader agenda. I found him quite willing to discuss ways in which to avoid dangerous incidents. And at the end of the meeting I took Yazov aside. It was after a breakfast that included vodka and caviar at the Soviet Embassy in Bern. I said to him, "Look, we've had good discussions. We want to continue this dialogue, but it is not going to continue unless we get an apology for the Nicholson affair." He said, "Well, Major Nicholson was where he shouldn't have been." I said, "Look, let's get this all behind us. I don't want to discuss the details, but in our next meeting we need to have worked this out and I will raise it with you."

In the next meeting he invited me to Moscow. When I raised it at the table, I was stonewalled. They always had a lot of people at the table—I dealt not just with Yazov, but with Yazov and Akhromeev. They functioned in tandem. My staff wanted me to come right back at him at the table and I said, "No, I'm not going to do that." I grabbed him at the end of the meeting and I said, "Let's go have a discussion." So he took me into his office. I dare say, I'm probably the first American ever to go into the Soviet minister of defense's office with just him and the Soviet interpreter, if I recall correctly. I said, "I told you it's going to be all off unless we have an apology for Major Nicholson, and I mean it. I'm prepared to walk out right now." Then he began to pull out a lot of pictures on where Nicholson was. I said, "Once again, I told you I'm not interested in that. Let's start drafting." I could see he was reluctant to draft, so I drafted. And the Soviet interpreter, I could see, was trying to be helpful in translating the language. I worked out some language which didn't have the word *sorry* in it, but I think it had regrets of some sort, I'm not sure how it translated into Russian, but after about an hour-and-a-quarter session I finally heard the *da* out of Yazov and I said, "Okay, this is sufficient. We will go ahead." That enabled us to allow our military, which had been shunning all social functions, even national days in Washington, to go ahead and renew contacts. As I recall, Major Nicholson's wife took it rather well but there was some static from his father. He didn't feel we had gone far enough. But it enabled us to continue the military dialogue.

Mr. Oberdorfer: What was your impression of the relationship between the military leadership in the Soviet Union and civilian authority?

Mr. Carlucci: They didn't like the civilian authority. I couldn't tell what the relationship was between Yazov and Gorbachev. Of course subsequent events [the August 1991 coup, in which Yazov participated] indicate that he was not totally loyal, but he always seemed to be respectful of Gorbachev. The group of folks over there from the Foreign Ministry were not very high on his hit parade. That was quite clear. And I have been interested in the comments from the Soviet side here that the relationships between the Foreign Ministry and the Defense Ministry weren't as cordial as they might have been. I also had the impression when I was talking to Yazov about Nicholson that he wasn't an entirely free agent. I really had to drag him into doing something. He was very nervous.

Mr. Oberdorfer: And who would have been the person or the institution that would have put the clamps on him? The General Staff, or somebody like that?

Mr. Carlucci: I once again defer to our Soviet friends. I'd be very interested in their speculation on this. Maybe I'm wrong. Maybe it was Akhromeev, but I would doubt that. Maybe it was the KGB.

Mr. Oberdorfer: Could some of you tell us what you think about this relationship between civil and military authority in the former Soviet Union, and the extent to which this affected the developments that took place in the 1980s?

Mr. Bessmertnykh: The first issue is the quality of the problem you are solving. It's very hard to present a single picture of that relationship. It's always fluctuating depending on what kind of issue is dividing us, what kind of issue we are both trying to solve. Contacts between the military and the diplomats started to develop very intensively after we got involved in the arms control negotiations. So since the '70s, those contacts became an integral part of foreign policy making. Before that, the contacts and mutual interest existed only when some border issues were discussed. But since the '70s it was always arms control. And that was a very touchy field. The military felt that this was their own turf [and resented] the diplomats eventually getting into their own territory [in cases such as] Major Nicholson's. Sometimes they were like guys from another planet. So very often their relationship was tense in general because the Foreign Ministry was trying to find a compromise, trying to find an agreement, and the military were assigned to protect the national security of the country and sometimes they optimized their role in that.

Second, the personal nature of the relationship. There were good diplomats and bad military and vice versa. I would say that in the '80s, the period we are discussing, the major figure on the scene was Marshal Akhromeev. Later, to a small degree, General of the Army Moiseev, and before Akhromeev, Marshal Ogarkov. These three gentlemen of the army played a very important role. I think it was good for the Soviet military machine that the top-level military went through the negotiations. Not only were they changing their policy, but they were changing themselves through meeting the other side, not from the trenches but at the negotiating table. They were getting educated about the interests, the concerns, and the views of the other side.

I observed this through my personal experience with General Moiseev. When we were [negotiating] the final articles of the START Treaty, they brought Moiseev and myself to Washington. It was probably the first time when, at the negotiating table in the State Department, there was not only the foreign minister but the chief of General Staff and quite a number of generals in uniform. They noticed that those generals who, while in Moscow, felt one way became different men after the first sessions of tough talks with the Americans. They understood that diplomacy is not just drinking glasses of champagne. So, I believe that sometimes we exaggerate the obstinance of the military, especially when we talk about such a man as Akhromeev.

There was an interesting Soviet practice which was called "initiatives." Before major events in the country, the general secretary would have to present some "initiatives" to impress our own people and the world. Several months before the event, all of us were given the task of finding what these initiatives could be. At the end of the '70s and the beginning of the '80s it was almost always an arms control initiative. Of course we had to involve the military. Without them, we wouldn't be able to create an initiative. The military knew that in connection with a Party congress, for example, they would be asked to prepare an initiative so that the general secretary could surprise the world with tremendous new ideas. And Akhromeev always had something in his pocket. He would always work out several positions beforehand. So when Gorbachev would ask him to do something, he would very often present some good ideas, and then it would be for us, the military and the Foreign Ministry to work together. This applies to the famous 1986 declaration by Gorbachev on complete nuclear disarmament. On January 15, 1986, it was unveiled as a great initiative before the Twenty-seventh Party Congress. Akhromeev was very helpful. He rescued situations.

But on many occasions, when we would clash, we would just come to the clinch and would not be able to move each other. Then we would use the president as the referee, but in a different sense of the word. He was a referee who would support only one side in that clinch. We would use his powers to squeeze some positions from the military. And Gorbachev was good at that, especially in the first years of his presidency. In 1988, for example, when he could really decide, he said, "Yes, there are two positions: the Foreign Ministry's position and the General Staff's. I think we should do this." Of course he wouldn't say that was the Foreign Ministry's position. It was his position to say, "I believe" or "This is the way it should be done." So that's why Shevardnadze was disliked so much by the military, because he used Gorbachev on several occasions to squeeze positions from the military.

Mr. Oberdorfer: Shevardnadze, as Mr. Bessmertnykh just mentioned, came into conflict with the military on a number of occasions when shaping policy. We'll talk tomorrow about Afghanistan, on which he was an important shaper of policy. Sergei, what was your sense of the real relationship between Shevardnadze and the generals and admirals who he was trying to get to do what he felt should be done, or from whom he was trying to get information about what was going on?

Mr. Tarasenko: First of all, I'd like to put something on the agenda. It concerns military openness in our society. The society was closed.

The budget was closed. There was no flow of information between the military and diplomacy. We knew nothing about what kind of programs they were working on, what to expect next, or when a new generation of missiles would appear. That was a hushed affair. Nobody had access to this—nobody, ever, until Shevardnadze insisted on giving his deputy Karpov special clearance to have special access to military papers and documents. So that was a big problem. We did not know how many troops were in Afghanistan at a given moment; how many advisors were in Angola or Ethiopia or Mozambique. So even on this level, the Foreign Ministry was just not informed—and not only on a constant basis but even if the ministry would request specific information on particular cases we [were] lied to almost every time. Every single time.

Let's take this Nicholson affair. They invented a lot: that he was dressed in this kind of camouflage uniform, although it was just standard fatigues; that he slipped into some window and went inside this installation, though it was just a section containing propaganda material.

Mr. Carlucci: That was what Yazov was telling you?

Mr. Tarasenko: Yes. They will usually sell you an awful story that makes no sense; [one could not] connect the events. So the first time we would bring the story to the American side they would say, "Look, nothing of the kind, the situation was thus." This was a real problem. Before the negotiations on strategic weapons, there was no way for us to know about any numbers, colors, types of weapons. We had been completely shut out from any sources. The Military Council had been activated around '87. I saw a guy coming to Shevardnadze with folders from time to time, and they had regular meetings of this council which Politburo members were on. So there was some institutionalized relationship. Then again, as you remember, we had this committee of five chaired by Politburo member [Lev N.] Zaikov. It was a clearing house for all the negotiations on arms control. So that was another source. And to be honest, Shevardnadze used this committee a lot, particularly Zaikov. He calculated his relationship with Zaikov. They lived next door to each other. So he was particularly careful about his relationship with Zaikov. And he would ask Zaikov to help him in pushing some proposals or in taking decisions, for example.

But certainly, to get any information, to get the military on board, was extremely difficult always, and lack of information handicapped us. I remember in one case, the chemical weapons issue, we started to look into that seriously, preparing to change our position. Shevardnadze asked all the bosses from the chemical department of the Defense Ministry to come to his office for a talk. So the commander came, a four-star general, and a number of other generals. They never told Shevardnadze how much it would cost, where these things were located. He was a Politburo member. He was a member of the Defense Council. But no information. "Well," [they would tell him,] "we have something that's difficult to estimate how much." Then he [would have to] use this committee of five just to extract this information.

Mr. Oberdorfer: Mr. Chernyaev, from your vantage point, what did you observe about the relations between President Gorbachev and the military? How did he work with them?

Mr. Chernyaev: It would be better to try to describe that using some specific examples. Perhaps to anticipate the next subject a little bit and to speak about Afghanistan, I would say that here the situation was really unique. You might be surprised if I told you that our top generals were against the invasion of Afghanistan in 1979. Marshal Akhromeev and Marshal Sokolov were against it, and so, even, was General Varennikov, who subsequently played such an ominous role in the August coup of 1991.[5] And even though all those three generals were decorated and got the golden star, the hero of the Soviet Union, for their role in fighting in Afghanistan because they faithfully executed the strategy that was decided by the political leadership, they still, from the beginning until the very end, thought that the invasion of Afghanistan was a reckless mistake, and they were very critical of it. Akhromeev even told me that the three of them had written an official paper containing their objections to the decision to move troops to Afghanistan when that decision was being taken. But Ustinov was then the all-powerful minister of defense, and he made them stand to attention. He asked, "So, are generals now defining policy in the Soviet Union?" He said, "Your task is to develop specific operations and to implement what you are told."

But that, of course, was when Gorbachev was not yet general secretary. Later, under Gorbachev, I participated twice in Politburo meetings in which Marshal Akhromeev, upon his return from inspection trips to Afghanistan, reported to the Politburo about the situation there. Each time he reported to the Politburo, his reports were, I think, brilliant and very critical. He lashed out against continuing to fight that war in Afghanistan. He said, "This is a war against the Afghan people." He said, "We have lost this war. We lost this war a long time ago." He said that neither [of the Afghan leaders] Karmal [and] Najibullah was worth one Russian soldier's life. He was all for withdrawing from Afghanistan as soon as we could. Then later I said that to Gorbachev—"Look, that really was a brilliant report by Akhromeev." And he said, "Well, you understand it was an arrangement between us that he would say that." I will later speak about how Gorbachev was engaged in an educational campaign among the members of the Politburo, trying to prepare them for the withdrawal of troops from Afghanistan.

The withdrawal of our troops from Eastern Europe was the moment when the stability of the Soviet armed forces was really shaken, when they complained bitterly and criticized Gorbachev, and when relations between Gorbachev and the military began to deteriorate. I would say that until that moment, Gorbachev was the full and complete master of the situation both in political and in military terms. You may remember that scandal [in May 1987] when a German boy [Mathias] Rust landed a small plane on Red Square. And Gorbachev really lashed out against the Ministry of Defense and all the commanders who had allowed that to happen. The minister of defense, [Sergei] Sokolov, was dismissed. Several dozen top generals were retired. I think 157 generals and colonels were retired, were dismissed, and some were even put on trial. Gorbachev later said to me that in purely human terms it was difficult to do that. But at least, he said, the one advantage to doing that was that they will finally stop saying in the West that Gorbachev is subservient to the military-industrial complex and the generals, rather than they obeying him.

Sergei mentioned the role of Politburo member Lev Nikolaevich Zaikov, and I support what he has said. He was responsible in the Politburo for the military-industrial complex. He was a very soft-spoken man, a very balanced individual, extremely competent in military-industrial matters and totally loyal to Gorbachev. And when some problem emerged in managing armaments, or some problem between the Foreign Ministry and the minister of defense, Gorbachev assigned that problem to the commission headed by Mr. Zaikov. They would fight it out in that commission, and Zaikov would inform Gorbachev about how the decision was going. In many cases they found a solution under the auspices of Mr. Zaikov. If not, they went over to the general secretary, and the general secretary settled the dispute.

[Then-chief of staff Marshal Sergei] Akhromeev later became advisor to Gorbachev. I must say that Akhromeev of course met a very tragic end, and he was politically and ideologically a very conservative person, but he was profoundly an honest military man, a decent man with certain inner convictions.[6] You could disagree with him on military and political issues, but still we all had the feeling that he was a decent man. He was totally faithful—he really was totally faithful to Gorbachev, and he played an enormously important role in the decision to destroy the SS-20s deployed in Europe. Gorbachev valued Akhromeev's role in pushing through that decision.

When Akhromeev became advisor to Gorbachev on military matters, clashes emerged not just between the Foreign Ministry and the Ministry of Defense but also between Akhromeev, marshal of the Soviet Union, a military man, and the Ministry of Defense.

Mr. Oberdorfer: I'd like to ask one specific question that's always intrigued me. In December 1988 Gorbachev came to the United Nations for a final meeting with President Reagan and to meet Vice President Bush and for a luncheon at Governor's Island in New York harbor. In that visit, which he initiated, he announced at the United Nations a unilateral reduction of five hundred thousand Soviet troops, and the withdrawal of all kinds of bridge-building and other threatening sorts of equipment from Eastern European countries. At the same time it became known that Marshal Akhromeev was retiring as chief of staff of the Soviet armed forces, and the theory was around in the press—I confess to having generated a little bit of it myself, about half on the basis of not very good information—that the reason that Akhromeev was stepping down was that he disagreed with the unilateral cutbacks in Soviet armed forces. On the other hand, he immediately joined Gorbachev as his military advisor. So I guess my question is, what was Akhromeev's position? How did Gorbachev convince the military, if he did convince them, to agree to accept a unilateral cutback which they were known to have opposed in the past?

Mr. Chernyaev: It's quite untrue that Akhromeev was against that initiative. He had participated in a very positive way in developing that unilateral reduction initiative. I know that because we worked together with Akhromeev on that, and also, of course, with the Ministry of Foreign Affairs.

Mr. Oberdorfer: Why did he step down?

Mr. Chernyaev: Akhromeev had been asking Mr. Gorbachev to be allowed to step down from that position because he had felt tired. It was a very difficult position involving a lot of long hours, and he said there should be a younger man to do it. It was Akhromeev's own decision. He said to Gorbachev, "I am prepared to work for you in any other capacity, but I want to step down as chief of the General Staff because it's just too hard for me." But then he complained to me, "Anatoly Sergeievich, I really have got myself from the frying pan into the fire because working as advisor to Gorbachev is sometimes even harder for me than as chief of the General Staff." He said, "I sometimes really become desperate in situations when Gorbachev and I take some decision on a military matter and then I have to go to the Ministry of Defense and the General Staff to discuss it with Marshal Yazov, General Moiseev, and other top generals. It takes me hours and hours and sometimes days and days to fight it out with them and to try to persuade them of the wisdom of that decision. And sometimes," he said, "one just wants," as he put it, "to take one's hat off and throw it on the floor." And Gorbachev just laughed it off, saying, "What kind of advisor to the president are you if you cannot insist with the military that this decision is correct?"[7]

The fact that General Moiseev was appointed chief of the General Staff after Akhromeev was one of the mistakes that Mr. Gorbachev made, because Moiseev was a very mediocre general. I would think that he was fit to be a commander of a division rather than the chief of the General Staff. But at least twice he was really able to impress the U.S. administration. [For example,] he sabo-

taged a decision in the CFE [Conventional Forces in Europe] process in 1990. And I remember discussing it with Mr. Bessmertnykh. We said to each other, "Well, what a situation! We look
stupid because we take a stubborn attitude on certain aspects of
the CFE Treaty that was concluded in Paris. It is a clear violation
but we have to defend that clear violation, and both of us who are
close to the president and Foreign Ministry look really silly defending those positions." And then President Bush calls Mr. Gorbachev and says, "Mikhail, my friend, please send over General
Moiseev because we know that we will find a solution working
with him." This happened at least twice. Moiseev went to Washington and wrapped up an agreement on the issue that he had created as for months he stubbornly resisted any agreement. Then
twice he went to Washington and wrapped up that agreement and
he looked like an arms control knight in shining armor. President
Bush calls Mr. Gorbachev on the phone and praises General Moiseev to the skies, and that, of course, leaves us, all of us in Moscow, laughing about this whole thing.

Mr. Oberdorfer: Chances are that President Bush had some pretty
good information about who was the blocking point. Maybe that
is what his tactic was about. I'd like to ask about Sergei Akhromeev. Perhaps Mr. Nitze knew him best. I'd like to preface this by
saying that the Russians referred to Mr. Nitze as "the old man."
He came into the arms negotiations with this immense prestige of
a person who had been at the heart of the American government
policy making going back to the World War II strategic bombing
survey, the Marshall Plan, the design of his U.S. policy for the Cold
War, NSC 68, the decision to build the H-bomb, the Cuban missile
crisis, when he sat at the right hand of John Kennedy, and the negotiations on strategic arms. The Russians were perfectly well
aware of who he was. And then at Reykjavik for the first time
came this other remarkable figure, Marshal Sergei Akhromeev,
who had been a junior officer in the siege of Leningrad during
World War II and had risen right through the ranks through a regular military career to be marshal of the Soviet Union, with the big
boards on his shoulders and the stars and a number of battle ribbons that you couldn't even count. I think there were nine or ten
rows of battle ribbons on his tunic. What was your sense of dealing
with Akhromeev?

Mr. Nitze: It seemed to me and to the rest of us that he was the most intelligent man on the Soviet side that we had seen or heard of. He stuck to the reality of the situation. He understood the basic factors of the nuclear relationship and the overall military relationship. He never said anything which was inconsistent with a correct evaluation of what the real facts were. That seemed to us to be a brand-new phenomenon. Later, when we met Akhromeev regularly, he lived up to all of our anticipations. He was direct, he was straightforward, and he was a first-class military man. We never had any doubt about his complete loyalty to the Communist Party: *(a)* he was a dedicated member of the Party, and *(b)* he was a dedicated supporter of Gorbachev. He was wholly loyal. He was highly regarded by his own military. We could find no flaw in Akhromeev. He was a marvelous person.

Ms. Ridgway: I'd like to tell two stories which may seem frivolous, but I think they illuminate a couple of points. One does relate to the negotiations that were held between Paul and Marshal Akhromeev on INF. It was later in the game, and it illustrates the relationship on the Soviet side between the military and the military-industrial complex. At the very end of the INF process Secretary Shultz led a team to Geneva to finish the numbers and the like. We had a couple of very tough issues, but one had to do with the aggregation and the disaggregation of SS-20 numbers. We were having a terrible time getting a number to finally fit in the last block on the SS-20s. The group in the room included the secretary, Paul, Mr. Shevardnadze, and Marshal Akhromeev. Finally Marshal Akhromeev said, "I can't give you that number until Thursday because I don't know what it is." We were quite astounded that, in fact, he did not know what his SS-20 number was. And he went on to say, "I know what I have in my count, but I cannot give you a figure that includes what is being produced and what is on the factory line and what is on the shelves because I don't get those numbers. The numbers I get relate to what I have asked for, but they keep moving this product through and I don't know what the rest of the numbers are." It struck us, since we had dealt with him in such an open fashion before and had Paul's estimate of the man, that we should wait. And he went back and got numbers. But he suggested to us that he himself did not have certain pieces of information that were held by the industrial side.

The second story, Don, I might chide you just a little bit on, because sometimes, even as late as 1988, the press walked by a story because it was wasn't mysterious enough. General Secretary and President Gorbachev gave his speech in the morning at the United Nations, and it was seen that Marshal Akhromeev was not there. The parties then moved down the street and took the ferry across to Governor's Island. And already the press corps was beginning to surmise that there was trouble at home with the military. A consistent story throughout this period was of an imminent military coup. While we waited for the leaders to turn up, because we had sort of gone on in advance, I talked with Ambassador Bessmertnykh and said, "Why isn't Marshal Akhromeev here? What about this story?" And he said to me, "Roz, it's very simple. He has been tired for a long time. He has been suffering from headaches. He wants to leave his current position. He wants to move on to a different job. He is not here for that reason." We went out and informally briefed the press. And that story was so unsexy that we couldn't get anybody to believe it.

Then, if you recall, Mr. Gorbachev turned up late because on the ferry over from Manhattan to Governor's Island he had felt compelled to call home to see what was the story about this earthquake in a place called Armenia. He arrived at Governor's Island and apologized for being late but said he had to make this telephone call, and it seemed that something terrible had happened in Armenia. He said that he didn't have all of the numbers, but he thought the numbers were going to be quite large and he was very concerned. So we went on with the meeting, and then he changed his plans and went home. Instead of doing the Armenia story and the story of a political leader going home because it was now clear that twenty-five thousand people had died, [the press persisted in doing the story] of the UN speech on the military and an imminent military coup, and Marshal Akhromeev. As a result, I think there's a bit of skewed history still lingering in the archives on something that was really quite straightforward and which people were trying to tell us about, but it didn't seem to be as much fun to listen to that story.

Mr. Oberdorfer: Before I defend the press, I think George has something to say.

Mr. Shultz: Well, I don't want you to be too self-conscious, but it seems to me that the press also missed the story of Mr. Gorbachev's address to the UN because you were captivated by the hard news, which was the troop withdrawal. But the first half of the speech was philosophical, and if anybody declared the end of the Cold War, he did in that speech: It was over. The press walked right by that.

But I wanted to make a comment about Marshal Akhromeev. He told me and he told Paul and others, "I'm the last of the Mohicans." And we said, "What do you mean by that?" He said, "Well, I'm the last person on active duty who served in World War II." I said, "Yes, but where did you get that 'last of the Mohicans?' " He said, "I was brought up on James Fenimore Cooper." And that gave you a little window into the man. He told me about his experience in the battle of Leningrad, which must have been heroic. In a social side-moment standing by ourselves during the Washington Summit, during the White House dinner, he just volunteered to me, "I'm the marshal of the Soviet Union and I have all these honors and I have done all these things, but nothing that I have ever done has made me as proud as my service as a sergeant in World War II in the battle of Leningrad—until now. Now my country is in deep trouble and I'm trying to help Mikhail Sergeevich, and I'm very proud to be doing that." I was very gripped by that comment of his.

Mr. Chernyaev: I'm very pleased to hear what Secretary Shultz just said about the UN speech of Mr. Gorbachev. At that time, very few people, unfortunately, really noticed the extent to which this speech was a turning point in Gorbachev's New Thinking. If you read that speech carefully, you will see that for the first time Gorbachev publicly renounced Marxism-Leninism as an approach to the analysis of international issues and international processes.

Mr. Oberdorfer: The troop cuts were definitely not trivial, they were important, but they paled compared to the international relations philosophy that Gorbachev set out at that time, including, by the way, a statement that "we will not dictate to any other nation. We are not going to try to tell any other nation what to do"—meaning, in all of our minds, Eastern Europe. Compared to what he said, what he did does not hold up in historical significance, but that is the reason that historians write history and journalists write tomorrow's newspaper, because we can't always have twenty-twenty eyesight about what is the significance of what is being done, even when officials are almost jumping up and down trying to tell us.

Mr. Bessmertnykh: I think it was in that speech that Gorbachev pronounced the freedom of choice as one of the principles of New Thinking. And I was a little perplexed by the fact that the American side didn't like it. I mean, they wouldn't buy it. They wouldn't even introduce it into joint documents . . . What was behind it? Why was freedom of choice was not accepted?

Mr. Shultz: Are you speaking of the Moscow Summit?

Mr. Bessmertnykh: No, but it was mentioned by Gorbachev in that United Nations [speech].

Mr. Shultz: He gave the president some language in his first private session at the Moscow Summit. But at least as I read that, and I think Frank and Roz also have very much the same view, it was basically the détente-like wording and therefore, we thought, rather misleading. It had in it, for example, this notion of non-use of force. As a general proposition, you wouldn't say you would never use force, but then this dictum had been there when you invaded Afghanistan. So we said, "Why are we going around this circle again?" And that was why we resisted. I thought it was successfully resisted when I saw the joint statement that you and Roz negotiated. We went into the final meeting and all of a sudden out of the blue he [Gorbachev] threw this on the table again and we had a little—

Mr. Bessmertnykh: Yes, I remember that very vividly.

Mr. Shultz: But, Frank or Roz, do you have the same recollection?

Mr. Carlucci: I think it was described very accurately in Don's book. Ronald Reagan was taken by complete surprise and, not having the background, was inclined to say yes; and both you and I slipped him notes at the same time saying no.

Mr. Matlock: That language was unacceptable. But if it had been explained what he was trying to achieve, what he was getting at, I believe we could have worked out language acceptable to all sides. If we had needed a statement on some of these topics, we could have probably worked it out if we had known a couple of weeks beforehand he wanted it. I think the element of surprise didn't help in this case.

Ms. Ridgway: Mostly it was, as the secretary said, we had been trying since before the Geneva '85 summit never to use the phrases that were identified with an earlier period, with 1972 and '74. It got so bad at one point, I remember, the president told this story: We were talking in Geneva about having a one-on-one, but it was called tête-à-tête, and finally somebody said, you know, "Why don't you knock off this 'tête-à-tête' stuff. If we keep having all this French around here, next thing you know we'll end up with détente." There was that sensitivity to all language and misunderstandings and the sense of violation that was associated with it.

Mr. Bessmertnykh: I remember that pretty well because Roz and myself were struggling with a paragraph, we were sitting on the balcony of the guest house, it was raining, and we finished that very successfully. But I'm talking about only one concept, that of freedom of choice, because I've always thought that by declaring the freedom of choice we actually accepted one of the principal philosophies of the United States. And when we found that it [the concept] was somehow uncomfortable in that particular period we could not understand it initially.

Mr. Oberdorfer: In the speech to the United Nations, the one that we so brilliantly reported, Gorbachev went on to say, "The new world which we are entering requires the freeing of international relations from ideology." He said, "In the new world it is evident that the use or threat of force no longer can or must be an instrument of foreign policy. This applies to non-nuclear force as well as nuclear weapons." And then, in what was immediately interpreted as a message about Soviet intentions in Eastern Europe, Gorbachev declared, "All of us, and first of all the strongest of us, have to practice self-restraint and totally rule out any outward-oriented use of force." He went on to say "that the principle of freedom of choice is a must for all nations. A universal principle that knows no exception."

Mr. Bessmertnykh: Yes. This is exactly what was said.

Mr. Oberdorfer: We've been promising this for a while, now here it is. Does somebody have questions? Please, state your name so the panelists and others will know who you are.

Mr. King: My name is Captain Chris King. I teach politics at the U.S. Military Academy. My question is: Yesterday, Secretary Shultz, you mentioned several times this notion of unlinking negotiations . . . Could you elaborate on whose notion this was? Was this something that you emphasized, detecting that Reagan wanted to establish a firm dialogue with the Soviets ever since that first snowy night, or was this something that he came out and said that we need to move forward with, despite other events that might have taken place?

Mr. Shultz: The notion of linkage was a concept of how we should deal with the Soviet Union that started in the Nixon-Kissinger days and carried right up on through until the Reagan administration. And I think in the case of the Korean airliner, as I mentioned, there was a very explicit operational discussion of that and a rejection of it as we went back and picked up on the arms control negotiations. If when we faced the Daniloff case, the Korean airliner, and a half a dozen other things, we still had had the same notion of linkage as in the past, everything really would have just shut down. That would have been a great mistake. I think that the emergence of a different concept was important.

I set it out in a speech devoted to that subject at the opening of the new Rand-UCLA Soviet Studies Center back in 1984. It was a big problem getting that speech done because I knew what I wanted to say and the speech would get sent to our Soviet group and [the State Department's] European Bureau. This was before Roz was there. She and I are kindred souls on the linkage question. And back it would come, changed all around. That happened several times. I told them, I'm not going to send it to you for your views any more because you're trying to change my mind and my mind is made up. But it was deeply embedded in all the people who worked on Soviet affairs for a long time. It was rejected in a kind of doctrinal way, but more important in an operational way, as we worked our way through these issues.

My recollection is that the first people to drive this thing home to me were from the Russian side, when, during the Nixon administration, we hit targets in Cambodia. This was unacceptable to the Russian side. They read us a lecture in the negotiations that were going on, saying that this was a dreadful thing that we had done—violating the restrictions on hitting the Cambodians—but that [what we were trying to do] was too important to let that [the bombing] interfere with the continuation of our negotiations. So they were the ones who didn't want to link our actions in Cambodia to calling off the negotiations.

Mr. Oberdorfer: Mr. Chernyaev wanted to make a comment.

Mr. Chernyaev: Mr. Gorbachev appreciated very highly the wisdom of the secretary of state in his concept of delinking those things, because the negotiations on arms control were under way at the time when Mr. Gorbachev thought that we could develop a good relationship with the United States and even become friends on the basis of just arms control. It was only later that Mr. Gorbachev accepted and even became convinced that without a solution to the human rights problem the Cold War could not be brought to an end, a new relationship with the United States could not be built. His idea of the primacy of universal values simply did not work if no decisions were taken on the specific human rights cases—but that came later.

In the initial years, as late as—I think—February 1988, Gorbachev said, "Secretary Shultz, do you accept that human rights are our internal affair?" I don't recall your specific answer, but I do recall your saying generally, "Of course it's not your internal affair because there are the UN Charter and the CSCE, signed by your country, etcetera. But I'm not saying there will be no progress until all those humans rights cases are resolved." That is essentially what you said. I believe that decision that you took in the initial years of arms control negotiations was very helpful because it saved the arms control process and made it possible later to make progress also in other areas. In my book I say that this was really the unique contribution of Secretary Shultz in preparing the end of the Cold War: he delinked those areas, even though in real life all of that was not separated and eventually there was progress in all those areas.

Mr. Shultz: Let's be clear about one thing. The idea of not being tied to linkage didn't mean that we didn't have a broad agenda. And right from the beginning we set out the four-point agenda that Jack Matlock referred to. And we always insisted on talking about all the parts, not just arms control, but not necessarily in a linked manner.

Mr. Chernyaev: But there's a big difference between this approach and the approach that many senators and other people took. Gorbachev was sometimes irritated by that, because to each discussion, to each conversation, they brought another list of human rights cases. He was just waiting for them to produce that list. President Reagan sometimes began talks by producing a list of human rights cases and putting it on the table.

Mr. Oberdorfer: I think Secretary Shultz has emphasized, though, that [he's] not saying the United States didn't put forward these proposals or requests in the four areas. The four areas were arms control, regional matters/conflicts, human rights. What was the fourth?

Mr. Shultz: Bilateral affairs.

Mr. Oberdorfer: Bilateral affairs, right. Let's go to another question.

Mr. Hershberg: Jim Hershberg from the Cold War International History Project. Two very brief questions. First, on the Gorbachev speech in New York in December 1988—when the Russian panelists say that they understood that they were committing themselves to the principle of freedom of choice, does that mean that in December 1988 they and Gorbachev understood and accepted that the principle would lead to Eastern European countries leaving the Soviet bloc and that was the implication, not simply satisfying some American negotiating principle? Second, on the Geneva 1985 summit, maybe Pavel Palazchenko can clarify a legend about that meeting. The story goes that Ronald Reagan, to break the ice and create a bond, told Mikhail Gorbachev that if the earth were invaded from outer space, the U.S. and the Soviet Union would cooperate militarily, as in World War II, to defend the species. And since you presumably were there, perhaps you could clarify what exactly was said and in what tone, and what General Secretary Gorbachev's reaction to it was.

Mr. Oberdorfer: Well, we want to dispose of the outer-space men first. Pavel, do you remember?

Mr. Palazchenko: Yes, I recall. On a number of occasions President Reagan used the Mars analogy in my presence, and I think in the presence of most people around this table. So I don't see anything very unique in that. Generally both Gorbachev and Reagan, from time to time, told stories and used language and spoke in ways that are not considered normal or routine in diplomatic discussions.

Mr. Carlucci: Colin Powell and I used to refer to it as the "little green men" speech.

Mr. Oberdorfer: The first question that Jim Hershberg raised was, did the acceptance of non-use of force mean that as early as 1988 Mr. Gorbachev and Mr. Shevardnadze, and all the people who were dealing with these matters, understood that the posture of the Soviet Union was such that Eastern Europe was going to change its political orientation and break away from the Warsaw Pact and the relationships that they had up until that time?

Mr. Bessmertnykh: That was one of the most important elements of the speech. It was a turning point in the development of the New Thinking. It is exactly so. That speech definitely reemphasized that the Soviet Union was not going to use force either against East Europe or any other place. But you asked whether at that time the Soviet Union would have accepted the breakaway of East Europe from the Soviet Union and whether that position was supported by Gorbachev in 1988. No, I don't think that was the case, because Gorbachev believed that the East Europeans would go through reforms, would change their systems, but it did not necessarily mean that there would be a very deep breakdown in the Soviet–East European relationship. He believed that the reform would unite us more than any other kind of ties.

Mr. Chernyaev: At the time he believed the choice would be a good kind of socialism, but he was not going to interfere if they chose something else.

Ms. Patt Derian: These flashpoints seem to be those which have aggrieved the United States,[8] and it makes me wonder, surely in all of those years, there must have been some in which the Soviet Union felt that it was the aggrieved party?

Mr. Palazchenko: Well, we both [Palazchenko and Chernyaev] recall
that Shevardnadze felt that we were the aggrieved party when, for
example, right on the eve of some important negotiation something would happen, such as the U.S. decision to cut the personnel
of Soviet missions in the United States by, let's say, one hundred
persons. That happened on the eve of important negotiations, and
Shevardnadze always asked, why now? Why is it that some spy
case or, you know, Daniloff's [seizure], for example, without looking at the merit of this, why do it on the eve of Shevardnadze's
coming to the United States to discuss Reykjavik? Of course, it
became much more difficult to settle the final details of that in
an atmosphere in which Mr. Shevardnadze, by his account, spent,
all in all, twenty-four hours with you, Mr. Secretary, discussing
the intricacies of the Daniloff-Zakharov exchange. So he felt
aggrieved.

Mr. Oberdorfer: People here may not remember that first the United
States arrested a Soviet citizen who was working in New York at
the United Nations but did not have diplomatic immunity, on
charges of spying by trying to recruit the Guyanese employee of a
U.S. defense contractor. After that happened, in retaliation, so to
speak, the KGB arranged to have somebody hand a paper to Nick
Daniloff, *U.S. News and World Report* correspondent in Moscow,
and then they immediately grabbed him. It was almost exactly the
same method of arrest as had been used in the case of Zakharov,
the Soviet citizen who had been arrested. The arrest of a promi-
nent, well-respected, obviously-not-a-spy American journalist
created a grand furor in this country and, as you say, led to hours
and hours of negotiations between Secretary Shultz and Foreign
Minister Shevardnadze to try to get it resolved. In the end Zakharov was sent back home, and Daniloff was released and freed
from the Soviet Union. But the question was asked, is this an accident or just somebody's way of interfering with the process?
Does anybody over here have any comment?

Mr. Shultz: I think the sequence has to start earlier. You have to start
with the fact that the Soviet Union had a gigantic mission, under
the rubric of the mission to the UN, that was larger than any other
* mission—including the U.S. mission—by, I don't know, 100, 150
people. So it was a platform for espionage that was a big problem,

and it seemed as though we had to deal with that somehow. I think the timing had to do with not wanting to do it right in the midst of an important Soviet meeting. So when that meeting was over, it was done. It wasn't done in connection with Shevardnadze's visit at all.

Mr. Matlock: That was the personnel cut, yes.

Mr. Shultz: But I don't think it's fair to say that the Daniloff seizure and [the] Zakharov [case] were identical. Those were very different things.

Mr. Oberdorfer: It may have been different in terms of their substance, but in fact, the way the whole thing went, Zakharov went to meet his contact on a subway platform in New York and the guy who was working for the FBI handed him this paper, and a whole bunch of people grabbed him and hustled him off to the pokey. The same exact thing happened with Nick Daniloff in the Moscow park somewhere. Maybe there are lots of things that weren't identical, but the arrest procedure truly was.

Mr. Shultz: Yes. But I don't think it's right to say that these are two identical cases. The fact is that there were aspects of the Daniloff case that weren't known, in which things done in the U.S. government complicated Daniloff's situation, and they have never been fully revealed. But when you read my book in April, you will find out about them.

Ms. Ridgway: Before it became the Daniloff case it was, let me call it, the Zakharov file. And I'm not going to draw judgments, but it certainly was very clear, as the request for interagency clearance to seize/arrest Mr. Zakharov made its way through the United States executive branch, that everyone who had ever dealt with U.S.-Soviet relations knew that the last case in which the FBI had seized a Soviet citizen who did not have diplomatic cover had produced immediately the seizure of an American businessman in Moscow. Everybody knew the game. If you picked up KGB, they picked up CIA. If you picked up CIA, they picked up KGB. And if you picked up uncovered, nondiplomatic personnel, you were going to get an American citizen not protected by diplomatic cover picked up. There wasn't a person in Washington who didn't know that. The process of raising the question "Do you know what you're doing?" to the interagency intelligence community produced a situation in which no one was prepared to sign a piece of paper that said, "Do not seize a spy." It's deadly. You don't want your name on a piece of paper that says, "Let a spy go." Once the question had been posed, no one was prepared to stop it. In consequence, there was an interagency clearance of the seizure and arrest of Zakharov, and all of us spent the rest of August waiting to see who was going to get nailed in Moscow.

Mr. Oberdorfer: Very interesting.

Mr. Hershberg: Was it considered [whether] to expel him instead of detain him and thus avoid tit-for-tat?

Ms. Ridgway: It was not a style that was popular with those who were in that business.

Mr. Matlock: Look, we could spend a long time on this, but there are certain things that I think have not been brought out. First of all, our internal security agencies felt very much at a disadvantage because of the presence of this large UN mission plus the Soviet citizens at the [UN] secretariat who we knew were working for intelligence agencies. Now, there was no comparable organization in Moscow, nor did we use international organization coverage for that sort of intelligence activity in other countries. So it was a continual irritant that these international organizations were used for this purpose. It was bad enough to have their own missions used where they had cover, but when they began to use people from the secretariat who didn't have diplomatic immunity, this just had to be considered unacceptable.

There had been cases in the past, and Roz is right that this had happened, although the U.S. reaction was different. I think the KGB hadn't yet gotten the point that we wouldn't simply arrange an exchange without a cost to them. You remember, as far back as the Kennedy administration Professor Barghoorn was picked up under exactly the same circumstances. Kennedy certified that he was not a spy, and everybody knew he wasn't. Khrushchev said, "Well, release him." The story went around that Khrushchev said—I don't know whether it was true or not—that he told the KGB, "I said you can pick up an American, but I didn't tell you to pick up a friend of the president's." That's probably apocryphal.

We had another case, actually at the time of one of the first summits in '72, where an American scholar was picked up. In this case, Kissinger arranged for a quick exchange, which I felt set a very bad precedent. Then you had the case with the businessman, Mr. Crawford, during the Carter administration. These things had happened in the past, but there was very great resentment that innocent Americans would be picked up whenever we arrested on legitimate grounds staff officers of the KGB engaged in espionage, people without diplomatic immunity. That has to be considered in the background. It wasn't just a matter of saying, "Look, we shouldn't arrest, you know, a spy without diplomatic immunity." The question was, how far can we tolerate the use of the UN mission and the UN itself as a cover for espionage. It was a very serious issue within the U.S. government.

Mr. Oberdorfer: If I may just add my own one comment on this. There were so many meetings going on in this period [that] practically anything you did was going to be either just before or just after some U.S.-Soviet diplomatic meeting. How many meetings did you [Shultz] have with Shevardnadze? Twenty-eight or something? A large number.

Mr. Tarasenko: Thirty plus.

Mr. Shultz: I think it was widely interpreted that Cap Weinberger's letter to President Reagan just before the Geneva Summit was designed to make it very difficult for the president in Geneva.[9] As it turned out, it didn't disrupt it, but it was a deliberate attempt on his part. Some things like that did take place.

Chapter Four

∴ *The Makers of History*

What were the strengths and limitations of the key personalities in-volved in the turn away from the Cold War, especially Mikhail Gor-bachev and Ronald Reagan? What views did each side have of the other? How did each leader influence the other? And most important, how did they influence the course of events that culminated in the end of the Cold War? The Princeton Conference participants take on these questions here, and Fred I. Greenstein returns to them in chapter 7.

Mr. Oberdorfer: We've got a lot of people around the table who have had considerable experience with both of these men. I might turn to Frank and ask him to explain his own sense of the two leaders, having seen them both close up.

Mr. Carlucci: One was clearly a visionary, the other was a tactician. One liked detail, the master of the subject; the other had a few broad principles that he abided by, and those were almost immu-table. One liked to tell jokes; the other, while he had a sense of humor, was not particularly interested in telling jokes. One liked to talk from his own handwritten notes; the other, the sooner he could get the notes out of the way and get on with the more infor-mal conversation, the better he liked it. The one had an abiding interest in human rights questions; the other one wanted to get on the major subject of arms control. And the amazing thing is that the alchemy between these two disparate personalities seemed to work, that it somehow came together. There is no question that Ronald Reagan was very taken by Gorbachev; that he understood this was a new figure in the Soviet Union; that this was a historical moment. And as our former Soviet friends have said, there's no question that Gorbachev recognized that this was a new, unique opportunity to establish a personal relationship and change the whole dynamic of the relationship.

Mr. Shultz: Let me comment on Ronald Reagan, in part because it's a parlor game in the United States to cast aspersions on him—to a degree, I'm afraid, led by the Bush administration. I think that one needs to step back and say that, after all of the criticisms of Ronald Reagan, people have some explaining to do. He was elected governor of California, where I reside, and he was reelected governor of California by a huge margin. When he left office, he was very popular because it was clear that the state was a great deal better off when he left than when he started. And I believe that the same thing can be said about the United States, generally, and particularly about the foreign affairs situation when Reagan left office as compared with what he confronted when he entered office. So after people have gotten through talking about his distaste for detail, and about how he liked to tell jokes and stories, they have some explaining to do.

Historians also will have some explaining to do. The question they'll have to answer is, why was this man so successful? When Bud McFarlane left as national security advisor, he came around to me shaking his head and said, "He knows so little and he accomplishes so much." I felt that many of his staff had that view, and they didn't understand their man and understand the role of the staff. If a person has some weaknesses, it's the staff's job to protect him against the weaknesses and help use the strengths. Many of them seemed to me to be acting exactly in the opposite way. That's why I had so many fights with the NSC and White House staffs. As I have struggled to understand Ronald Reagan, here are some of the things that come to my mind and which I think have a very considerable bearing on the way U.S.-Soviet relations went.

First of all, Reagan was and is comfortable with himself. He had his views: you could argue with him, you could argue with him vociferously, and he didn't resent it. Maybe you would have some impact on him, maybe you wouldn't. He was a very decent person. He had a basic set of ideas and principles that he held to. And in a very nice way, if you tried to move him away from those ideas he understood what you were trying to do and you didn't get very far. He had a consistency about him, and he would stick with things. Sometimes you'd wish that he wouldn't.

On the other hand, there was a presidential instinct that was very strong. I saw this on display many times. One that has always struck me particularly was the Bitburg experience, which many of you remember.[1] It was excruciating. It's one of those things that gets out of control and pretty soon you can't do anything about it. It just takes place and you try to manage it as best you can. But what people observed, whether they were for or against the visit, was that Reagan had made this commitment to go, and he had made it to his friend Chancellor Kohl, who had played a very important role in the INF deployments. Unless Kohl backed away, he wasn't going to back away. What other politicians observed was, here is this man being assaulted on all sides—the Senate and the House were voting practically unanimously that he shouldn't go—and he went. He took all this heat and stood there and carried through. He would stick with things, and that, in the end, impressed people.

Reagan was not a person who was very much concerned about going against the conventional wisdom—didn't bother him in the slightest. In that sense he was a very revolutionary guy. A great many of the things that he advocated were derided when he advocated them, but in the end they came to pass. He was also, as Frank suggested, a person who had a vision of what he thought would be a better United States, a better world, and a confidence that the things that he believed in were good things. And because they were good things, somehow he could persuade other people to go along with him.

As far as the U.S.-Soviet relationship is concerned, I think that these characteristics were important because there were a great many people in the United States—and very heavily in what you might consider his constituency, Reagan country—whose view was that the Soviet Union couldn't change, that any new personality, like Mr. Gorbachev, would talk one way but it didn't really matter. So when Reagan said, "I think this man is different," and when he took positions that went against what this conservative base thought, that was an expression of this internal confidence, as I see it, and willingness to stand against people all around him if he felt that this was the right course. It took a little bit of that confidence and willingness to appraise things as changeable and changing that led him to move forward with a certain amount of confidence and without as much nervousness as the people around him often expressed, and thereby to get a great deal done.

It is amazing to go back and look at the campaign that was waged against the INF Treaty even after it was clearly going to come to pass. Nixon was against it. Kissinger was against it. [Former national security advisor Brent] Scowcroft was against it. All of the far right was against it. The NATO commander [General Bernard Rogers] was against it. Reagan was convinced it was the right thing. He proceeded. We were assaulted in the ratification hearings in a major way. People like Dan Quayle did everything they could to derail it, attaching amendments of one kind or another, all in considerable part to try to derail START. And I might say, in slowing START down they did a great disservice.

Reagan faced a lot of criticism for managing a change in U.S.-Soviet relations and in the particular things that he did. He was also quite prepared to take it right to Gorbachev. And at least as I watched it, the Reagan-Gorbachev relationship was not based on these two leaders going out of their way to accommodate each other. On the contrary, I felt that Gorbachev laid it on the line and so did Reagan. One reason they respected each other was that they both could see that the other guy was saying what he thought. Maybe you didn't agree with him and maybe you did. But there it was. It wasn't maneuvering and manipulating and trying to make some obscure point. It was right there. It was real. What you saw was what you got.

Mr. Oberdorfer: I think that gives us a good lead-in to ask one of our Russian friends to talk a little bit about Gorbachev as they saw him, and then we'll have sort of a crossfire, and let the Russians talk a little bit about Reagan and the Americans about Gorbachev. George Kennan, an eminent citizen of this community, said on a television interview a year or two ago, after Gorbachev became very well known, "Numbers of us who have known that country"—meaning the Soviet Union—"for a long time simply stand without explanation as to how a man of these qualities could have emerged from a provincial Party apparatus in the North Cauca-

sus." For Kennan, who is about as shrewd an observer of the Soviet Union and Soviet history as there is, to say that he is baffled
by the emergence of this figure says something about the difficulty of coming to grips with Gorbachev and who he is. A much
more complex figure, obviously, than we thought, just as Secretary
Shultz suggested that Reagan was a much more complex figure
than it seemed on the surface.

Mr. Bessmertnykh: Let me say a little about both men. It so happened that I knew more about Reagan, and knew him earlier, than
Gorbachev himself. I was minister-counselor of the Soviet Embassy in Washington at the time that Reagan became the president
and when he carried on the pre-election campaign. So of course
our task was to analyze the man, his views and positions, and to
report them to Moscow. As always, we had to present to our people
in Moscow the personal profile of the man: whatever we could
gather about him. This is the regular job of any embassy in any
country.

We believed we had a pretty good picture of Reagan. It was more
political than personal because we didn't know about him in a personal way. The political picture was, I think, correct. He was a
conservative, a man who had already put his views forward many
decades ago in a very straightforward way. But the mood in Moscow was "anyone but Carter," because Carter was so irritating to
us at the end of his presidency that anyone would have been better
than Carter. When Reagan won the election, everyone was happy
in Moscow. But very soon a certain concern started to appear when
Reagan started to make his positions clear on the Soviet-American
relationship.

As for Gorbachev, I first heard about him from my ambassador
Dobrynin, who went on vacation to Moscow and when he came
back, I asked him what interesting talks he had in Moscow. He
said: "Listen. There was an interesting man who has just come to
Moscow. I walked around to consult with the leaders of the Politburo and almost no one asked me any questions. They said, 'Well,
how's life?' I said, 'Well, it's okay,' and that was it. There is one
man, one man who asked me twenty, thirty questions. His name
was Gorbachev. He is so interested in doing that these days. And
what's surprising is, he's read so many books about the United
States."

I said, "How come? What books could he read about the United States?" But it so happened in the Soviet Union in previous years almost everything was published, but certain books were published only in numbers [large] enough for the Politburo and Central Committee to read. So Gorbachev took those books and read them all. He was kind of preparing himself, perhaps knowing that he would have to deal with the United States.

Of course, then I worked with him after 1985. It was so interesting to watch how they handled their first meeting in Geneva. Everyone is trying to emphasize the difference between the two. Of course, they were different in age and in background and philosophical attitudes, maybe in the level of knowledge about the world, but I would like to emphasize the common things about the two because it is the commonality of certain elements that made them friends. They were real friends. In 1990, when Gorbachev made his farewell visit to the United States, he specifically went to the West Coast to meet the Reagans. There were no other reasons for him to do that. When Reagan invited him, he went there because he liked that man very much.

As for the common things, I would say those two men were very idealistic. They each had their own ideals which they tried to follow all through their lives. The ideals were not similar, but the dedication to those ideals was similar. They both believed in something. They were not just men who could trim their sails and go any way the wind blows. So that was the thrust, the essence of the two men. This is what they immediately sensed in each other, and this is why they made good partners. I never believed the stories that were published in the American press that Reagan couldn't handle the negotiations with Gorbachev, because I knew it was not correct. Especially after Reykjavik there were many stories saying that Gorbachev had outplayed Reagan and that Reagan had been duped by the energetic young Soviet president. It was not true at all. Reagan handled negotiations very, very well. He might not have known all the details. He used little cards when he would come to details. He didn't like the formal part of negotiations. He was unhappy with it. He would try to rush through this formal part, and then he would throw away the cards and then he would start talking the direct way.

I was across the table at all the summits and followed this president for all those years, and I personally admired the man very much. He was a good politician. He was a good diplomat. He was very dedicated. And if it were not for Reagan, I don't think we would have been able to reach the agreements in arms control that we reached later, because of his idealism, because he thought that we should really do away with nuclear weapons. Gorbachev believed in that. Reagan believed in that. The experts didn't believe, but the leaders did.

Mr. Oberdorfer: Mr. Chernyaev, would you like to say something about it?

Mr. Chernyaev: I believe that Gorbachev became what he became, the kind of person and the kind of statesman that he became, first of all because he is morally and ethically and also physically a very healthy man. It is the consequence of his general health as an individual. At a certain point, that helped him in his activities as a statesman to abandon Marxist-Leninist orthodoxy and to adopt a policy of common sense. He is proud of having tried and of having succeeded, to a certain extent, in introducing an ethical principle in international politics and also in our country's politics, even though he understands from his personal experience how difficult this task is and how many years it will probably take to really produce something practical from this combination of morality and politics.

I think it would probably be more interesting for you to hear me speaking about the chemistry between Gorbachev and Reagan, Gorbachev and Shultz, Gorbachev and other leaders. I've already said that after the first summit in Geneva, particularly during the months when there was some backsliding in the relationship, for a number of reasons Gorbachev developed a general view of President Reagan that was not particularly favorable. He did not like, for example, that Reagan sometimes wanted to teach him, that Reagan sometimes insisted on taking the upper hand in the conversation. And once Gorbachev even said to Reagan, "Mr. President, you are not a prosecutor and I am not in the dock, so let us try to develop a relationship that is not based on that." Gorbachev did not immediately understand the strength and the message of Ronald Reagan as a statesman. Initially, Gorbachev did not particularly like the fact that Reagan did not want to discuss the details of, let us say, arms control and some other questions. As soon as those details emerged in the conversation, Reagan immediately said, "Let us call in George and Eduard."

It was only later that Gorbachev understood that Reagan, maybe because of his instincts, maybe because he was so programmed, played his role as the president of a superpower in a somewhat different way. I think that the first voltage arc, so to speak, happened between those two leaders in Reykjavik. Gorbachev felt in Reykjavik that Reagan was someone who was concerned about very human things, about the human needs of his people. He felt that Reagan behaved as a very moral person. He also saw in Reagan a person who was capable of making very big decisions. And even though Reykjavik did not achieve practical results, Gorbachev felt that there were grounds for hope that there would be a chemistry between him and Reagan that would produce very important results in the future.

You should have seen at Reykjavik, when Gorbachev and Reagan were leaving Hofdi House and all of us watched them coming out of that very small, white building, apparently having failed, but we saw that they both were really feeling for what had happened and they both were behaving in a very human way. Gorbachev had his arm around Ron Reagan's shoulder, and Mr. Shultz was walking behind them. I think it was at that time that Gorbachev decided to do what he did twenty minutes later at that famous press conference in Reykjavik in which he said that this was not a defeat; that this was indeed a breakthrough. It was at that time that Gorbachev decided that he could and would work together with Reagan. Even though there was again after Reykjavik, just as after Geneva, some backsliding—and I heard Mr. Gorbachev make some very harsh remarks about the president of the United States and the positions he took, sometimes using language that cannot be translated—still, things were put back on track. Through joint efforts, and particularly the efforts of George Shultz and also Eduard Shevardnadze, a very important treaty, the INF Treaty, was prepared. Mr. Gorbachev's visit to Washington took place and the treaty was signed.

Mr. Oberdorfer: Let me just add, here, that we have had other instances in which leaders of our two countries have gotten to know each other. You can go back to Franklin Roosevelt and Stalin, and to Nikita Khrushchev and Eisenhower. I traveled around the country with Khrushchev when he came here in 1959. People were charmed by him—for a while, anyway. Then there were Nixon and Brezhnev, in the days when Brezhnev was more vigorous than he later became. Yet none of those people, despite the fact that they broke the ice, was able to produce the great changes in our relationship which were produced by these two unusual figures that we have been talking about tonight, Reagan and Gorbachev.

I'd like to throw out for discussion these two points: first, the extent to which underlying circumstances contributed to the tremendous change which took place in international relations; and second, the way in which others, especially Secretary Shultz and Foreign Minister Shevardnadze, worked in a special and cooperative way, despite the turbulence and tension, to try to put together the pieces of a relationship. I guess maybe I look to Paul Nitze, who's seen so many interactions between those two countries going back to the 1940s, with different personalities and in different circumstances: What is your sense of why this time it took, but on previous occasions it did not?

Mr. Nitze: In my view, George Shultz had an enormous impact on making it work. I can remember one day in particular when Mr. Gorbachev was furious at the U.S. side and he began the discussion that day by denouncing, first of all, me, for what I'd said at the Atlantic Council the day before when I briefed the council about the upcoming negotiations and took a very firm line as to what I thought should be the American position. Then he denounced Roz Ridgway, who was also of the same view, and said that she was even worse than I, and maybe even tougher. Having warmed to his task, he then began to denounce the president of the United States for a speech he had made in Maine, quoting verbatim from that speech. Having gotten that off his chest, he began to denounce Secretary Shultz, and he capped this particular attack on Shultz by saying, "The trouble with you, Mr. Shultz, is that on matters of foreign policy you think you're always right." At that point George Shultz said, "On matters of foreign policy, Mr. Secretary General, I am always right." And I've never seen such a warm reaction. Gorbachev thought this was really very funny, and he began to laugh. That was the breakthrough that really made that particular session. But there are not that many people who have the instinct for the right remark to head off problems, and Secretary Shultz certainly had that ability.

Mr. Oberdorfer: Do you think this was fated? I mean, suppose it hadn't been Reagan? Suppose it had been Ronald Jones or some other kind of character who had been president of the United States with Gorbachev in Moscow, knowing he had to change the policy of his country. Would we be in the same place today?

Mr. Nitze: Frankly, I was never quite clear in my mind about what made Mr. Gorbachev tick. I didn't quite feel comfortable about what made him operate the way he did. From time to time he would say, "Don't get me wrong. I'm a dedicated Marxist-Leninist. And what is more than that, I believe in the eventual triumph of socialism worldwide." I thought he was serious when he said that. He repeated it several different times. Clearly that was not a formula designed to endear [his viewpoint to the United States]. But I would like to hear comments from the Soviet side as to whether he spoke truth when he said that, or whether there was some other, more complicated explanation.

Mr. Chernyaev: Almost throughout his work as leader of the country, Gorbachev would say that he was committed to what he called the "socialist choice." He only rarely called himself a "consistent Marxist-Leninist," and that was only in the beginning of his career. But if you look at his speeches, at least those that have been published, you will see that in speaking about the "socialist choice" he was less and less speaking about purely socialist content. He spoke to his public, and it was quite clear that he could not drag this society that considered itself socialist out of that overnight. But in the company of his friends, he very often said, "Look, this is our socialism. This is what it brought our country to." For him, the idea of being committed to this socialist choice was basically the idea of changing the country gradually from its state of total stagnation and inadequacy. Even though Gorbachev spoke about the people being committed to socialism and not willing to abandon socialism easily or overnight, what he really meant was that he understood very well that people identified with socialism not as high ideals but as a certain kind of society in which they had certain guarantees—not much, but they knew that they had a certain safety net that they were not willing to give up. They relied not so much on socialism but on the state, and he knew that this could not be abandoned easily.

Mr. Oberdorfer: When did he come to understand that the reforms which he had begun and other developments in the Soviet Union were leading to the breakup of the political system?

Mr. Chernyaev: I think that happened sometime around the Nineteenth Party Conference, in mid-1988. His concept of that conference from the very outset was that the conference should begin the process that would liquidate the Party as a monopoly, and as a state structure. The *nomenklatura* soon understood that.[2] It is starting in the fall of 1988 that the conscious resistance to Gorbachev's policies among the Party nomenklatura really worked.

Mr. Oberdorfer: The other night, our Russian friends had a little seminar here in Princeton, and the questions were, what happened in 1989, in 1990, and to some degree, 1991, when this all came crashing down? Sergei Tarasenko told us about a conversation he had with Shevardnadze prior to the collapse of Eastern Europe and the sense of inevitability of what was happening. Could you repeat for this general audience what you told us that night?

Mr. Tarasenko: That was connected with the Polish developments when Solidarność won the election in Poland [in June 1989]. We'd been vacationing on the Black Sea in Georgia when I was wakened early in the morning by an urgent cable our Moscow office said they had received from President Ceaușescu of Romania. Ceaușescu proposed a collective military action against Poland, and he asked for an urgent meeting. He asked Shevardnadze to come to Bucharest for preliminary talks; then he proposed to organize a conference of the Warsaw Pact to take action to save socialism. While Shevardnadze was at the beach, I went and reported this information to him. He took it calmly: there was no way he was going anywhere. There was no question of taking any action. Forget about it.

In a couple of days the Romanian minister came to our place for talks. Nothing came out of that. But it was a signal to us, and it certainly was an emotional moment that forced us to think about the situation. I remember that we stayed on the beach and started to discuss things, and we posed a question to ourselves in our discussion: "Do we understand what is going to happen?" The collective opinion was, "Yes, we do." That inevitably we will lose our allies—the Warsaw Pact. These countries will go their own ways. And we even acknowledged between ourselves that the Soviet Union would not manage to survive. The logic of events would force the breakup of the Soviet Union, specifically the Baltics. Because a lot of guys were from Georgia, and we were in Georgia; we were well aware even then of the problems in the Caucasus—that there was a lot of opposition there to Moscow's rule and that there could be some problems. So we did acknowledge it, even saying to ourselves, "Yes, we'll suffer. We'll lose our jobs, we'll be punished for that."[3]

So, on a theoretical level, it was no problem to project the collapse of the empire. Our empire was doomed. But we didn't think that it would come so soon and in such a fashion.

Mr. Oberdorfer: Jack Matlock has spent nearly all of his adult life studying the Soviet Union and other Eastern European countries as Soviet desk officer, as National Security Council official for Soviet matters, as ambassador to Czechoslovakia, ambassador to the Soviet Union. Ambassador Matlock, was this whole thing kind of an inevitable play that was fated to take the historical course that it took?

Mr. Matlock: I think personalities have a very important effect on history. I've never shared Tolstoy's theory of history, though I'm very much in love with Tolstoy as a writer. I think it made a great difference that these two people, Ronald Reagan and Mikhail Sergeevich Gorbachev, were in power in their two countries at the time they were. I come to this as a professional. I was not a politician. I didn't know Ronald Reagan. As a matter of fact, I didn't even vote for him the first time he was elected because I couldn't really identify with the image. However, as a professional, dealing in my area, I think I was totally loyal in working for him, and I came to appreciate certain things. I agree 100 percent with what Frank Carlucci and George Shultz have already said. I would just add a few things because I do think that President Reagan, particularly among other intellectuals, is simply not understood.

He knew what he wanted but he didn't know how to get there, and he was quite open about recognizing that. He was an ideal person to work for on the staff because if he made a mistake, you could say, "Mr. President, hey, you really made a boo-boo there," and since he was comfortable with himself, he wasn't uptight and you could be very frank. I recall on one occasion he had said publicly, "Well, the Russians don't have a word for 'freedom.'" The next day I went in and said, "Hey, you know, they do have a word for freedom. I think you mixed it up with 'compromise.'" And he said, "Gee, Jack, you know, I guess I did mix that up." You felt perfectly free to correct him. I quickly learned that you could tell him what you thought. He was comfortable with it. He didn't take it as a personal insult. He knew he didn't know everything. He knew he didn't know much about the Soviet Union. He had various ideological assumptions, and he had read some book by someone which had a lot of pseudo-quotes from Lenin, most of which were false, by the way, which we finally had to demonstrate to him.

But at the same time he had an open mind. It was an interesting combination. I know how hard it is to get fifteen minutes with the president, but if we said, "Mr. President, we'd like to put on a two-hour briefing on the Soviet Union," they'd make time for it. I organized several of these briefings because he loved to chew the fat and listen. He also liked to read, and he would read voluminous materials over the weekend—more than the other presidents that I worked with. Most presidents really feel that they know, so they don't really listen that well. Ronald Reagan knew what he didn't know, and he was willing to listen. And papers would come back. When I was asked to do a paper about the values and shortcomings of summitry, the first paper I was asked to do, I said, "Yes, what do you want, two pages or so?" And they said, "No, we can go to eight or ten. He's going to read it over the weekend." He would read and annotate it. I remember he wrote at the end of one paper, "This was something I felt that I couldn't articulate myself. Thanks for explaining it."

But where Reagan had a real instinct—an instinct that was instructive to all of us—was as a politician. He understood politicians. We could say about Gorbachev, for example, particularly after he got to know him, "Hey, Gorbachev's got a problem at home. He's facing pressure on this, pressure on that. We've got to understand this." He would pay attention to that, and he would be willing to take it into account.

Ms. Ridgway: I would argue that while it may have been true that each of our countries would have continued on a course which, for the Soviet Union, would have produced in the late 1980s what it did, how all of that turned out would have been different had the two men not met and established a relationship between the United States and the Soviet Union. Had they not had people who brought them together, they could very well have, like ships, passed in the night and passed each other by in history, not having had an influence on the nation of the other. You also have to say that only a President Reagan, like Nixon in China, had the kind of political unassailability at home that made it possible for him to be the one to reach out. And he could not have done it had he not been supported by people who took over the process of engagement and protected it from the continuous assault from people who really did not think that it was in the interest of the United States to proceed on one or all of the parts of the agenda. It was the extent to which the two men came together, stayed together, developed a relationship, and worked some issues, that at the end of the day made it possible for the Cold War to end as it did: that is, in a political setting without enormous amounts of bloodshed. And it made it possible for the Soviet Union's leadership to address its own problems without wondering where the United States was, where the NATO alliance was, and whether they were standing by to take advantage.

But all of that could not have happened if it hadn't been for George Shultz and Eduard Shevardnadze. Now, how those two people came together is probably another story, but I really don't think you can do a twosome in discussing this. I think you must discuss a quadruple set of figures. And the process players cannot be separated from the policy players.

Mr. Oberdorfer: Let me ask you one further thing. Shevardnadze was a person from Soviet Georgia. He'd been the Communist Party boss of Georgia. He had absolutely no diplomatic experience whatever—barely any experience in the Soviet capital, even. He had been outside the country only a few times. And yet, he ended up with some kind of instinctive feel for diplomacy. Ambassador Ridgway once recounted to me the story of her impression of the first meeting between Secretary Shultz and Minister Shevardnadze in Helsinki, which was in the context of a meeting of the

CSCE that took place in the summer of 1985, only a few weeks after Shevardnadze was named to be foreign minister. But could you tell us that?

Ms. Ridgway: Well, I remember vividly because, in addition to being a believer in policy, process, and procedure I also believe in the importance of courtesies: the human side of official contact. The tenth anniversary meeting of the Conference on Security and Co-operation in Europe, which was held in Helsinki, was the occasion. The United States delegation was seated in the front of the room. The alphabet was French.[4] We were seated in the front of the room with the two Germanys. The delegation of the Soviet Union was in the back. Everyone was waiting to see what would happen when the secretary decided that he would walk from the front to the back of the auditorium to shake the hand of the new Soviet foreign minister appearing on the scene for the first time. Silence reigned in this huge international hall—the Finlandia Hall in Helsinki—as the American secretary of state first walked across the front of the room and then walked up all of the steps to the back of the room. As the news media and the world's photographers realized what was happening, they all began to gather where the juncture would take place. And as George Shultz put out his hands to extend the welcome to the new Soviet foreign minister, there was this explosion of light and commentary along the sides.

With that kind of a welcome, the people wanted to know what the first meeting would be like, and it was my own first meeting of this kind as well. What I saw was the beginning of the assembling of a new Soviet team—as was the case on the American side in large part. But I saw a new foreign minister who had been given all of his papers, who was accompanied by a team of advisors old and new and, as with the American delegation, had enough extras to fill up the sofas in the back of the room. And each time he began to go through his notes, someone would jump up and try to tell him how to read his notes. I see that Mr. Bessmertnykh is smiling. He probably remembers some of this. Finally it was just very clear he was going to talk on his own. And we started through an agenda that was traditional.

This was a man who was not yet free of some of the old way of doing things in terms of assembling delegations, preparing notes, and making long speeches. But it was also very clear that he wasn't going to be putting up with this for very long and was going to have his own style. The secretary's answer to this was to encourage the informality. We've talked about the simultaneous translation and the different way of organizing the remarks so that it was not a half-hour presentation on each side. On the outside of the meeting, I believe Mrs. Shultz and Mrs. Shevardnadze were participating in sightseeing. This was the first time that a wife had accompanied a Soviet foreign minister on such a trip, and consequently there was an opportunity then to begin to build a very human dimension around this relationship involving someone who was very new to it. It was an incomplete introduction, in that not all of the topics perhaps were covered the way we wanted. But it was very clear that a different road had been started down as to how the two sides of this table would communicate: the manner in which they would speak and the fact that they would try to include this human side in it.

Mr. Shultz: Actually, having read that Mrs. Shevardnadze would be present, my wife O'Bie and I talked it over and we said, this relationship has lots of tension in it and it will have lots of ups and downs, but we have a new foreign minister who has brought his wife. They're from Georgia, and we understand Georgians are gregarious, so let's try to get to know them as human beings. Whatever policy differences we'll have, let's try to establish a human contact anyway. We did make a big effort there, and I have a feeling that the Shevardnadzes must have said to each other something rather similar, because it wasn't difficult to work with them.

I wanted to comment earlier that these personal relationships that we've talked about this evening were proceeded by a lot of very tough substantive interactions of these two countries during the Reagan period and earlier. I do think that if we are trying to explain how it is that the outcome that came about took place, we have to look at these historic forces. We have to look at the strategic decisions that were made, and at the difficulties of implementing those decisions and a lot of the trauma that was experienced. Then we have to look at the personal factors and see how they interplay and not get ourselves feeling that that's really the whole story.

As Roz said, at that first meeting Shevardnadze had this gigantic stack of talking points which he faithfully but obviously reluctantly went through. I was told that there was a big argument in your delegation, and he didn't want to have this big bunch of talking points, and that he was basically told, "You don't know enough about this. You've got to read these things out." So he did, but obviously with a lot of resentment. He much preferred to become the master of his brief and then be much more free-wheeling and conversational, which is where he wound up. Is that true? Did you have that argument with him?

Mr. Bessmertnykh: Yes. When Shevardnadze came to the Foreign Ministry, he started to meet with the chiefs of the departments just to get aware of what is going on, what he should do. As the chief of the U.S.A. Department, I was among the first ones he received. I told him immediately, "Mr. Minister, you are going to see the U.S. secretary of state in about two weeks." Shevardnadze just groaned. He said, "Oh, why? What shall we be talking about?" I said, "There is a whole agenda. The main item will be arms control and nuclear weapons." And he said, "Well, I should not have accepted the job." He didn't know what it was all about. I said, "We should prepare the talking points for you." This is what you were referring to just now. I said, "Even for Gromyko we would always prepare talking points, and he would use those talking points and he would hold negotiations based just on what we prepared for him." We trained Shevardnadze every day on the various subjects. By the moment of his going to Geneva, he realized he still wouldn't understand what it was all about. So he said, "What should I do at that meeting with the secretary of state?" We suggested that he should just read that briefing book because it was the official position of the country. And he said, "All right, I'll do that." But he absolutely disliked that idea, because he was not that kind of man. He wouldn't just repeat somebody else's points.

He told me many times after that first meeting with you that he had felt immediately relaxed; that you didn't put him in an uncomfortable position by pressing on specifics which he didn't know. I think you liked his statement when he said, "I brought this thick book, but I don't know what's in it, so I'll start reading to you." The openness and frankness that was displayed by the two of you immediately set the foundation for the personal kind of relationship. Shevardnadze had this kind of uncomfortable feeling for the next year. I remember meetings in which he was interrupted by the first deputy foreign minister, and then he would be interrupted by a deputy minister, and he would be looking at one, and looking at another, unable to follow the difficult discussion of arms control. But in about a year he grasped the subject, and then he carried on all the talks easily.

I would like just to tell the story about Tarasenko. After about a week of Shevardnadze's [tenure] as minister, he called me and said, "Would you suggest a person who could advise me daily about all those foreign policy issues that come to my desk. I receive cables. I receive papers. But I have got to understand what it's all about." I said, "Well, there is a nice man, a very knowledgeable and good man—Sergei Tarasenko." So he took him as a temporary advisor, but then he liked him very much and Sergei was with Shevardnadze until he went to Georgia, and he even stayed there for another year in Georgia. I put him in a very difficult position for six years. And I think he could add something to the story.

Mr. Oberdorfer: Sergei, would you like to say something about Shevardnadze? Maybe about Shevardnadze and his relationship with Shultz.

Mr. Tarasenko: Yes. First I accompanied him to the Helsinki meeting as the second man in the U.S.A. Department, carrying this huge bag of papers, you know, just in case issues came up. I took notes, so I actually didn't deal with him in any way, I just sat in the corner and wrote notes. I liked the way he behaved in a general way. Then he invited me to come over to his office. I would say that was the first time I performed this role of explaining to him something specific about arms control, and then, for the first time, I was amazed at what we wrote in these [briefing] papers. All these abbreviations. Half of the page [was] abbreviations: GLCMs, SLCMs— Terrible. He would look at these abbreviations. But he was a normal guy, he'd never seen [such things]. So I would say, "This stands for . . . ," and so on, and we redid all the papers.

I would say that at least during the period when he started things, he relied on my advice on some matters, [but this phase] ended rather quickly. It ended actually in New York when he came to the General Assembly session. It was funny. I knew that he would be calling me, so I stayed ready. Then around 11 o'clock in the evening he called me: "Please, come." I came to his office. He looked at the watch. He said, "We are both tired. It will not be good to proceed with these papers. Maybe we will meet at four o'clock in the morning." I said, "Okay, I'll be here." So I was back at four o'clock, he was there, and we started a new custom. Very soon I got accustomed to his odd hours, you know. It didn't mean anything to him. He would call you any time. Usually he would call whenever he felt he had something to tell me, not bothering about where I was. And after that, actually, he was on his own. He was a surprisingly quick study. He has this Georgian pride, you know. He's a very proud man. And he is not used to a situation in which he is inferior and has to depend upon somebody. He doesn't like it. So he did a lot of learning on the job, and within a couple of months he was on his own except for some part of the main conflict areas [on which he] needed some reference.

I'm partial, obviously. I liked the man. I followed him all the way. I resigned with him. So I'm partial. I want to say that. But the quality I would rate the highest was his personal charm and personal attention. I do not want to put some negative attitudes out, but just to note a difference between the two guys. I was not for Gorbachev the first time [I dealt directly with him]. In Reykjavik, I was with the minister in his cabin, and Gorbachev came in and they started talking. I wanted to get away, but he said, "Stay." I stayed. But what surprised me [was] that Gorbachev actually looks through you. He doesn't see. Maybe he wasn't in a good mood then, but he's cold, personally cold. That was my impression. Shevardnadze, on the other side, is extremely warm. He will not pass you. He will smile. He will notice you. He will pat you or make some move, you know, to take notice of you. And he's specifically generous with gratitude. Whatever you will do for him, he will say to you, "Thank you."

I remember we were working on the exchange of New Year's greetings between Gorbachev and President Reagan. So, with my colleague Stepanov, we did a piece for this Gorbachev presentation on TV and we sent it over to the minister, and I thought that's the end of it. I went home, and around ten o'clock in the evening a call comes and a guy from the office says, the minister wants to talk to you. "Okay." I took the phone. And the minister said, "I like this piece." "Well, thank you very much." "For what you did, it's a good piece, so I appreciate it." A member of Politburo reaching some small guy down there, you know, and saying thanks to him. While I worked for Gromyko, you never expected even a nod or any reaction from Gromyko, whatever you did for him. And now this new guy takes [the] care of phoning me late at night. So he was good at creating loyalty. You were hooked on him. He had this kind of personality. You would like to work for him. That makes the difference.

Mr. Oberdorfer: Mr. Gromyko, who said in answer to a question from a reporter about how he felt about something, "My personality doesn't interest me," was somewhat different. Shultz wanted to say something—

Mr. Shultz: You introduced the subject of Shevardnadze by observing that he was inexperienced in foreign affairs and hadn't been out of the country, and that has been confirmed on the Soviet side here. Yet he turned out to be a very successful foreign minister. Sergei has given some of the reasons. But I think your introduction and his success raises the question, what does it take to be a successful foreign minister? In addition to his personal qualities, his energy and hard work, there are two things that seem to me to be very important. One of them became more and more obvious to me the first time I met with him and Gorbachev together, and this was in Moscow before the Geneva Summit, and then at the Geneva Summit: he had a very easy relationship with his boss, the general secretary. They worked confidently together, and that's essential if you're going to be effective.

And the second factor is that Shevardnadze knew his country. He had struggled with the problems in Georgia, and he had lots of discussions with Gorbachev and others about what was going on in other parts of the country. So he understood his country, I would say, much better than Gromyko could possibly have understood it. Gromyko had never spent much time there, as we know. My impression is that the rulers of the Soviet Union, before Gorbachev and company came along, for a long period of time basically lived in a little cocoon in Moscow and where they went on vacations. Their feel for what was going on was quite limited. I think that a person who wants to be a foreign minister of a country but who doesn't know his own country pretty well is not going to wind up doing that well. This was one of Shevardnadze's strengths.

Mr. Oberdorfer: Mr. Chernyaev—

Mr. Chernyaev: I wanted to respond to something Ambassador Ridgway said because I think that she mentioned something very important about the influence of the people who surround the leaders. With respect to Gorbachev, you should also speak about another very important influence, and that is the influence of people he met, particularly the Americans he met, and he had hundreds of contacts with all kinds of Americans—senators, congressmen, writers, scientists, schoolchildren, students. Through those contacts he—as he liked to say—he was learning the reality about the world and he was learning to respect the world. This had a tremendous impact on his attitudes and also on the process of shaping the New Thinking.

Paradoxically, I would say that in a certain way Mr. Shultz had more of an impact on Gorbachev than Eduard Shevardnadze. I have memorandums of Gorbachev's conversations with foreign leaders that Gorbachev intends to publish gradually. This is a source of enormous importance for understanding what was really happening and how the personal element was combining with political positions and principles. I recall two visits by Secretary Shultz to Moscow in February and in April of 1988 that preceded President Reagan's visit to Moscow. Let me quote from this memorandum of conversation a couple of passages that illustrate Gorbachev's attitude toward people of a certain level.

The first thing Gorbachev said to the secretary of state on April 22, 1988, was, "I am glad to welcome you, Mr. Secretary of State, and I welcome you as a person who has done a great deal to put our relations on their current track. You and your colleagues present here are our old friends, and are people who we know and respect." He said, "It seemed to me that over the past two or three years we have been engaged in a very productive search for new approaches toward our relations, and the results are there for us and for the whole world. Both of us have had to overcome many obstacles along that path and we have done a lot of difficult and necessary work, and I would like to say once again, as I have done publicly, that I value very much your contribution toward this. I would like to salute the efforts of you, Mr. Secretary of State, also of others present here." And he mentioned Mr. Nitze, Mr. Matlock, Mr. [Thomas] Simons [director of Soviet Affairs at the State Department], Ms. Ridgway, and General Powell, who had recently joined our common efforts.

Then he began to get fired up in his very emotional and rather critical manner, because on the eve of your arrival President Reagan had delivered a speech that Gorbachev did not like. I don't recall exactly what was in that speech by Reagan, but probably something that reminded Gorbachev of the bygone times of anti-Communist crusades and of the times of mistrust of Gorbachev. But then, after the conversation was over, I spoke with him and Gorbachev said, "Look, did you note how when I was criticizing the president they did not rush to defend their president immediately? Maybe they feel that there was something wrong in that speech by the president, that his recent speech was not in the spirit of the kind of work that we have done together with President Reagan."

Then he recalled how he had been saying goodbye, shaking hands with every member of the U.S. delegation; and he said, "You heard what Nitze and Ridgway said to me when I was shaking their hands." So he remembered their every word, and that shows that he really held in very high regard those people and their contribution, and it illustrates, I think, a totally different character of the relationship. But specifically what both of you were saying to him as you were saying goodbye after that conversation, he will recall that for you in his memoirs, because he really said great things about that in his book.

For Gorbachev, Secretary Shultz was an extremely important and interesting interlocutor. And in addition to their discussions about missiles and aircraft, there was, from time to time, that very important philosophical theme about mankind and its future. Now that Gorbachev is working on his memoirs and he is dictating the draft, each time he comes to a point at which he discusses some conversation with Secretary Shultz, he always emphasizes his great respect for Mr. Shultz, describing him as one of the greatest, an outstanding statesman of our time. Gorbachev's words are, "He helped me very much both in developing and in implementing my policies."

Mr. Oberdorfer: I hate to tell Mr. Chernyaev this, but before Mr. Gorbachev gets his memoirs too far along, this conversation is recounted in some detail in my book. I agree with you, it's one of the most interesting conversations that Gorbachev and Secretary Shultz had. President Reagan had made a stem-winding, anti-Communist speech in Springfield, Massachusetts. I doubt the State Department ever saw the speech. It was his boiler plate, more or less. Except that what he didn't realize was that now there was a transcript service which had just started not too long before then, in which the transcripts of speeches are published and made available to embassies. The Soviet Embassy in Washington took all this stuff and they sent it over electronically to Moscow. I doubt that there were a hundred Americans outside of those at the rotary club in Springfield, Massachusetts, who had the slightest idea of what Reagan had said. But as far as Gorbachev was concerned, this was probably a major policy pronouncement.

Mr. Shultz: I didn't know what Gorbachev was talking about. I looked over at Colin Powell, the national security advisor, having replaced Frank when Frank went to be secretary of defense, and said, "What's he talking about, Colin?" He didn't know about it either. So we drove on by.

Mr. Oberdorfer: Mr. Palazchenko would like to say something.

Mr. Palazchenko: I recalled a joke about a Russian teacher assigning junior high school students to write a sentence about a Russian writer of their choice, and so one student wrote about Nikolai Gogol: that Gogol was very special because he stood with one foot in the past and with his other foot he was saluting the future. This, I think, can be said about Reagan and Gorbachev and about basically all of us here. That speech was his one foot in the past, I guess. But he did, I think, a great deal to salute the future.

Chapter Five

Afghanistan and the Limits of Empire ∴

The fateful decision to invade Afghanistan and the painful process of withdrawal are the main subjects discussed in the transcript below. The Russian participants reconstruct the Soviet decision to dispatch troops to bolster the embattled "progressive" regime in Kabul, providing a fascinating window on the Brezhnev-era Soviet policy-making process. The give-and-take between the Russians and the Americans on the prolonged struggle over withdrawing the Soviet troops brings out eerie parallels with the U.S. experience in Vietnam. The participants also discuss the complex negotiations that facilitated the winding-down of other Cold War regional conflicts.

Mr. Oberdorfer: Several months ago, former foreign minister Bessmertnykh told me of a group of documents on Afghanistan that was so secret that only the foreign minister himself could open them. I would like to start off by asking him what he has learned about the decision to go into Afghanistan.

Mr. Bessmertnykh: To me it was always a mystery why Gromyko, who was very cautious in foreign policy, would support the introduction of troops into Afghanistan when even a schoolboy knows that Afghanistan is a territory you should never touch. The history of the Russian-Afghan relationship shows that the Afghans are a people who would always die for their freedom and who may not be won over. You may recall the story about the Russian Cossacks who were hired by the British to go and fight the Afghan tribes, and those Cossacks took the army and their horses and went south, but then turned right and found themselves in Africa. They simply avoided Afghanistan: They knew it was a dangerous spot.

It was a conventional wisdom that Afghanistan is an area which should not be invaded.

Now that we have all those documents, we can read into parts of the story, but at the time it happened it was a complete secret and we didn't even know who participated in making that decision. I personally learned about it when on a nice short home leave to Moscow from Washington in December 1979. It was a short announcement on the television. When I heard that military [force was being introduced into Afghanistan], I immediately recognized that we were getting into big trouble in the Soviet-American relationship. So, it's very hard now to differentiate what you knew at that moment from what you know now. But by the time I became the minister of foreign affairs, I still knew nothing about the participants in that fatal decision. So we started to search the archives of the Foreign Ministry, as I think was done in the Central Committee and other places. Gorbachev wanted all materials to be collected.

Suddenly, in the safe only for the foreign minister, we found a package of documents sealed, with a signature on it, not to be opened. It didn't even say, "Except by the minister." So no one, except maybe God, was allowed to open it. It was not to be opened, and that was that. I had that package on my desk for about ten minutes thinking about who should give the instruction to open it. Then I felt that I should do it myself. So I opened the package. It was a set of papers prepared for the Politburo on the day the invasion occurred that described all the measures that should be taken to protect the action, politically and propagandistically— what to say to the foreign audience, what to say in domestic quarters. There [were] signatures, of course, of those who prepared the document. The name which struck me as most interesting was [Boris N.] Ponomarev, chief of the International Department of the Central Committee of the Communist Party.

It was clear that Andropov, Ustinov, and Gromyko were heading the foreign policy at that time, after Brezhnev had had a heart attack in 1976. Foreign policy was in the hands of those three men, and so I was not surprised that they were ones who had made the decision. But the fourth name [Ponomarev] was very important. So, looking back and hearing the rumors and the talks with the people who were involved, we knew that the military were against it. Kornienko told us that at that time. Akhromeev told us on a number of occasions that the military didn't like the idea of going with troops to Afghanistan.

Kornienko remembers that Gromyko, who would always discuss Afghanistan with him, suddenly stopped discussing Afghanistan with him sometime in October 1979. He suddenly became very silent about this subject. That surprised Kornienko, because it was always an item on almost every day's agenda. So from October to December people were thinking about the advisability of moving into Afghanistan, probably weighing the pros and cons. And in December it was decided.

My personal feeling is that it was decided on the basis of several considerations. There was a lot of information coming to the leadership at the time from different sources, especially from the intelligence sources, both military and KGB. Intelligence said that things were turning out very badly in Kabul as far as the Soviet interests were concerned, and that [Hafizullah] Amin, who had taken over after [Nur Mohammad] Taraki as the general secretary [of the People's Democratic Party of Afghanistan], was not trustworthy because he had started to play games with the Americans and with some other suspicious people.[1]

Mr. Oberdorfer: Mohammad Taraki had been the revolutionary leader of Afghanistan, and he was on good terms with Moscow. He was overthrown by his deputy, Hafizullah Amin, who had been a student at Columbia University and was suspected by some of being pro-American. Taraki, whom the Russians knew and liked, was killed.

Mr. Bessmertnykh: That incident definitely brought a lot of concern to the government. But the general public didn't pay very much attention to what was happening there. Because for the Russians, Afghanistan was always a friendly country—[whether] under Daoud,[2] [or under] the King of Afghanistan. There was always . . . historically an excellent relationship between Afghanistan and Russia. When the so-called April Revolution of 1978 occurred, no one knew about the sources of that revolution, but it was wholeheartedly accepted. Here I come again to Ponomarev's role.

Since 1978, when Afghanistan went the "revolutionary way," I think that the interests of the Foreign Relations Committee of the

Central Foreign Relations Department of the Central Committee grew, and with all those ups and downs and domestic developments, the concern was growing that a "socialist country" on the southern border of the Soviet Union might be in trouble. When Amin took power, I think the basic consideration that overwhelmed the decision was that we were losing a socialist country, rather than that we were in danger of losing a country that would become associated, say, with the United States. So it's not so much a strategic as an ideological consideration that, in my view, overwhelmed those people who made the decision.

As for Gromyko, in instances when Andropov and Ustinov had the same opinion he would almost always accept it. He was very cautious with those two men, and I don't know of an instance in which Gromyko opposed any joint view that Ustinov and Andropov had. I think that usually they would work this way: The ministers—of course, Ustinov was minister of defense and Andropov was the chief of the KGB—would just consult between the two of them, and then they would work on Gromyko, and Gromyko would accept. I think he just yielded to that pressure and became a part of that decision. But after the decision was taken by the Politburo on December 12, as we now know from the documents, of course, he supported that as a soldier.

The story goes—I heard it from people very close to Gromyko—that he believed that we would be in Afghanistan not much longer than three months. In the minds of those older men, the plan looked like a very temporary, short exercise, though, of course, with a lot of problems for the Soviet Union. Gromyko was an experienced man. He knew that the United States would react strongly, as Carter did. But all the same, I think they felt that they would survive it. In three months they would withdraw the troops, and the dust would settle down, and the people would forget about it and things would return to normal. And the men who were pro-Soviet would be sitting in Kabul, protected by that military intervention.

Mr. Oberdorfer: The papers that you saw that were not supposed to be opened by anybody, except maybe God or Karl Marx, what did they say about what was anticipated in terms of international reaction or what the Soviet Union would have to do?

Mr. Bessmertnykh: It was clearly indicated that this action would definitely cause an alarm in the press of the West, and there would be certain quarters in the West that would try to use it to undermine the international role of the Soviet Union and its positions and influence. So you have got to have a certain set of measures to counteract that forthcoming reaction. A lot of things were said there about what should be done in the press, the radio, the TV, and through diplomatic channels and policy generally. It shows that there was a certain amount of preparation, so it was not done on the spur of the moment.

Mr. Oberdorfer: Something puzzles me, and I think it puzzles a lot of people who know a whole lot more about it than I do. You mentioned Yuri Andropov, who was head of the KGB, and Marshal Ustinov, who was head of the Defense Ministry, yet we know from what you've said and what Marshal Akhromeev told me himself when I interviewed him that the professional military were opposed to it.

Mr. Bessmertnykh: That's true.

Mr. Oberdorfer: They thought it was impractical. [Akhromeev] asked, "How would anyone think that a country like that, with so many thousands of miles, could be occupied by a small number of people?" The KGB had experts who had been in and out of Afghanistan not for three months but for their whole lives. They must have known very well something about the history and external conditions, and yet the top political people, the chief of the KGB, and the minister of defense totally disregarded all this expertise to make this decision. How do you explain that?

Mr. Bessmertnykh: I think this is a case that indicates the complete breakdown of the policy-making standard. The decision was taken without consulting the experts. Gromyko didn't even consult Kornienko, who was very close to him.

When we talk about the professional military, people should realize that Ustinov, although he was the defense minister, wasn't a professional military officer and he did not represent the views of the professional military. He might rather have represented the views of the military-industrial complex. But when Akhromeev talks about the professional military, he means the General Staff.

It's similar to comparing the secretary of defense of the United States and the chairman of the Joint Chiefs of Staff. Their views are different sometimes. The same stories occurred in the Soviet Union. So it was a failure of foreign-policy-making procedure, but it's still a little bit mysterious to me. I still can't understand why Gromyko accepted it, because I respected Gromyko. I knew the man, and I just can't understand why he went wrong. Maybe just because he felt it would be a short exercise.

Mr. Oberdorfer: To what extent—from what you have been able to learn, or from the documents, or from your conversations with other people in Moscow—was this, in your opinion, part of some more general expansionistic drive by the Soviet Union to assert itself in places in the third world?

Mr. Bessmertnykh: I'm absolutely confident that it was not on the leadership's mind. There was always the proposition that whenever Russia did something in the south, it was immediately interpreted as an intention to get to the warm seas. You know, people would immediately [start] saying, "Aha! Russia is now trying to get to the Persian Gulf or to the Indian Ocean." It was almost never the case. Maybe someone in the eighteenth century had this notion. But in practical policy there was never a need for that because we already had access to the seas, and the vastness of the Soviet Union is so great that just to get an extra one thousand or ten thousand square kilometers was nothing. So it was never a strategic consideration. I think it was more ideological.

After the Russian empire had composed itself at the end of the nineteenth century—and certainly strengthened in certain elements after 1917—there were really only two places where Russia fought for land: the northern Caucasus and Central Asia. Otherwise, it just gained land by moving to the east like Americans moved to the west. And after the development of our world-circling navy, really, there was no necessity of getting the land, even from that point of view. So it was more ideological, or a part of the Cold War game. It was double vision. First, ideological, because this was a socialist country; and second, the United States, it was feared, might get Afghanistan after losing Iran.

Mr. Oberdorfer: Mr. Tarasenko wanted to say something.

Mr. Tarasenko: The problem with us is that we are trying to be too rational in respect to Afghanistan and the motives and the goals of the decision makers and the gains [they envisioned]. The story is simple, it seems to me, if you look back at the Soviet system at the time: Brezhnev was ailing. The matter of succession was up in the air. These guys were cynical, they valued personal interest above the interest of the country. They were positioning themselves at least to stay on the Politburo when the guard was changed. Over this period there was a gang mentality: to stick together, to be tough, to show that you are a true believer, that you are indeed a Communist, you are a Leninist, you do everything to guard the system. So if you will not take this cynicism into consideration, you will be wrong. You cannot find a believable motive why those guys did it. I know that Gromyko, for example, valued his Politburo position above anything else. He would do anything to keep his position on the Politburo. That explains what Mr. Bessmertnykh said. He [Gromyko] would usually side with Andropov, Ustinov, the guys who mattered in this respect. So this is a story of personal cynicism.

It just happened that at this juncture "socialism," broadly speaking, was under threat. They [slid] into this mess, but what were the options that faced them? Just to do nothing? Well, then you would be accused of being "not vigilant enough from the socialist point of view." So I would say this was a gang mentality: Let's go together and do that, and a lot of other questions will be removed. [This "psychological picture," and not strategic aims, explains the decision.] But in practical terms, when they got into Afghanistan, they tried to find a justification for this action. Well, really, why had they done it? So they picked clues from the Western press that it might be valuable to be there because you are close to the Gulf, because you might project your power, and for other practical reasons.

By the way, I was the one who worked on the Afghan government statements that we in Moscow issued. We issued two Afghan government statements on how the thing could be settled. Those two famous papers were done within the U.S. desk and had nothing to do with the Afghan government.

Mr. Oberdorfer: These were papers that pretended to come from the Afghan government?

Mr. Tarasenko: Yes.

Mr. Oberdorfer: But actually they were drawn up by the Soviet Foreign Ministry?

Mr. Tarasenko: Yes, they were written on the thirtieth floor of Smolenskaya Square [where the Foreign Ministry's skyscraper is situated]. We had been working on the terms of a proposed solution, and I was told, "Make it so that we will have an opening in case we would like to get a permanent military base or bases. You should not foreclose this eventuality." So that [did seem to matter, as] I was ordered to do [this]. We maneuvered around what words to use in order to leave this opportunity open.

Mr. Shultz: I want to come back for a second to what Mr. Bessmertnykh said about the ideological reasons—that there was concern about a country that was in the socialist camp going out of the socialist camp. We always interpreted that as the Brezhnev Doctrine. Once you were in the socialist camp, you never leave. As I put it once in a speech, "What's ours is ours, what's yours is up for grabs."

Mr. Bessmertnykh: I think that was the mentality. Sometimes the country did not go a "socialist way," because it was very hard to identify whether a country was socialist or nonsocialist. So a new concept was devised, which was called a "noncapitalist way." If a country went a noncapitalist way, it was presumed that it was almost a socialist way. Afghanistan, of course, could not be a socialist country without a working class and with its backward social and economic structures. But the Afghan leaders were saying that they had made a socialist revolution. The people who were in charge of that part of the foreign policy—protecting the ideological states—thought that their task was to protect those states and not to let them go. We never used the word *Brezhnev Doctrine,* but it was essentially correct.

Mr. Oberdorfer: This to me is a very revealing story, and it's pretty scary. Because with power comes responsibility, and here was a case of an empire that had a tremendous amount of power. And we have heard today that it made what seems to me a totally irresponsible decision based on factors which had very little to do with its international responsibility.

Mr. Bessmertnykh: Even as far as [its own] national interests are concerned.

Mr. Oberdorfer: Mr. Gorbachev and his friend Eduard Shevardnadze were then candidate members of the Politburo. They said later, I think, that they had heard on the radio that this invasion had taken place. They did not have any prior knowledge. Would somebody over here like to talk about the consequences of this decision?

Mr. Shultz: There was a major military operation in Afghanistan, and the Soviet troops numbered on the order of 150,000, with a lot of armor, aircraft, helicopters, and so forth. They successfully controlled Kabul, controlled all of the large cities. I don't know what a military person would say might have happened in Afghanistan if the Afghan people had been just left to themselves. But there were times during that period when I was in office when the analysts thought that the situation looked pretty dismal, from our point of view, in Afghanistan. The United States initially reacted under the Carter administration, but in the Reagan administration there was a huge reaction and gigantic support for the Afghan people, organized collaboratively with China and with Saudi Arabia. Something like a billion dollars worth of materiél a year was supplied to the mujaheddin. Even with that, it was back-and-forth in terms of the war.

It always seemed to me that a critical point came with the introduction of the Stinger ground-to-air missile from the United States. And I believe the lineage of the introduction of that is that it was suggested to me by Morton Abramowitz, who was head of our intelligence group at the time, and that it made its way through the decision-making process with a considerable amount of controversy. This was an instance in which I was very much on the same side as Bill Casey and the CIA, while the Defense Department was rather reluctant. Not because they didn't want to see help to the mujaheddin, but they were afraid that this wonderful weapon might somehow fall into Soviet hands or in some ways be used against us. They were very reluctant to let it out of their control, which is understandable.

President Reagan did make the decision to use that weapon, and it did, I think, make a big difference in countering the Soviet advantage in the use of close air support by low-flying aircraft and helicopters. In the kind of terrain involved, where you couldn't support your troops with close air cover you were not able to operate effectively. The tide shifted, and before long it was easy to say that Soviet control went no further than the fringes of the cities where [Soviet] troops were located. The Afghanistan mujaheddin held everything else in the countryside and threatened the cities. We have heard about this decision to intervene and the questions raised about its wisdom and so on, but if there had not been a powerful reaction and support for the people of Afghanistan who were ready to fight for their freedom on a massive scale, the Soviet Union might well have succeeded in at least having an Afghanistan that was satisfactorily kept in its orbit.

Mr. Oberdorfer: Two footnotes to this. The decision that Stingers be included as part of the support for the Afghan resistance was made in the spring of 1986. The weapons started showing up in September, and the first of the Russian planes was shot down by Stingers. Basically, their air force became grounded not too long thereafter. And then in November of that year was the decisive meeting at which Gorbachev decided to remove the troops.

We have with us Hal Saunders, who was the assistant secretary of state for Near Eastern and South Asian affairs at the end of the Carter administration, when the invasion took place. I very well remember, from the days immediately preceding the invasion, briefings about what was going on as the U.S. began to see these flights of airplanes coming in from the southern part of the Soviet Union. I remember what a shock it was. Hal, do you have anything you want to add about the reaction of the U.S. government?

Mr. Saunders: We watched the buildup, and the increasing Soviet military activity during the three or four months before that. I think it's a fact that the decision to invade in force was a surprise. We saw the buildup, we knew there was increased advice and help from the Soviets for the Afghan government's resistance to the mujaheddin, but I don't think we really expected a full invasion, for all of the reasons that would be laid out here in terms of the consequences. So it was a surprise when it happened, and of course, the Carter administration reacted very sharply to it, as we all know. The reaction was sharp in the political, psychological sense, first in terms of strong verbal reaction, and then the gradual winding down of certain aspects of the U.S.-Soviet relationship.

The decisions to support the mujaheddin, I think, were very slow in coming in the Carter administration. What was remarkable in those first months was how much the mujaheddin could do themselves, with captured equipment from the Afghan depots. The first decisions we made were simple things like supporting a radio for the resistance to use, and things like that. The major decisions to actually help the mujaheddin came later on, after the 1979 invasion, as I recall. Then, as Secretary Shultz pointed out, we were very serious in working not only with the Saudis but with the Egyptians at that time, and then with the Pakistanis, of course, to get equipment in. But it was a gradual decision. As I recall, the serious equipment didn't begin to flow until after the summer of 1980, by which time, of course, we were also coping with the Iran hostage crisis. We had a major fleet in the Indian Ocean in connection with the hostage crisis, which our Russian colleagues saw, in some ways, as related to the Afghan invasion.

Mr. Oberdorfer: To what extent was it your sense, or the sense of the people in the Carter administration, that this was part of the general outward push by the Soviet Union?

Mr. Saunders: I think the prevailing view in the Carter administration was just what Mr. Bessmertnykh said, that this was not a major Soviet strategic offensive. There were, however, people in the Carter administration, some close to the president, who seriously feared that. The military, for understandable reasons, must prepare for the worst case. So a lot of the meetings in the situation room in the White House were built around the question of what if this were a first step toward the Persian Gulf—which was, of course, a very great center of our attention at that time because of all the activity in Iran with the hostages and everything that surrounded that. So I think the military had to prepare for it, but I really think the normally articulated assessment in the situation room over at the White House was that it was an unlikely possibility. But it got a lot of public attention. You remember, ABC News did a simulation—I can't remember exactly when—on *Nightline*, which focused on the question of a Soviet military thrust toward the Gulf. It was a war game done by very high-level people.

Mr. Oberdorfer: There was an announcement of the Carter doctrine in 1980: Any threat to the Persian Gulf would be responded to by the United States. Something which didn't come into play that time, though it did during the Bush administration.

Mr. Shultz: That was in the Reagan administration, too, and it's still out there as far as I know.

Mr. Saunders: It was actually written into a presidential speech at the last minute—again, without broad government consensus. Here is another decision, this one on the American side, in which things happened at high levels without necessarily thinking through the long-term implications.

Mr. Oberdorfer: Mr. Chernyaev—

Mr. Chernyaev: We really very often are amazed at how much analytical ability goes into explaining why the Soviet leadership decided to invade Afghanistan. There is the assumption that it was a rational decision. The U.S. analysts seem to think for the Kremlin, the KGB, and the Central Committee, and they try to rationally explain what happened and why it happened. But the trouble is that there was nothing of the kind going on in the Central Committee or in the KGB in the way of rational analytical work.

Mr. Bessmertnykh speaks about ideological reasons. I would agree with that, with one correction. It was mostly ideological justification. As far as the initiators are concerned, people like Ustinov—and also, I would say, Gromyko—really did not care much about any ideology. The argument that we were trying to strengthen the security of our southern borders, or even that we were pushing toward warm seas, is really total nonsense because everyone understood that we had no need for strengthening security over there at that time, with the overall strategic situation the way it was. Those who initiated the invasion were smart enough to understand that making Afghanistan a socialist country, a part of what was called the socialist community, was utterly absurd; it was totally crazy.

So what was it? It was the manifestation of a totally arbitrary and irresponsible approach to policy making that was typical of the Soviet leadership at that time. There is no document that shows who first had that crazy idea of moving troops into Afghanistan. Of course, in the International Department of the Central Committee, we tended to blame Gromyko, and I still do not rule out that he was the one into whose head this kind of idea came. But I know that before that formal meeting of the Politburo at which the formal decision was taken, most members of the Politburo, even those that voted, had nothing to do with developing that decision.

It was a decision of four persons: Ustinov, Gromyko, Andropov, and Ponomarev. Ustinov and Gromyko were totally in favor of acting boldly, of moving with troops, sending Karmal down there and installing him in Kabul. The idea was very simple: "Well, it's there, why not move in? Why not do it on the cheap?" There had been the assassination of Mr. Taraki, the previous Afghan leader. Amin was behaving in a way that looked like he could not be controlled. So why not install a person with whom it would be easier to deal? That was the entire theory behind that. That was all.

It is said that there were some doubts and hesitation on the part of Andropov. I don't believe that very much, because I feel that a lot of the decision would not have been possible without the reports from his people. So had he had doubts, he would have said so. As for Ponomarev, he knew that even in the Communist parties and the democratic organizations this wouldn't be welcomed, and therefore he rather weakly expressed some doubts. But of course, then he very quickly reoriented himself, saluted, and toed the general line.

Ponomarev was aware of my previous discussion with Mr. Wallace, who was a member of the British Communist Party and who knew the situation in the region very, very well. He was an expert. After the Taraki assassination, Wallace came to see me and we discussed the situation. He asked me, "What are you going to do?" I said, "What should we do? We won't do anything, I think." I said that Taraki had invited Soviet troops to come in thirteen times and we had refused. Then he laughed and said, "Well, if you choose to do it, ask us, the British, because we have a lot of experience being there."

And a week after the invasion a group of Soviet scholars sent a report to the Ministry of Foreign Affairs. Gorbachev later said in a meeting of the Politburo that he became aware of this report after he became general secretary. The group of scholars who sent that paper was headed by Professor Gankovsky.[3] I know him from my university years. He was a major expert on Afghanistan. In that memorandum, a week after the invasion, they analyzed all the possible consequences of the invasion from the standpoint of history, psychology, sociology, politics, national experience, the balance of forces, the surrounding countries, the Muslim world, everything. Their conclusion was that this is a reckless adventure that will end very badly for us, that this is trouble, that this is bad, that this is destructive. And I know that Kornienko afterwards was very much in favor of withdrawing the troops. I heard his reports to the Politburo, and afterwards he stood very firmly for withdrawing the troops from Afghanistan. But Gorbachev, at one point when he was very emotional—he was seething—said to me, "You know, Kornienko is for withdrawing troops now, but that memorandum from the scholars was in his room, in his desk, locked up, and no one saw that for years and years." It was just sitting there—until the decision was taken to withdraw the troops.

And now about Gorbachev. Right after his election as general secretary on March 16, 1985, Georgiy Arbatov [head of the Institute of the United States and Canada in Moscow] had a talk with Gorbachev. By that time they had already established a good rapport. In the initial years of perestroika, Arbatov was something like a foreign policy confidant of Gorbachev. Arbatov and I had known each other for thirty years, so he also wanted to give me an idea of how to deal with big people and with international affairs. Arbatov told me that when he met with Gorbachev soon after his election as general secretary, Gorbachev had showed him a piece of paper on which there was a list of international questions that he had prioritized [as to] what he wanted to deal with first. Item 7 or item 8 was Afghanistan. Arbatov, who was a rather bold man, said, "Mikhail Sergeevich, I would place Afghanistan first." Gorbachev said, "Yes, I agree." He said to me afterwards, "This is the number one task that we have to resolve." It would take a long time to discuss why Gorbachev, who from the very outset believed that this was a problem that had to be solved quickly—why still it took four years for us to complete the withdrawal from Afghanistan. I'm trying to address that question in the book that I have written.[4]

But as early as the summer of 1985, Gorbachev began to work

to educate the members of the Politburo. He brought huge stacks of letters from the mothers of soldiers, from soldiers and officers, to the Politburo. He even brought letters from two generals who were fighting in Afghanistan. He read those letters, which really were very dramatic documents, to the members of the Politburo. The main point made in all of those letters was, why are we there? what are we doing there? In those letters, officers were saying, "We cannot explain to the soldiers why we are in Afghanistan." "How come this is called internationalist duty, when we are destroying villages and killing innocent citizens, and we see terrible things happening?" Those letters also complained that what the newspaper *Pravda* wrote about Afghanistan was all lies. "The Afghans are not fighting mujaheddin. We are fighting against mujaheddin." At least three times he read out those letters to the members of the Politburo. However, at that time he was not yet saying that the invasion had been a mistake. His conclusion was that Karmal, the Afghan leader, would have to be removed and there would have to be another person with whom you could discuss the withdrawal from Afghanistan.

Mr. Oberdorfer: I just want to add something to this. According to conservative estimates, about 1 million of Afghanistan's 12.5 million people had been killed by the time the Soviet troops departed. About 5 million out of 12.5 million people had fled as refugees to neighboring Pakistan or Iran. At least another 1 million had been displaced from their homes within the country. Most of the deaths were civilian, but close to 100,000 resistance fighters, the mujaheddin, were also among the dead. The official Soviet Defense Ministry figure for Soviet military deaths was 13,831, but that included only those who had been killed in action. A more comprehensive estimate of Soviet war deaths from all causes was 36,000. By 1989 it was estimated that three-fourths of Afghanistan's villages had been severely damaged or destroyed, in addition to large sections of the country's few major cities. Mr. Nitze—

Mr. Nitze: During the days when this occurred I was persona non grata to the Carter administration, and I was very much persona grata to the Joint Chiefs of Staff, as a consultant on strategic matters. From our standpoint, the importance of Afghanistan strategically was very obvious indeed. You measured the distance, par-

ticularly, from the airfields in the western portion of Afghanistan
to the Persian Gulf. It was really very short, I think a hundred miles or so. You looked at what would happen if the Soviet Union
had direct access and permanent bases there in western Afghanistan. We would compare the logistics of our situation in the Persian Gulf. With the Soviets in control of those bases, with our lo-
gistic situation, we would have been in an impossible position in
the whole Persian Gulf area. So this question of what happened in
Afghanistan, on a long-range basis, was to us of immense importance, and I believe that's why our military were always for [pro-
viding] the most serious help to the mujaheddin in order to keep
that from happening.

Prof. Greenstein: Well, I'm the one person that hasn't yet plugged one
of their own books—Mr. Nitze has a fine book with a chapter on
Reykjavik which we will plug in the afternoon. But one of mine
does deal with a very close examination of American intervention
in Vietnam, and the parallels in terms of decision making are really quite extraordinary.

I would not describe the American decision makers as cynical
in going in, but I would describe them as having very short time
horizons due to a very, very sloppy decision-making process. And
interestingly, four seems to be the magic number, in that most of
the decisions were made over the dining room table on the second
floor of the White House [at the] so-called Tuesday lunches. Without staff support or systematic study, and with very little consultation with the military, President Johnson, Secretary of Defense
McNamara, National Security Advisor MacGeorge Bundy, and
Secretary of State Dean Rusk made the key decisions on Vietnam.
No minutes were kept of those meetings, so we have to look at the
doodles that Mac Bundy kept during the meetings, but we know
that all those people's subordinates were unclear about what was
going on.

We also know that at the beginning of the year 1965 there was
no plan at all for American troops to fight on the ground in Vietnam, and nobody ever decided to have a ground war. Instead, what
they did was start reinforcing air bases as a consequence of a not
very carefully thought-out decision to engage in retaliatory air
strikes. By the summer of that year, large numbers of American
troops were in an unannounced war. In the middle of the summer,

President Johnson finally made an announcement in a news conference that General Westmoreland would get all that he wanted. Interestingly, General Goodpaster, who is here in the room, was asked to do a systematic study of what would be involved in winning in Vietnam. That study was not done, however, or ordered by the White House, until we were already fighting. As far as we can tell, it never came to the attention of these decision makers in any careful way until they had made their decisions.

Mr. Oberdorfer: As a person who was a correspondent in the Vietnam War and who watched our country go through extremely difficult times making the decision to get out of Vietnam—a folly, I think, comparable to that of Afghanistan—I know how tremendously difficult it was for the United States to deal with this. The repercussions among the people and government of the United States last until this day, to some degree. So it was with great fascination, beyond simply the question of news, that I watched the Soviet Union grappling with its decision—Gorbachev having realized, as Mr. Chernyaev has told us, that this was a dead-end street. But realizing that and getting out of there in one piece were two very different things. Sergei Tarasenko was the closest aide to Foreign Minister Eduard Shevardnadze, who was the chairman of the special commission of the Soviet Politburo whose objective was to arrange for the withdrawal of Soviet forces. I would like to ask Sergei to describe what happened and what kind of problems Shevardnadze encountered in trying to get this job done.

Mr. Tarasenko: I will start on a personal note. I went with Shevardnadze to Afghanistan six times, and when we were coming into Kabul airport, believe me, we were mindful of Stinger missiles. That's an unpleasant feeling. You were happy when you were crossing the border and the loudspeaker would say, "We are now in Soviet territory." "Oh, my God. We made it!"

Shevardnadze started by visiting Afghanistan. He's a believer in knowing the situation on the ground. First of all, he went there for a talk with Najibullah, and they established a good relationship, and then a friendly relationship. It was important later in persuading the Afghan side to face the eventual withdrawal of the Soviet forces, because, well, it was not easy. The way I understood it was that Najibullah would be left alone in Kabul like the cowboy in the western films, you know, just waiting for the guy who will come and shoot him. We were consistently told by the American side that Najibullah would have his throat cut three days after the Soviet troops left.

So Shevardnadze got this mandate to withdraw Soviet forces from Afghanistan and keep Afghanistan a friendly state.

Mr. Oberdorfer: Those were the two parts of his charges?

Mr. Tarasenko: Yes, and make it within two years. He was allotted two years for this job. When I first heard about his appointment as a chairman for this commission, I thought this was a one-way ticket. We cannot do that. It would take a miracle. Knowing the Vietnam experience, certainly I thought that they are there for a long time. But he started working with the Afghans, specifically on that idea of forming a national guard. Not to change our involvement in Afghanistan, [but] to rely more on financial support, not on the Soviet Army's fighting support. And it made a difference. Because by the time of withdrawal, Najibullah was in a better position, because he had his guards, some forces which he could rely on. He endured longer than the Soviet Union did, you know.

So the mandate was fulfilled. We withdrew from Afghanistan and kept Afghanistan a friendly state as long as the Soviet Union existed. But this Politburo commission was delicate. There were Yazov, defense minister; Kryuchkov, KGB chief; Dobrynin, from the International Department; the guys from the government, [including] Deputy Prime Minister Talyzin, [who] was in charge of the aid program; Katushev, the economic relations minister; and some other people, mainly from the government and the Party's Central Committee. Ostensibly everyone agreed that it was a good idea to get out. But there was a lot of resistance, and people just dragged their feet. They did not want to do anything. And I recall that Shevardnadze had to maneuver cautiously in dealing with these people. Some of them were members of the Politburo. He would usually say, "This is not my idea. This is Gorbachev's idea. I have to report to Gorbachev. If you are not in agreement, go to Gorbachev and explain to him your position, but I need some consensus and need to perform these duties."

I remember when they prepared a letter to the Party and the

Soviet people explaining the Afghanistan situation, and they
needed to [include] some figures on casualties. They asked Yazov,
"How many were lost there?" He said, "About . . . , around . . . ,"
and Shevardnadze said, "Look, we cannot use this 'around.' These
are human lives. On this we should be specific with the exact
number, because people [will] say you do not know how many
were lost there. It's impossible. These are people, families, mothers, fathers, kids." So they pressed Yazov maybe for half an hour,
and then at the end he came up with the figure thirteen thousand
or something, and they accepted it. There was not much discussion. Nobody doubted this figure. It's official. Yazov tells us that.
Certainly it was, at best, a conservative figure.

And the KGB guys on this commission were not happy with
this withdrawal either—for practical reasons, as far as I can guess,
because they had a lot of people depending upon them there in
Afghanistan. What to do with them? It was a tricky issue for everyone involved. But they did have a good working relationship
with Kryuchkov. Kryuchkov and his deputy, Shebarshin, were always on these trips to Afghanistan, and they were instrumental in
getting things straightened with Najibullah. Before the Tashkent
meeting [held on April 17, 1988] there was a preliminary meeting
between Gorbachev and Najibullah. Just [when we] thought that
Najibullah had agreed to the plan of the Geneva settlement, when
Gorbachev actually was in there with Najibullah, he [Najibullah]
said that Wakil, his foreign minister, objected to this settlement.
He would not sign on, and it was a big, big problem on our hands.
Then at the crucial moment Kryuchkov said, "Leave it to me, and
I'll persuade Najibullah. I know how to talk to him." He went to
Najibullah, and in half an hour he was back and said, "It's okay.
Najibullah will convene the Politburo meeting at the airport, and
he will go with you to Tashkent." So it happened.

But, I recall, it left a deep impression with me how we talked in
the [U.S.] State Department over this Afghanistan situation,
whether the American side will join in the Geneva process and
[whether it] will sign up or not. If you remember, Mr. Secretary,
there was a long, protracted discussion. Your team went to another
room. And if you recall, we didn't agree. A couple of days later you
sent a message to Moscow that, yes, the United States would join
the Geneva process. It was such a relief, you know. It actually

helped us a lot. But indeed, maybe we were in a solid position anyway, because we had decided to go on irrespective of what the
United States' position would be. We decided that we would go on
alone anyway, without the agreement or with the agreement. This
was a firm decision. But the United States agreed to join this process in Geneva during this ceremony. It helped us to overcome this
process.

Mr. Oberdorfer: Mr. Tarasenko referred to meetings with Secretary
Shultz, and—at least to me—the most notable one was in mid-
September 1987, when Mr. Shevardnadze had come to Washington ostensibly to work on the INF Treaty, which was then still
under negotiation. He had Afghanistan much on his mind, and he
came to see Secretary Shultz. I would like to ask Secretary Shultz
to tell the story.

Mr. Shultz: By this time, Shevardnadze and I had evolved what was a
very productive pattern of working, under which we would be
joined by one or two people. Roz Ridgway was always there, and
usually the national security advisor, who at this time was Frank
Carlucci. We would then commission people to work on different
subjects. Paul Nitze was the ringmaster of all the different arms
control discussions on our side. Dick Shifter was our person who
managed the human rights group. We had a bilateral relations
group, and then we had attention to regional issues, Afghanistan,
Nicaragua, Cambodia, and so on.

We came to a point in our meeting when we were going to hear
from our working groups on regional issues, and particularly Afghanistan, and Shevardnadze asked to see me privately. He came
into my back office, and he said that he just wanted to tell me that
the decision had been made to leave Afghanistan and it was not
sometime [far] in the future. It would be prompt. And of course I
welcomed that, and I asked about the pattern of withdrawal and
the importance of having it be front-end loaded. That is, you move
a lot out quickly, so that you are far beyond the point of no return,
so to speak, on a relatively short timetable. All those things he had
thought about, and he raised the problem of Islamic fundamental-
ism and expressed his concern about that in Afghanistan. It was
not as though it was any decision for me to make. He just told me
that the Soviet decision had been made. Then we proceeded into

my larger office, where the working groups were gathered. That was a weird discussion, because people went back to us with arguments, and I looked over at Shevardnadze at one point and he looked at me. He sat, and the argument went on. But it was kind of irrelevant by that time. I had had many meetings with Shevardnadze by this time, and what he told me I believed. I didn't think he would tell me something like that if it was wrong. So I was convinced that was so, and, of course, I told that to the president.

Mr. Oberdorfer: How well was that accepted throughout the government?

Mr. Shultz: Well, there were very large elements in the U.S. government that didn't believe the Soviet Union could or would change, and many particularly doubted that the Soviets would ever withdraw from territory that they regarded as in their domain. The CIA people didn't believe that the Soviet Union would leave Afghanistan. On the whole, people that you associate with the word *hardliners* didn't believe it. But I believed it, and I think the president did. I spoke with [Undersecretary of State] Mike Armacost, and after I told him, he believed it. As I recall, before the actual withdrawal took place Mike had some bets with [deputy director of the CIA Robert] Gates and with Fritz Ermath [CIA national intelligence officer for the Soviet Union]. Mike bet that they would withdraw, and the CIA people bet that they wouldn't. They put fifty dollars or so on the line, but we were sure, and I was sure, because Shevardnadze had told me that.

Then in 1988 they had another meeting on this process of withdrawal, and this is the one I think Sergei was referring to. Shevardnadze said, "We have done everything that you have said was important, front-end loading, short timetable, and so on." But, he went on, what would happen was that the Soviet Union would continue to supply the Najibullah regime, and we would presumptively have to agree that we wouldn't continue to supply the mujaheddin. We said that there had to be a reciprocal arrangement: if they would agree not to supply any more arms, then we could agree to that. But if they were going to supply arms, we would have to be able to supply arms. We went around that circle. I guess our meeting went on for well over two hours. As you said, the group with me adjourned and sort of caucused, and we concluded that we didn't see how it was proper for us to change our position. Somebody asked me last night if the relations with Shevardnadze were of such a nature that we tried to bend our policy to accommodate him, and I said no, they weren't. They were of such a nature that we discussed things frankly, and obviously if there was something that was in our interest that we could do, we would do it. But we could see that he very much wanted us to agree to this, and we couldn't agree to it.

Now, not too long thereafter the Pakistanis became very worried because they wanted to sign the Geneva protocols, and they came back to us. Our problem was that we couldn't supply the mujaheddin except through Pakistan, and if they signed those protocols, they would be saying that they wouldn't support the actions of the mujaheddin in Afghanistan. Therefore we wouldn't be able to deliver our supplies. We said that, of course, we would have to assert that we would continue to supply, and what would they do? An elaborate set of phone calls was arranged, Prime Minister Junejo called me, and then the real authority in Pakistan, [President Muhammad] Zia [ul-Haq], called President Reagan and assured us that no matter what they signed, they would be the place from which our supplies could flow. And I remember President Reagan asking Zia, "How can you do that?" He said, "We have been doing it all these years and we never said we weren't." I think he said something like, "It's all right in Islam to lie in a good cause." So we accepted his word, and we did make a public statement. Then I told Shevardnadze that we would come and sign those protocols, but he should know that we would say publicly that we intended to continue supporting the mujaheddin—but, of course, if they wanted to diminish the flow of arms [to Najibullah], we would [reduce shipments to the mujaheddin].

One reason why the CIA thought the Soviets would never withdraw was their assessment that the minute the Soviets withdrew, the Najibullah regime would collapse. I went back two or three times to be sure. I asked, "Is that your assessment?" Of course, they were the ones who were managing this so-called covert operation, and so they had the people on the ground. In fact, they said that merely the announcement that the Soviets would withdraw might precipitate the collapse of the regime. They were absolutely certain of it. I got a different point of view from John Glassman, who was our chargé in Kabul. We had kept a small group there, and he was not so sure. His view only reinforced my view and the president's view that we had to have a reciprocal arrangement. So this to me was another illustration of how far off the CIA is when it comes to making political and economic estimates. I think they have been very good at estimating numbers of tanks and missiles and things of that kind, but they misread situation after situation in political and economic terms.

Mr. Oberdorfer: Let's move along to the broader implications of some of the things that we have been talking about today and in the last two days. I would like to ask Secretary Shultz and some of the other Americans, and then the Russians, about the decision-making process. I mean, we have heard kind of horrendous stories about how four people in the Kremlin sat there, cut off from their experts, and made a decision which was calamitous not only for them but for millions of people in and around Afghanistan. And we have our own experience making some not-well-thought-out decisions, such as that to go into Vietnam. What do the discussions of the last couple of days tell us about the way in which decisions have been made or ought to be made?

Mr. Shultz: I think it's important to draw on the knowledge and expertise that you have in coming to important decisions. At the same time, at least in the U.S. government context, it's difficult because people fear that the more people who are knowledgeable and involved, the more chance there is for a leak that can be debilitating to the decision-making process. There's a tension there. My own feeling always was to err on the side of inclusion and take my chances on the leaks, but the leaks can be very debilitating. We had lots of leaks in the Reagan administration, and we also had lots of arguments. To some extent the arguments were counterproductive. But on the whole, when important issues are being considered, I think it's much better to have arguments. If I see an administration where nobody ever argues with anybody, I think you are headed for trouble.

Prof. Greenstein: Let's turn to our Soviet friends and ask a little bit about decision making, particularly in the Gorbachev period. The description we had—at least of the earlier period—was of an almost unnatural consensus, and failure to engage in vigorous discussion of the sort that Secretary Shultz is advocating. Could one argue and debate?

Mr. Bessmertnykh: In foreign policy, you face several components of the policy-making process. First, you have your own plans. Second, you have your own actions. Then you have the actions of the other side—in this case I mean the United States, which was always our conflict partner. Fourth, you have the actions of third parties; and then you have accidents in foreign policy. Out of those five components, only two are under your control, three are not. So you're never in a situation when you are completely confident about a foreign policy line because even if you come up with a brilliant idea and you have brilliant operators who'd implement the policy, there are still three more components that could either neutralize or act against your programs.

I think that the importance of the quality of information is enormous in foreign policy making. When we discussed, for example, Afghanistan, certain parts of the decision were influenced, first, by the nature of information that was coming from our people in Kabul. The second factor is the quality of analysis of this information, and here we come to a point at which the analysis could be different. Information could be cut to satisfy the needs either of the president or the government, or of someone else.

Then you come to the formulation of the policy itself. I think we can refer to Afghanistan as a case study: Why did those four men make this kind of decision? For the Soviet Union at that time, I think it was because we were dealing with a totalitarian system of government. Those four people could simply make that decision without expert advice because they had the power. They were the ones who controlled the country, they were the gods, they knew better than anybody else. My greatest respects to Gromyko, for example, but I don't remember a case in which he would react to somebody's advice by saying, "Oh, that's great. I never thought about that before." He would [never] make such remarks because he always believed he knew better than anybody else. I think the same happened with Ustinov, the defense minister, and some other leaders of that time.

It was only with Gorbachev that this policy-making procedure greatly changed. He was the first leader who created informal advisors groups. Previous leaders never even thought about them. Maybe Arbatov in his personal capacity would be doing something with Brezhnev, and probably more [often] Bovin and Inozemtsev with Andropov.[5] Several individuals had access, but it was not a [formal] system. So Gorbachev was the first one who created bodies of knowledgeable men, intellectuals from academia and journalists, whose opinions he would listen to. There were lots of discussions, and he welcomed these discussions. I don't know whether there was any decision he would make on his own—just sitting in his office. He would always ask advice. This is a strength of a leader, when he relies on his advisors more than on his own instincts. Perhaps Gorbachev relied on experts' advice less at later stages, but during his first years he did it. This style of decision making came down to the lower layers. Suddenly this group of five [appeared], which Mr. Tarasenko mentioned yesterday, when arms control decision making was referred to interagency discussions. There had never been such a system before Gorbachev.

So, I think that the pre-Gorbachev system created the situation in which any decision could be made, right or wrong, and you would never know. Gorbachev's period produced, I think, a system which was very close to the American one. When we discussed it, we found a lot of similarities in decision making in Gorbachev's time [that brought it] closer to a Western type of decision making. Sometimes he overdid it with the official advisors. He would send them two weeks before his summit to a country to prepare the turf, and they would report to him in absolutely unrealistic terms that now the country was ready to receive him because they spent two weeks before him. And that was ridiculous. Maybe my professional envy is working now. But in any case, Gorbachev brought a new system with new people, and advisors actually started to play their role.

Prof. Greenstein: Secretary Shultz has a comment, and then Roz.

Mr. Shultz: I think there's another aspect of decision making that underlines the importance of having a natural process of exposure to a wide flow of information and ideas. When people speak about decision making, they generally have in mind the big decisions, and they want to see an orderly process. Well, there are big decisions, but I don't think that most important decisions are like that. Life in these posts consists to a very considerable extent of coping. All day long there are problems. Some are big, some are little, and you are coping with them, and you have got to do something about them and try to get them resolved. I think one of the big distinctions between somebody who does it well and somebody who's mediocre or poor is that a person who does it well has a sense of where you are trying to go. Problems come up and you have to cope with them, and you have a natural flow in which you can easily be informed. You can't be informed automatically about everything. You have got to have developed relationships so that when people see a problem, they know they can have access to you and you've got this information.

Then, instead of coping with problems in a random way that doesn't go anywhere, you know what you are trying to do. As you cope, you move things incrementally in that direction. Over a period of time it adds up to something. This is the unobserved aspect of decision making, but probably in many ways it is more important than the big decisions that get focused on all the time. These little things do wind up adding up to big moments, and sometimes when they don't go right they get you in very serious trouble. All of a sudden there was President Reagan going to Bitburg. It wasn't as though he said, "I want to go to a cemetery where there are only Germans and where there are a lot of SS and so on." He didn't decide that. He decided something altogether different, but there was a process which wound up bringing that about, and then all you could do is cope with it and try to make the best you could out of it. But that happens a great deal, and sometimes, obviously, it can happen in a positive way.

Mr. Oberdorfer: Before Ambassador Ridgway says something, I would like to ask what we call, in the trade, a follow-up question. You mentioned that it's crucially important to have an idea of where you are trying to go. Did Gorbachev, in your view, have a fairly clear idea in his mind where he was trying to go, and was it a realistic idea?

Mr. Shultz: I felt that Gorbachev and his team had a very clear idea that the situation that they had inherited was not satisfactory and they should change it. As we worked on these problems, I thought that a reasonably good idea evolved in the arms control area. We came to an agreement that there were going to be very large reductions in nuclear weapons. That's what his objective was, that's what President Reagan's objective was. So in that broad sense we were on the same track. Although there was a lot of difficult work in bringing things together, there was a clear sense of objective, and an underlying rationale for it. The rationale was not that different between the two sides. In addition, we also came to share the notion that it would be good if these hot spots around the world could get dampened. It wasn't only Afghanistan but the Namibia negotiation, which I thought was one of the most interesting bits of diplomacy you could imagine. By that time we were going to work in a collaborative way with the Soviet side. The Iran-Iraq War was another instance in which we were able to work together. Our interests were a little different and there was a lot of edginess to it, but nevertheless, I believe for the first time in the history of the United Nations, there was a unanimous vote on a Section 7 matter, involving the most severe sanctions in the UN arsenal.

Where it seemed to me the Soviet side was uncertain was brought out most sharply to me in a meeting I had in the Kremlin with Mr. Ryzhkov, who was in charge of economic policy. It was very clear that he saw the problem and he described it accurately. But it was also clear—and he was frank about it—that he was struggling to try to figure out what to do about it. We talked, for instance, about how inefficient barter trade is and how you have to get into the international market on a currency basis to be efficient. That means you have to have a convertible currency, but you can't really have a convertible currency unless you have a market that helps to give it some value. But how do you get to these things? Ryzhkov was at sea as to where to go, but he was very conscious of the problems. I think the economic area was also a hard one for Gorbachev. As I talked to him, it was evident that he knew the system they had wasn't working. He had a hard time accepting the tenets of a more market-based system and kept wanting to reform the system they had and make it work better. I felt—and I remember Margaret Thatcher kept telling everybody— the problem is not to try to make the system work better, the system is the problem. You have to change it, and that was very hard for him.

Mr. Oberdorfer: Ambassador Ridgway—

Ms. Ridgway: I was interested to hear Minister Bessmertnykh say that as the Soviet Union was changing the nature of its foreign policy there was—and he put it in positive terms—an adaptation of the American decision-making process. I would be hard put to tell you what the American decision-making process was or is, and I think it's important to understand the extent to which formal and informal systems exist alongside each other. In the case of this particular period in history, 1985 to 1989, not only were formal and informal systems residing alongside each other, but congenial and adversarial systems within the U.S. government were residing alongside each other. I recall coming back to take up my steward-ship of my piece of this four-year effort in the summer of 1985, and being handed the list of all the interagency committees which now had a place for me at the table and which I was to begin to attend. And the first one that I went to I simply left. It wasn't an Alice in Wonderland reaction, but certainly I asked myself, what-ever can be produced by this kind of committee? because in an interagency process the people who are deputized to represent agency or departmental views for the most part are not entitled to change that agency's position. They come with minds that will not be changed, even though they have been given the responsi-bility of producing a coherent set of rational choices for leaders. The arguments become very small and very personal.

So you say to yourself, "No decision, no rational set of choices, can come out of this mechanism. There must be another piece of machinery around town that is more effective." As you become more familiar with the issues, you begin to identify those formal institutions to which you must pay some respect, because if you don't, they will rise up and snatch you. Then you have to identify those people and those informal groups in which, in fact, you can get something done. It's very difficult when there is no agree-ment—as I thought was the case—that the bureaucracy ought to follow the president. There were still people who, when the presi-dent made the decision, instead of going out and marching to that decision, [they] went out and continued either to behave as before or to try to change it.

Mr. Shultz mentioned the problem of leaks. There are a couple of kinds of leaks. I recall once I did a press briefing. It was my first press meeting. The secretary was leaving for Helsinki, [it was] the first trip I took with him as the briefing officer, and I went down to the press room. After I talked about what the agenda was in Helsinki, someone asked, "Well, what's the secretary's schedule?" So I just turned the page and I read what the secretary's schedule was. I stepped off of the podium and about six people stopped me and said, "You mustn't ever give out the secretary's schedule." I remember I asked why, and I was told, for security reasons, for one; and second, it's just not done. Some kinds of leaks come from people who have the schedule and who just want to feel empowered. So when someone calls them up on the phone and says, "Look, I can't get the schedule from the press office, do you have it?" they just feel big by saying, "Yeah, I have it, and they are going to do X, Y, and Z." That kind of leak is from small people trying to feel important.

The dangerous leak is the leak that is intended, in fact, to take the president's choices away from him. It was that kind of leak that one had to guard against so that as choices were being prepared, legitimate arguments were taking place. These were tough issues. There were people who could see that the argument might well go against them. They didn't like what they thought the president might do or what seniors in the government might do. And the next thing you know, you would see the headline which took the most likely outcome and, having distorted it somewhat, had it in the paper before it even got to the president. That has become apparently an accepted method of behavior in the bureaucracy, and I would hope that any bureaucracy that is taking shape in emulation of the American system would try to find a way to avoid that. I happen to think it just requires discipline, and my personal view is that you should fire people. You hardly ever find out who they are. All you can do is guess, but it's dangerous to guess. So your circle gets smaller and smaller based on trust, based on confidence.

One of the reasons I think there was success in this endeavor is because the argument between the hard-liners, or whoever they thought they were, and those who wished to pursue the course the president had chosen never was resolved. And another major reason is that the interagency process never got hold of the non–

arms control agenda. I can hear Jack [Matlock] saying "yes" on that. Somehow those people who had captured the arms control agenda—and Paul [Nitze] had to fight his way through that mess—did not give enough credit to the importance of human rights, regional issues, and the bilateral relationship—which, as Jack has said before, was a different way of describing something that never would have been approved if we called it anything else. It was the opening-up of the relationship. That's what was tucked away in the bilateral relationship, and it included exchanges of people in scientific, educational, and trade cooperation. But if we had called it "the opening up of a different relationship with the Soviet Union," we never would have gotten anywhere. So we just called it "bilateral relations," and very important people decided it wasn't worth their time.

Mr. Shultz: It was interesting that Don Oberdorfer couldn't even remember the fourth part of the agenda.

Ms. Ridgway: That's right. So there were a lot of people [who could not fathom the importance of] Chet Crocker spending eight years going back and forth, in maybe one of the most underappreciated diplomatic feats that's ever been accomplished, or people struggling away on the question of fusion cooperation. They [thought] that human rights, for example, which the president always put first, was something that didn't touch on what you would call strategic perceptions of this relationship. So, fortunately, it became very clear that those three pieces of the four-part agenda were not engaged in this very elaborate and very complex arms-control machinery. We kept it out of the formal interagency process, and usually it was only very, very close to a departure for a trip that it would begin to emerge. And then people could say, "Well, you know, what's in that? Let them go play the game of Cambodia or Namibia while we are going to do the big stuff on numbers and weapons."

So it was important to have different circles, and different methodologies and different relationships and memberships in who did what, to keep this whole thing going forward, otherwise I think we would not have succeeded. Another feature of this was that while a very small group of people were a part of the secretary's circle, he certainly knew that behind each of us were other small circles of people whose sense of what was important for the country was essential [to their being included]. Even though someone says, "Don't tell anybody else," they knew perfectly well there were one or two other people you did have to tell. We could not do all of this. That made it possible for us to manage successfully that kind of confidence, which was something Minister Bessmertnykh touched on.

You can have high policy, and you can have lower-level policy, but at some point in a relationship as difficult as this, you have the unexpected crisis. I recall one that is not on the list here but that best demonstrates the requirement for a bureaucracy that has had confidence placed in it and has been assured that it can make decisions. If decisions are seen as intelligent, they will be supported. That cannot be underestimated. We had been in New York. The secretary had been meeting with Minister Shevardnadze. It was very, very bad weather. In fact, some of us had come back from New York [as the] things that we were interested in had been concluded. Minister Shevardnadze's airplane had suddenly been moved from New York to Andrews Air Force Base. There was a hurricane coming up the east coast of the United States. I think I was one of the last people to get out of New York, and I walked into the office on a Friday afternoon to find that the Immigration and Naturalization Service the day before had taken a young Russian sailor who had jumped ship in New Orleans and had sent him back forcefully to his vessel, which was in the harbor at New Orleans. If there had not been a bureaucracy, in the best sense of the word, that had felt it could take decisions and could act within an understood framework of the relationship, we would have had an even bigger mess on our hands. But as it was, people several layers down in the bureaucracy knew they could act. And by the time the issue came to the secretary's attention, State Department people had already left Washington to go to New Orleans. Tom Simons [the State Department's director of Soviet affairs] had flown to New Orleans. We had already worked with the Soviet Embassy in Washington to alert the vessel that we would put somebody on board to take that man back off the ship. All of the right pieces of machinery were in place and were functioning at a level far below that of ministers.

While that was a very difficult story and took some time to resolve, I think it could have been more difficult and more damaging to the relationship if there had not been throughout the system the identification of an informal system. Those would be my only points: [First,] that the informal [system] cannot be too shallow in its reach into bureaucracy if you are going to cover all the levels of possibility in the relationship. And second, in the American experience, I think that we now have an interagency structure that no one should emulate unless you really like gridlock in policy. The way things did work was outside the system.

Mr. Oberdorfer: We have gotten a bit far afield from looking at the Cold War, in a sort of natural progression of things. I'm not going to answer about the press, and leaks and so on. That's another conference and another occasion. We [journalists] have a different way of looking at it. Mr. Nitze and Ambassador Matlock wanted to say something.

Mr. Nitze: I just wanted to dwell on how decisions are made at the practical level of the U.S. government. In the days when McNamara already knew he was on the way out, he was succeeded by Clark Clifford. Neither of them wanted to run the Pentagon. So I found, as deputy, that I had to run the organization, and that required that fifty decisions a day on the average had to be made. You had to reserve part of your day for the important things that needed to be done. So, how did you make fifty decisions within an hour or two? There the techniques I found that were useful were, first of all, to have a judgment about your staff, which ones in your staff you could rely on. And from past experience I knew that certain ones would almost certainly be right; I would just okay it right away if they recommended the position. The second criterion was whether decisions are inherently self-correcting. If you decided this way and it's wrong, would it come up again? If they are inherently self-correcting, make those decisions very fast. But if there are ones that are for keeps, that can't be changed, then you really have to take it seriously and you have to take the time and put that in the box that you are going to spend your afternoon on.

Mr. Oberdorfer: Jack, did you want to add something?

Mr. Matlock: I just wanted to add a couple of examples to points already made. The first has to do with the fact that before you can really make a big decision effective, an awful lot of small decisions have to be made, and sometimes mechanisms need to be put in place. Our consultations on Afghanistan, for example, depended upon earlier decisions that we had made to engage in a broad dialogue on regional issues, which were very controversial in the government. I think that half of our assistant secretaries of geographic bureaus opposed them. I remember arguing very strenuously on one of your [Shultz's] trips that we needed to do this, and I warned that the first year or two would not show any results, but the people working on these areas should get to know each other and should start comparing notes. But gradually, if it worked, we would at least have a mechanism when we were ready to engage to deal with these issues, and I think that this mechanism did serve us well right through—whether it was Afghanistan or Libya, or later Nicaragua, Cambodia, and so on.

Second, on the issue of informal or ad hoc coordination methods, I think back to the way we put together two of the points on the agenda before Geneva. I wrote a memo pointing out first to McFarlane, who was our national security advisor, that we hadn't put much content into two of the points on the agenda. We said that the Soviets should get out of the third world immediately, but we hadn't really provided any concrete ideas for that. On the whole issue of exchanges, whereas people generally were in favor of them, again, we hadn't made that many concrete proposals. So I made a number of suggestions, and I think McFarlane showed it to you [Shultz] and you liked it, and then he said, "Look, we've got to make sure that Defense and CIA don't oppose us. Check it out with Weinberger and Casey." My method, since I was a little lower down in the bureaucracy, was to call their deputies. I called [Deputy Defense Secretary] Will Taft and I called Bob Gates, and I asked them to try these ideas out on [their] superiors. They got back to me in a day or so, and Taft said, "Well, Weinberger's all for it. Anything to take people's minds off SDI." The word back from Gates was, "Well, Casey doesn't think it's going to produce anything, but he doesn't object. Do it if you want to."

So, in effect, we sort of got carte blanche at the top, and then we set up very small working groups from State and NSC. Then there were two presidential speeches that gave us a policy recommendation. And although, as Roz says, people didn't always salute when the president made a speech, within the bureaucracy it was a powerful argument to make in order to get others to do something. "Look, the president is committed to do this."

Prof. Greenstein: Let me cut in for a second. We've clearly just scratched the surface of decision making, but an element which has been striking to me, and I would like to see whether I'm correct in taking this from the discussion, is a sense in which the personalization of your adversary seems to have been extraordinarily important here. The material reductions in forces really were not very profound during this period, yet in some intangible way the transformation of the climate was absolutely extraordinary. What people seem to have been saying again and again is that at a certain point we stopped seeing the other people as types. They no longer were categories, they were individuals with flesh-and-blood qualities. And I would be curious to know whether I'm appropriately interpreting this.

Mr. Chernyaev: I'm thinking of this in terms of what I think is the main question: when did the Cold War end? The Cold War ended at Malta, but the preparation of this dramatic turn took place in the Reagan years, and we have to appreciate the role of the Reagan team and also the role of Gorbachev, and the fact that Gorbachev and the U.S. side were able to establish a relationship on a certain level. At Governor's Island in New York in December 1988, when the three presidents met, we saw the transfer of that experience from the years of hard work together with the Reagan administration to the new administration.

Then there was a pause, unfortunately, an overly long pause, when the new administration was trying to collect its thoughts and to develop its thinking about what it was going to do. You should know that Gorbachev was very concerned about that pause, and he was very worried that perhaps the new administration might even intend to ruin the assets that had been accumulated during the previous years. After that pause, Secretary Baker came to Moscow and the process was resumed, leading up to Malta, where the two leaders were able to say to each other that they did not regard each other as enemies, and their two countries as potential enemies, but that they regarded themselves as partners in building new international politics. Bush said that on the plane coming into Malta he had decided to say to Gorbachev that he had changed his view of perestroika totally, 180 degrees, and that he wanted to help perestroika succeed. But I do believe that the process became irreversible even before Malta, and at Malta it registered as irreversible.

Mr. Beichman: Will you entertain a question [that] bears on this [subject], off the floor?[6]

Mr. Oberdorfer: If you make it short.

Mr. Beichman: In the new book *At the Highest Levels,* by Strobe Talbott and Michael Beschloss, it is reported that Vice President Bush, while driving with Gorbachev in Washington, told him that he, Bush, would be running for president and that they should not worry about—the quote was "the marginal intellectual thugs surrounding President Reagan." Did that, coming from Bush, then have any effect on relations with the Reagan administration?

Mr. Palazchenko: They misreported. Not "around Reagan," but "on the right of Reagan." And that I think is a very important correction. This is what Vice President Bush did say, that Reagan was very well placed to make deals with the Soviet Union because he was conservative. To the right of him is just the lunatic fringe and thugs. In back-and-forth translations, probably coming back to Beschloss and Talbott, it kind of came together into that formulation, which was not exactly what Vice President Bush said.

Mr. Beichman: Now we have the formulation straightened out. Was that remark registered with President Gorbachev?

Mr. Palazchenko: Let me say that it's important to set straight what Vice President Bush really said at that time, and I think it did register. Gorbachev actually talked with Mr. Beschloss and Mr. Talbott about that conversation, and he did say that the conversation was of some importance to him. He did expect President Bush to take a consistent attitude in continuing to develop U.S.-Soviet relations along the lines of the work that he began with President Reagan, and that's why I think he found it so unfortunate that there was that rather long pause. At that time there was a lot of discussion in the Foreign Ministry of the Soviet Union about that pause, and there were some people who really were worried that this pause might presage a turn for the worse in the relations. Gorbachev was, I think, worried about that pause. But on the basis of that talk—Bush assured [Gorbachev] that he would work with him if he was elected—Gorbachev expected Bush to work together with him.

Mr. Bessmertnykh: Of course, Pavel, you were in the car when the talk was had; but Gorbachev several times referred to this car conversation on the way from the Soviet Embassy in Washington to the airport. This part that we are discussing I didn't hear from him. He would sometimes say, even in some of his correspondence and telephone conversations with Bush, "I remember what we discussed in the car," [or] something like that. The thrust of this, as far as I understood from Gorbachev, [was] that Bush told him during that drive that if he's elected and when he assumes office he will look at the Soviet-American relationship as a priority item of his foreign policy, and he's dedicated to the improvement of the relations, and to continuing the best of what has been done by the previous administration. This is how Gorbachev saw the conversation. That was the main thing, as far as I understand.

Mr. Oberdorfer: Well, Pavel was there, and Michael and Strobe weren't there. Secretary Shultz has a couple of things to tell us, and then we are going to break for lunch.

Mr. Shultz: I'll tell three stories that come up in connection with questions and comments that have been made. First, on the question of leaks, particularly in the arms control field: I remember, Paul, hearing that in your frustration about leaks in the interagency process, you said in one meeting that we should have periodic recesses for filing breaks. As far as the decision-making process in different kinds of institutions is concerned, I'm frequently asked by students at Stanford, "You have administered in government, and in business, and in the university. What's the difference?" I have a long scholarly answer, but I also have an apocryphal answer, which goes: I quickly learned when I became a businessman that you had to be very careful when you told somebody who was working for you to do something, because the chances were very high that he or she would do it, whereas in the government you really didn't have to worry about it, and in the university you weren't supposed to tell anybody to do anything in the first place.

On the personal level with Mr. Gorbachev, one little incident sticks in my mind about personal relationships and how people feel about each other. At the end of the Washington summit meeting, one big event was a press conference by Mr. Gorbachev. It was known that when the press conference was over he would go back to their embassy, and from there go to the airport. I had to take off right after he did. I couldn't leave until he left. But the next day I had to be in Brussels briefing our NATO allies on what had happened at the Washington Summit and signing the agreements that were necessary on INF with the various basing countries. So I'm anxious to get going because I want to get there in time for the meeting and I would like to get a little sleep in the process.

So I tune into Mr. Gorbachev's press conference. His opening statement took almost an hour. Then somebody asked him a question, and forty-five minutes later he finished the answer to that question. Then another one, and it went on and on. It was interesting, but it went on and on, and I was chomping at the bit. He finally ended, and I whipped over to the Soviet Embassy because I was to ride out to the airport with Shevardnadze. The Soviets put me in a little holding room, and before long, in comes Gorbachev. He was obviously feeling very good. He clapped me on back and said, "Well, George, I understand that you watched my press conference." I said, "As a matter of fact I did." "How did you like it?" I said, "It was much too long. Your answers went on and on." And he laughed and slapped me on the back. I said, "Well, at least there's somebody around here who will tell you what he thinks." And he laughed then. So I thought, "Well, he was all right. We've got a human relationship."

Mr. Bessmertnykh: See, I think the human part of the relationship between the two superpowers was very important in the Reagan administration and somewhat later. It so happened that Roz and myself were always working on the final documents of the summits. All the final summit documents were done by us. We spent days and nights on that, and it was a pretty tough job. But Gorbachev knew, and the president knew, that [we] would be doing that. Usually at the end of the final documents there would be a statement that "[in these] negotiations participated," [followed by a list of] names always [including] Assistant Secretary Ridgway. And once my wife came to me and said, "Listen, I want to know. I learned that Assistant Secretary Ridgway is not a gentleman, it's a lady. Who is she?" Because for years she knew that days and nights I worked with Ridgway, and she never suspected she was a lady.

Mr. Oberdorfer: Well, there is something to this question of human interaction and values. I'm sitting here between these two groups of people. You can sort of feel the flow going back and forth, and in fact, in a remarkable way, you think that eight or ten years ago we were thinking about having a fight with one another.

Chapter Six

The Riddle of Reykjavik ∴

All of the Princeton Conference participants were at the Reykjavik Summit, and all agreed in the final conference session that it was among the most dramatic diplomatic exchanges of their lives—if it was not the most dramatic. Ensconced in Hofdi House, an abandoned diplomatic residence high on a windswept hill outside the Icelandic capital, the Soviet and American teams bargained, in marathon negotiating sessions, over the entire range of their nuclear arsenals. On the last day of the two-day summit, Presidents Gorbachev and Reagan ended up talking about eliminating all ballistic missiles in the arsenals of the two countries, and even broached the idea of eliminating nuclear weapons altogether. The meeting foundered when Gorbachev insisted on linking agreements in all areas to restrictions on SDI which Reagan found unacceptable.

Discussion at the Princeton Conference revolved around two central issues: Was the summit well handled or bungled? And what were Gorbachev's motives? Was he trying to trip Americans up on the SDI issue? The interpretation was widespread at the time that Gorbachev had set Reykjavik up as a trap, and that the Reagan administration walked right into it. Here, the American participants defend their handling of the summit and make the case for its role in history. The Russian participants defend Gorbachev's role, insisting that Gorbachev's fixation on SDI was not a trick and was not related to domestic political considerations, but reflected the Soviet leader's personal conviction at that time.

Mr. Oberdorfer: The subject of this final panel of the conference is the summit which took place in Reykjavik, Iceland, in October 1986. The Reykjavik summit meeting has been described as perhaps the most unusual Soviet-American meeting of the post–World War II era, with the exception possibly of the Kennedy-

Khrushchev meeting in Vienna. The first question in my mind is, why Reykjavik? Why did Mr. Gorbachev decide after the Geneva Summit—after a period when relations seemed to bog down somewhat—to propose a working meeting with President Reagan in a brief period of time, at which he was prepared to put on the table a big pile of very tempting concessions, in return for which he insisted upon some restrictions on the U.S. SDI program? Why did he do it, and why did he do it in the way that he did it?

Mr. Bessmertnykh: Nineteen eighty-six was a very important year for Gorbachev. He devised in the beginning of that year the plan of complete elimination of the nuclear weapons by 2000. As we discussed earlier, it was partly an initiative presented to the public, but it was also a program which was very carefully worked out with the General Staff and Foreign Ministry. It was the result of a very intensive effort to devise, once in a lifetime, a scheme which may work. In the beginning of 1986 Gorbachev had made up his mind that we should go deeper and deeper with the reductions, and slowly come to the complete elimination of nuclear weapons.

Some people regarded that initially as a propaganda ploy. To a certain degree it was, but it was basically a program which Gorbachev believed in. This is, I think, a starting point [for answering the question of] why he brought to Reykjavik the program he did. We were preparing for the summit meeting. It was after a certain period of uncertainty after the Geneva Summit. We were concerned about the loss of the tempo in the relationship.

And since, as we have already agreed, Gorbachev and Reagan had developed a certain kind of trust with each other in Geneva, Gorbachev wanted to try with that particular president to achieve progress in arms control, because Reagan was saying all of the same things about his inner feelings with regard to the necessity of eliminating the nuclear weapons. So emotionally and ideally they really were thinking on the same level of doing something at last with those terrible mass-destruction weapons. The two leaders were ready. The turn was ready.

As for the Soviet Union, we were already feeling the pressure of the arms race. Gorbachev wanted to go on with the reforms; and the continued arms race, especially in the nuclear area, was a tremendous hindrance to the future of those reforms. Anatoly Chernyaev has confirmed on a number of occasions during this conference that Gorbachev had never thought his reform was possible without drastic reductions in nuclear arms. So when Reykjavik was on the agenda, he said, let's try in a very serious way to talk with the American side. Of course, we didn't think that we would come to the point at which the two leaders came to the final, complete elimination of the nuclear weapons. I think they got carried away during the negotiations, but [we saw a] 50-percent reduction as a possible proposition.

We had two positions with which we went to Reykjavik. The first was to cut each type of the strategic triad by 50 percent: 50 percent of the ICBMs, 50 percent of the SLBMs, and 50 percent of the heavy bombers. But the American side didn't accept it immediately. So [during the negotiations at Reykjavik] Marshal Akhromeev said, "Well, I will be back at 3 A.M.," because he already had in his pocket the second position, which was exactly what he wanted. But he decided to check with General Secretary Gorbachev whether it was time to go to the second, backup position, or whether we should still try to trade with the Americans a little bit. But since time at Reykjavik was very short, he went to Gorbachev and Gorbachev said, "All right, let's go to the second position." So after Akhromeev went back, he presented our backup position. Of course, we didn't know that you were planning to give us an extra number of missiles. So we had a fallback position and presented it, and that was the limit. But it is important to note something else besides our insistence on the ABM Treaty. Another thing which we have been very strong about in the working groups—I think that Paul would remember that—was the test ban. We were pretty active in insisting that there should be a complete ban on nuclear tests. So that was another [issue hooked] on the proposal to cut down by 50 percent.

Mr. Oberdorfer: There were two things that strike me as somewhat different about the invitation to go to Reykjavik, and I wonder if Mr. Chernyaev can shed any light on how General Secretary Gorbachev decided on these two things. One was that it was to be a working meeting, not a regular summit meeting as Geneva had been. Second, it was to be in a short period of time in a mutually agreeable country, neither Moscow nor Washington. How did Gorbachev get the idea of having an early working-level meeting at that time with President Reagan? What was he after?

Mr. Chernyaev: Let me recall once again that for many reasons, and some of them Mr. Bessmertnykh has just recalled, Gorbachev at that time believed that we could end the Cold War mostly or exclusively through a process of disarmament, while putting aside all those other questions, such as human rights, etcetera. During the first three years he stuck to this approach. Almost right after Geneva, on January 15, 1986, Gorbachev made a statement offering his proposal for the complete elimination of nuclear weapons by the year 2000. No one really believed at that time that this was a serious proposal, and even now many people really think that Gorbachev did not really mean it.

I was close to Gorbachev at that time, and I spoke to him almost every day. I saw each time this question was discussed that he was serious, that he really was a believer, that he really believed in this goal, that this had to be done. He recalled that again and again in subsequent years. He said, "I was called the 'Kremlin dreamer,' and people were saying that this was all an illusion on the part of Gorbachev. But look, the process of real arms control and real disarmament is on the way."[1] Beginning in 1986, particularly after that January initiative, he began to follow extremely closely the progress of arms control negotiations. He was mad at the way the negotiations were progressing because he believed that negotiations were not moving ahead in the way that he thought they should.

And he accused not only the American negotiators, but even more his own Soviet negotiators. He often said—it was his favorite phrase—"This whole thing smells of moth balls. We really should give a shake-up to all of this old clothing in Geneva." I think it happened in March or in April of 1986. Sometime in the spring of 1986 he set a task for himself to somehow try to draw President Reagan out and to make him come to this kind of special meeting to discuss disarmament. He sent a letter to Reagan. He was waiting for an answer. He was very impatient. He was looking forward to an answer, and the answer finally came, I think, in July or in August.

Mr. Oberdorfer: July.

Mr. Chernyaev: He was not satisfied with that answer. When we went on vacation to the Crimea in early August 1986, he said to me, "We'll think of something there, some kind of move there [on vacation in the Crimea]." First he instructed the Foreign Ministry to prepare a new arms control platform for a summit, and I remember how the idea of Reykjavik came up. On an extremely hot day in August we were sitting at the veranda [of Gorbachev's dacha] working through the papers. Finally a paper from the Foreign Ministry came, and it was on his desk. It contained the Foreign Ministry's proposal or arms control platform for the summit.

Shevardnadze was on vacation, Bessmertnykh was on vacation. This was signed by Deputy Foreign Minister Kovalev. I put it on his [Gorbachev's] desk and I said, "This is the proposal that the Foreign Ministry wants us to make on disarmament." He said, "What do you think?" I said, "Well, you have a look and shape your own opinion." When he had a look at that paper, he said, "Well, this is a paper that you can easily send to Karpov [in] Geneva, and he will spend another three years talking away with the Americans and living in a comfortable setting in Geneva, getting paid well for his work."

So he said, "Let us ask the Foreign Ministry to prepare a different kind of letter to Reagan proposing a meeting in late September or early October, or at any time that he would set." "Where?" Then he said, "Well, either in London or in Reykjavik." I was surprised. I said, "I understand London, but why Reykjavik?" He said, "Well, Reykjavik is something that people will understand, because if we meet in London, then, you know, some other great powers might get jealous, and the Americans might not like it. But Reykjavik—well, people will understand. It's just halfway." Then he said to me, "I will propose something really dramatic, and that is to cut in half all the legs of the strategic triad. And then, of course, the generals and the Foreign Ministry people will look into how to adjust this to our different arms structures, but my proposal will be to cut it in half."

So this is how the idea of Reykjavik was born, and then, of course, there were two discussions in the Politburo in September and October, and he came to Reykjavik with this proposal.

Mr. Oberdorfer: Mr. Chernyaev, to what extent in this initial discussion, or in the Politburo discussion, was the objective of curbing the SDI plan an essential part of his thinking? Was that central to it, or was that just peripheral?

Mr. Chernyaev: No, I don't recall any particular focus on this.

Mr. Bessmertnykh: A big part of the SDI insistence was introduced into the follow-up system of working up the documents. The president gave us this idea of 50-percent cuts, and then Akhromeev worked with him every day on that. They were completely confident that they would go for 50 percent if there were no SDI. That was the price that the military asked for this deep cut. We discussed certain possibilities, and Akhromeev said, "No way. We just couldn't give them that." So Gorbachev didn't have a chance. He also believed himself, after being briefed by Akhromeev, that without [a U.S. commitment to limit SDI] the Soviet Union would not be able to go that deep into the reductions.

Mr. Oberdorfer: So if I understand, his original conception was 50-percent cuts in all parts of the triad, and it was only later, when this thing went to the General Staff to be staffed out and so on, that the conditions regarding a strict, limited, laboratory interpretation of SDI was introduced. Is that correct?

Mr. Bessmertnykh: Yes, I think that's correct.[2]

Mr. Oberdorfer: Because it seemed possible at least, looking back on it, that Gorbachev was kind of setting up a trap for the president. He was offering these big cuts, but on a condition which the president was very reluctant to or would not accept, namely [the limiting of] the SDI program, which, as Secretary Shultz has said, was so important to him. Some people have theorized that the whole point of it was to catch Reagan in this contradiction in which he would have to choose between his baby, the SDI program, and the big reduction, which he also wanted.

Mr. Bessmertnykh: It was already a technical part of working out the position. When the whole interconnected system of our position was created, it included complete disbanding of SDI, as part of the package.

Mr. Palazchenko: He had this idea about the ABM Treaty, that it had to be strictly observed.

Mr. Oberdorfer: At the same time, something else was happening in the United States that was to come to the fore at the Reykjavik

Summit, and that was a discussion that arose partly as a result of Gorbachev's dramatic proposal of January 15 on eliminating nuclear weapons by the year 2000. There was a sense in the American government, as I understand it, that some major idea should be proposed on the American side, not to allow Gorbachev to be the only person who was suggesting to the world that something new and dramatic should be done. I believe Mr. Nitze and others went to work on bringing forth some kind of proposal to compete with Gorbachev's big idea. Then in June, in a very restricted meeting in the White House, Secretary of Defense Weinberger for the first time suggested the idea of banning all ballistic missiles. It was a rather surprising idea coming from the defense secretary. Maybe Secretary Shultz could give us an idea of what the thinking was at the time.

Mr. Shultz: We thought that the interesting thing about the Gorbachev proposal in January was its timetable. That is, it set out an end objective, but there was also a timetable and there was clear evidence of the notion of interim steps. What we talked about was front-end loading these interim steps in terms of the search for proposals for the drastic reductions of nuclear weapons that President Reagan had proposed. One of our problems was that we were sort of stuck in the START negotiations with an inability to change our positions very much. At least as I viewed it, the Defense Department was kind of dug in, and you couldn't get anywhere. So when Secretary Weinberger made this suggestion, I had some intimation about it beforehand. I welcomed it in part because it was a way of breaking open the log jam on our START position, and in part because it always seemed to me, as I said earlier in the meeting, that the most threatening thing to the United States was these ballistic missiles. If they were done away with or largely done away with, we would be in much safer shape.

So we worked on this proposal, with a lot of ins and outs and some screwy versions—I think of the Weinberger proposal—combining it with the notion of a period of nonwithdrawal from the ABM Treaty. Then there appeared the July 25 letter that did contain a formulation of nonwithdrawal, along with proposals which included the notion that in the end there might be the elimination of all ballistic missiles. It's interesting that hardly anybody noticed that. It was a breathtaking concept. I might say that all along President Reagan stated his vision and his dream that nuclear weapons be eliminated, and nobody took that seriously. I suppose that what startled people in Reykjavik was not what was said, because both Reagan and Gorbachev had said that before, but the fact that here were the two leaders in an operational setting talking about timetables. All of a sudden this vision had a certain reality to it that would have changed the scene dramatically, and that really did grab people's attention.

Mr. Oberdorfer: I gather that no one thought that this July 25 letter, when you got it, was all that dramatic, or you didn't quite catch the idea that it implied elimination of all ballistic missiles?

Mr. Chernyaev: Well, Gorbachev was not impressed. He did not like that approach. He wanted a different kind of wide-ranging approach toward overall nuclear disarmament.

Mr. Bessmertnykh: It was even more than that. When the military analyzed the proposition of complete elimination of ballistic missiles, they had reported to the president that it was a trap, because if that proposal was accepted the United States would keep its heavy bombers and cruise missiles, while the Soviet Union was very weak on heavy bombers and hadn't developed cruise missiles. So the picture looked very bad. The United States develops SDI, which protects its territory. And there are all those bases around the Soviet Union, with aircraft capable of carrying nuclear weapons sitting next to the borders of the Soviet Union, and cruise missiles being deployed. So it was immediately reported to the president that the proposal was unacceptable.

Mr. Oberdorfer: I'm not going to go through all the back-and-forth about the discussions over the table at Reykjavik, because they involved all the incredible complexities of these weapons. But at the end of the day, on the last afternoon, President Reagan, with Secretary Shultz and General Secretary Gorbachev, accompanied by Foreign Minister Shevardnadze, and their interpreters, one of whom was, I think, you, Pavel, and their note takers, one of whom at least at some point was you, Ambassador Matlock, got down to the question of offers on the table. These offers had been reformulated by Secretary Shultz's team during a break, reformulated again, and discussed back and forth. What they called for on the American side was cutting in half the ballistic missile strength on the two sides and cutting in half all offensive strategic offensive weapons within five years.

Mr. Shultz: To equal final numbers.

Mr. Oberdorfer: Yes.

Mr. Shultz: That was a very important point that Paul negotiated.

Mr. Oberdorfer: And then in the second five years, elimination of all the rest of the ballistic missiles, so that at the end of ten years you have no ballistic missiles on either side and you have only half of the other strategic offensive forces. Now it's easy to say that in a phrase, but this would have been by far the most revolutionary arms control agreement in the history of the world. That agreement, in principle, was to eliminate all of the most powerful weapons that both sides had in their arsenals—ballistic missiles with nuclear warheads on them. The question that I've always wondered about, and I guess maybe historians are going to wonder about: Suppose they hadn't gotten hung up on SDI and they had been able to come to this agreement, what would have happened then? If President Reagan and Mr. Gorbachev had come out to the steps of the Hofdi House in Reykjavik and announced to the world—which had no preparation, by the way, for any of this— "We have just agreed to eliminate all of our ballistic missiles and atomic bombs on the warheads in ten years," what do you think would have taken place? Would this have been able to be accomplished? Would Congress have raised holy hell? Our allies? Would the American public and the publics everywhere have said, "These people have lost their minds," or would it have been the reaction "Thank goodness somebody is using some sanity?"

Mr. Nitze: We had grave worries about how our NATO allies would look upon this. As I remember it, I was sent over to talk to somebody about it, and they were really deeply concerned. I think we were prepared to go forward with it in any case; isn't that right, George? That's my recollection.

Mr. Shultz: Yes. But just to set it absolutely straight, recall at the end Gorbachev's SDI proposal—namely, to restrict activity to laboratories—and President Reagan's proper rejection of that. There was also a disagreement about what we would eliminate. The Soviet proposal was that we would eliminate all strategic weapons, and ours was that we [would] eliminate all ballistic missiles, and there's a big difference between those two proposals.

Mr. Oberdorfer: They were not that close?

Mr. Shultz: There was a great deal of argument involved in that difference, as well as the SDI difference. I think it's interesting, when you go back and look at the record, how many times Reagan or Gorbachev said things like this. Yet the world was caught by surprise. One can well respond, "Why were you surprised?" After all, Reagan was in favor of eliminating all nuclear weapons. He said it to the Japanese Diet, he said to the Korean Assembly, he said it during his election campaign, he said it endless numbers of times, and practically everybody, all the arms control people, tried to talk him out of it. He said, "Well, I hear all your arguments, but I still think we'd all be better off if we didn't have nuclear weapons hanging over our heads."

Mr. Oberdorfer: Do you have your own theory as to why people never registered on this?

Mr. Shultz: Because they didn't think. They said, well, he's a visionary. That's what he's saying, but it's not a practical possibility. I myself didn't think it was a practical possibility. You can't uninvent nuclear weapons. They are already invented. But you can sure cut them way down. In that sense, I think he was very much on the right track.

Mr. Oberdorfer: Roz—

Ms. Ridgway: I think you don't want to lose track of the fact that you could ask the same question about Paul's negotiations with Akhromeev on INF. Certainly, when we briefed the allies by phone the next day as to what had been accomplished and everybody was acting very surprised, you have to ask, why were they surprised? We had been on the course of reducing one set of that class of weapons, and down the road a piece [toward] eliminating the second, but they all acted as if they had never heard of it before. You can trace today's European interest in the so-called European se-

curity identity and the Western European Union right back to
Reykjavik. Immediately following Reykjavik there was a Western
European Union declaration on this topic. And when, in a very
quiet session with a group of Europeans, we had a chance to ask,
"Why were you surprised? Why did you react the way you did,
since you were briefed in, for example, the July 25 letter that was
carried by Paul around to major capitals?" the European answer
was, "Because we were not at the table." They had not treated certain strategic, political concerns as real before, and suddenly the
reality of the new age was with them.

Mr. Matlock: You know, we're so often accused of not consulting the
allies. It simply was not the case. The president wrote a letter to
the chiefs of the government of every basing country before Reykjavik. This is in addition to the July 25 letter which they had gotten earlier. The president reviewed these proposals [in his second
letter], and every one of them answered approvingly. I personally
collated those answers for Reagan, and later you had people like
[Manfred] Wörner, defense minister in West Germany, saying, "We
weren't consulted." Well, we had on record a letter from Kohl. He
was consulted. Now, whether he talked to Wörner—that was his
affair; but frankly, there was a lot more consulting than the Europeans were willing to recognize.

Mr. Shultz: This goes back to something we discussed when we
talked about the nature of these two leaders. They were both
people who were self-confident enough to be very bold and not to
be troubled if they broke away from the conventional wisdom. But
from the U.S. standpoint, it has always seemed to me that Reykjavik has been grossly misunderstood, in part due to our immediate reactions. I gave a talk on Reykjavik to the National Press
Club the week following, and I was asked during that, why did I
look so tired and disappointed at the end of the Reykjavik meeting
and my press conference? And I said, "Because I was tired and
disappointed."

But when you look at the content, from our standpoint, we
practically had agreement from Gorbachev to the INF proposals
the president had made in his initial statement of the U.S. position. We had agreement by Gorbachev to the basic structure of the
strategic arms reduction treaty that was very much along the lines

of Reagan's proposal in his Eureka College speech on this subject. Two very tricky matters had been worked out by Paul Nitze with Marshal Akhromeev. One was not only reductions by half, but reductions by half to equal numbers of strategic weapons. That's key, because if you start from different levels and you are reducing by half, you can end up with unequal levels. And the other important thing, given the disparity that Mr. Bessmertnykh referred to in bomber weapons, was the bomber-counting rule, which you [Nitze] and Akhromeev negotiated. That was very difficult: how do you equate a bomber with a ballistic missile? Obviously, a ballistic missile's warhead is much more significant, and so how do you count a bomber? And what you were working out with Akhromeev was, I believe, that a bomber counts as one no matter how many bombs it has on it.

So Reykjavik introduced the basic INF Treaty and settled, in an immense amount of detail, the basic structure of what became the START I agreement. Furthermore, on nuclear testing, though we never got the language on that, we did have a discussion [suggesting] that we would have some tests in each country, which would be mutually observed. Out of that would come a verification scheme that would allow us to ratify these two treaties that were around. I've always felt in some ways that what was most important of all was something that happened as a result of our insistence on and your recognition of our four-part agenda. We kept hammering on that all the time.

This was not solely an arms control summit, in our view. At the end of the first morning, we could see that there was an immense proposal there. We worked on the president's talking points. As I recall, Paul, you and some others stayed back in the afternoon because we could see there was going to be an all-night session working on this material. We had to get ourselves lined up. At the end of the afternoon session, the president proposed—Gorbachev was very agreeable—that we have a working group to work over these proposals, and I suggested that there should be a second working group that would address human rights, regional issues, bilateral issues, and Gorbachev agreed to that. So Roz and Sasha [Bessmertnykh] worked that out, and they agreed, I think, for the first time on a reciprocal basis that human rights will be a recognized, legitimate, regular part of our agenda, as distinct from the position in the Gromyko days that this was not a subject that they were willing to discuss. I consider that to be a huge breakthrough.

What came out of Reykjavik was sensational. As we all know, once you put positions on the table, you can say, "I've withdrawn them," but they're not withdrawn. They're there. We've seen your bottom line and so we know where it is; and they all came right back up on the table before long. So it pained me to hear the Bush administration people saying about summits, "Now the worst thing in the world would be like Reykjavik, a random, unprepared, crazy summit like that"—when what they were describing was the most productive summit that was ever held, and also one that was very well prepared. Not that we knew what they were going to be proposing, but there was hardly anything that was discussed that we hadn't worked over endlessly. We had a full panel of advisors there, and we were ready.

Mr. Oberdorfer: The summit in Reykjavik has already been subject to a great deal of historical reinterpretation, because it ended up seemingly a total failure. As you pointed out, you were disappointed and frustrated. Reagan came out furious. The next meeting in Vienna was horrible: you and Mr. Karpov got into a big shouting match.

Mr. Nitze: He called me a liar.

Mr. Oberdorfer: People said this was a total disaster. Now they are reconsidering Reykjavik, because many of the things that were proposed there came through within the next year or two. I want to ask one more question of Secretary Shultz. The last discussions between Gorbachev and Reagan, on the second afternoon, were really the most famous part of this summit, one that was contested for a while. They were discussing how to structure the reductions in this second five-year period, and finally Reagan said, "It would be fine with me if we eliminated all nuclear weapons." Gorbachev says, "We could do that: let's eliminate them. We can eliminate them, all nuclear weapons." Now, you were there. Was this reality or discussion? Is there any way that the president could have caused the United States to eliminate all nuclear weapons?

Mr. Shultz: I think that the United States, Russia, and the world would all be much better off if there were far, far, fewer nuclear weapons. These weapons of mass destruction are terrible. Let's not kid ourselves. Look at Chernobyl. If you say your dream is to eliminate them, well, okay, but let's have a schedule for getting them way down. I think in the end, you do need a very small—I will call it an insurance-policy arsenal—because you have to have something, in view of the fact that you can't uninvent the nuclear weapons, and people all around the world are smart enough to figure out how to get them. Politics, in the best sense of the word, would tend to support bringing the levels of nuclear weapons way down. We probably could have gone quite some distance. But our Joint Chiefs of Staff went up the wall about the whole idea of deep reductions, despite the fact that they were represented in the secretary of defense's proposal. They clearly had not taken the proposal seriously. And then Margaret Thatcher came over and preached us a lesson about how important ballistic missiles were because they can reach way into the Soviet Union. So obviously, there was a big negative reaction to doing something sweeping.

Mr. Oberdorfer: What was your frame of mind at the time as you heard those two guys talking about this, if you remember?

Mr. Shultz: I personally have felt for a long time that the first thing— since we really kicked out the British—that could devastate our country is the strategic ballistic missile with a nuclear warhead on it. If we were able to obviate that, we'd be way ahead of the game. So I was sitting there cheering this on, although I think that maybe we would have been better off if we hadn't had that last go- around and that last proposal.

Mr. Nitze: My recollection is, Mr. Secretary, that you said to the president, "Mr. President, I think you misunderstood. Our position is the elimination of all *ballistic* missiles."

Mr. Shultz: I think the exchange there was when Gorbachev made his proposal . . . for the elimination of strategic weapons rather than ballistic missiles. The president said, "Well, that sounds just like our proposal." And I said "No, it isn't, Mr. President. It's different. It's very different, and it is an issue."

Mr. Oberdorfer: Then you went on to all nuclear weapons.

Mr. Shultz: I'm sort of reacting to your question about whether this was desirable, in my opinion. Obviously, there were all sorts of things that would have to come along if you went down this road, and particularly the huge asymmetries that were present then in conventional forces.

Mr. Oberdorfer: Mr. Chernyaev wanted to talk.

Mr. Chernyaev: I, too, believe that what happened really ought to have happened. In principle, it would be hard to imagine some different course of developments in the area of disarmament. The proper way of studying this, particularly from the standpoint of today, is to look at it in light of the dictum that the two presidents adopted at Geneva when they included in that communiqué the famous phrase that nuclear war cannot be won and must never be fought. I believe that, moving in that direction, Gorbachev never wanted to outsmart the other side, as many of you have heard him say. He has said many times that in our day and age it is simply impossible to outsmart the other side in the arms control process. Why, then, was there such a difficult, agonizing process? That brings back to me the words of Secretary Shultz, something he once said in his discussions with Mr. Gorbachev. He said that the devil is in the details; and the devil is that reality that made it so difficult to move forward this process and that created those retreats and backslides.

Mr. Oberdorfer: This probably is a little bit unfair, but what the hell. I want to ask a question of Pavel, who was in that room. There were only eight people in the room. Everybody in the whole world is watching. There's Gorbachev, Shevardnadze, an interpreter, and a note-taker. And on the American side there was Reagan, and Shultz, and an interpreter, and note-takers. Interpreters and note-takers would change from time to time. Pavel was there interpreting at some of those most crucial points; Sergei Tarasenko and Jack Matlock were there taking notes at crucial points. Quite apart from this policy stuff, I would just like to ask each or any of you, what was your impression of the human interaction in this room—the two leaders of the most powerful countries of the world talking about destroying the main parts of their arsenal, in an intense two-day discussion? What was your own sense of what was going on, just on the human level, between these people?

Mr. Palazchenko: Well, I agree with Secretary Shultz that the most impressive thing was the fact that the two leaders were discussing, as he puts it, in an operational setting, the elimination of nuclear weapons. This is really something that impressed me at that time, and the interaction between them was a difficult one, obviously. That was not yet the time when they really had already become friends. But I was impressed, and I was just wondering, asking myself whether this is something that will really begin a process, that will really set the ball rolling, or whether this is something that might evaporate. Afterwards, as you know, there was a difficult period when there was a period of misunderstanding between Moscow and Washington, and a war of interpretation about what really happened and what was said in Reykjavik. But Sergei and I have discussed this many times, and we agree that the difference between problem periods under Gorbachev and Reagan, on the one hand, and similar periods in the previous administrations was that these two men never said, "Well, so be it. Let the process evaporate."

Mr. Oberdorfer: Sergei, do you want to add anything?

Mr. Tarasenko: Well, I was not supposed to be there in that room. Our assumption was that there would be just bosses and interpreters for the first meeting. So I was left on the ship. Then a security guy rushed in, grabbed me, and brought me to this house and pushed me into the room where Jack was sitting. I saw that there was another guy on the American side. This was a reciprocal arrangement, so we [had to] have the same number of people on our side. I was completely, utterly unprepared, and maybe for fifteen or twenty minutes they talked one-on-one. Well, I'll be frank in my reciting this. Gorbachev felt after this fifteen minutes that he could not get any attention from President Reagan. He was not sure that he was getting through to the president, and he wanted to present this arms control package.

Mr. Shultz: Sergei is speaking about the initial meeting, which was just between the president and Gorbachev.

Mr. Tarasenko: [For] fifteen minutes they talked one-on-one, and then Gorbachev decided to invite foreign ministers just for this delivery, for his presentation of the big proposal. So then the secretary and ministers came in, and they started talking in a more orderly, organized way about arms control. But when suddenly they started to talk about big cuts everyone was elated, on the one hand, but [on the other hand] a little bit frightened with what was going on. [We were] in a big game with high stakes, and the stakes were being raised every five minutes. The discussion was fascinating, you know. It seemed like you were at a movie. There [was] some touch of unreality to that. Something historical [is] going around you. You are not recognizing exactly what it is, but you feel that it's something beyond what you can guess or expect.

But on the second day [when the last effort to overcome the SDI/ABM impasse had failed], everyone felt let down. Everyone was in a gloomy state then. I don't know why, because after a rational analysis, it could be seen that it was a good meeting indeed. It was a fine, productive meeting, but maybe it was so quick, so rapid, with [such] high stakes [that agreement wasn't possible].

Mr. Oberdorfer: You nearly went to the moon and you fell short?

Mr. Tarasenko: Yes. It's really an eerie feeling. But I have to report that after the meeting Shevardnadze was angry with Akhromeev. He said that Akhromeev had blocked the agreement.

Mr. Oberdorfer: By insisting on SDI?

Mr. Tarasenko: Yes. Akhromeev had a fallback position which allowed some room to find a compromise, but he stalled.

Mr. Oberdorfer: You mean something beyond laboratory testing?

Mr. Tarasenko: Yes. I'm not sure because Shevardnadze never told me details about it, but he said, "I will not forgive Akhromeev. He ruined the meeting."

Mr. Oberdorfer: Do any others of you believe this?

Mr. Nitze: My recollection of the final departure of Mr. Gorbachev is that he had Akhromeev right behind him. I came down those stairs from the room upstairs where they had been negotiating, onto the ground floor. I was standing at the bottom of the stairs coming down the Hofdi House. Akhromeev passed me as he came down the stairs, and he said, "I am not to blame." Those were his words.

Mr. Tarasenko: He tried to disclaim his involvement.

Mr. Oberdorfer: Before I get to Ambassador Matlock, let me just follow up on that question. Do any of the rest of you know anything about whether there was a fallback position on the SDI question?

Mr. Bessmertnykh: As far as I know, there were no backup positions.

Mr. Palazchenko: Right. Gorbachev was not free to do anything. There was probably a Politburo decision, so he had to stick to it. He was general secretary, but he was not a czar.

Mr. Bessmertnykh: But I think what Shevardnadze meant is not that in Reykjavik there was a fallback position that we didn't use. That was not the case in Reykjavik. But when the position was formed in Moscow, Akhromeev insisted that the [curtailing of] SDI should be a completely ironclad condition on the 50-percent reductions.

Mr. Tarasenko: My understanding is that right there in Hofdi House they could have made a deal, and Shevardnadze thought that it could be done. He certainly knew the framework, the limits, but he thought that there was room to maneuver. I got in the car with him, and he talked a lot. He was distressed. He said more than once, "Look at this guy. He ruined everything." He was very emotional about that.

Mr. Oberdorfer: That's the first time we've heard of this, and it's very interesting. Several of you mentioned that Mr. Gorbachev was bound. Suppose, in the Soviet system of that time, Gorbachev goes to the Politburo and says, "I'm going to do this at Reykjavik in this particular case. This is my proposal that I'm going to make to the Americans." Could he have—on his own authority or by contacting other members of the Politburo—shifted his position, or was he locked into it there?

Mr. Bessmertnykh: My personal feeling is that he could do it. At that moment, at that time, he was very powerful, and he had the control of the Politburo, but he would have had to do some explaining after he was back. But probably he was not sure that he should do it, because the military position was so strong, and I think he felt that he might be blamed for selling out the national interest.

Mr. Shultz: During the course of Reykjavik, there was a considerable amount of movement on other issues. It wasn't as though a position was taken and never challenged.

Mr. Oberdorfer: I was thinking just on this one sticker that was the final obstacle. But, Mr. Chernyaev, did you want to add anything to this?

Mr. Chernyaev: My view is somewhat different. At that time, Gorbachev could decide. I don't think that he would have encountered any resistance at the Politburo. The program that he took with him to Reykjavik had been discussed in the Politburo, and there was no objection at all. But at that time he himself was sincerely convinced that if SDI were to continue, it would create a circumvention channel that would devalue the agreement about drastic reductions in nuclear weapons. It was his sincere conviction at that time. He said to Reagan, "If it were a question of grain—how much you want to sell, how much you want to buy, etcetera—I would be ready to compromise, but this is something that is a problem for us because this is our security. Our security is at stake." This is what he believed. It was his inner conviction, and he was not afraid of someone scolding him back in Moscow. That was a different situation.

Mr. Oberdorfer: Ambassador Matlock was also sitting there. I'll ask for his personal thoughts about it, and then we will go on to other things.

Mr. Matlock: I was not sitting in the final session. I took notes on the first day, in the one-on-one meeting. In general, I think my emotions went up and down, with everybody else on our side and, I gather, on the Soviet side. I did think, in addition to the fact that we did make the basic breakthroughs for at least two major arms control treaties that were subsequently signed, that the proposal for elimination of ballistic missiles was something which was dismissed too readily, and subsequently dropped by the United States too readily. It was a serious proposal that had been prepared within the U.S. government, but on what we call a close-hold basis. Key specialists were consulted—not all 2,536 people who thought they were specialists and therefore would have said it's not prepared if they didn't have a hand in it. But it was seriously prepared, and what many people didn't recognize was that it was not just about ballistic missiles carrying nuclear warheads, it was about ballistic missiles, period.

Now, this is really a quite revolutionary proposal when you consider the fact that it is ballistic missiles that are particularly given to surprise, that are the most useful if you are the attacker, and that are the principal delivery system for chemical weapons. It was the Soviet ballistic missiles that made all the airfields in Europe absolutely vulnerable even without a nuclear war. I just suggest that people who want to understand Reykjavik fully should research that question. If we made a mistake, it was that we didn't really have time to explain the implications of this.

And the Soviets' conclusion that it would have left them with only bombers and cruise missiles was true. We were talking ten, twelve years. On the nuclear side, we thought that you can build a bomber force and you can build cruise missiles in that period of time much more cheaply than you can maintain submarine-launched ballistic missiles, for example. Although we were asking you to give up your heavy missiles, we were willing to give up our submarine-launched missile force, which was the jewel in our offensive crown. In any event, without belaboring, I will just say I think that was a serious proposal. It is too bad it was dropped, because in the future the world community is going to have to grapple with the proliferation of ballistic missiles. I would suggest as one legacy of Reykjavik that both of our governments go back and take another look and see if we can't get it on track.

Mr. Shultz: I would like to just insert a logical connection. The president proposes the Strategic Defense Initiative because he wants us to be able to defend ourselves against ballistic missiles. However impractical it may be, if you could come up with an SDI that provided a complete shield, then you would have completely defended yourself against ballistic missiles. Turn that coin over. If you eliminate ballistic missiles, you have achieved the same result. In addition, one of the arguments against the SDI that was advanced immediately by the Soviets was that [SDI] is offensive because if one side is able to defend itself against ballistic missiles and the other side isn't, then you are all set up to make a first strike and the other side can't retaliate against you effectively. What is the answer to that bit of logic? Again, it is to eliminate the ballistic missiles. Then you don't have the first-strike capacity, and you've squared this business. So there is a certain internal logic here.

You were talking about atmospherics at Reykjavik. That house, Hofdi House, was insisted upon by the security agencies of both the Soviet and the U.S. side because it was an isolated house that they could control. But it was moved out of by the British ambassador, I believe, because he was convinced it was a haunted house. It was unoccupied, and on the side of the room where we met was a big picture window. At that time of year Reykjavik gets dark most of the time, but you do get the rhythm of the season. It alternately rained, then cleared and brightened up, and back and forth. When you looked out this picture window you could see a kind of counterpart, in an odd way, of the discussions inside the room that were going through this same process of alternating between dark and light.

Mr. Oberdorfer: There's one other thing about Reykjavik that's not on arms control, but it has really appeared much in the discussions that we have had in the last couple of days, and it's about human interaction. I was very much impressed with the statement that was made to me by Charley Hill, who was Secretary Shultz's executive assistant at the time of Reykjavik and who had previous experience dealing with Communist governments in some of his earlier foreign service assignments. He said to me that in the past it seemed to him that conversations with Soviet diplomats always stayed so close to the Party line. He said (I quote), "You knew you were talking to someone who wasn't a real human being. You were talking to a programmed mind of someone doing something for some reason other than what an individual human being would do on his own hook. And suddenly, somebody at the top said it's okay to be a human being again, and their officials from top to bottom changed. Their personalities changed, their approach changed, their scathing wit changed. Somehow, suddenly, the lid was off, and you could be yourself to a certain extent."

Now, Hill said that came to him in the discussions around the coffee pot upstairs, and so on, while these four, six, or eight, as it turned out to be, were meeting. The rest of the people were talking to each other, milling around. But his view was that that was the time when people who had been under kind of Party-line instruction were suddenly free to say what they thought, within the bounds of policy. Charley is a diplomat, too. Quite apart from the question of whether Reykjavik was the time, do you all recognize this? Do you think there was some kind of a constriction on what you as individuals could say or think, but somehow at some point earlier in the Gorbachev years it was taken off and you could be much more yourselves in interaction with other people than you could ever be before?

Mr. Bessmertnykh: You know, for us, of course, there were no instructions to change ourselves into human beings, but there was something that influenced us, and that was Gorbachev himself.

We had been with him since 1985. We saw him talking, we saw him participating in the preparation of the talks. He was an absolutely new type of top leader. He was absolutely human, accessible—a man who could love, who could curse, who could use good and unprintable language. He was an absolutely normal man, very intellectual at the same time and knowledgeable. So just the example of that man probably made us better. In Geneva, in Reykjavik, we were getting more and more open to each other, and this pattern of interrelationship existed for the rest of the presidency. I think a lot of things were done just because we were open to each other. We could sometimes tell each other things which in normal diplomatic practice would not be said. You would say, "Listen, this is the limit. We just can't go beyond it because of this and that reason. Here we can maneuver. Let's try it." So I would agree that one of the major elements of changing the Cold War was changing ourselves. We were the products of the Cold War, all of us. But we became softened by the new realities.

Mr. Chernyaev: I agree totally with what Alexander Bessmertnykh said. Glasnost had raised the dome that existed over our society. That dome was not totally removed, but there was a lot more intellectual freedom in our society. Those people who went to Reykjavik were not, I would say, selected—hand-picked—by Gorbachev, but he knew who was going. The team that went to Reykjavik went there with his knowledge. He was, at that time, selecting people who he believed were capable of being personalities, of being authentic individuals. I would only disagree with any particular emphasis or focus on the Party line, the Party nomenklatura, the Party apparat. There were people at Reykjavik who were from the Party apparat, and it's incorrect to think that people who were at some point working in the Party nomenklatura were stupid, incapable of thinking, or that they were bound. Some people in the Party nomenklatura had understood many things even earlier than other people in our society. So you shouldn't generalize too much on this. Ninety-five percent of the first generation of perestroika supporters, the Gorbachev generation of perestroika supporters, were Party members, and many of them were members of the Party apparat.

Mr. Oberdorfer: Ambassador Ridgway—

Ms. Ridgway: I would like to try the American variation on the same issue. It is slightly different, but there certainly grew up over a period, over the decades of the U.S.-Soviet relationship, the school of thought that said when you negotiated with Soviet Communists you could scream, you could shout, you could play games, and that was answered from the other side as well. As the relationship became serious, as opportunities were created to really move forward, it was very clear on the American side that if you wished to be a part of the serious, substantive negotiations, you would adopt a standard of professional behavior which did not eliminate the human side of all of this, but in which argument was conducted as arguments should be conducted; in which disagreements were carried out, either resolved or not resolved, but with civility; in which there was respect for other people; in which language was cautious; and in which there were not ad hominem references to counterparts that were not attractive.

If you wanted to know who was going to be around at the end of the day doing serious business, there was a behavior standard, and it was matched on the other side. It is quite noticeable that with both sides it was a combination of professional and personal. I think it's important to say that they were continuing to serve the national interests of their own countries. At no point did this common commitment to taking these huge opportunities make anybody sloppy with respect to the national interest. At no point was it ever said that in order to work in the national interest you had to be rude and uncouth.

Mr. Oberdorfer: I think it's time, nearly at the end, to take a very brief retrospective look at this retrospective look at the end of the Cold War. In this last couple of days we have gone over a huge amount of territory: trends and personalities; the interaction of people and policy and government; the crises back and forth, ranging from the shooting down of Korean [Air Lines] flight 007 to a number of others; the leaders and how they interacted—Reagan, Gorbachev, Shevardnadze, Shultz; the extraordinary decision-making system or nonsystem which [got] the Soviet Union into Afghanistan, how the American government dealt with it, how the Soviets managed to get out; and now this most extraordinary of all summits. Secretary Shultz, I think, called it a "high-stakes game." It was perhaps the highest-stakes game in diplomatic history.

Before we end, I would like to ask first Mr. Bessmertnykh and then Secretary Shultz to give any thoughts they have about what they bring out of this several days of discussions, and then ask Professor Greenstein to give us his final analysis.

Mr. Bessmertnykh: I think the Cold War ended for several reasons, some of which maybe we have not completely comprehended yet. But it was ended by human beings, by people who were dedicated to eradicating this part of history. It was an enormously difficult task, and we have discovered during these discussions that the result was successful because both sides tried to reach the same goal. If you had different goals, even if you were the nicest people in the world, you wouldn't get where we got. We have discovered how much mistrust there was and how many misjudgments there were, and I think this is one of the basic lessons for the future leaders and for the present leaders: Please check two or three times before you make a decision, because the information may be wrong, the inclinations may be erroneous, and the advice you receive may not be perfect.

The third thing I would like to emphasize is that the Cold War is over, but the remnants of it are still spread all over the world. We are not through with the job. There are still great tasks to do. We must participate in that, because if you don't clean the world of the remnants of the Cold War by, say, 2000, [they] will grow into the twenty-first century and will do a lot of harm to everyone. So I'm happy that the Cold War was ended. The United States and the Soviet Union didn't want to be cold warriors initially, but somehow they became the commanders of two camps. But they had really good intentions to [rectify] the situation and have intentions to destroy the beast. This is what we have discovered here during this discussion.

Mr. Shultz: As you look at the forces that were at play in the Cold War and in bringing the Cold War to an end, it seems to me you reflect on where we go from here. We are at a period in the history of our world that cries out for creative statesmanship on the order of what Paul Nitze participated in. To my way of thinking, weapons of mass destruction combined with ballistic missiles are a big threat to everybody. Getting a real handle on these is important. I think—particularly in the information age—there are the connections among our economies that are intense. The international economic institutions that were created at the end of World War II, and which have basically served well, nevertheless have become somewhat obsolete. It seems to me not only that a fresh look is needed at security issues and regional problems but also that there needs to be a thorough review of economic arrangements so that it's possible to take maximum advantage of the huge opportunities that are before us.

And as we do that, I think there are lessons to be learned from this exchange that we've had here. From our reflections on the efforts that we reviewed, the lessons would be to maintain your basic principles, to keep working at it, to—as Roz suggested—conduct diplomatic relations in a civil, professional way, with the expectation that sooner or later you are going to be able to break through and make some achievements. This session has been, for me, very interesting, and quite a few things have surprised me. From my standpoint it's been a very informative and interesting occasion, and I express my thanks to you, Fred, and the Woodrow Wilson School, and Don as a person who has orchestrated all of this very skillfully. I express my appreciation to you both.

Prof. Greenstein: I think rather than opening some metaphoric fortune cookie and coming up with a little conclusion, I would like to propose that we . . . continue these discussions. It strikes me that often, august groups are pulled together and they immediately attempt to reach lofty conclusions, and often these come out as platitudes. I think the fact that this discussion has been so experienced, and so grounded in the hard work of unraveling the past, made this is a sort of ex post facto ghost summit, as it were. Maybe *ghost* is the wrong adjective, but I hope that we can continue this kind of process, and I suspect that most of the people here would feel motivated to do that under appropriate circumstances. So, thanks to all of you for coming.

Part II

Analysis and Implications

∴

The Search for Causes to the End of the Cold War

∴

WILLIAM C. WOHLFORTH

For the former diplomats and officials at the Princeton Conference on the End of the Cold War, the question was tough but straightforward: How did they bring about a decisive improvement in superpower relations in the face of domestic and international resistance? No scholar worthy of the name can resist asking a further question: *Why* did they succeed? Their predecessors had failed to achieve such a degree of cooperation for much of the preceding four decades, but these two diplomatic teams forged ahead to reach unprecedented agreement on almost every item on the Cold War agenda. Did they just try harder, and if so, why? Was it the nature of the circumstances, the quality of the strategies, the personalities of the key players, or just luck?

The Cold War's end presents major puzzles that are relevant not only to scholarly theories but also to policy and politics. As of 1984, the two superpowers had been locked in rivalry for nearly four decades and their relations were at their lowest point in over twenty years. Three years later, they were well on their way to achieving a détente deeper than any in the history of the Cold War. By the end of 1989, the détente had blossomed into a full-blown concert of two powers with more interests in common than in conflict.[1] This dramatic emergence of cooperation between rivals is all the more striking when one notes the rarity of analogous occurrences in the history of international politics. George Shultz, Alexander Bessmertnykh, and their bosses were working against the odds. Most enduring rivalries between states have been ended only by war, and the few that have ended peacefully did so only when both rivals turned their attention to a third power they perceived as a greater threat.[2] It is no wonder that the process of engagement described above in chapters 1 through 6 was so often almost derailed.

The diplomatic breakthrough achieved by the Princeton conferees was in many ways unprecedented, and therefore unexpected. Surprise at an outcome—and especially one with such important consequences—leads naturally to a desire to explain it. And that basic drive to explain is wedded to longstanding and often highly partisan debates about competing theories and policies. All parties to these debates were caught unawares by the sudden end of the Cold War. Everyone involved—from unilateral disarmers to obdurate hawks, and from tough-minded realists to world-order visionaries—had adjusted intellectually to the ongoing superpower rivalry. Suddenly, the strategic conditions that had anchored the discourse for forty years were gone. Anyone who had been active in the debates faced two basic questions: "How do I reconcile this outcome with the interpretation of the Cold War associated with my favored policy or theory? And does this outcome call into question any of the basic premises underlying my favored policy or theory?"

Intellectuals' efforts to get their bearings in the new circumstances led to a mild cold war over the question of why the Cold War had ended. Among scholars of international relations, the debate always centered on realism, a theory that predicts conflict among states and highlights the importance of international as opposed to domestic causes.[3] For most scholars, the end of the Cold War dealt realism a serious blow. These scholars argue that the negotiated conclusion of the Cold War confounded realist expectations of continued conflict, and moreover, that the variables featured in that theory had little or nothing to do with this major upheaval in international relationships. They suggest that this outcome reflects fundamental changes in the international system which have altered the costs and benefits of rivalry and cooperation, rendering realism out of date.[4] Realist theory grew up with the Cold War, and its fortunes varied in proportion to the level of superpower tension. Now that realism's silent ally is dead, say its foes, the theory should make an equally graceful exit.

Other scholars respond that the outcome is consistent with realism, reflecting the Soviet Union's exhaustion in its rivalry with the United States.[5] They contend that the rise and decline of powers is central to realist theory and was a central element behind Moscow's eventual decision to sue for peace in the Cold War, and that the causes highlighted by realism lay behind the intricate diplomacy of the Cold War's end and will continue to shape international politics in the future. Yet a third group of scholars rejects the idea that this event contains any lessons for international relations theory. They insist that the end of the Cold War was mainly the by-product of domestic changes, especially in the Soviet Union, and had little to do with realism or any other theory of international politics.

It is clear even from this brief description of the theoretical debate that determining the implications of the Cold War's end for theory requires a determination of the causes of that event. And the debate over theories is linked to a more politically charged debate about policy. The inescapable fact with which any analysis must come to terms is that this decisive turn toward cooperation followed four years of Ronald Reagan's extremely hard-line anti-Soviet policy: a massive military buildup; a high-technology threat in the form of the Strategic Defense Initiative; blistering anti-Soviet rhetoric; an open-ended doctrine of aid to anti-Communist "freedom fighters" around the globe; renewed emphasis on Soviet violations of human rights; and a diplomacy focused more on public opinion than on real negotiation. It is true, as Don Oberdorfer first documented, that within the Reagan administration the turn toward engagement with Moscow occurred in 1983.[6] But the public at large and the Soviets themselves were not aware of this change until at least a year later.[7] In any case, Reagan and his key aides firmly believed that it was their tough policy that had set the stage for the new turn in relations by shifting the real balance of power and the perceived "psychological" initiative toward the United States.[8] And although the Reagan team eventually opted for negotiations, it gave Gorbachev the honor of making most of the concessions.

For decades, critics of deterrence theory had argued that just such "peace-through-strength" policies would only further the arms race and could even lead to war.[9] For decades, Sovietologists skeptical of

American policy in the Cold War had argued that hard-line policies only helped Soviet conservatives and that superpower détente was a precondition of Soviet reform.[10] But the virulently anti-Communist policies of Reagan and his Southern Californian friends, whose extremism shocked even establishment Cold War hawks, immediately preceded the deepest superpower détente to date, and the most thoroughgoing imaginable reform of Soviet domestic and foreign policy.

Either Reagan's policy helped to end the Cold War, or it actually delayed the emergence of cooperation, or it had no effect on changes that derived exclusively from domestic Soviet politics or Gorbachev's personality.[11] Once again, a search for causes is necessary in order to reach a conclusion about this debate. And the search must be careful if we are to take any lessons away from this episode, for the effects of any given policy may be highly contingent. It is perfectly possible that Reagan's policy did speed the Cold War's end, but only because of the presence of specific enabling conditions. For example, Jack Snyder has argued that hard-line U.S. policies "help Soviet soft-liners only when Soviet hard-liners are in power," by discrediting the Kremlin hawks' peace-through-strength arguments. But hard-line policies "simply discredit Soviet doves when they are already in power" by discrediting their argument for peace through accommodation.[12] It is also possible that the tough policy may have had precisely the effects that the critics had always alleged—aiding Kremlin hawks and hindering Soviet reform—but that these effects were simply overwhelmed by other, more powerful causes specific to this case, notably the ripening general crisis of Soviet Communism.

The cold war over the question of why the Cold War ended may have generated more contention than clarity at first, but now it is settling into a prolonged competition that will surely generate important new insights for historical and theoretical scholarship. In the following three chapters, Fred Greenstein, Robert Jervis, and Alexander George begin to think through the causes of the Cold War's end. Using the transcripts of the Princeton Conference as a referent, these scholars develop key aspects of their earlier work on personality (Greenstein), perception (Jervis), and learning (George). They show how the personal qualities of central decision makers, the changing content of mutual images, and the evolution of elite beliefs about the political world can contribute to fundamental change in international politics. Despite their differences of emphasis, all the contributors to this book agree that the evidence is still incomplete, and we should not rush to judgment; that any explanation of this event will feature many causes operating at many levels; that it is likely that different causes at different levels will be responsible for different aspects of the complex event we call "the end of the Cold War"; and that any explanation will contribute to a general understanding of politics only as it is integrated with other findings about other cases.

These assumptions may sound like social-scientific truisms, but it is remarkable how often scholars of international relations write as if they do not accept them. For decades, international relations scholars discussed the problem of explanation according to the three "images" or "levels of analysis": the individual; the state; and the international system.[13] Partly because theoretical debates were linked to disputes about policy in the Cold War, and partly because of the natural tendency in any debate to overstate one's position, many scholars argued that one level of analysis is somehow "primary." This led to the inevitable retort that, no, it is really some other level that "matters" and that needs to be "brought back in" to the analysis. For anyone involved in the empirical study of international politics, this sort of debate is beside the point. All levels "matter" to different degrees at different times. Further, all levels interact, making them hard to separate empirically. For example, the international system (conceived of either as an abstract "structure" or more prosaically as the concrete actions of other states) may influence a state's domestic politics.[14] And there are plainly many more than three levels. The domestic political system (level 2), for instance, obviously contains many levels itself, including bureaucracies, economic interests, and ideologies.

The important issue for scholars and policy makers is to determine which levels of analysis tell us what information about any given event or class of events. In a complex world, no theory that says anything meaningful can be true all the time, and no policy can be right for all situations. As Jervis's and George's earlier work has demonstrated, the main task for scholars is to determine the conditions under which different theories capture important causal relationships, in order to lay a foundation for suggesting the policies that are most likely to work.[15] Part of that task is determining what causes were at work in key cases in which particular policies were applied.

The chapters that follow begin this investigation in the crucial case of the end of the Cold War.

In chapter 7, Fred Greenstein argues that the end of the Cold War is an example of a very consequential event in which top decision makers were influenced but not strongly constrained by either the domestic or the international system. If leaders have some autonomy in reacting to the conditions they face, then what they do depends in part on who they are. If this was true of the Cold War's end, then both scholars and politicians need to exercise care in drawing general lessons from the case. And if international politics consists of many such crucially important events whose outcomes depend on the personalities of key decision makers, then many scholars will have to rethink their essential approach to theory-building. Heavy investments in complicated and mathematically elegant deductive structures that are supposed to model the choice calculus of any and all decision makers may yield poor returns. And the assumption that personality effects "wash out of" the explanation if large numbers of decisions are analyzed may offer small comfort if the importance of personality can be shown to be large in such history-making events as the end of the Cold War.

Greenstein documents the effects of key personalities on the emergence of cooperation throughout the series of superpower interactions from 1983 to 1989. On the American side, for example, the initial impulse to cooperate stemmed in part from Reagan's personality and even predated Gorbachev's arrival on the scene; the political ability to cooperate was provided by Reagan's total invulnerability to charges of being "soft on the Russians"; the organizational ability to translate Reagan's proclivities into action and get the unwieldy American government to effect a turn toward cooperation was due in large part to George Shultz's determination and practical Washingtonian savvy; and the ultimate success of the negotiations was partly due to the personal rapport that developed between the two leaders and their diplomatic teams. The experienced decision makers who gathered in Princeton had no doubts about the importance of personality. They spontaneously cited numerous instances in which they had perceived strong personality effects at work in overcoming domestic resistance to international cooperation and in reaching compromises at the bargaining table.

Jervis, in chapter 8, focuses on another powerful strain of evidence to which the Princeton Conference participants returned repeatedly: the convergence in perceptions of the two superpowers' decision-making elites. Jervis identifies a set of perceptual processes that had kept the two sides "living in different worlds" throughout the Cold War, complicating all efforts to cooperate. A large body of empirical scholarship—much of it inspired by Jervis's earlier work—documents the vast gap between Soviet and American self-images, views of each other, and views of the international situation during the Cold War. The Princeton Conference and other new sources on the end of the Cold War document how, after 1985, the two sides began to see each other and the world in increasingly similar ways, easing the path to agreements on the issues. But Jervis cautions that the causal role of changes in perceptions is unclear and may be difficult to establish. Changed perceptions may correlate with changes in policy but may themselves be caused by other changes in material interests. Gorbachev may have called forth the New Thinking to justify a policy he felt compelled to adopt to meet domestic or international challenges.

This brings us to George's analysis of Soviet intellectual change in chapter 9. George agrees with Jervis and Greenstein that the international environment of the mid-1980s was permissive. The superpowers could have adapted to those same circumstances in many different ways. But the striking feature of the Cold War's end, according to George, was the Soviet political elite's unusually "creative adaptation" to the circumstances it found itself in: a wholesale revision of the previous class-struggle ideology. Thus, the perceptual convergence that Jervis discusses was precipitated in large part by intellectual change on the Soviet side, change that helped convince the Americans that something new and important was afoot which distinguished this from the previous experience of détente. George acknowledges the key role that Gorbachev played in this revolution of ideas but stresses that it is necessary to explain the revolution's widespread acceptance among the Soviet political elite. Gorbachev's leadership skills and the Soviet Union's domestic travails were important in winning adherents to the New Thinking, but so too was the plausibility of the ideas themselves, given the Soviet elite's experience in international politics. In other words, a complex process of political learning which transcended the immediate instrumental needs of the moment must form part of the explanation.

Most participants in and early chroniclers of these events agree that the factors highlighted by Greenstein, Jervis, and George lie at the heart of any explanation.[16] Further, most agree that "second image" factors will loom largest in accounting for the turn. Domestic constraints, changing configurations of political and economic interests, political learning based on accumulated decades of experience trying various policies, and innovative leadership all seem to outweigh the more amorphous causes featured in systemic theories of international politics. But it is also true that all these changes took place in an international context of bipolarity, Soviet decline, secure nuclear deterrence, relative prosperity among the Western allies and Japan, and the "information revolution" about which Shultz enthused to Gorbachev so frequently. Further, the two superpowers reacted to initiatives by important allied leaders such as Margaret Thatcher, Helmut Kohl, and François Mitterrand—inspired in part by their own personalities and domestic imperatives—as well as the activities of peace movements on both sides of the East-West divide. All these factors constitute the raw material of an explanation; the difficulty is in assembling them in the proper order and mixing them in the proper amounts.[17]

The daunting complexity of the Cold War's end highlights one of the toughest questions for empirical researchers seeking general knowledge about international politics: whether causes at various levels can be identified separately and added up to a whole explanation.[18] We can and should show the causal importance of individuals, perceptions, ideas, domestic constraints, and many other factors. But can we show how much each matters for the specific aspects of the events or phenomena we wish to explain? As noted, reaching some judgment of the causal importance of various levels is a virtual requirement of settling the theoretical and policy disputes that swirl around the ending of Cold War. Using the Princeton Conference transcripts, other sources on the end of the Cold War, and the insights provided by Greenstein, Jervis, and George, I turn to these issues in the final chapter.

Chapter Seven

Ronald Reagan, Mikhail Gorbachev, and the End of the Cold War

What Difference Did They Make?

FRED I. GREENSTEIN

One was clearly a visionary, the other was a tactician. One liked detail, the master of the subject; the other had a few broad principles that he abided by, and those were almost immutable. One liked to tell jokes; the other, while he had a sense of humor, was not particularly interested in telling jokes. One liked to talk from his own handwritten notes; the other, the sooner he could get the notes out of the way and get on with the more informal conversation, the better he liked it. The one had an abiding interest in human rights questions; the other one wanted to get on the major subject of arms control. And the amazing thing is that the alchemy between these two disparate personalities seemed to work, that it somehow came together.

> Frank Carlucci III, former secretary of defense
> and national security advisor

In Geneva, in Reykjavik, we were getting more and more open to each other, and this pattern of interrelationship existed for the rest of the presidency. I think a lot of things were done just because we were open to each other. We could sometimes tell each other things which in normal diplomatic practice would not be said. You would say, "Listen, this is the limit. We just can't go beyond it because of this and that reason. Here we can maneuver. Let's try it." So I would agree that one of the major elements of changing the Cold War was changing ourselves. We were the products of the Cold War, all of us. But we became softened by the new realities.

> Alexander Bessmertnykh,
> former Soviet deputy foreign minister

It is common to assume that events of momentous proportions and consequences must be the result of large historical forces that dwarf the human agents who take part in them. The sequence of decisions and nondecisions that brought about the dramatic and unexpected reduction of Cold War tensions during the second term of President Ronald Reagan provides a fascinating body of evidence for testing such Tolstoyan assumptions.

This chapter explores the role of personality in the rapid transformation of relations between the Soviet Union and the United States in the period from Mikhail Gorbachev's accession as general secretary of the Soviet Communist Party in March 1985 to the end of the Reagan presidency in January 1989, the year that was to see the collapse of Communism in Eastern Europe, which was to be followed two years later by the collapse of the Soviet Union. My main focus is on Reagan and Gorbachev, but I will also discuss the parts played by various of their key subordinates, most notably American secretary of state George P. Shultz and Soviet foreign minister Eduard Shevardnadze.

My interest is not only in Reagan and Gorbachev themselves but also in the unfolding relationship between them and, more generally, between the two nations' leadership teams. As I shall argue, the development of often-quite-personal links among the individuals who led the United States and the Soviet Union was one of the most significant outcomes of the East-West diplomatic activity of the period that concerns us. The importance of personal chemistry in the superpower politics of the late 1980s is a pervasive and unexpected theme in the discussions reported in this volume. Virtually to a man and woman, these participant observers testify to the extent to which the striking improvement in relations between their nations was accompanied by the growth of warm, friendly relations between the two groups of national representatives. Putting it differently, persons who had hitherto been viewed as mere representatives of their systems emerged from their stereotypes as flesh-and-blood individuals. This transmutation appears to have been not just an offshoot of the intense diplomatic activity of President Reagan's second term but a contributor to its outcome.

In reviewing the events of the Reagan-Gorbachev years, I make no assumption that all the details of my historical account will stand the test of time. Much presently unavailable evidence has yet to emerge. Still, a great deal is already known, and we need not wait for a fuller historical record to clarify the conceptual issues raised by the problem at hand. As a specialist in political psychology and the American presidency, I devote more attention to the better-documented American side of the story than to the Soviet side, drawing on the Princeton discussions that are reported in this volume, as well as Don Oberdorfer's interview-based reconstruction of the events in question, the expanding body of memoirs and other primary source records of the Reagan presidency, and the emerging scholarly literature on the end of the Cold War, especially Raymond Garthoff's systematic mining of American and Soviet sources.[1]

My concern with human agency should convey no implication that political actors are unmoved movers. Quite the contrary. Without contextual preconditions, without environments that are at least pervious to human intervention, even the most gifted leader can make no mark. A devastating forest fire may be the result of a human agent, but there is little likelihood of such a conflagration in a rainforest. Moreover, much of the impact of leaders takes the form of unintended consequences and therefore does not constitute leadership in the grander sense of informed strategic action.

Assumptions and Conceptual Distinctions

What is entailed in the claim that some individual has been historically consequential? When we say that an individual has had an impact on a particular historical outcome, we usually mean that three conditions have been met: the individual's actions were not ones we would have expected from other similarly situated actors, the actions were ones that made a difference for the outcome, and the outcome was important.

There is no doubt about the importance of the end of the Cold War. The outcome of the events in which Ronald Reagan and Mikhail Gorbachev were central protagonists could scarcely have been more significant for a world that had existed for four decades in a precarious equilibrium that at any point could have been shattered by a nuclear apocalypse. There also is no doubt about the capacity of each of the two men to take consequential actions. In the United States, the ubiquity of the military aide who carries the "football" that would enable the president to trigger the nation's nuclear arsenal is a reminder of the chief executive's ability to take autonomous action, even though in many areas of policy he also is subject to the powerful constraints on a chief executive in a pluralistic democracy. The specifics of nuclear command and control in the former Soviet Union are less well known, but the Russian participants at the Princeton Conference confirmed that Mikhail Gorbachev also had a very substantial capacity for independent decision making during much of the period that concerns us.[2]

It is less evident, however, how one can even address the question of whether, and to what extent, the individual leadership qualities of the two national leaders made a difference. In effect, the claim that a leader's personal qualities mattered in a particular historical outcome is a counterfactual proposition about a universe of potentially available leaders who might have figured in the events that led to that outcome. The presumption is that at least some, and possibly all, members of that universe would have acted differently from the leader in question in the given circumstances. Such thought experiments are the very stuff of assertions about historical causality, even though many historians (including some who implicitly engage in them) deny their utility.

Thought experiments have a bad name, in large part because many of them posit complex and unverifiable chains of causality. But thought experiments about specific, short-run causal links are another matter. Their very stipulation can be the first step toward clarifying questions about historical causality and suggesting the means of addressing them. Consider, for example, the claim of some analysts of the American involvement in Vietnam in the 1960s that the U.S. military intervention in that nation was an inevitable consequence of the realities of the American political system, which works to prevent leaders from taking actions that may be desirable in the long run but that are politically unpopular in the short run.[3] That claim, with its implication that the particular characteristics of President Johnson and his associates made little difference, is too broad to be subjected to systematic examination. But it implies a variety of more concrete claims about specific short-run links in American decision making on Vietnam during that period.

Rather than debating in general terms about whether American intervention in Vietnam was inevitable, it is more instructive to look at particular turning points in the American intervention. Episodes that are appropriate candidates for such analysis include President Lyndon Johnson's initial authorization of the bombing of North Vietnam in February 1965 and his incremental commitments of ground troops in the subsequent months of that year. The hypothesis that Johnson did (or did not) "have" to take those actions cannot be falsified in any strict sense, but it *is* subject to an appeal to evidence. Editorials and interpretative news stories in the leading newspapers and periodicals, for example, shed light on whether the climate of opinion in the political community mandated Johnson's actions. And the record of deliberations in Johnson's advisory circle provides evidence of whether the necessity of those actions was self-evident to other similarly situated political actors.[4]

The foregoing example has a number of implications for the problem at hand. One of them is that it is essential to assess the context in which the actions and events of concern took place. Under some circumstances, the political context is sufficiently unstructured to leave room for different actors to vary in the actions they take. But other situations virtually dictate some courses of action and preclude others. (No conceivable American president would have proposed a wait-and-see policy in the immediate aftermath of Pearl Harbor.) If it seems evident that a leader's political environment dictated a particular course of action, there is little reason to ask what difference that individual's personal qualities made for the action.

Another implication is that it is essential to establish precisely *what* outcome is to be explained. In the present instance it is not particularly instructive to ask in the abstract whether the personal qualities of the American and the Soviet leaders of the late 1980s contributed to the improvement in relations between their nations. There needs to be a further specification of the particular outcomes to be accounted for. Since the aim of such an analysis is to assess the impact of individuals, a further implication is that the leadership qualities of those individuals must be identified. Finally, other relevant actors in the events and outcomes under consideration must be examined, including any who might under other circumstances have been available to fill the positions of the leaders being assessed.[5]

The Political Context in March 1985

The sea change in Soviet-American relations during the second half of the 1980s was clearly *not* a necessary consequence of the political context in which the United States and the Soviet Union found themselves at the time of Gorbachev's accession in March 1985. At that time, Soviet-American relations were marked by mutual suspicion and wariness, as they had been since 1979, when the Soviet invasion of Afghanistan spelled an end to the détente that had prevailed since early in the decade. While the two sides took a number of steps in the direction of improved relations in 1984, that movement was cautious and inconclusive.

Reagan had entered office in January 1981 committed to the premise that the Soviet Union had for some time been engaged in a massive military buildup, leaving the United States in an increasingly unfavorable strategic position that he was bent on reversing. In 1981 he proposed and Congress approved a full 10-percent increase in American military spending. From the Soviet standpoint, the new administration's words were as provocative as its deeds. Its strategic planners advanced doctrines that called for the United States to go beyond mutual deterrence and acquire the capacity to "prevail" in the event of war with the Soviet Union, doctrines that were paralleled by those of Soviet military theorists who advocated a "war fighting" strategy.

President Reagan himself oscillated between making rather general statements about the necessity of maintaining peaceful relations with the Soviet Union and castigating the Soviets in terms that denied the very legitimacy of their political system. His anti-Soviet rhetoric had primacy in the early years of his presidency. In his first press conference, Reagan appeared even to rule out workaday relations with the Soviets, dismissing détente as "a one-way street that the Soviet Union has used to pursue its own aims." As late as March 8, 1983, in one of the most widely publicized speeches of his presidency, Reagan denounced the Soviet Union as "the focus of evil in the modern world" and declared that since the leaders of the Soviet Union were "good Marxist-Leninists . . . the only morality" they recognized was "that which will advance their cause, which is world revolution."[6]

Even more provocative from the Soviet standpoint than Reagan's "evil empire" speech was his advocacy, later in the same month, of a revolutionary new space-based strategic weapons defense system. Reagan himself appears to have viewed the proposed Strategic Defense Initiative (SDI) as a defensive shield that would remove the dangers of nuclear war, but his proposal had precisely the opposite significance for the Soviets. In their view, the American aim was to extend the arms race into space, force massive new military expenditures on the Soviet Union, and eliminate its capacity to deter an American nuclear strike.

Initially, the Soviet leadership was slow to respond. Soviet restraint appears to have been a function of the disarray of the Soviet leadership in a period when the health of Communist Party general secretary Leonid Brezhnev was failing. It also seems to have resulted from a Soviet tendency to discount public professions of anti-Communism on the part of American politicians, which led Soviet leaders to hope that the new chief executive would prove to be another Richard Nixon, whose public castigations of Communism were a cover for arriving at a modus vivendi with the Soviet Union. In November 1982, however, just two weeks before his death, Brezhnev responded in kind to the anti-Soviet pronouncements of the Reagan administration, declaring that "the ruling circles of the United States of America have launched a political, ideological, and economic offensive on socialism and have raised their military preparations to an unprecedented level."[7]

During the brief tenure of Brezhnev's successor Yuri Andropov, relations deteriorated further. On September 1, 1983, the regularly scheduled Korean Air Lines flight KAL 007 was shot down by a Soviet fighter plane and all of its 269 passengers were killed. The resulting recriminations on both sides were of unprecedented virulence. In the following month, the Soviet Union withdrew from disarmament negotiations to protest the planned deployment of intermediate-range missiles in Western Europe. For the first time in twelve years there were no ongoing arms reductions discussions between the two nations. So great had Soviet distrust of American intentions become by the end of 1983 that in November, when NATO forces conducted a routine test of the procedures for release of nuclear weapons in the event of war, the KGB appears to have instructed its agents in Western Europe to be alert for signs of an imminent attack.[8]

In 1984, during the even briefer tenure of Konstantin Chernenko as general secretary, the superpowers inched back from the brink. President Reagan made a number of addresses in which the accent was on the two nations' common interest in finding a means to end their mutual enmity. Similar statements were made by Soviet leaders. In spite of the resistance of hard-liners in his administration, Reagan held a highly publicized White House conference with Soviet foreign minister Gromyko on September 28, 1984, the first such meeting of his presidency. Some time thereafter, the two nations agreed to explore the resumption of arms talks. But these halting steps toward improved relations were not sufficient to reverse the overall deterioration in relations of the previous three years.

As President Reagan entered his second term and still another Soviet general secretary, Mikhail Sergeevich Gorbachev, appeared on the scene, the circumstances in which the leaders found themselves were unsettled and uncertain. They were as conducive to a return to the confrontation of the previous three years as to the mutual accommodation of the 1970s. Certainly there was no expectation that change of the magnitude of that of the next several years was even conceivable. Instead, as Raymond Garthoff points out, there was a whole series of imponderables. It was not clear whether President Reagan and his associates would make a genuine effort to negotiate, especially on arms control. It was equally unclear whether the Soviet leaders would "recognize and accept a serious Reagan interest in dialogue and negotiation." And it was uncertain whether each side would understand the perspective of the other well enough to negotiate with any degree of success.[9]

What Changed between 1985 and 1989?

World War II ended unambiguously in Europe on May 7, 1945, and in the Pacific on September 2 of that year. The undeclared Korean War ended on July 27, 1953, with the signing of an armistice at Panmunjom. It is far less evident what it means to speak of the end of the Cold War, a confrontation that was a war in name only.

It of course made no sense to continue to speak of the existence of a Cold War after December 1991, when the Soviet Union itself no longer existed. But in January 1989, when President Reagan stepped down, it was not even anticipated that the Communist governments of Eastern Europe would all be gone by the end of the year, much less that the days of the Soviet Union were numbered. Still, by the standards of all but a few observers it was plain that Soviet-American relations had undergone a night-and-day improvement between 1985 and 1989.

Some of the change took the form of concrete agreements. In December 1987, the Soviet and American leaders signed the first Cold War treaty that actually mandated a reduction in nuclear arms, the Intermediate-Range Nuclear Forces (INF) Treaty. In December 1988 Gorbachev announced a unilateral five-hundred-thousand-troop reduction in Soviet military force levels and declared that henceforth the Soviet Union was renouncing "the use or threat of force" to advance its interests. The INF agreement reduced the nuclear arsenals of the United States and the Soviet Union by only 4 percent, however, and Gorbachev's 1988 actions still left the Soviet Union with a huge military establishment.

The great bulk of the change in superpower relations during the second term of the Reagan presidency took less tangible forms than arms control agreements and efforts to reduce force levels. In large part it consisted of transformations in mind-sets, perceptions, and expectations. Where suspicion and animosity had been, guarded trust and goodwill came to be. One indicator of that change was the responses of the much-surveyed American public in opinion polls. By 1989, Americans were giving more favorable ratings to Mikhail Gorbachev than to many American public figures. Americans had come to view the Soviet Union in glowing terms that were reminiscent of the high point of Soviet-American amity during World War II.[10] But changes in public attitudes were mainly a function of changes in the attitudes of the leaders of the two nations and the way they and their nations came to relate to each other.

As the testimony of the Princeton Conference participants makes evident, the new relationships themselves were a significant part of the change. For at least some of the actors, those links came to be deeply personal and individual. To this I shall return. But much of the change was at the level of routines and working arrangements. From the top down, communications became more frequent, more open, and less inhibited by earlier strictures. Ronald Reagan, who met with *no* Soviet general secretary during his first term and did not meet the Soviet foreign minister until 1984, participated in four highly publicized summit meetings and one additional gathering with Mikhail Gorbachev during the course of his second term, with results that were both tangible and intangible.

The 1985 Geneva Summit was not an occasion for serious negotiations, but it conveyed the symbolism of a new beginning. The 1986 Reykjavik Summit more than made up for the absence of negotiations the previous year. It witnessed a veritable frenzy of high-stakes bargaining as the two sides debated (but finally rejected) the revolutionary possibility of scrapping their nations' nuclear arsenals. The 1987 Washington Summit saw the signing of the INF Treaty. Capping the sequence, the 1988 Moscow Summit was marked not only by the exchange of final INF documents but also by the spectacle of the two leaders ambling through Red Square and Reagan's disavowal of his characterization of the Soviet Union as an evil empire. ("I was talking about another time, another era.")[11]

The Reagan-Gorbachev meetings were the most visible manifestation of a burgeoning of diplomatic activity, at a variety of levels, in which the two foreign ministers played a crucial part. One of Gorbachev's earliest acts after assuming power was to appoint Eduard Shevardnadze as foreign minister. That intensely idealistic, outgoing Georgian could scarcely have been less like his predecessor, Andrei Gromyko. Shevardnadze was without prior experience or commitments in the area of foreign policy, but he and Gorbachev were friends and fellow New Thinkers, and Shevardnadze undoubtedly had other qualities that commended him to Gorbachev. Secretary of State George Shultz immediately reached out to establish a personal bond with his Soviet counterpart. Before long, the two had entered into a remarkably open relationship in which position-taking progressively yielded to mutual efforts at problem solving.[12]

Developments within the two nations contributed to the growing concord between them. Even before 1988, when the Soviet leadership showed how thoroughly it was breaking with the past by announcing that all Soviet troops would be withdrawn from Afghanistan, the dizzying pace of change in Soviet politics and society had already begun to have a potent demonstration effect in the West. It was difficult for Westerners to remain distrustful of a Soviet Union whose highest official bore so little resemblance to the medal-bedecked apparatchiks of the past and in which Soviet politicians of varying convictions could be seen on television in unscripted debate, even criticizing the general secretary of the Communist Party. The appearance of so different a Soviet reality reduced the tendency of American and other Western leaders to make statements that the Soviets viewed as provocative. And the Soviets were further reassured when it became clear that in the changed international climate, the Strategic Defense Initiative was unlikely to be funded at a level that would make it a serious threat.

The course of improvement did not run smooth. As late as the eve of the 1988 Moscow Summit, the speech-writing staff of the Reagan White House (a bastion of hard-liners) provided the president with an anti-Soviet oration, which Reagan then dutifully delivered. There were other setbacks, such as the arrests of the Soviet physicist Gennadi Zakharov and the American journalist Nicholas Daniloff in 1986 and the controversy in 1987 over whether the Soviet Union had penetrated the U.S. Embassy in Moscow. It was in connection with such potential disruptions that relationships came into play—both the diplomatic working arrangements to which Alexander Bessmertnykh refers in these pages and more personal affinities.[13]

At one level, the sheer existence of a continuing process of negotiations provided what Bessmertnykh describes as a "safety net" by providing forums in which damage control could come into play when untoward events occurred. At another and somewhat more personal level, the leaders on both sides came to know their counterparts well enough to give one another the benefit of the doubt in situations that might have led to confrontations in the past. Thus, when President Reagan's 1988 anti-Soviet speech (which had not been cleared with the secretary of state) reached Gorbachev, his initial response was outrage. Then, as his foreign affairs advisor Chernyaev reports, he noted that the American negotiators who were meeting with him at the time did not "rush to defend their president." Putting a favorable light on the matter, Gorbachev concluded that "there was something wrong" in Reagan's speech—it "was not in the spirit of the kind of work that we have done together."[14]

As Bessmertnykh points out, the evolving personal relationships between diplomats on the two sides made it increasingly possible for them to "tell each other things which in normal diplomatic practice would not be said . . . 'Listen, this is the limit . . . Here we can maneuver.'" On a similar note, Shultz comments that "the Reagan-

Gorbachev relationship was not based on these two leaders going out of their way to accommodate each other. On the contrary, I felt that Gorbachev laid it on the line and so did Reagan. One reason they respected each other was that they both could see that the other guy was saying what he thought."[15]

But there was a still more personal level at which relations between the two groups improved. At the Princeton Conference there was repeated testimony to the genuine nature of the attachments that were formed across national lines. Secretary Shultz *and* his wife became personal friends with *Mrs.* Shevardnadze as well as her husband. General Secretary Gorbachev chastised aides who made fun of President Reagan's reliance on cue cards in negotiations. Gorbachev went out of his way to pay a visit to Reagan in California at a time when the latter was no longer in office and such a trip was not a political necessity. Personal bonds such as those forged between the two groups of leaders are likely to have political consequences. It is possible to envisage mutually assured destruction as a means of deterring an impersonal representative of an alien political system; it is repugnant to rely upon such a mechanism when that individual is a genuine friend.[16]

Personalities and Their Impact

From what has preceded, it should be evident that the metamorphosis of the Soviet-American relationship during the second half of the 1980s was multifaceted and multiply determined. So far, I have recounted that transformation without focusing directly on the qualities of its agents, but now the stage is set for their consideration.

Stated baldly, my argument is as follows: The redirection of international relations of the late 1980s could not have occurred without structural preconditions, the most obvious of which was the dire condition of the Soviet economy and Soviet society, which had been in extended decline for many years and which were further taxed by the demands placed on them by the Reagan administration's military buildup.[17] Mention should also be made of the norms and institutions of authoritarian political systems, which contributed to Gorbachev's ability in the early period of his incumbency to neutralize opponents of his policies.[18] But that alteration did not have to take place when it occurred, and it did not have to take place peacefully. It might have been thwarted, and violence might have ensued within the Soviet Union or between the Soviet Union and the United States if there had been a different outcome to the succession struggles within the Soviet Union during the early and mid-1980s and Mikhail Gorbachev had not emerged as general secretary of the Communist Party of the Soviet Union.

Gorbachev was a necessary but not sufficient agent of change. His impact, which was as much an unintended as an intended consequence of his actions, depended not only on structural circumstances but also on the unexpected and seemingly out-of-character contributions of Ronald Reagan. And Reagan, who in one sense was the overpowering presence in his own presidency, was in another sense a political innocent who required skilled assistance in whatever he sought to accomplish. He had that in the person of his often-beleaguered secretary of state, George Shultz, whose steady, clear-headed direction of American foreign policy was crucial to the turn in the Cold War. None of the foregoing actors were ciphers in a deterministic political process. At every stage, they encountered the disagreement and opposition of various of their contemporaries. Those individuals, if they had been placed in the positions of the three above-mentioned leaders, would almost certainly have behaved differently and in so doing would have altered the course of events.

How a leader with as open a personality and as much openness to political innovation as Mikhail Gorbachev "could have emerged from a provincial Party apparatus in the north Caucasus," or indeed could have emerged at all in the Soviet Union, has puzzled even observers who devote their careers to the analysis of Soviet politics.[19] The question is outside the competence of a student of the American presidency. One need not be a Soviet specialist, however, to recognize that Mikhail Gorbachev was far removed from the typical, hidebound products of the Soviet political system and that he was endowed with exceptional leadership skills.

To a student of the American presidency, that son of a Soviet peasant farmer bears a surprising resemblance to an American scion of a rural patrician family: Franklin Delano Roosevelt. Both were highly tactical reform politicians who lacked detailed overall preconceptions of the end-states they proposed to bring about. Both nevertheless were acutely aware of their nation's shortcomings and sought to seize whatever opportunities they could find to remedy them, even when it was not certain what the precise outcome of their efforts would be. Roosevelt appears to have taken office without an explicit legislative program and probably even without the intention to convene the epochal One Hundred Days legislative session of early 1933, which produced a deluge of New Deal reform legislation. Gorbachev too seems to have assumed power without a detailed blueprint. His foreign policy departures appear to have initially been by-products of his efforts at domestic reform, and even the latter were not clearly foreshadowed by his initial statements and actions.[20]

Both men had conventional beliefs for their times and contexts. FDR never rejected capitalism and Gorbachev continued to view himself as a socialist, even after the failed coup against him in the summer of 1991 foreshadowed his fall from power and the imminent demise of the Soviet Union. But their acceptance of the dogmas and assumptions of their milieus did not prevent the two men from being proactive (as well as active) and from being prepared to take the lead in changing their respective nations in ways that would have been unlikely in the extreme if other potentially available leaders had taken their places. If, for example, the would-be assassin who narrowly failed to take Roosevelt's life in February 1933 had succeeded, it is unlikely that the sweeping domestic innovations that constituted the New Deal would have come into being, and it is even possible that the United States would have succumbed to authoritarian rule or internal war. If the Soviet leadership had selected virtually any member of its inner circle other than Mikhail Gorbachev as general secretary in March 1985, it is likely that the Soviet Union would have limped along for additional decades very much as it had in the era in which Leonid Brezhnev was general secretary.

Unlike FDR, Gorbachev lacked mass appeal, but he was not without charismatic qualities within his own inner circle. Just as a Roosevelt aide declared that FDR seemed to have been "psychoanalyzed by God," the ex-Soviet participants in the Princeton Conference attributed out-of-the-ordinary, if somewhat less awesome, qualities to their chief. Chernyaev describes Gorbachev as a "morally and ethically and also physically . . . very healthy man," whose "general health as an individual . . . helped him . . . to abandon Marxist-Leninist orthodoxy and to adopt a policy of common sense." Bessmertnykh refers to Gorbachev as a role model whose personal example led his aides to abandon the rigidities of Cold-War diplomacy: "He was an absolutely new type of top leader. He was absolutely human, accessible—a man who could love, who could curse, who could use good and unprintable language. He was an absolutely normal man, very intellectual at the same time and knowledgeable."[21]

If there is a question about how a leader with Mikhail Gorbachev's political skill and capacity for innovation could have arisen in the Soviet Union, there is an even more puzzling question about how an individual with Ronald Reagan's seeming limitations could have played a significant part in the momentous events that spelled the beginning of the end of the Cold War. That actor-publicist-ideologue, whose muddled responses to journalists' questions bespoke the most rudimentary acquaintance with his own administration's policies, is an improbable candidate for the role of historical prime mover. The short answer is that while Reagan was the antithesis of a "detail man," he had other qualities (some of which are more common among "real people" than among politicians) that account for his contribution to the Cold War endgame. These qualities were parts of a political style that (more so than the styles of most politicians) was not all of a piece.

Ronald Reagan's political style differed sharply in its public and private manifestations, and the latter were themselves markedly differentiated. In his public capacity as his administration's chief spokesman and salesman, Reagan was the model of a presidential activist. In veteran Reagan-watcher Lou Cannon's phrase: for Ronald Reagan the presidency was "the role of a lifetime."[22] In this century, only the two Roosevelts, Woodrow Wilson, and John F. Kennedy were Reagan's match as presidential communicators. If, however, Reagan was the star performer of his presidency, he was also its producer. He may not have composed the detailed script of his administration or directed every scene, but his values and his premises, no matter how vaguely articulated, were at the core of its policies.

In the more private aspects of presidential leadership, Reagan was in some respects breathtakingly passive. This was especially the case in connection with the largely off-the-record activities through which an administration determines the specifics of its policies, strategies, and implementation procedures. The many memoirs of his presidency are consistent in their testimony to the extent to which Reagan was uninformed about and inattentive to much of the specific content of policy. Perhaps the most telling evidence of Reagan's remoteness from policy and political specifics comes from the commission led by Senator John Tower which Reagan himself appointed to look into the Iran-Contra affair. The commission conducted extensive interviews within the Reagan administration and had detailed access to classified information, and it concluded that Reagan had been abysmally uninformed about such matters as the diversion of arms profits to the Contras and the case of the sale to Iran. He had been inattentive not only to the minutiae of his administration's operations, but also to their broad outlines. As a result, he had permitted members of the White House staff to pursue policies that were internally inconsistent and contrary to his administration's overall objectives.[23]

Yet in spite of his failure to master a good bit of the content of his administration's policies and politics, Reagan had a number of qualities that enhanced his ability to win the confidence of the Soviet general secretary, who eventually receded from his demand that SDI be confined to the laboratory and agreed to move ahead on arms control negotiations. Reagan had the courage of his convictions, but he also was amazingly open-minded for a putative ideologue. It did not bother him that so many of his advisors were appalled at his antinuclear views. Neither his distrust of the motives of the Soviets nor the attitudes of his conservative aides prevented him from seeking to win over Gorbachev. His efforts in that connection were advanced by his ingratiating manner and style, his skill as a negotiator,[24] and his readiness to participate in the promulgation of his administration's policies. By his manner and his actions, he provided a permissive climate in which Gorbachev could continue his domestic and international initiatives. A less forthcoming president might well have created a siege mentality on the part of the Soviet leadership and in so doing discouraged Gorbachev and his associates from bringing about change.

Reagan also radiated an idealism that appears gradually to have contributed to reassuring Gorbachev of his intentions and those of the United States, perhaps in part because it contrasted so sharply with the rhetoric and policies that had marked his first term. In a curious sense, the absence on Reagan's part of the sophistication that is commonly taken to be a hallmark of effective leadership worked to his advantage by freeing him from commitments to the status quo.

As the Soviet specialist on American politics Alexander Bovin put it, Reagan was not the sort of professional politician who "slices off small bits of decisions, bit by bit." Instead, he was "a figure with a bold approach and a keen intuition, even if he did not understand many of the important details."[25]

The best account of how the disparate elements of Reagan's style fit together is that of his first-term domestic policy advisor, the economist Martin Anderson. To begin with, Anderson points out, Reagan's strong general convictions enabled him to set his administration's general priorities. Everyone knew that he placed the defense buildup and the economic program ahead of everything else. What was far less well known is that he had other, quite different convictions that would also shape his administration's policies. In particular, his strongly anti-Soviet views prove to have been combined with equally strong antinuclear convictions and a more general belief in the desirability of finding a means to coexist with the Soviet Union without relying upon nuclear deterrence to do so.[26]

Anderson also points out that as strong as Reagan's tenets were, he was nevertheless tactically flexible, showing no remorse when he had to adjust to political opposition. This contributed to his ability as a negotiator, in that he set his demands higher than the minimum he would accept and accepted what he could get. Moreover, the remarkable self-confidence to which Secretary Shultz referred at the Princeton Conference appears to have enabled Reagan to make decisions easily and promptly. And the basic humility to which Jack Matlock alluded undoubtedly contributed to another of his qualities—a willingness to delegate authority.

But delegation, Anderson observes, was Reagan's Achilles heel. Reagan's practice was to make decisions on the basis of the options his aides presented to him. He neither questioned those options nor refined or shaped them himself. Therefore, when he had competent aides, as in his first term and in those foreign policy actions in which George Shultz was preeminent, things tended to go well. When his aides were deficient, as was the case with the triumvirate of Donald Regan, John Poindexter, and Oliver North in the Iran-Contra affair, the results could be catastrophic.[27]

Ronald Reagan was consequential for the winding down of the Cold War not just because of *what* he was but also because of *who* he was. As several of the conference participants stress, Reagan was uniquely situated to lead the United States and the Soviet Union to accommodation. He was so well known for his intense, vociferous anti-Communism, and he did so much to reinforce this image in his first term in office, that he was for all intents and purposes invulnerable to attack from the right for seeking accommodation with the Soviet Union. The failed efforts by hard-liners to make such attacks do, however, show the limitations that would have been encountered by a centrist president or even by a president such as George Bush, who was suspected of being a closet centrist.

The quintessentially conventional George Bush is instructive in other respects. As we have seen, Reagan's accommodating approach to the Soviet Union encountered regular opposition from within his own administration. Bush was one of the skeptics, at times even abandoning his usual cautiousness and publicly voicing his skepticism about whether there had been significant change in the Soviet threat. There is good reason to believe that the man who would have been Reagan's successor if the 1981 attempt on Reagan's life had succeeded would have been less prepared than Reagan was to come to terms with the Soviets in the period that concerns us. The actions that Bush took immediately after entering office indicate as much. His response was to step back, institute what became known as "the pause" in East-West relations, and wait for the dust to settle.[28]

It remains to add the two foreign secretaries to the picture. Shevardnadze was less influential than Shultz. It served Gorbachev's purposes to employ an associate with Shevardnadze's political skills and flexibility as foreign minister, but precisely because Gorbachev was so much of a force in and of himself, Shevardnadze did not have a substantial independent effect on events during the period that concerns us. He was, however, a remarkable figure. What other leader of an established power would have been as disposed as Shevardnadze was to confront his associates with a fundamental moral and intellectual challenge to the very principles under which their nation operated?

The belief that we are a great country and that we should be respected for this is deeply ingrained in me, as in everyone. But great in what? Territory? Population? Quantity of arms? Or the people's troubles? The individual's lack of rights? Life's disorderliness? In what do we who have the highest infant mortality rate on our planet take pride? It is not easy answering such questions: Who are you and who do you wish to be? A country which is feared or a country which is respected? A country of power or a country of kindness?[29]

George Shultz *did* have an important and distinctive impact. His actions were informed not only by his unusually extensive background as a player in Washington bureaucratic politics but also by his training as an economist and his experience as a labor mediator. Moreover, he had an influence on Gorbachev as well as on Reagan. Shultz's impact on Gorbachev (to which Gorbachev's aide Chernyaev testified at the Princeton Conference) was at the intellectual level. Shultz took the unusual tack of playing the part of pedagogue with Gorbachev, providing the Soviet leader with what in effect was a continuing tutorial on developments in the global economy, even preparing charts on trends in world economics for Gorbachev's instruction. Shultz was seeking (as one of the secretary of state's aides put it) to "get inside of Gorbachev's mind" and persuade him that the Soviet Union could not hope to maintain its status as a great power in the future unless it opened its society and permitted its citizens to participate in the global "information revolution" of the final decades of the twentieth century.[30]

But Shultz's most significant contribution to the changed international climate of the period was with respect to Reagan and his policies. Proceeding persistently and stoically, in the face of relentless opposition on the part of the many hard-core conservatives in the Reagan administration, Shultz enabled Reagan to implement the unexpectedly visionary aspect of his world view. Precisely how Shultz accomplished that and why he was so necessary is neatly summarized by Oberdorfer:

The role of George Shultz as U.S. Secretary of State was of central importance . . . given the paradoxes in Reagan's views and the endless disputes on Soviet policy within his administration which lasted until its final year. Reagan knew that he wanted a less dangerous and more businesslike relationship with the Soviet Union, but he did not know how to go about achieving it . . . Shultz provided two ingredients that were otherwise lacking: a persistent and practical drive toward improved relations through the accomplishment of tangible objectives, whether they were arms control pacts, the settlement of regional conflicts, human rights accords or bilateral accords; and organizational skills to mobilize at least parts of the fractious U.S. government to interact on a systematic basis with the Soviet government. Reagan wanted it to happen; Shultz was the key figure on the U.S. side who made it happen.[31]

Conclusion

I opened this chapter by noting that the politics of the end of the Cold War shed light on perennial questions about whether and to what extent individuals can have an impact on major historical outcomes. The body of the chapter should be viewed as a discussion of the analytic requirements of identifying such effects and a presentation of illustrative evidence in support of the proposition that such effects were indeed significant. The complexity of the topic precludes definitive findings, especially in such brief compass. I have stated the broad outline of my argument at the beginning of the previous section, but I have two more general sets of observations, one about the utility of studying the impact of personalities on events and the other about the political qualities evinced by the individuals to whom I have been particularly attentive.

Some will argue that it is not useful to direct an analytic beam at personalities, maintaining that doing so diverts attention from their larger political contexts and pointing out that the occurrence of particular actors with particular qualities on the stage of history is fortuitous. The first claim has some merit. In focusing on actors, the analyst is likely to underplay the full array of contextual factors. Training a searchlight on one area leaves others in the shade. But different analyses will illuminate different facets of reality, with complementary results: one emphasis does not preclude others.

The second claim seems to me simply to be wrong. The very randomness of the distribution of individual qualities in political roles adds to the urgency of studying those attributes. One way to illustrate this assertion is to visualize the institutions and other channels of political process as if they were the circuitry of a highly complex computer and leaders were circuit breakers. Attention to the qualities of the circuit breakers would be all the more urgent if their performance characteristics were random, with some capable of tripping at inappropriate times, losing valuable information, and others failing to trip, exposing the system to the danger of meltdown.

As one scrutinizes the "performance characteristics" of Mikhail Gorbachev, Ronald Reagan, and George Shultz, what becomes particularly evident is that in spite of their very different personal qualities they resembled one another in important respects. All three of them combined a general vision of the importance of defusing the nuclear stalemate of the previous four decades with an ability to transcend ideology and persist in seeking to bring about a fundamental improvement in superpower relations. Their overall mentalities and actions (and particularly those of George Shultz) bring to mind Max Weber's celebration of leaders who have the "calling for politics" and his characterization of politics as "a slow, strong boring of hard boards." Weber's further statement about the requirements of responsible political leadership seems to me to capture the blend of idealism and pragmatism that marked the actions of those individuals and in so doing to provide this chapter with a suitable ending: "It takes both passion and perspective. Certainly all historical experience confirms the truth . . . that man would not have attained the possible unless time and again he had reached out for the impossible."[32]

Chapter Eight

∴ *Perception, Misperception, and the End of the Cold War*

ROBERT JERVIS

> We have discovered how much mistrust there was and how many mis-judgments there were, and I think this is one of the basic lessons for the future leaders and for the present leaders: Please check two or three times before you make a decision, because the information may be wrong, the inclinations may be erroneous, and the advice you receive may not be perfect.   Alexander Bessmertnykh

Even colleagues much younger than I will spend their lifetimes thinking about the origins, course, and end of the Cold War. There is so much to learn that much of what we say now is likely to be quite wrong. In this way, the situation of scholars resembles that of statesmen as described by Alexander Bessmertnykh. Our conclusions are not likely to do as much good or as much harm for the world as did those of the decision makers we are studying, but it is not entirely self-importance that leads us to think that the lessons we learn from the recent half-century will influence what is done in the future. In seeking this understanding, our closeness to the events is both a handicap and an advantage. A handicap because we lack the perspective and the still-secret information that our successors will have; an advantage in that we can draw on our own experiences, and more importantly, on the still-vivid memories of the participants.

These reports and the recently declassified documents that accompany them say much about the patterns of perception and misperception that characterized the Cold War. Before discussing them, however, I want to note that while this fascinating information can shed at least some light on other fundamental questions, it cannot fully answer them. Most obvious is the issue of the origins of and responsibility for the conflict. Put most crudely, was the United States an expansionist power or was it largely reacting to a perceived Soviet menace? Were its perceptions accurate? Were its responses prudent? If it overperceived the threat and overreacted, is this to be explained by normal cognitive biases or was it the product of the need to justify expansionistic impulses by the apparent perception of external menaces? Of course, one can ask the same questions of the Soviet Union.

New information will certainly be of value here. For example, learning that Stalin sanctioned the North Korean attack on South Korea makes it hard to see Soviet policy as simply defensive.[1] But multiple interpretations will remain. We are still unsure about the origins of World War I even though all of the archives have been open for years.[2] Arguments about the sources and motives for American policy at the start of the Cold War are driven not primarily by new documents but by broader intellectual and political trends and perspectives. Of course, we know much more about how American statesmen saw the world and what they were trying to achieve in the late 1940s now that the records are open, but the fact that we can still debate the reasoning behind American policy implies that even when we have read the Kremlin archives we will not agree on the answers—and perhaps we will not even agree on the questions.

The Princeton Conference shed some light on a second broad issue, although it too is partly beyond the reach of documents and memories. This is the question of whether the Cold War can be best explained by the structure of the international system or by the nature of the states involved. Proponents of the political theory known as traditional realism argue that foreign policy is a product of the state's external environment. More rigorously and singlemindedly, structural realism argues that in a bipolar system the two dominant states will be adversaries and the resulting configuration will be stable.[3] The United States and the Soviet Union were then enemies by position.[4] With only two dominant powers in the system, each could only menace the other. *Only* has two complimentary meanings here: no other state could menace either of them, and each had no choice but to menace the other because the threat posed by the other was generated not by a specific policy but by its very existence as a state that had the capability to challenge if not destroy its rival.

Those who see the basic source of foreign policies as coming from within the state reject this explanation. For them, the Cold War was a clash not of two abstract states but of two differing social systems. Right at the start, after all, Stalin had accurately predicted, "This war is not as in the past; whoever occupies a territory also imposes on it his own social system."[5] The other side of this coin is revealed toward the end of the Cold War, when Gorbachev declared that the West could have faith in the sincerity and the permanence of the changes in Soviet foreign policy because they were accompanied by enormous domestic changes. This argument comes in two main variants, one attributing responsibility for the Cold War to the United States and the other attributing responsibility to the Soviet Union. The latter stems from the Kantian and Wilsonian tradition that argues that democracies are peaceful, or at least do not fight each other.[6] The Soviet Union, by contrast, was expansionist because it was a dictatorship—a country that cannot live at peace with its own people cannot live at peace with the world. Parallel in form but quite different in content is the attribution of the Cold War to American expansionism growing out of the U.S. economic system, on the grounds that a system that is exploitative if not oppressive at home has to be exploitative and repressive abroad if the domestic order is to be maintained. Of course, each of these arguments does not exclude the other—both the United States and the Soviet Union could have been driven to challenge the other because of domestic impulses. Alternatively, the clash could have come not from the nature of either regime but from the fact that they were very different from one another. Because their governments were based on very different forms of legitimacy, the very existence of each challenged the other's right to exist.[7]

Both the way the Cold War ended and the comments by the Soviet participants at the Princeton Conference lend credence to the importance of domestic sources of the Cold War, especially those within the Soviet Union. Bessmertnykh argued that Gorbachev's "first step" toward ending the Cold War had been to remove "ideology from foreign policy" and that the decision to intervene in Afghanistan had been based on ideological rather than strategic considerations.[8] As Soviet leaders came to place less weight on socialist values, both the importance and the possibility of building socialism in Afghanistan diminished. If socialism was not that different from capitalism—and certainly not much better than it—why spend blood and treasure to establish it? If socialist countries did not necessarily follow foreign policies different from those of countries with different economic systems, why would establishing socialism abroad aid the Soviet Union? This train of thought was highly subversive. Soviet foreign policy had been underpinned by the assumptions that socialism was morally and economically superior and that the dominant sources of foreign policy were domestic. If international politics was no longer to be seen as a reflection of the class struggle, the basic postulates of Soviet foreign policy had to be called into question. Thus, rather than quibbling over words, Gorbachev and Ligachev were engaging in a fundamental dispute when the former argued that national and international interests had primacy over class ones and the later reasserted the traditional Soviet view.[9]

Evidence from the last years of the Cold War, although not yet definitive, parallels the emphasis placed on ideological changes by the Princeton Conference participants. On the Soviet side, the decline in faith in Marxism-Leninism preceded and produced changes in Soviet foreign policy. The case of Afghanistan has already been noted. More dramatic, of course, was the freeing of Eastern Europe. As I will discuss later, Gorbachev does not seem to have expected the results to be as dramatic as they were. But even a willingness to allow a diversity of regimes in those countries would not have been possible without the sense that no one social system was best for all countries and that domestic changes were compatible with a pro-Soviet foreign policy. Furthermore, the basic reorientation of the Soviet policy toward the West was premised on the twin beliefs that countries with different social systems did not need to be enemies and that the American hostility toward the Soviet Union was the product not of the capitalist regimes' need to control the world or their fear that socialist states, by their very existence and example, menaced them, but rather stemmed from ill-conceived Soviet policies. The profound shift epitomized by Gorbachev's December 1988 speech to the United Nations—the adoption of a view that saw the Cold War as unnecessary and mutual security as feasible—was made possible by the belief that the problem was Marxism-Leninism, not Western, American, or capitalist ideology.

Those who stress the importance of the international structure and a state's external environment are not without replies, however. They could start by noting that whereas Gorbachev saw his predecessors' misguided ideology as much of the source of international conflict and argued that a democratized Soviet Union would be peaceful, his UN speech focused on the systemic level. Even more than did Robert McNamara in his speech in San Francisco decrying the arms race a generation earlier, Gorbachev in New York accepted the centrality of the security dilemma. If the attempt by one state to increase its security has the unintended consequence of making others less secure, then understanding this dynamic can lead not only to a fruitful arms control treaty but also to unilateral moves such as the withdrawal of large numbers of Soviet troops from Eastern Europe, which by making the other side more secure can in turn increase the state's own security.[10] Thus, Gorbachev recognized that structural sources of rivalry are hard to overcome even if all of the major states have social systems that are conducive to peace and cooperation.

More fundamentally, those who stress the importance of the state's external environment can argue that the domestic and ideological changes were—if not mere superstructure—at least produced in large measure by external pressures. That is, Gorbachev did not renounce Communism as the result of careful intellectual study, nor did the domestic changes occur in a vacuum. Rather, the extent of the domestic failure, the need for drastic change, and Gorbachev's recognition that he had to change Soviet foreign policy in order to carry out internal reforms grew out of the pressures of the external environment. Indeed, Waltz's neorealist argument catches the essence of what happened quite well: the Soviet Union lagged badly behind in the competition with its rival and was in grave danger of "falling by the wayside"; it therefore had to emulate the policies, including the domestic policies, of its more successful competitors.[11] To return to the example of Afghanistan, had the West not supported the mujaheddin in a way that allowed those fighters to deprive the Soviet leaders of an easy victory, the imperative to re-think the Soviet position would have been much less.

More broadly, the perception of domestic failure was vivid only because it could be contrasted to what was happening abroad: if the capitalist countries had not been growing as fast as they were, the state of the Soviet economy would not have been seen as so deplorable and few would have argued that liberalization would improve it. Of course, the West was not only a standard against which the success of socialism could be judged but also a rival whose successes compelled matching efforts. As the Princeton Conference participants noted, even when SDI no longer was seen as a potential grave menace to Soviet security, the kind of technology it embodied epitomized the Soviet Union's inability to compete in areas that were likely to be vital in the future. It was also clear that it would be dangerous if not impossible for Gorbachev to embark upon wide-ranging domestic reforms in the absence of much better relations with the West. Trade and technical assistance, if not aid, were necessary, and the domestic groups that opposed perestroika would be greatly strengthened by international tension. Thus the Soviet Union had to end the Cold War not only because it was unable to stay in the competition but also because maintaining hostility to the West would have prevented those domestic changes that held out some promise of eventually rebuilding Soviet strength.

In this view, while it is true that the end of the Cold War coincided with the change of the Soviet domestic system, the major sources of change were external. The sort of de-ideologization of Soviet foreign policy that the conference participants described was real, but was itself the product of the failure of Cold War policies. Many of the changes in thinking were then rationalizations for change rather than reasons. The decision makers were not fully aware of this process, and so even the most perceptive memories are less than fully revealing. "Motivated biases"—the impact that powerful needs have on perceptions and beliefs—were at work, and the sources of the pressures that drove the changes were external.[12] The issue at this point is undecidable, and indeed, there is no reason why ideological disillusion could not have been both genuine and motivated. But whether as a cause, an effect, or both, the reduced ideological distance between the two superpowers was associated with reduced hostility between them as well.

The pattern of changing Western perceptions of threat provides other clues about the degree to which the Cold War was driven by differences in social systems, as contrasted to either bipolar rivalry or specific menacing actions taken by the adversary. From what Secretary of State Shultz says, it appears that the United States was more impressed by the renunciation of ideology in Gorbachev's UN speech than by the concrete promise to reduce troop levels in Eastern Europe.[13] But since domestic reform in the Soviet Union, changes in foreign policy positions, and reductions in military strength all proceeded along the same trajectory in fairly close order, separating out the impact of each element is difficult. Those who stress material factors can point to the importance of the freeing of Eastern Europe in 1989, which eliminated the Soviet threat to Western Europe and the danger of war growing out of a conflict on that continent. The Soviet withdrawal would have ended the Cold War even if it had not been accompanied by significant changes in the Soviet domestic system. Indeed, those who feared Soviet power rather than Soviet ideology should not have been impressed by the latter changes in the absence of the former. But many people were impressed, which provides evidence for the importance of beliefs about states' domestic systems. Thus, when Ronald Reagan went to Moscow in 1988 Soviet power appeared unchanged, and although the INF Treaty had been signed and the Soviets had begun withdrawing from Afghanistan, Soviet foreign policy behavior had not yet been radically altered. But Reagan's beliefs about the USSR had been. When asked how he could be so friendly toward the "evil empire," he replied, "I was talking about another time, another era."[14] A realist, and certainly a structural neorealist, would be hard pressed to explain why American perceptions of the Soviet Union changed in response to Soviet domestic changes. A follower of Wilson or Kant would not be. On these points, further discussions between American and Soviet policy makers will be extremely helpful in allowing us to compare each side's action with the other's perceptions.

In at least two other respects, a realist would have trouble understanding Reagan and Gorbachev. Put another way, these two statesmen were not realists. Realists are supposed to seek to ameliorate problems, not solve them. Tallyrand said that a diplomat's motto should be "Pas de zèle," and when Dean Rusk was appointed secretary of state he is reported to have said that he would be pleased if he finished his term with the world in no worse shape than it was in when he took office. The attitude of Reagan and Gorbachev was very different. They thought that they could fundamentally change U.S.-Soviet relations. Reagan initially believed that the main instruments would be strength and firmness; Gorbachev used concessions and accommodation. But more striking than the difference in means was that both sought drastic change. More specifically, the two leaders were not realists in their rejection of nuclear weapons. All respectable experts believed that such weapons were here to stay; indeed, many—myself included—argued that mutual second-strike capability helped maintain U.S.-Soviet peace. Furthermore, the experts thought that it would be foolish to seek to eliminate these weapons or even to limit stockpiles to a very low number. If such an effort were successful, the result would be great instability because the side that cheated just a bit could obtain first-strike capability. The knowledge that this was the case would encourage cheating, even on the part of a country that only wanted to be secure. Reagan, and apparently Gorbachev, would have none of this. Thus Reagan not only yearned for SDI but really did mean to share it with the Soviet Union if it were developed. For Reagan and probably for Gorbachev as well, the desire to abolish nuclear weapons did not stem from prolonged analysis. Rather, it came from the instinctive feeling that, as Reagan told a press conference in 1983, "To look down an endless future with both of us sitting here with these horrible missiles aimed at each other, and the only thing preventing a holocaust is just so long as no one pulls this trigger—this is unthinkable."[15] The conclusion, of course, may be correct. But realists are supposed to rely on rationality, not feelings.

Living in Different Worlds

The sharing of documents and memories from the Cold War makes it increasingly clear that each side lived in its own world. Each thought that its perceptions were universally valid and failed to realize that others saw a very different world. This is not unusual: it is hard to find any case of international conflict, or even of sustained international interaction, in which each participant was able to grasp the others' perceptions.

Of course in the Cold War, as in previous conflicts, each side realized—or believed—that the other held different values and sought different goals than it did. It is only a slight exaggeration to say that each side saw itself as good and the other as evil; itself as protecting and furthering the best values of mankind and the other as destroying them; itself as honest and moral and the other as deceptive and hypocritical; itself as seeking security and the other as aggressive. But the sense of these deep differences did not make it easier for either side to understand how the other saw the world; indeed, each acted as though the other's deviant values did not prevent the other from sharing some of its rival's basic perceptions. Thus it is not surprising that the Cold War was filled with cases in which one side or the other was taken by surprise. I suspect that only rarely could one side's statesmen write a position paper as the other side would have written it.

The reasons lie in four interrelated perceptual processes that characterize international politics. First, Rashōmon effects are common: different states see the same situation very differently.[16] Because leaders proceed on their own understanding of situations, they will often be in their own perceptual and conceptual worlds. Furthermore, leaders are not likely to understand this and will assume that others see the world the way they do. Second, in what can be called mutual perceptions, to understand events statesmen must try to explain why the other state is acting as it is, which calls for reconstructing how the other understands its environment. Each state must do this and must try to estimate its role as target of and influence on the other's policy. Third, behavior is influenced by leaders' perceptions and beliefs about their own nation (self-perceptions).[17] A state that sees itself in decline is likely to see others and to behave very differently from one that conceives of itself as continuing to be strong, if not dominant. Self-images thus often become the battleground for policy. Furthermore, appreciating others' perceptions of the state is especially difficult and painful when this view contradicts the state's self-image. Finally, second-order perceptions—perceptions by leaders of how their nation is viewed by other nations—are also important.[18] Does the state think that the other side believes that the state is aggressive? That it will retreat in the face of demonstrations of strength? That it is acting on the basis of a long-range plan? These perceptions are likely to be a major influence on the other's behavior, and so the state needs to grasp them if it is to understand and affect what the other does.

It is rarely easy for a statesman to see that others view his country and the acts he undertakes on its behalf very differently than he sees them. Part of the difficulty is cognitive: adopting a perspective different from one's own calls for mental agility and the ability to interpret information from alternative perspectives, often employing alien concepts. This is one reason why scientific breakthroughs are so difficult.[19] Where self-images are concerned, additional barriers are in place as well. To realize that others see you in a different, and presumably an unflattering, light is to acknowledge the possibility that they are right, or at least that you did something that could have given rise to this impression. Thus, most American statesmen—and members of the general public—have difficulty understanding how sensible and well-motivated people abroad might see the United States as overbearing if not aggressive. It is clear to most Americans that when their country supported foreign dictators, there were overriding considerations of national security at stake and the alternative was a violent left-wing regime that would have been even worse for the people of the country. To see an alternative interpretation would be to call into question many deeply held beliefs about American life and society, as well as the wisdom of specific policies. It is thus no accident that the citizens of a country who are most critical of its foreign policy usually hold very different beliefs about the government—if not the country as a whole—than do most other citizens, and that Gorbachev and his colleagues changed their views of Soviet society as they carried out radical changes in foreign policy.

Even in the absence of extreme ideological differences, the Rashōmon effect and related processes can defeat a state's policy, as is shown by two important cases in which American policy makers were taken by surprise: the Japanese attack on Pearl Harbor and the Iranian revolution. In 1941, Japanese and American leaders lived in very different perceptual as well as material worlds. Each side interpreted the unfolding events of that year very differently and, to the extent that it paid any attention to the other's interpretations, it saw them as deceptive or as rationalizations. This is part of the reason why neither side was able to predict how its behavior would affect the other. Although American leaders realized that the oil embargo was pushing Japan into a corner and that Japan was therefore likely to strike at its enemies, they could hardly imagine an attack against Pearl Harbor: this would mean total war with the United States, which Japan could not possibly win. An alternative course of action—attacking the Dutch East Indies and Malaya, coupled if necessary by a move against the Philippines—made much more sense. But Japanese leaders believed, on the one hand, that a move southward would automatically lead to an American attack against their supply lines from the Philippines, and on the other hand, that faced with immediate defeats, the United States would be willing to lose a limited war. The former belief did not make much sense to the Americans because they knew that it would be difficult for them to attack Japanese forces if the United States itself had not been struck. The latter prediction was, from the American perspective, even more bizarre: the idea that the United States would fight a limited war hardly crossed anyone's mind because it was so discrepant with the American self-image and view of the world.

Some of the reasons why the United States failed to understand the unrest in Iran in 1978 are to be found in similar cognitive processes. Despite the fact that relations between the United States and the shah's regime were close and the level of communication was high, neither understood the other and its perceptions. The Carter administration called for both liberalization and stability in Iran but failed to see that its double message was interpreted as confusing, contradictory, and even menacing. To American analysts, the fact that the shah had not used all the force at his disposal indicated that he thought he had the situation under control; to the shah, the fact that America was urging continued liberalization in the face of unrest indicated that it was sympathetic to the opposition and perhaps had turned against him. The Americans believed that the shah was strong and decisive; the shah and his advisors knew that this was not the case, assumed that the Americans perceived the shah accurately, and therefore read strange and disturbing meanings into the American refusal to urge him on. To Iranians, whose history had predisposed them to see plots and disguised external interference, a conspiracy among the shah's enemies—which to an increasing number appeared to include the United States—seemed the best explanation for the unfolding events; American officials were less prone to perceive conspiracies and so could not believe that the Iranians truly were concerned about them.

Indeed, almost every intelligence failure is a mutual and second-order failure. One reason that American analysts did not expect the Soviets to put missiles in Cuba is that they believed that the Soviets knew that the United States would respond very strongly if they did;

American leaders did not think that it was necessary to issue explicit deterrent threats to protect Kuwait because, even without carefully considering the situation, they knew that the United States could not permit a successful invasion; in 1967–68 American officials in Vietnam knew that a Viet Cong uprising would lead to a military defeat and thus were taken by surprise by the Tet offensive.[20] In each case the United States made an error because the other side made an error—and that error was at least in part a misjudgment of the United States.

The propensity for people to live in different perceptual worlds—and to fail to understand that they do—is not limited to relations between adversaries. Even under the most propitious circumstances actors may misperceive each other and fail to understand the other's perception of them. Thus Richard Neustadt has shown that the two most serious Anglo-American crises of the postwar era (the Suez crisis and Kennedy's cancellation of the Skybolt missile program) were occasioned by a failure of each side to understand the other's interests and perspectives and, even more strikingly, the second-order failure to understand the extent to which the other failed to understand them.[21] Indeed, even people in the same society may reveal the same pattern of perceptual differences: after all, *Rashōmon* was not about international politics.[22]

Further evidence of the pervasiveness of these problems, and the propensity for statesmen to underestimate them, is revealed when two countries' records of the same conversation are laid side by side. In the most extreme cases—which are not infrequent—it is hard to believe that the two accounts are reporting the same conversation. In other cases, each participant records more of what he said than of his counterpart's remarks, loses crucial nuances, and confidently tells his superiors that his message was received as intended.[23]

As the Cold War came to an end, perceptions converged and statesmen realized that others could see them differently than they saw themselves. As usual, the strong adjusted much less than did the weak; indeed, to a considerable extent, many of the standard American beliefs about the origins and sources of the Cold War were confirmed by what the Soviet leaders said at the end of the conflict.[24] But we should not be too quick to assert the accuracy of various perceptions. Finding and explaining divergences and convergences may be the more appropriate task, at least at this stage.

It would also be incorrect, or at least premature, to argue that the convergence of perceptions was a cause rather than an effect of the diminution of the conflict. As I noted earlier, beliefs provide rationalizations as well as reasons; they can follow as well as precede policy. Wesley Wark nicely shows how changes in British assessments of the strength of Nazi Germany took place after, not before, shifts in policy.[25] Related arguments concern whether the New Thinking influenced Gorbachev's policy or was used by him to justify what he had already decided to do.[26]

Nevertheless, without resolving these arguments we can still try to see how, when, why, and with what apparent effect the adversaries saw the same reality. Most obviously, we want to know whether states saw the military balance in the same way.[27] Although much more research is needed for a complete picture, it seems clear that in at least some instances both sides tended to engage in "worst case" analysis. The result was that each feared that the other was superior to it in strength, that trends were running against it, and that the other would be likely to exploit this imbalance. In the early 1980s, for example, both the United States and the Soviet Union saw the situation as dangerous and deteriorating. As Bessmertnykh put it:

In a certain way I was happy to hear the CIA's appraisal of our efforts, because almost the same story was reported to the Soviet government by our own intelligence services . . . As for prevailing in a nuclear war, which the United States suspected the Soviet Union believed it might do, I think that in the minds of the Soviet leaders it was completely an opposite picture . . . We thought the American idea of "prevailing" in the Cold War might include the possibility of a first strike. So you see the two mirrors, the two reflective situations, which were caused by tremendous suspicion of each other.[28]

It will be very interesting to learn whether earlier periods in which American leaders felt insecure were also characterized by Soviet perceptions of falling behind or whether there was greater agreement on the state and meaning of the military balance. In 1949–50, for example, American leaders were extremely disturbed about what they saw as growing Soviet strength that would permit aggression. This view, epitomized by NSC-68, was seemingly confirmed by the Korean War. But we now know that while some of the American perceptions of the war were accurate, others were not. It seems clear that the war was started by the North with Stalin's approval, but that the initiative was Kim Il Sung's, with Stalin acceding to his wishes somewhat grudgingly. Furthermore, contrary to what the Americans believed at the time, he did not view this as a test of American resolve and indeed did not think that the United States would respond.[29] Of course, this does not answer the important counterfactual questions: would Stalin have authorized the attack if the American army had been larger? Would he have seen the United States as weak if it had not fought, and would he have been more adventuresome if the United States had behaved as he expected?[30] We may never be able to answer these questions, but I suspect that as we learn more about how the Soviets saw themselves, the United States, and the world around them the Soviet view will not fit the pictures found in the American archives. That is, the strength the United States attributed to the Soviet Union was probably not felt by its leaders, who I suspect saw the American military posture as stronger and more threatening than the Americans did.

Many Americans were also deeply pessimistic in the late 1950s and early 1960s. Although fears of a "missile gap" were in large part a product of lack of access to highly classified intelligence data (reinforced by partisan desires to attack the incumbent administration), the general sense of unease was fueled by more than missile estimates.[31] American domestic institutions seemed weak, American education ineffective, economic growth slow, and American ideals decaying and lacking in appeal abroad. The Soviet Union, by contrast, was seen as growing stronger. Soviet second-strike capability—the timing of whose arrival would be only slightly affected by which intelligence estimate was correct—would undermine the credibility of the American threat to protect Europe. The Soviet appeal to the decolonialized states in Africa and Asia seemed great and menacing. Henry Kissinger's stark opening of *The Necessity of Choice* embodies much of the mood of the times: "The United States cannot afford another decline like that which has characterized the past decade and a half. Fifteen years more of a deterioration of our position in the world such as we have experienced since World War II would find us reduced to Fortress America in a world in which we had become largely irrelevant."[32]

Khrushchev hoped to benefit from this American mood, but it is not clear that he thought that it was any more accurate than the American fears of inflated Soviet missile strength, which he deliberately reinforced. His pressures on the West, especially in Berlin, were real, but it has yet to be shown whether they were driven by optimism and feelings of strength or by pessimism and fear of weakness. He needed victories abroad partly to hold together his domestic coalition, and this generated pressures on him to believe that he could wring concessions from the West.[33] But it still is not clear that he thought that the world was moving in a desirable direction; his frantic efforts indicate a fear that it was not.

Despite—or perhaps because of—the fact that the Cuban missile crisis has been more thoroughly studied than any other episode in the Cold War, much about it remains in dispute. The declassified documents and discussions among the participants indicate clearly, however, the Rashōmon effect. The symmetry between American deployment of intermediate-range ballistic missiles in Europe, felt by Americans as clearly defensive and necessary to maintain deterrence and reassure the Europeans, and a Soviet deployment in Cuba seemed obvious to Khrushchev but escaped the attention of most Americans.[34] That pressures on the Soviet Union would be increased by the Kennedy administration's defense buildup also seemed implausible to Americans.

The Soviets called these events the Caribbean Crisis. The name is not arbitrary: it argues that the confrontation was caused not by the Soviets placing the missiles in Cuba but by the American threats to Castro. Whether Khrushchev's desire to protect Castro was a major motivation behind the deployment remains unclear, but there is little reason to doubt that the Soviets did believe that Cuba was in danger. This the Americans failed to understand because they did not intend to invade.[35] They were not prepared to use large-scale force to oust Castro, and they assumed that the Soviets realized this. The result was not only that they overlooked an impulse that might reinforce the Soviet desire to deploy missiles to Cuba, but also that American officials were blinded to a diplomatic instrument that was available to them during the crisis: they were slow to realize that a pledge not to invade could be a significant inducement to the Soviet Union to withdraw.

Statesmen often fail to understand that they live in their own worlds because they assume that the other has the same information that they do. Most obviously, the leaders of a state that does not seek to threaten others generally does not expect the security dilemma to operate because they believe that their benign intentions are clear to others, who therefore will not feel threatened by the state's security measures. As John Foster Dulles put it, "Khrushchev does not need to be convinced of our good intentions. He knows we are not aggressors and do not threaten the security of the Soviet Union."[36] Similarly, after the Chinese entered the Korean War, Dean Acheson argued that "no possible shred of evidence could have existed in the minds of the Chinese communist authorities about the open [peaceful] intentions of the forces of the United Nations."[37] The United States may be particularly prone to self-righteousness, but it is not unique in assuming that its knowledge and understanding of its own behavior and intentions are both valid and clear to others. Eyre Crowe's famous "Balance of Power" of 1907, which laid out the evidence for German aggressiveness, was built on the premise that Germany understood that England did not threaten legitimate German interests.[38] To take an earlier case, the skirmishing between France and England in North America developed into the Seven Years' War partly because each side incorrectly thought that the other knew that its aims were sharply limited.[39]

In these cases, self-image was one of the causes of the informational discrepancies. But strong and incorrect assumptions about what the other side must know can operate in the absence of this factor. A good example is provided by one reason why the United States was taken by surprise in the Tet offensive. We usually think that states are taken by surprise because they lack information. In a sense, of course, this must be true. But in this case the United States had information that was too accurate for its own good. That is, the United States was sufficiently well informed about conditions in South Vietnam to know that an enemy offensive would not trigger a mass uprising. The problem lay in the next step in the American reasoning: because the Viet Cong and the North Vietnamese had extensive intelligence networks, they too would realize that the offensive could not bring about a revolution. We now know, however, that the latter parties did expect a general uprising; contrary to what the United States assumed, they were quite ill-informed about conditions in the south.[40] While the U.S. failure was not driven by self-image, North Vietnam's may have been: Ho Chi Minh and his colleagues deeply believed in the justice and popularity of their cause; it would have been not only cognitively difficult but also emotionally painful for them to realize that their support in the South was less than overwhelming and that a "people's war" could not bring victory.[41] The fact that the North's information was in part distorted by motivated bias made it more difficult for the United States to realize that the information it had would not be available to the other side. Even when statesmen can intellectually grasp the fact that the other's perceptions are driven by impulses that they do not share and that they literally find alien, it is next to impossible for them to get a sense of the emotional power of these biases.

The Princeton Conference reveals two cases in which statesmen were misled by the assumption of informational symmetry. Both sides report that the start of a meeting between Shultz and Gorbachev was very stormy because the latter complained vociferously about a hostile speech that Ronald Reagan had just given. Shultz's response was vague and less than completely satisfying, in part because he and his assistants did not understand what Gorbachev was talking about. Policy had not changed; no major speech by the president had been given. It turned out that in order to rouse the faithful, in a routine address to Massachusetts Republicans, Reagan had repeated the old Cold War themes. Presumably he gave it little thought; he certainly had no expectation that it would reach Soviet ears. But modern communications techniques did him in. "The full texts of this and other Reagan speeches, most of which were reported at modest length or less in the U.S. press, were routinely obtained by the Soviet Embassy in Washington and propelled by the latest electronic means to the desks of Politburo members only a few hours after they were made."[42]

The difficulty was that Gorbachev assumed that the speech had a foreign policy purpose.[43] It showed, he said, that "the U.S. administration is not abandoning stereotypes, not abandoning reliance on force, not taking account of the political realities and the interests of others, the balance of interests."[44] Gorbachev further assumed that Shultz would know all about the speech. He and the secretary of state lived in the same informational world: Shultz would certainly understand Gorbachev's concerns and react accordingly. Shultz could not. As he explains: "I didn't know what Gorbachev was talking about. I looked over at Colin Powell, the national security advisor . . . and said, 'What's he talking about, Colin?' He didn't know about it either."[45]

This incident did not have major effects. The shooting down of a Korean airliner, and the Soviet defense of that action, did. Later reports confirm what seemed apparent from the public record: American leaders' outrage at the destruction of the airliner was compounded by the Soviet reaction. Far from apologizing, or even claiming that they had made an understandable if unfortunate error, the Soviets went beyond the argument that they were within their rights to shoot down a plane violating their air space and claimed that the aircraft had acted as though it were on a spying mission by taking evasive actions, keeping the running lights extinguished, showing no lights from inside what purported to be a passenger compartment, and failing to respond to tracer fire. The Americans not only knew that these claims were preposterous, they knew that the Soviets knew this, because they were able to read the conversations of the Soviet air defense network. They assumed—as I expect even the most sophisticated observers would have done—that the facts that were known to the local officials had been accurately transmitted up the chain of command to the Politburo. In fact, the report that Ustinov, the defense minister, had given to the Politburo was incorrect on all these points.[46] Whether he meant to mislead his colleagues or whether he himself was being misled by his subordinates is not yet clear. But in either case, the Soviet behavior is now more comprehensible. Had Ustinov's report been true, there would have been reason to believe that the flight was a provocation if not a security threat. The American claims of outrage would have been hypocritical, if not part of a plot to paint the Soviet Union as evil.

Coming into the Same World

It would be too extreme to say that the end of the Cold War was caused by perceptual convergence. But it does seem that cases of the Rashōmon effect became fewer in the late 1980s. Three aspects of this that I think were causal as well as symptomatic were discussed by the conference participants. First was the seemingly minor matter of switching from consecutive to simultaneous translation. As Shultz notes about the first meeting with Shevardnadze in which this was done: "We got eight hours' work done in four hours. But more important, it allowed there to be conversation. It may be a small point."[47] Small but perhaps not insignificant. It not only allowed listeners to match the speaker's gestures and facial expressions with his words, and so to gain a deeper understanding of what was being said, but also permitted a more natural and easier exchange of views. Informational asymmetries and incorrect assumptions about what the other knows and believes were a bit less likely to survive in this environment.

More broadly, the Americans (particularly Shultz) were able to convince their counterparts (especially Gorbachev) that in the modern era information and knowledge were power, that a freer flow of information between East and West would benefit both sides, and that the Soviet Union could not thrive internally unless it utilized more—and more honest—information.[48] Many Soviet policy makers were aware that the information they received from the bureaucracy was suspect. Thus Shevardnadze's assistant, Tarasenko, notes in passing his habit, upon arriving at his office, "of listening to a BBC broadcast . . . just to hear the world news."[49] The Chernobyl catastrophe apparently had great impact not only because the damage was a vivid reminder of what a nuclear war would do, but also because it proved extremely difficult for the Soviet leaders to learn what had happened from their own bureaucracies: the West often provided faster and more accurate information.[50] This must have alerted Gorbachev and his colleagues to the possibility that in other instances as well the information he was receiving about both the West and his own country was not accurate.

Most generally, of course, the end of the Cold War coincided with democratization and glasnost. Although this was not a central topic of the Princeton Conference, it is clear that foreign policy change and the desire for better information went hand in hand. An attitude of openness, of testing one's ideas against evidence, of considering alternatives, and of developing conflicting sources of information was perhaps a necessary condition for seeing that previous Soviet policies were self-defeating, in part because they were based on inadequate perspectives. A willingness not only to try to understand Western points of view but also to consider their possible validity both supported and was supported by glasnost. Without these efforts to see the world differently, Gorbachev could not have thought it possible to end the Cold War or developed strategies for doing so.

This is not to say that all his beliefs proved to be accurate. Indeed, many of his crucial decisions were based on incorrect premises. Although he saw how deep the domestic problems ran, he underestimated the difficulties of reform from above and believed that the Soviet system not only required but also could survive radical reforms. It is not yet clear whether Gorbachev understood that pushing the Eastern European countries to liberalize would result not in their putting into place the kind of system he was seeking in the Soviet Union, but in the end of Communism in those countries. Bessmertnykh argues that Gorbachev expected the Eastern Europeans to "change their systems, but . . . not necessarily . . . that there would be a very deep breakdown in the Soviet–East European relationship. He believed that the reform would unite us more than any other kind of ties."[51] But Tarasenko argues that by the time the Solidarity government took office in Poland in August 1989 he and his colleagues foresaw not only the revolutions but the partial break-up of the Soviet Union as well.[52] I suspect that we will never have a definitive answer to this question, in part because different people had different expectations and the same person may have believed one thing on a cognitive level and another on a more instinctive or emotional one. Nevertheless, there is much to the statement by Bessmertnykh with which I began this chapter. Decision makers often assume that the information they receive is correct and think that their way of seeing the world is the only possible one. They are likely to live in a world that is quite different from that of their counterparts. Often the first step toward dealing with serious conflicts is to understand this. But there is a tension if not a paradox here. The realization that information may be incorrect and that Rashōmon effects are possible may reduce a statesman's confidence in his ability to chart a new course. Fortunately, the leaders at the end of the Cold War were both confident and willing to try to live in a common world.

Chapter Nine

∴ The Transition in U.S.-Soviet Relations, 1985–1990

An Interpretation from the Perspective of International
Relations Theory and Political Psychology

ALEXANDER L. GEORGE

My purpose in this chapter is to discuss the transition in U.S.-Soviet relations during the period from 1985 to mid-1990 from the standpoint of theories of international relations and political psychology. In considering whether to take on this daunting task, I recalled the remark made in early 1990 by one of my colleagues who is—as I am not—a specialist on the Soviet Union. He said, "If you asked me five years ago whether such remarkable developments in the Soviet Union and Eastern Europe could take place, I would have replied: 'Impossible.' However, if you ask me today, I say, 'They were inevitable.' " So far as I know, my colleague has not been asked more recently whether the subsequent dissolution of the Soviet Union in December 1991 was either predictable or inevitable.[1]

If I were to take to heart my colleague's good-humored disparagement of his expertise, this would be a very short chapter indeed. However, I will try to make a case for the relevance of theory, both international relations theories and theories associated with political psychology, for understanding the remarkable improvement in U.S.-Soviet relations discussed by the former decision makers in chapters 1 through 6 and will comment very briefly on this development. In doing so I will be constrained by two propositions concerning the limitations of theory to which I have subscribed for many years: First, I believe that theory inevitably struggles to catch up with reality and often has great difficulty trying to cope with real-world complexity; second, I believe that theory does better in explaining what has happened than in predicting it.

The study of international relations lacks a single comprehensive, coherent theory; rather, theory is fragmented, much of it is not very well developed, and unsurprisingly the field is marked by often-intense controversy. However, international relations theory is evolving in important directions as specialists broaden the spectrum of problems to which theory should be applicable and pay increasing attention to developing theories that have greater policy relevance. Moreover, if the remarkable developments in the Soviet Union and Eastern Europe and the transition in East-West relations are properly studied, our theoretical understanding of international relations can be significantly enriched, particularly with regard to the two-way interaction between changes in the international system and changes in domestic systems and politics.

Not only international relations theorists but also political psychologists will find the study of these developments in East-West relations rewarding for the assessment and refinement of the various theories they bring to bear in understanding international conflict and its amelioration. I will not attempt to offer anything like a comprehensive discussion of the transition in U.S.-Soviet relations from the standpoint of political psychology. This is a field (if indeed it can be regarded as a single field or discipline) that embraces so many different paradigms and theories that few of us can claim competence in all of them. The political and psychological milieu of East-West relations profoundly changed in the years after 1987 largely because Mikhail Gorbachev changed the "reality" of East-West relations by setting into motion fundamental reforms in the domestic structure of the Soviet Union and by introducing a radical reconceptualization of the Soviet approach to international relations.

In chapter 7, Fred Greenstein establishes the critical role that Gorbachev (and, to a lesser extent, Ronald Reagan) played in the development of U.S.-Soviet relations. Clearly, it would be valuable to bring to bear our theories of creative, transformational leadership.[2] I will take a broader approach, however, one that will focus more generally on the role that political learning and adaptation played in paving the way for Gorbachev. It was the process of learning and adaptation that led to changes in fundamental beliefs and policy assumptions held by quite a few, though by no means all, politically influential persons in the Soviet Union who supported his policies of perestroika and glasnost. Moreover, political learning and efforts at creative adaptation continued after Gorbachev came to power in March 1985. Gorbachev's diagnosis of the shortcomings—political, economic, ideological, and moral—of the domestic system became more sober and led to the increasing radicalization of his prescriptions for change. Thus, I shall address the prerequisites of the perceptual convergence that Robert Jervis analyzes in chapter 8.

As for theories of international relations, I will call attention to the limited relevance of structural-realist theory and emphasize the necessity of using an alternative theoretical approach that focuses on the impact of domestic structure and politics on a state's foreign policy. Then, in order to characterize the remarkable change in the political and psychological milieu of East-West relations, I will focus on changes that took place in three fundamental variables that profoundly affect the character of international relations: (1) the "security dilemma"; (2) ideology; and (3) geopolitical aspects of U.S.-Soviet competition in the third world. I refer to these as variables because each changed in ways that facilitated the transition in East-West relations. These three variables are of interest here also because they provide a link between international relations theory and political psychology.

The Uses and Limitations
of Structural-Realist Theory

Many would regard structural-realist theory,[3] or neorealism as it is sometimes called, as the dominant theory in international relations. This theory argues that in order to understand international relations one has to take into account the "anarchic" nature of the international system, which lacks a central governmental authority; the fundamental importance of the distribution of power among states; and the fact that the primary objective of the state in this anarchical society is security, which leads states to seek to increase their power either through their own efforts or by means of alliances in order to preserve their territory, independence and political integrity, and economic well-being. Structural-realist theory is appealing for several reasons. It calls attention to fundamental forces ("anarchy," "distribution of power") that do indeed affect relations among states; it lends itself to relatively rigorous and systematic formulation; and it offers a parsimonious theory of the behavior of states and the outcomes of their interaction with each other. In comparison, other theoretical approaches to international relations are more diffuse; they deal with many variables neglected by structural-realist theory and attempt to describe and explain complex processes of decision making and strategic interaction among states which do not lend themselves to systematic, parsimonious formulation.

My own view, shared to some degree by many if not most scholars in the field, is that structural-realist theory is indeed necessary but quite insufficient by itself either for the study of international relations or, certainly, for the conduct and management of international politics. As its foremost proponents acknowledge, structural-realist theory is not a theory of foreign policy or of statecraft. In fact, neorealists claim no more than that the few structural variables encompassed by their theory operate as constraints on choices of foreign policy and on the outcomes of state interactions. To be sure, they regard these as rather severe constraints, but in applying them to analysis of international relations, structural-realist theory makes probabilistic predictions, not deterministic, straightline predictions.

Other variables not encompassed by this theory—such as domestic structure and politics, ideology, belief systems, images of the opponent, bureaucratic politics, strategic interaction, and bargaining— need to be brought into the analytic framework in order to try to predict or explain specific foreign policy decisions and specific outcomes. When one brings these other variables into the equation, then one must draw upon various aspects of political psychology. This, then, is how international relations theory and political psychology intersect.

Among the limitations of structural-realist theory is the restricted scope of its predictions and explanations. As structural-realists have increasingly conceded, their theory by itself does not give us much help in understanding how to promote peaceful change in international relations; how to achieve cooperation among states; how states define their interests and how their conception of interests changes; and finally, of particular relevance for my purposes, how and under what conditions political learning by states, their leaders, and their people takes place.[4]

More specifically, the argument advanced here is that the increase in the relative power advantage enjoyed by the United States over the Soviet Union—relative power being a causal variable to which structural-realist theory attributes great importance—was of limited and indirect value in explaining the transition in U.S.-Soviet relations. Far more relevant, I will argue, is a central proposition advanced by other international relations theorists which emphasizes the causal impact of a state's domestic structure, politics, and other domestic attributes on its foreign policy. This is by no means to ignore the impact that changes in the international environment can and do have on these domestic variables.[5] Certainly it is true that Soviet leaders were forced to come to grips with the unexpected shift favoring the United States in what they call the "correlation of forces" during the late 1970s and early 1980s. The relative decline of overall Soviet power contributed indirectly to pressures for domestic changes in the Soviet Union. But, as the comments of Alexander Bessmertnykh and Anatoly Chernyaev in the chapters above attest, it was the abysmal deterioration in the performance of the Soviet economy, especially in comparison with the much better economic performance of many nonsocialist states, that motivated Soviet leaders to undertake fundamental changes in foreign policy as well as in domestic policy.[6] I emphasize, that is, the complex two-way interaction between international politics and domestic politics as experienced by Soviet leaders. However, I will not attempt to sort out the complex causal interaction of external and internal changes that brought about dramatic changes in both Soviet domestic and foreign policy. Instead, I shall focus on learning by Soviet leaders and on their adaptation to changes in their international and domestic environment. And similarly, I shall discuss learning that has taken place among some influential American leaders and the efforts of U.S. policy makers to adapt to new developments in their domestic and external environments.

The Impact of Some Important Variables on Relations among Adversaries

It is well to begin by providing a brief description of three key variables—the security dilemma, ideology, and geopolitical thinking—and of how they aggravate relations among adversaries. It was changes of a benign character in these important variables that help to explain the remarkable transformation of the psychological and political milieu of U.S.-Soviet relations in the period 1985–90. The changes in these three variables have not emerged automatically or directly in consequence of changes in the relative power balance between the two superpowers, although, as was already noted, such a shift in favor of the United States in the past decade or so has played an indirect role in this respect. For these changes to have occurred, considerable learning from experience and adaptation to new developments on the part of Soviet and American leaders were necessary.

The Dynamics of the Security Dilemma

The phrase *security dilemma* is applied by specialists in international relations to identify a peculiar and aberrant type of interaction between adversarial states.[7] This dilemma arises because the measures that one state adopts to increase its sense of security, and to deter and defend against possible encroachments by a hostile (or potentially hostile) adversary, often are viewed by that adversary as a threat to its own security. This perception requires the adversary to take additional defensive measures of its own; and this response, in turn, requires the first state to take additional defensive measures, which then motivate the adversary to take further measures to strengthen its own capabilities. And so the cycle continues. In other words, the dynamics of the security dilemma force adversarial states to interact in ways that exacerbate the security problem for each. Exaggerating to make the point, one can say that each side's search for greater security can easily result in greater insecurity for both. The dynamics of the security dilemma tend to produce this kind of vicious result even when both states pursue essentially defensive objectives; the impact is greater, of course, when one or both sides actually pursue or are perceived to be pursuing offensive goals.

The interaction dynamics associated with the security dilemma can have three types of malignant consequences.[8] First, they can generate additional suspicion and distrust between states, thereby introducing a psychological overlay that exacerbates and rigidifies the real conflict of interests and thus severely complicates efforts at accommodation and conflict resolution. Second, the dynamics of the security dilemma not only encourage and feed an arms race among the contending parties but, as in the U.S.-Soviet experience, also severely complicate efforts at arms control. The motivation for more ambitious arms control agreements is diluted by concern over such agreements' possible security disadvantages. It is particularly difficult to achieve agreements that effectively control the technological component of the arms race because one or both sides believe that sacrifice of certain promising technological opportunities may have damaging consequences for their relative security position in the future.

Third, the dynamics of the security dilemma can have an adverse impact during a diplomatic crisis. The steps that one side takes in a crisis to reduce the vulnerability of its military forces, to increase their readiness, and to back up its diplomacy may be viewed by the other side as preparations to initiate or to escalate military operations, actions that require it to increase the alert status or to alter the deployment of its own military forces. As a result, a vicious cycle of interaction may occur which neither side anticipated or wanted and which can contribute to crisis mismanagement, escalation, and war.

The Impact of Ideology

Ideological differences between adversaries can severely exacerbate the malignant impact of the security dilemma insofar as ideology leads one to perceive the adversary as an implacably hostile and untrustworthy enemy. In the anarchic international system each state strives to enhance its security, safeguard its way of life, and ensure its basic economic needs. In such a system, relations among states would in any case tend to be competitive and conflictual, but the conflictual nature of world politics is much accentuated when states, viewing each other through the prism of their ideologies, regard each other as enemies. An enemy, in contrast to an adversary, symbolizes the antithesis of one's own core values and threatens one's preferred political and international order.

The image of an adversary is multidimensional, and some of its dimensions have particular relevance for foreign policy and interstate relations. In the first place, threat perception and threat assessment in the conduct of foreign relations are influenced by the general image one has of the adversary. Intelligence indicators of an adversary's intentions, both immediate-range and longer-range, tend to be interpreted on the basis of that image. Similarly, the explanations for an adversary's actions can also be distorted by one's general image of that opponent. As modern attribution theory reminds us, even under the best of circumstances a person who strives to make objective, scientific judgments is prone to a variety of attribution errors in assessing the character and behavior of other actors. A variant of the fundamental attribution error is of particular interest: When one's opponent takes a tough action one tends to view his behavior as a demonstration of innate hostility rather than as a logical response to the situation or to one's own behavior. But when the opponent behaves in a conciliatory fashion, one assumes that he was forced to do so, either by the situation or by one's own behavior, rather than because of his character or general dispositions. An ideologically inspired image of a hostile opponent can accentuate attribution biases of this kind and complicate efforts at accommodation. When policy makers hold a "bad-faith" image of the opponent it can distort their processing of incoming information about the opponent's behavior. Policy makers operating with such an image all too readily resort to cognitive dissonance reduction mechanisms in order to ignore or explain away behavior by the adversary that is "discrepant"—that contradicts the bad-faith image of him that they hold.[9]

Another critical dimension of the image of an opponent has to do with how one explains his animosity and whether one regards his animosity as permanent or subject to change. This dimension has a significant bearing on judgments concerning such fundamental questions of foreign policy as, What are the causes of the opponent's hostility, and can one do anything to alter them so as to reduce that hostility? Is it realistic to try to develop a more constructive type of relationship with the opponent which includes cooperative as well as competitive elements? It is precisely questions of this kind that for many years dominated discussions of what policies the United States should adopt toward the Soviet Union.

The Impact of Geopolitical Thinking on a Superpower's Foreign Policy

Let us turn, finally, to a consideration of how geopolitical thinking in foreign policy can further intensify the adverse impact that the security dilemma and ideological antipathy have on the rivalry between great powers. As has often been noted, great powers with global interests have tended to expand the concept of their "security requirements" ever outward. Once a great power establishes advance outposts or enters into commitments with distant allies, its conception of threats to its security interests and of its security requirements expands. One may recall in this connection Arthur Balfour's complaint many years ago that Britain's security requirements tended to snowball over the years and to take on an open-ended character: "Every time I come to a discussion—at intervals of, say, five years—I find there is a new sphere which we have got to guard, which is supposed to protect the gateways of India. Those gateways are getting further and further away from India, and I do not know how far West they are going to be brought by the General Staff!"[10]

One would assume that, logically, great powers should find it relatively easy to limit their competition in those parts of the world where they have nothing approximating vital interests. But in fact, great powers often have responded to a contrary logic—the metalogic of geopolitical thinking—which encourages them to believe that it is precisely in areas in which both sides have only modest interests that policies to increase one's own influence at the expense of the opponent's can be safely pursued. Involvement in such areas may be perceived as offering opportunities for marginal but nonetheless useful gains. A great power may regard competing with its rival in such circumstances as offering tempting opportunities for pursuing a long-term strategy for gradually weakening the other power's regional, and eventually its global, influence. A series of cumulative marginal gains in different areas, each of which is admittedly of limited value, could eventually weaken the other power substantially. Such a strategy may be regarded by one or the other of the adversarial powers as an attractive, low-cost, and low-risk way of enhancing its own global security position. As this reasoning goes, any weakening of the opponent's influence and control, even in peripheral areas, puts him on the defensive, ties up his resources, distracts him, and thereby reduces his ability to threaten and damage one's own more central interests.

In these ways the abstract commonsensical "logic" of what should be limited competition, if any, in areas of peripheral interest tends to be displaced by the quite different metalogic of global competition driven by geopolitical thinking.

Once the game of geopolitical competition is under way, neither side is disposed to accept the other's assurances that it is acting in a particular region solely for defensive purposes. Since an adversary's intentions, particularly the relationship of his current actions to possibly more ambitious long-range goals, are difficult to ascertain reliably, one is inclined to judge those intentions not by the opponent's words but rather by how one judges the possible implications and long-range consequences of his current actions.

The Soviet Union's Profound Domestic Crisis and Gorbachev's New Thinking

One need not dwell on the profound, pervasive crisis that gripped all aspects of Soviet society—economic, political, social, and moral—to emphasize the impetus it gave to a rethinking of the Soviet approach to international relations.[11] At risk of oversimplification, one might say that Gorbachev perceived that an effort at thoroughgoing reform of Soviet society would be facilitated by—indeed, required—a new approach to international relations. But for our purposes it suffices to call attention to the close relationship between Gorbachev's political and economic reforms at home, symbolized by the terms *glasnost* and *perestroika,* and his New Thinking in foreign policy. Both his domestic and foreign policies reflected a substantial rejection of Marxist ideology and an effort to replace it with new concepts. Gorbachev's approach to international relations explicitly abandoned the ideological prism of a Marxist class struggle among states and substituted for it new concepts of "interdependence," "mutual security," and "comprehensive security."[12]

The changes that the Soviet leader introduced and was pursuing in foreign policy reflected a highly self-conscious effort to get rid of or at least minimize the adverse effects of the security dilemma, ideology, and geopolitical thinking which I have briefly summarized. He and his closest associates spoke openly of their effort to "deideologize" international relations, to "demilitarize" the foundations of security, and to "degeopoliticize" competition with the United States for influence in the third world. Before spelling this out more fully it will be useful to provide some historical perspective on the efforts the two superpowers made to move beyond the worst aspects of the Cold War toward a nonconfrontational form of competition, one that would be gradually leavened by cooperation and collaboration on significant issues of mutual concern. It is from this historical experience that both superpowers derived important lessons that were applied in the development of their relations.

A Historical Perspective on Moves toward Superpower Cooperation

The serious search for a less confrontational, more constructive relationship between the two superpowers began with the move toward détente which followed the Cuban missile crisis. I shall focus here, however, on the period beginning with the Nixon-Brezhnev détente of the early 1970s and will address the following questions: What lessons did leaders on the two sides draw from the abortive Nixon-Brezhnev détente? How did Soviet and American leaders assess the implications for their relationship of new developments that occurred in the international environment and in their domestic situations since the early 1970s? What new conceptions emerged regarding the development of a more constructive and stable relationship?

The erosion and collapse of the Nixon-Brezhnev détente of the early 1970s led to a revival of the Cold War in the late 1970s and early 1980s. Not only were these years marked by rising tensions and lack of constructive engagement between Moscow and Washington; many observers feared the possibility of nuclear war should the two superpowers get into a new crisis comparable to earlier ones in Berlin, Cuba, and the Middle East. However, despite the harsh rhetoric of the second Cold War, various ugly incidents, and accentuated militarization of foreign policy, the superpowers managed—as they had in previous decades—to avoid a shooting war of any kind between their military forces. And in fact, they worked their way out of the second Cold War without drifting into any dangerous war-threatening crisis.

Some useful learning had evidently taken place in Moscow and Washington as to the modalities of crisis management and crisis avoidance, and this served the superpowers well in managing the tensions of the second Cold War. Shared understandings and patterns of behavior that helped U.S. and Soviet leaders to avoid crises and war have been discussed elsewhere.[13]

In the early 1970s the efforts of Nixon and Kissinger to improve U.S. relations with the Soviet Union stemmed in part from their recognition that they were operating in a new situation, in which there had been a relative decline in the position of the United States in the world. And indeed, Brezhnev believed that it was rising Soviet strength—a shift in the "correlation of forces"—that had forced détente upon the United States. In the late 1980s, however, it was the Soviet leadership that sought an improvement of relations from a position of weakness.

Evident, too, was a certain asymmetry between the superpowers as regards the desire for and receptivity to change in the international system. The Soviet Union under Gorbachev aimed for substantial, indeed in some respects radical, change not only in its relations with the West but also in the structure and modalities of international relations. To be sure, Gorbachev's general concepts for such changes and their implementation evolved slowly, and many of them were not fully specified. The United States, much less dissatisfied with the existing situation, was concerned lest the momentum for change get out of hand and undermine the gains the West had made in stabilizing the situation in Europe and in containing and, to some extent, eroding Soviet expansionism in the third world. Moreover, the two superpowers had different as well as overlapping agendas for change which had to be sorted out and explored, and this was most strikingly evident with reference to the problem of how to reconcile German reunification with new security arrangements for Europe.

This problem illustrates another difference between the two eras. In the late 1970s it was President Carter who tried at the outset of his administration to shift U.S. foreign policy away from a geopolitical preoccupation with the Soviet "threat" to a set of "world order" goals that he favored; but at that time the Soviets seemed more interested in exploiting opportunities to increase their global influence. In the late 1980s, however, it was Gorbachev who promoted the vision of a world order toward which he wanted to move boldly and quickly, and it was the United States that wished to move more slowly and cautiously. Dissatisfaction with the general state of international affairs was much greater in Gorbachev's Moscow than in Washington. Convinced that changes in the structure of relations in Europe were necessary and desirable, the Soviet Union was much more ready to accept the substantial risks of fluid, uncharted change than was the United States. Although the United States recognized that the existing structure of peace and stability in Europe must and would change in ways that could not be clearly foreseen, it was more concerned with managing the risks of change and the transition to new forms than the Soviet Union appeared to be. More generally, because the two superpowers differed somewhat in their readiness to move away from traditional concepts of security and instrumentalities for achieving it, there was a certain lack of synchronization in their efforts to create a more constructive and stable relationship, and beyond that to restructure the international system.

Still another important difference between the two eras concerned the People's Republic of China. In the early 1970s, both the United States and the Soviet Union, though with sharply divergent goals, attached considerable importance to China as a factor in superpower relations. Brezhnev wanted to use détente with the United States to serve as a kind of alliance for isolating and weakening China. For his part, Nixon rebuffed Brezhnev's overtures; instead he exploited the Sino-Soviet conflict, attempting to use détente with China to exert leverage on the Soviet Union. These differences, some observers feel, contributed to the erosion of the Nixon-Brezhnev détente. In contrast to its role during the 1970s, China in the 1980s held a more neutral, balanced position vis-à-vis the two superpowers and was not a complicating factor in the development of U.S.-Soviet relations. At the Princeton Conference, for example, China was never mentioned as a factor in the evolution of U.S.-Soviet cooperation after 1985.

Learning and Adaptation to New Developments

In addition to drawing general lessons from the abortive détente of the 1970s, both superpowers began the task of adapting to important new developments in their internal and external environment.[14] The ways in which they responded enhanced the possibility of a significant improvement in their relationship. These new developments and their implications are mostly well known and hence can be dealt with briefly:

1. Both superpowers experienced serious economic difficulties, the Soviets in a much more acute and immediate form than the United States. As a result, Soviet priorities shifted from the pursuit

of global aspirations in the early 1970s to efforts to deal with serious domestic problems in the 1980s. In the 1970s Brezhnev attempted to expand the global position of his country, proclaiming that the Soviet Union was now the political as well as the military equal of the United States. Such claims were strikingly absent in Gorbachev's era; instead, Soviet leaders and writers acknowledged that their country could no longer afford an expensive foreign policy and that it needed to curtail military competition with the economically stronger Western powers.[15]

2. A remarkable shift occurred in the Soviet Union's conception of its superpower role. There was a sober recognition that the acquisition by the Soviet Union of strategic parity and military equality with the United States did not yield the type of "political equality" Brezhnev desired and the benefits that such a status was expected to yield.[16] The favorable "correlation of forces" that Brezhnev heralded in the late 1960s and early 1970s did not turn out to be as advantageous as expected; instead of enabling the Soviet Union to achieve hoped-for gains, it provoked the United States into strengthening its own military capabilities and pursuing a more assertive foreign policy. Besides, Soviet gains in the third world proved to be more expensive and, for the most part, less stable than had been expected. Competition and rivalry with the United States led to misallocation of resources which exacerbated domestic Soviet problems. Gorbachev's New Thinking emphasized that the Soviet Union must no longer allow its conception of superpower status and its foreign policy to be shaped by the imperatives and modalities of the traditional game of geopolitical competition with the United States. Instead, the main foreign policy interest of the Soviet Union should be the creation of favorable circumstances for dealing with its domestic problems. The Soviet Union should reduce its involvement in existing regional conflicts and should encourage the United States to follow a similar path.

3. Not only Soviet internal difficulties but also a series of foreign policy failures forced a basic reconsideration of the assumptions, aspirations, and modalities of Soviet foreign policy. The list of flawed policies and failures included the invasion of Afghanistan, the sterility of Soviet policy in the Mutual and Balanced Force Reductions (MBFR) negotiations, the provocative deployment of SS-20s in Europe, the walkout in 1983 from the Geneva arms control negotia-

tions, and overly optimistic expectations and overinvestment in the superpower competition in the third world.

4. For its part, the United States encountered a number of difficulties and frustrations during the second Cold War which eventually made the Reagan administration willing to modify some of the policy objectives that it had proclaimed and pursued during the early 1980s. The administration's initiatives in the Middle East and in Central America failed to produce the hoped-for results. The Vietnam syndrome continued to constrain the use of force and threats of force as an instrument of U.S. diplomacy. Western European allies effectively resisted U.S. policies that they feared would undo the gains the first détente had achieved for Europe. The administration's threat to undo or bypass major arms control agreements made by previous administrations, Reagan's ambitious Strategic Defense Initiative (SDI), and his military spending plans eventually ran into stubborn resistance from Congress and public opinion. He was persuaded by public opinion and U.S. allies to resume serious high-level contact with Soviet leaders in the interest of reducing tensions, alleviating the fear of nuclear war, and reinvigorating efforts to develop a more constructive superpower relationship. And President Bush, although initially evincing a distinct preference for proceeding cautiously, recognized that it was time to move "beyond containment to a new partnership" with the Soviet Union and to try to bring it into a better relationship with the rest of the international system.[17]

5. Both Soviet and American leaders recognized a need to adjust—not passively but with new concepts and policy initiatives—to developments that were altering the nature of the NATO and Warsaw Pact alliances, their leadership role in their respective alliances, and relations between the East and West in Europe. Unlike the Soviet Union, which had exercised a dominating hegemonic position in the Warsaw Pact, the United States had considerable experience, and had experienced considerable difficulty, in trying to exercise a nonhegemonic leadership role in NATO. Under Gorbachev the Soviet Union drastically loosened its control over its Eastern European allies, and stood by as political revolutions in the region compelled the dissolution of the Warsaw Pact. The United States, for its part, entered a period in which some of its NATO allies were moving toward even greater autonomy within and outside the alliance. In particular, various developments combined to encourage and permit the Federal Re-

public of Germany and the reunified Germany to play a more influential role in Eastern Europe.

6. Both Soviet and American leaders recognized more generally that they would have to adjust to the ever-increasing multipolarity and pluralism of the international system as a whole. Moscow and Washington were increasingly aware that the trend toward increased turbulence in the third world and stubborn assertions of independence on the part of so many smaller countries meant that both superpowers would have to adjust to an era of declining control and influence in the rest of the world. In consequence, Moscow and Washington faced the challenging task of redefining what it meant to be a superpower in the emerging international system. By 1990, some Soviet commentators went so far as to acknowledge that the Soviet Union was no longer a superpower.

7. In the 1980s, opinion leaders and some strategic analysts in both the Soviet Union and the United States became increasingly uneasy over the extent to which the superpowers were relying on nuclear deterrence to keep the peace. Developments in military technology and deployment created deep concern that strategic deterrence, while stable and reliable in peacetime, could prove fragile—the much-discussed problem of crisis instability—during a tense crisis, when, as is likely, strategic forces would be placed on high alert. Concern over the vulnerability of their command systems to preemptive attack led both sides to move toward a "launch-on-warning" and "launch-under-attack" policy, thus exacerbating concern over the possibility of accidental or inadvertent nuclear war. In this context of rising concern over the possibility of nuclear war, President Reagan and other Americans found attractive the idea that advanced technology—SDI—might provide a perfect or near-perfect defense against incoming strategic missiles, an accomplishment that might even lead eventually to the virtual abolition of nuclear weapons. However, stubborn questions concerning SDI's feasibility, cost, and expected performance, and the fear of triggering an arms race eroded hopes that technology could prevent nuclear devastation.

As a result, although both the United States and the Soviet Union accepted some form of strategic nuclear deterrence as necessary for the foreseeable future, there was an increasingly strong feeling in both countries that they should attempt to reduce reliance on nuclear deterrence as a basis for their security. Not only should Moscow and Washington work together—through the Intermediate-Range Nuclear Forces (INF) Treaty, a possible Strategic Arms Reduction Treaty (START), and other bilateral arrangements—to develop a more benign, less dangerous form of nuclear deterrence but they should also, above all, give much more emphasis to creating stronger political foundations for improvement of the overall U.S.-Soviet relationship in order to enhance their mutual security.

8. In both countries there was growing awareness that relations in the past had been adversely affected by the impact of the "security dilemma" discussed earlier in this chapter. Greater sensitivity to the dynamics of the security dilemma encouraged thoughtful persons on both sides to raise questions about the offense-oriented military postures and doctrines the two sides had developed. Such postures and doctrines exacerbated both countries' insecurity and magnified distrust; they encouraged worst-case fears of possible threats from the other side, fed the arms race, and raised the specter of crisis instability and the possibility of accidental or inadvertent war. An important implication of this new awareness was that it created new opportunities for unilateral and cooperative steps for mutual threat reduction.

9. Similarly, leaders in both countries came to appreciate that the ideological dimension of their foreign policies had exacerbated the security dilemma, creating additional distrust and hostility, and magnifying obstacles to the exploration of cooperative arrangements to enhance mutual security. Significantly, beginning in the mid-1980s both sides began to abandon the heavy ideological cast that had permeated their rhetoric and their policies toward each other. Consider the remarkable shift within a few years from Reagan's "evil empire" characterization of the Soviet Union to his expression of friendship for Gorbachev. Even more striking was the Soviet Union's openly stated intention to "deideologize" its foreign policy and its view of international relations. This was accompanied by a concerted, well-orchestrated Soviet campaign to change the invidious, hostile image of the Soviet Union which was held in the West into the image of a reliable partner ready to cooperate in dealing with all global problems. It should also be noted that under Gorbachev's rule Soviet leaders and writers tried to alter the Soviet public's fear that the United States and NATO posed threats to Soviet security. On occasion they even admitted that unwise Soviet behavior in the past

had reinforced the negative Western image of the Soviet Union and that previous Soviet leaders had deliberately exaggerated the image of a hostile West. Quite obviously, this new position—that the Soviet Union was no longer threatened by the possibility of a deliberate, unprovoked attack from the West—created and legitimized important opportunities for considerable modification of Soviet military and arms control policies.

10. The more open Soviet political system that Gorbachev was creating had a benign effect on the Western image of the Soviet Union and encouraged new possibilities for significant cooperation. This shift manifested itself in many ways. Of considerable importance was the remarkable willingness of the Soviet leadership to open Eastern European and Soviet territory to on-site inspection in furtherance of arms control and confidence building. In addition, Gorbachev made significant moves toward creating a more pluralistic and more open domestic political system—one in which policy issues were publicly debated, the distortions of orthodox Soviet history were subjected to sharp revisionist attacks, and past Soviet domestic and foreign policy errors were admitted and criticized.

Another way in which the Soviet Union moved toward a more open system was the modification of its traditional emphasis on secrecy as essential for Soviet security. However necessary secrecy may have been in the past, the Soviets now recognized that it had serious negative consequences for relations with the West. Thus, Soviet secrecy had contributed to insecurity in the West; it had encouraged worst-case interpretations of Soviet intentions and given ammunition to Western proponents of the arms race. In consequence, Soviet secrecy had the paradoxical effect of indirectly increasing threats to Soviet security. Gorbachev and his colleagues recognized that greater Soviet openness was needed to reverse this process and that it would operate indirectly to strengthen Soviet security. As changes associated with glasnost continued, they eventually helped bring about a significant amelioration of the distrust with which the West viewed the Soviet Union, and thereby contributed to improvement in the overall political relationship. In fact, the development of a more positive image of the Soviet Union was well under way in the West by mid-1990. It had proceeded further in Western Europe and among the American public than among American foreign policy specialists, but by mid-1990 it had developed among all groups.

11. Over the two and a half decades following the Cuban missile crisis, American and Soviet leaders came to the sober recognition that their countries were inescapably vulnerable to nuclear devastation. Strictly unilateral measures by either side to promote its own security, although they continued to be essential, were no longer sufficient: each side was dependent on the restrained behavior and cooperation of the other to assure its own security and to lighten the burden of implementing security measures. Recognition of this mutual vulnerability and mutual dependence strengthened the superpowers' incentives to explore arms control, confidence-building measures, and other cooperative arrangements for enhancing their security.[18] Each side moved toward a recognition that the measures it took to increase its sense of security must not be measures that would have the effect, as they so often had in the past, of increasing the insecurity felt by the other side. In this important sense, objective conditions created the basis for the new concept of "mutual security" as the fundamental goal for developing a more constructive and stable relationship.

Conclusion

It is often said that history seldom gives individuals and states who have failed a second chance. But in the mid-1980s, U.S. and Soviet leaders had just such a second chance to do better than Nixon and Brezhnev had done in developing a less confrontational and more constructive relationship. The leaders of both countries avoided the temptation to reflect upon the past simply to discover how to be more clever the next time. This interpretation of the transition in Soviet-American relations credits important elements of the leadership of both countries with the good sense to rethink some of the fundamental assumptions, goals, and practices that had disturbed their relations for so many years. Contrary to the implications of structural-realist theory, although recognized in some of its formulations, leadership can make a difference. A leader's beliefs and policy choices are by no means always an epiphenomenon determined by external structural variables; in fact, it has been argued here that Gorbachev's New Thinking was influenced to a much greater extent by domestic pressures. Gorbachev's effort to "deideologize" Soviet foreign policy, to "demilitarize" the foundations of security, and to "degeopoliticize" global competition with the United States combined to greatly modify the Cold War image of a hostile, untrustworthy Soviet Union and to open the way for a more constructive relationship and the development of new concepts and modalities for mutual security.

Chapter Ten

∴ Scholars, Policy Makers, and the End of the Cold War

WILLIAM C. WOHLFORTH

The Princeton Conference was an example of productive cooperation between scholars and practitioners who shared the goal of understanding an important episode of change in international politics. But such cooperation is not always so easy, as people who routinely work in both policy and academia will attest. In a book on bridging the gap between theory and policy, Alexander George notes that "the eyes of practitioners often glaze over at the first mention of the word 'theory' in conversation."[1] And many political scientists, especially those who are skeptical of the importance of historical interpretation, discount the importance of knowledge about actual decision makers in the construction and testing of theories. Imagine the practitioner's reaction when informed that his or her recollections are nothing more than "noisy data" that will simply lead to "inferential blunders."[2] It is difficult to see how scholarly research can influence politics for the better if decision makers reject the very idea of theory and scholars try to treat decision makers as physicists treat subatomic particles.

The gap between theory and policy is a complex subject, but here I shall explore one element of it which has received little attention elsewhere and which is particularly well illuminated by the end of the Cold War and the transcripts of the Princeton Conference: the similarity between the decision maker's and the scholar's dilemma. The purposes of the two professions will always diverge—the one seeking immediate success in pursuit of the national interest, the other seeking empirically substantiated generalizations about politics—so there will always be something of a gulf between them. But both the scholar and the decision maker face the same problem: that of determining causes in ambiguous circumstances.

The chapters by Greenstein, George, and Jervis explore the causes of the turn in superpower relations at various levels of analysis. Determining how various causes acted together in this instance is vital for evaluating scholarly theories. But it is also vital for the policy makers involved. Suppose, for example, that Gorbachev could have had certain knowledge of the precise causal effect that Shultz and Reagan could have on the course of superpower relations. Such knowledge would have been of obvious and immediate importance for formulating policy. And the testimony at the Princeton Conference confirms that Gorbachev pursued that knowledge vigorously. The same goes for the perceptual and learning variables examined by Jervis and George. It was a vital matter of policy for the Americans to come to some assessment of the meaning of the intellectual revolution under way in Moscow. And again, George Shultz, Jack Matlock and their colleagues confirmed at the Princeton Conference that they had followed Gorbachev's New Thinking closely and had come eventually to view it as fundamentally important for policy.

The search for causes is the central task of the scholar, while the policy maker needs a rough-and-ready set of hypotheses about what is causing what in the situation he or she faces. And those rough hypotheses are hard to test, for exactly the same reasons that a scholar's hypotheses are. Here, I examine four basic and related problems that confront the decision maker and the scholar: the uncertainty under which decision makers must frequently operate, which can translate into an ambiguous historical record for scholars; the immeasurability of the variables that both decision makers and political scientists think are important; the complexity of the situations that decision makers face and scholars seek to understand; and the incomparability of these situations over time and across cases. All of these problems characterized the end of the Cold War and are illuminated by the transcripts of the Princeton Conference. My focus is on how these problems make matters difficult for scholars, but in each case I examine the similarities and differences between the challenges they present to academics and to decision makers.

Uncertainty

It is hard to imagine any strategic situation in which uncertainty is not a crucial issue. Decision makers bargaining over important issues want to know each others' preferences with regard to imagined outcomes and their capabilities for realizing those preferences. But certain knowledge about these parameters is virtually impossible to obtain in the absence of powerful signals or indicators. The end of the Cold War is utterly typical in this regard. The participants at the Princeton Conference discussed the fascinating process by which their assessments of each others' preferences (and—less discussed— each others' capabilities) underwent radical change between 1982 and 1989. They started out with a four-decade record of mutual hostility, and they ended up genuinely believing that their common interests far outweighed their differences. They began seeing the Soviet Union as a troubled but formidable superpower that might recover its momentum. They finished seeing it as a pitiable leviathan in its death throes. What the Princeton discussions and other sources reveal is the high levels of uncertainty that characterized all such assessments along the way.

The story of the Cold War's end might be told as a tale of the two sides discovering each other's "true" preferences and intentions, but it would involve a complicated plot with many twists and turns. As Anatoly Chernyaev recalled at the Princeton Conference, Mikhail Gorbachev and his team began the game with the conviction that earlier Soviet leaderships had overestimated U.S. hostility, but a considerable amount of hard bargaining and feedback was necessary before they could reach a new assessment they trusted (see chap. 2, above). On the American side, intense debates on "what the Soviets are really after" revealed the high degree of uncertainty. Each side devoted considerable intelligence resources to discerning the operative preferences of the other.

However, the discussions at the Princeton Conference showed how little trust key decision makers placed in such intelligence material. The evidence is in the extraordinary importance they placed on their own assessments, which were based on the personal relationships that developed in the series of ministerial and summit meetings beginning with the Geneva Summit. Like most leaders, Mikhail Gorbachev was a voracious consumer of intelligence material on his negotiating partners, but testimony also strongly suggests that face-to-face bargaining encounters had a powerful influence on his assessment of the Americans' intentions.[3] George Shultz reported, for example, the apparently deep impression that Reagan made on Gorbachev about his personal commitment to SDI at Reykjavik (see chap. 2). Shultz's own relationship with Shevardnadze led him to put more trust in the latter's indications of Soviet intentions in Afghanistan than in those of his own CIA (see chap. 5).

Of course, what gave those personal relationships substance were concrete actions. Roosevelt had a wonderful relationship with Stalin; Brezhnev and Nixon chummed around Camp David and San Clemente like old fraternity brothers. It was not just concessions in the Intermediate-Range Nuclear Forces negotiations or the unilateral reduction of a half-million armored troops in Europe that contributed to reduced American uncertainty about Soviet motives. It was those measures coupled with glasnost at home—with which Americans were quite properly impressed—as well, eventually, as important democratizing reforms. Furthermore, words were probably more important than many political scientists might be inclined to allow. The wholesale revision of Leninist ideology, the jettisoning of notions of "class struggle," and the statements about "freedom of choice" for East-Central Europe, coupled with the domestic reforms and foreign policy actions, made a powerful impression. But in the final analysis, only unambiguous choices clear away remaining uncertainty. For the Americans, the decisive moment was Gorbachev's decision not to intervene to stop the unraveling of socialism in East-Central Europe. As George Bush put it: "If the Soviets are going to let the communists fall in East Germany, they've got to be really serious—more serious than I thought."[4]

What is striking about the whole story is how many unprecedented signals and gestures were needed to reduce American uncertainty about Soviet intentions (and how few such signals the Americans had to send to reduce Gorbachev's uncertainty concerning their intentions). One reason for this is the history of hostility between the two states. Another important reason is the great difficulty of reaching a judgment about others' intentions under conditions of uncertainty. In particular, four key complicating factors are illustrated by the case of the Cold War's end. All of them make matters difficult for decision makers and the scholars who try to explain their actions.

Strategic Incentives to Misrepresent Preferences

In most bargaining situations, successful lying can increase one's payoffs. The buyer of a used car clearly would like the salesman to believe that her upper price is lower than it really is, and the salesman wants to inflate the buyer's perception of his bottom line. Since each bargainer knows that the others face similar incentives, signals about preferences will be discounted by all. It may be hard to convey one's preferences even if one wants desperately to do so honestly.[5] In international politics, states face similar incentives, but bargaining is complicated by the old realist concerns of anarchy and the security dilemma. The incentives to misrepresent become somewhat more complicated. An expansionist state faces incentives to appear satisfied with the status quo. A state satisfied with the status quo also wants to reassure its negotiating partner of its peaceable intentions, but in any bargaining it still faces an incentive to inflate its bottom line. Both sides may be able to read each other's incentives and thus may discount any information about preferences, just as a buyer ought to discount initial indications of a used car salesman's bottom line. Since each side knows that the other faces incentives to misrepresent true preferences, the question is, how do they update their assessments of the other side?

Part of the answer lies in the costs to a given state of taking an action or accepting a trade-off. If A thinks that B is aggressive, it will revise that assessment to the extent that B does things that would be costly for an aggressive state to do.[6] This helps to set the context for many of Gorbachev's bold moves in the diplomacy of the end of the Cold War, including the terms he accepted in the INF Treaty, the acceptance of an intrusive verification regime, and the decision to reduce Soviet military strength in Europe by five hundred thousand troops. All of these were actions that would presumably impose some costs on a state with hostile intentions. Indeed, precisely because many decision makers in the West still suspected Moscow of at least residual revisionist intentions, they did not expect Gorbachev to make those decisions. But even this relatively sophisticated "costly signaling theory" vastly understates the difficulty of the decision maker's task in general, and the uncertainties that both sides faced in reading each other's preferences in the superpower diplomacy of the late 1980s in particular.

The Ambiguity of Signals

It is difficult for both sender and receiver to assess the costs of signals. In hindsight, many of Gorbachev's signals were very costly indeed, facilitating if not causing the collapse of Communism. At the time, each and every one of those signals was subject to multiple interpretations. Some in the West argued that Moscow's INF concessions, for example, were intended to denuclearize NATO.[7] Policies are forward looking: any policy contains an implied prediction. A policy that accepts a cost today may be doing so for a benefit in the future. Any assessment of the policy's costs implies a prediction about its future effect, and prediction is a notoriously dicey matter in international politics. Much of the argument about Gorbachev's concessions concerned exactly this issue. Since many thought that Gorbachev expected great domestic and international gains from his concessions, they thought that such concessions were actually not costly to him and saw no reason to revise their estimates of his intentions. It will be difficult to ascertain even in retrospect what Gorbachev's operative expectations were, since he and those who supported him face an incentive after the fact to understate any earlier predictive failures. It seems likely, however, that they did not expect to pay the costs they eventually did.

Assessing the cost of any signal also implies an assessment of a given leader's domestic situation. If a particular move is essentially forced on a leader by domestic pressures, it contains little information about his intentions. For the Soviets, the constraints on Reagan were surrounded by uncertainty. In addition to the domestic American battles, there was the important constraint imposed by allied governments, themselves beset by powerful peace movements. The overall salience of these constraints was a matter of dispute, as was the basic direction in which they pulled (that is, for or against cooperation). Gorbachev seemed to begin his diplomacy on the assumption that Western Europe and most NATO publics were his allies against the Reagan administration; later, however, he appeared to have learned that many European NATO governments were actually more conservative about nuclear disarmament than was Washington.

In the case of Americans' assessment of Soviet intentions during the end of the Cold War, Gorbachev's domestic constraints also presented a puzzle. Gorbachev's domestic political situation was generally thought to contain incentives against cooperative moves, increasing the apparent costs of the concessions he made. At the same time, domestic economic incentives were thought to be pushing him in the opposite direction. Deep uncertainty surrounded American assessments of Gorbachev's domestic constraints, rendering the meaning of various moves hard to discern. Given all of these sources of uncertainty, it is not surprising that it took strong signals, coupled with changed rhetoric, domestic changes, and personal rapport among negotiators, to get the ball moving toward substantial cooperation on arms control.[8]

Incentives for Ambiguity and the Misrepresentation of Constraints

The problem of ambiguous signals is even more challenging if we consider the issue of private information.[9] Decision makers know that all parties face incentives to misrepresent their preferences. Further, they sense that changes in their assessments of each others' preferences will depend on the assessed costs of signals. Assessing the costs and benefits of actions is tricky, however, because the domestic and international environments are complex. It follows naturally that leaders and their diplomats face incentives not only to misrepresent preferences but also to misrepresent the constraints under which they operate, in order to influence the assessment of costs. And such tactics are possible, since leaders often keep information private, not only about their preferences but also about the constraints under which they operate.

The incentives to misrepresent constraints may be quite complex. Thus, American negotiators may have exaggerated the likelihood that the Senate would balk at certain treaty provisions or (less plausibly) that Reagan was constrained by his right wing; and Soviets could warn darkly that any further concessions would buy Gorbachev a one-way rail ticket to a Siberian health retreat. At the same time, leaders can use international constraints against domestic ones. The Senate is often told that its opposition to certain presidential positions in international negotiations is harmful to U.S. credibility with foreign partners. Gorbachev also used credibility arguments to help tame his military-industrial complex (which he wanted to do anyway for economic reasons).[10] And naturally each side tries to judge the nature of the other's incentives to misrepresent constraints, which colors the interpretation of incoming evidence. This is the basic stuff of diplomacy, but it complicates mightily the analysis of signals by decision makers in strategic bargaining situations and by scholars in retrospect.[11]

During the Cold War, analysts tended to assume that the Soviets possessed an advantage in any negotiation owing to their private information about domestic constraints. The constraints on U.S. presidents were wide open for all to see, while the Soviet general secretary's domestic political world was shrouded in secrecy.[12] In fact, matters were not so simple. Soviet negotiators actually confronted too much evidence about constraints on the U.S. side to reach an easy judgment. The Western side could thus concoct a great many plausible stories about constraints. Thus, U.S. presidents retained private information about their domestic (and alliance) constraints while possessing large amounts of material to utilize in any tactical effort to misrepresent them. Meanwhile, the myths of Communist Party infallibility on the Soviet side compelled Moscow to act *as if* the general secretary were completely unconstrained. It was only quite late in the Cold War's endgame that Soviet negotiators could plausibly play the domestic card. The Americans' negotiating position seemed much more helped than hurt by the apparent transparency of domestic and alliance constraints.

The more general point is that assessing the costs of signals would be complicated but manageable if the incentives to misrepresent were themselves obvious and cut only in one direction. In the bargaining over the price of a used car, everyone's incentives are obvious and easy to model. Unfortunately, this is very rarely the case in international politics. It is hard to name situations in which incentives to misrepresent all point in one direction, especially if domestic political considerations are part of the picture. That is, leaders usually do not face unidirectional incentives to misrepresent preferences and constraints; they face incentives to portray both preferences and constraints differently to different audiences.

Consider Gorbachev and the Cold War endgame. Gorbachev needed to convey generally benign intentions to the West. But he could not signal utter satisfaction with the status quo. If he did, the West would face no incentive to negotiate. It had somehow to be prodded. Gorbachev's method—typical for Soviet diplomacy—was to formulate proposals popular with some political elements in the West: certain factions in NATO governments, peace movements, and so on. They then would provide the prod for Washington, which, in the absence of some incentive, would be hard to bring to serious negotiations. Such prodding, however, could seem aggressive to conservative NATO leaders. Domestically, the general secretary wanted to cut defense and shift resources to the civilian sector, but he also needed to show that concessions were not harming Soviet security and were in fact "mutual." He wanted to appear less conciliatory to his domestic audience than he wanted to seem internationally. At the same time, he wanted his domestic audience to see the economic constraint as very strong, while he probably feared that if the West thought the economic constraint was too strong, it would simply stand back and wait for concessions. In short, Gorbachev, like most leaders most of the time, faced cross-cutting incentives concerning both preferences and constraints. And the result of cross-cutting incentives is not clear misrepresentation but ambiguity.[13]

Incentives for ambiguity make the costs and meaning of signals hard to read and explain even further why so many mutually reinforcing signals were needed in order for the two superpowers to agree to substantial arms cooperation. It is no wonder that experienced diplomats and leaders, proud of their unsentimental toughness, still seek to reach out and touch each other across the swamp of ambiguity in which they operate. Personal relationships may help in the interpretation and sending of signals. Such relationships can themselves constitute forums for signaling. They are unreliable indicators, to be sure, but so are all other indicators in the world of diplomacy.

Incentives for Ambivalence

Cross-cutting incentives foster ambiguity not only in governments but also in the individuals who lead them. Ambivalence is part of many stories of foreign policy and probably deserves a chapter in the tale of the end of the Cold War as well. Which was the "real" Reagan, the anti-Communist crusader or the antinuclear visionary, the ideologue or the pragmatist? The fact that it was not always easy to tell helped him lead his party and his country, and may have helped him in international negotiations. Which was the "real" Gorbachev, socialism's savior or its gravedigger, the tough Reykjavik negotiator or the one-world, antinuclear dreamer? Again, members of his inner leadership circle, politically active functionaries in his country, and American decision makers were often unsure. And that uncertainty was arguably functional for the reforming leader, helping him to keep critics at bay and maintain a reform coalition composed of many mutually antagonistic elements. Whether the contradictory strains in these two leaders' thought reflected a carefully crafted strategy or fundamental ambivalence will be an intriguing question for future scholars. It will be hard to answer, however, since the evidence is likely to be contradictory and since in hindsight both the leaders themselves and their biographers will be tempted to highlight that side of their personality which seems vindicated by history.

Indeed, ambivalence is an attractive response to a high level of uncertainty. One may know that an issue is important but be uncertain about the positions of key international and domestic actors and about the likely consequences of various courses of action. The wisest course under such circumstances may be to dodge the issue in the hope that it might become more tractable in time. Experienced politicians sense that unambiguous pronouncements in conditions of high uncertainty can be unwise. "Read-my-lips" statements can come back to haunt one when circumstances change. Procrastination has costs, but so does unambiguous choice. Indeed, the costs of making an unambiguous choice now may be much easier to reckon than the costs of putting off the decision to another day.

In short, the political environment may present actors with few incentives to formulate clear and ordered preferences prior to taking action. In the real world of the decision maker, James March argues, action often precedes thought: "Human choice behavior is at least as much a process for discovering goals as for acting upon them."[14] Decision makers may simply refrain from thinking through an issue before they act on it. They may not sit down and ponder goals until they are forced to do so by circumstances. Indeed, they may not settle on a consistent story about their preferences until after the fact, until after the nation has stumbled into and out of a major crisis or a diplomatic victory.

Uncertainty makes politics a risky business. A statesman can try to hedge decisions and obfuscate trade-offs, but eventually most have to take a leap into the dark, or at any rate, into a very poorly lighted area. And scholars would do well to bear this in mind when they evaluate the actions of decision makers from the comfortable vantage of hindsight. Arguably the most commonly posed "puzzle" in scholarly treatises on international relations is, why do states adopt self-defeating policies? The answer may often be that a policy can only be known to be self-defeating after it has been adopted and implemented.[15] Policies cannot be judged solely on the basis of the outcomes they yield. They also must be judged in terms of the expectations on which they were based. Many ultimately self-defeating policies may have been based on utterly plausible expectations. Many policies that are seen in hindsight to have been successful may have been based on patently absurd expectations.

It is important to fight the temptation to read the outcome back into the process and underestimate the uncertainty faced by both sides. The Princeton Conference is an extremely valuable source for scholars of international politics. The dialogue not only captured important new findings but recreated as no other source could the conditions under which these decision makers operated at a decisive moment both in their careers and in twentieth-century history. But it is important to bear in mind that those present at the conference represented the wings of their respective governments most interested in cooperation on arms control. Absent were representatives of the more hawkish, Cold War–oriented factions within each administration. That makes the story that emerged more coherent than it would have been had some hard-liners been present.[16] In particular, neither the Russian participants nor the Americans faced an incentive to subject the strategy of Gorbachev and Shevardnadze to much critical scrutiny. Even at a gathering as infused with a sense of the reality of diplomacy as the Princeton Conference, some of each side's daunting uncertainty about what they were doing and where they were going was absent.

Uncertainty is the answer to many scholarly puzzles. Indeed, it may be the answer to too many puzzles. The higher the uncertainty, the more permissive the political environment. Under uncertainty, many policies are simultaneously plausible. Why certain policies were adopted—and why some were successful while others were not—become highly contingent questions.

Jervis and George (in chaps. 8 and 9, respectively) both suggest that the problem with the main international relations theories is not that they are wrong but that they are indeterminate. They do not make unambiguous predictions about the behavior of real states in specific circumstances. It is thus hard to specify what outcomes in the real world should cause us to conclude that a given theory is wrong. Uncertainty is the twin of theoretical indeterminacy. When the scholar is armed only with indeterminate theory, much of his or her wisdom is an artifact of hindsight. When decision makers face uncertainty, scholars confront an ambiguous historical record, in which confirming evidence for many competing theories is all too easy to find. The uncertainty under which decision makers operate, and the incentives they face to misrepresent preferences before, during, and after major events, make measuring many independent and dependent variables harder than it is often thought to be.

Immeasurability

Decision makers and scholars both face a second problem: the difficulty of coming up with reliable measures of the variables they regard as important. For scholars, the absence of agreed-upon measures makes the testing of hypotheses difficult even if those hypotheses are rigorously formulated to make deterministic statements about behavior or outcomes. It is frustratingly easy for others to question the accuracy of the measures employed. For decision makers, measurement problems make it harder to monitor the effectiveness of policies, and contribute to the environment of uncertainty and unpredictability. For all, measures are like theories: very necessary but not necessarily very good.

The first major difficulty of measurement is that the material variables that lie at the heart of many international theories are much harder to measure than is generally recognized. The intractable difficulty of measuring "power" or "capabilities" is an important example.[17] All of the earliest writers on the subject, as well as the post–World War II "classical realists," recognized this problem. Even if power is defined narrowly as military capabilities, its measurement is still elusive, since the outcome of a military conflict is very difficult to predict. Military capability reflects an extraordinarily complex combination of factors, some of which are observable in peacetime but many of which are matters of conjecture until tested by battle.[18] Capabilities useful for defeating one kind of opponent may be useless or harmful when deployed against another. War outcomes themselves might be considered rough measures of fighting capacity, but wars (fortunately) occur relatively rarely, and many states interact over long periods without ever coming to blows. In all such relationships, the "real" balance of military power will always be debatable.

The U.S.-Soviet rivalry is an important case in point. The countries never fought each other. If the balance of military power between them was an important determinant of their behavior, it was one that was never tested and can never be tested. Evaluating realist theories against their competitors will therefore be a difficult business, as power is realism's central (in some cases only) variable. Competing systemic theories also highlight variables that are very hard to measure, such as interdependence and institutions. And theories couched at the domestic level often rely on domestic variables that are just as immeasurable as the balance of power. State action, for example, is often explained by reference to the power of various domestic interest groups. There is no reason to suppose that the balance of power among domestic interests is any easier to measure than the balance of power among states.

In all cases, the temptation is strong to assign values to immeasurable variables on the basis of known outcomes. Thus, the Cold War ended because the balance of power shifted against the Soviet Union—we know that because the Soviet Union collapsed in December 1991. Gorbachev was able to implement cooperative policies because modernization shifted the domestic balance of power against the military-industrial complex—we know that because Gorbachev implemented cooperative policies after 1987.

The second difficulty of measurement is that measuring behavioral variables is harder than scholars often appear to realize. Theories of international relations seek to account for overall patterns of cooperation. How do we measure patterns of cooperation? It is no easy matter to characterize long-term patterns of behavior nonsubjectively. We lack an agreed-upon theoretical baseline from which to measure observed cooperation. What, exactly, is cooperation? Was the behavior of a given state cooperative or competitive? It is often both. As noted, states face powerful incentives for ambiguity about their intentions, so there is likely to be evidence for competing interpretations of policy in most cases. U.S. policy in the Cold War endgame is an example. The Reagan administration's tough line against the Soviets is often taken as an example of successful containment policy. But the policy actually contained strong cooperative elements almost from the beginning.[19] Indeed, a key finding of Don Oberdorfer's *The Turn* is that the American impulse for an improvement in relations greatly predated Gorbachev's accession to power.

The third difficulty is that, as has long been recognized, beliefs or ideas are not subject to easy classification and analysis. The problem of uncertainty has led many scholars to a focus on ideas and beliefs as well as (or instead of) on the material factors that traditionally have lain at the center of international theory.[20] If the international political world is highly uncertain, then the ideas actors have about reality are important determinants of that reality. The rules and norms that political actors consider legitimate, the measures they agree to assign to variables, and the causal relationships their own political theories lead them to accept as true will all be central constitutive elements of the political environment.

The renewed focus on ideas is to be welcomed, but it is important to bear in mind that one reason for the discipline's original preference for material variables was precisely the difficulty of measuring ideas and beliefs. If "the distribution of military power" is hard to pin down empirically, so are preferences, ideas, norms, beliefs, and strategies. Indeed, the analysis above suggested that the political environment often presents decision makers with strong incentives for misrepresenting their real intentions or for deliberate ambiguity. In such cases, determining what decision makers "really" believed will be extraordinarily difficult. Policy makers face incentives to obscure their preferences, since private information is usually an advantage in bargaining; to seem to be different things to different parties; to keep options open; to misrepresent both preferences and constraints; and to tell a convincing story of strategic acumen (or helplessness) after the fact. The key to a successful strategy of misrepresentation or ambiguity is secrecy: that is, in such cases there will be a lot of misleading evidence about intentions and a small amount of very well hidden accurate information.

All of these incentives translate into a historical record replete with ambiguity and full of false trails. A leader may use his domestic critics to excuse the ambiguity of his policy before foreign partners. He may use the opinions of foreigners to tame his domestic opponents. The record of such a case would contain good evidence both for the proposition that domestic politics influenced foreign policy and for the proposition that foreign policy took primacy over domestic policy. In short, all of the uncertainty about intentions that decision makers have to contend with is also relevant to the scholar, with one important difference: the scholar usually knows the outcome before he or she goes about explaining it. And scholars face powerful professional incentives to resolve the ambiguity of the historical record in a manner favorable to particular theories. Thus, the danger of post hoc or tautological measurements is just as high when assessing beliefs and ideas as when gauging material variables.

These concerns about the dangers of hindsight all apply in spades to the end of the Cold War. Discussions of the Cold War's end rarely can avoid the subject of Gorbachev. The Soviet leader stood at the center of the vast array of competing forces that pushed and pulled the Cold War to an end. Perhaps for that reason, he seems to have faced the most intense incentives for obfuscation, ambiguity, deception, feinting, and maneuvering. Reading the memoirs of Gorbachev's key aides leads inescapably to the conclusion that these men were constantly unsure of where their chief stood and what he stood for. For many years, both centrist conservatives such as Yegor Ligachev and Nikolai Ryzhkov and more radical reformers such as Aleksandr Yakovlev and Eduard Shevardnadze all seemed simultaneously to see a different Gorbachev: one who ultimately was or was about to be "their man."[21] Who he really was at various points in the story is still a matter of conjecture.

Complexity

To understand the complexity policy makers have to contend with in any given situation, all scholars need to do is compose a list of the factors that appear to influence the outcome. In the case of the end of the Cold War, the picture is of a vast interacting array of forces for and against cooperation—in the international system, within governments and their publics, and even within the minds of individual leaders. On the American side, there was the Janus-faced President

Reagan, so aptly described at the Princeton Conference, who combined strong anti-Communism and peace-through-strength convictions with visionary antinuclear views.[22] Then there were the two factions within the government, each trying to draw out its favored "face" of Reagan. The victory of the more accommodative Shultz wing by no means predetermined the détente that followed. For that to occur, a similar set of independently indeterminate factors on the Soviet side had to work themselves out in interactions with the American side. In addition, there were other countries of lesser but still significant moment, within each of which forces for and against accommodation contended. And in the background were those conditioning factors highlighted by international relations theory: the bipolar distribution of power, the Soviet Union's relative decline, the security provided by nuclear weapons, the prevalence of democracy, interdependence, and the information revolution.

The system is complex, and its components are interactive. Exclusive focus on any one level of analysis is misleading, as is the assumption that influence flows from one level to the next unidirectionally. Governments influence the international system, which influences governments, which can influence their own societies but are also constrained by them; societies are penetrated by international influences, but societal groups also exert their reciprocal influences on international realities. One could draw lines connecting all these factors, but in all cases the causal arrows point in both directions. And the diagram would in any case look like a plateload of angel-hair pasta. Complex systems in which actors and environment constantly influence each other, in which the "environment" is inefficient in selecting behavior—and moreover, in which the "actors" are human beings who learn from experience and can quickly change their beliefs and behavior—may defy causal analysis. The point is made with special clarity by Jervis:[23]

A force may change the environment in which it operates such that amplifying or counterbalancing forces are called up; the kind as well as the degree of the effect may depend on the magnitude of the stimulus; and the combination of several factors may produce an effect that cannot be deduced from their independent influences. Indeed, the language of independent and dependent variables, actions and responses, and separate factors and forces may be misleading when we are dealing with a system . . . The dynamics of a complex system cannot be captured by arbitrarily labeling one set of elements "causes" and others "effects."

For scholars, this means that the task of demonstrating causality is very difficult in many cases and impossible in others. For policy makers, complex system dynamics can translate into unintended and utterly unexpected consequences. A small change can produce other, much larger changes. A policy might yield positive results when applied in small doses but disaster when applied in larger ones. Systems effects can be capricious. The end of the Cold War itself may be a vast tale of unintended consequences. The relationship between any given strategy and the relatively peaceful outcome may be utterly serendipitous. This is a hypothesis that must be borne in mind.

Consider Gorbachev's policies. It is clear that he intended perestroika to be a New Deal for Soviet socialism: he would do for Communism what Franklin D. Roosevelt did for capitalism. The policy unleashed the forces that destroyed socialism as he understood it. Foreign Minister Shevardnadze argued that in order to proceed with reforms, "we had to have confidence and eschew our weakness complex."[24] Western neoliberal theorists agree that a sense of confidence and security breeds liberalization and cooperation. But that turned out to be a disastrously illusory assumption from the standpoint of the Soviet Union's interests as Gorbachev interpreted them. The social and political system that Gorbachev pledged to improve appears indeed to have been critically weaker than its Western counterpart. A driving force behind Gorbachev's innovative arms control initiatives was the belief that reducing defense expenditures could rescue socialism by diverting resources to the civilian sector. This assumption was clearly revealed in the November 1988 Politburo meeting at which the unilateral conventional force reductions initiative was adopted. It appears to have been instrumental in convincing relatively conservative members of the Soviet leadership to accept unilateral concessions.[25] The belief that cutting defense expenditures could help rescue socialism via resource reallocation aided cooperation in achieving arms control, but the belief was an illusion. Cutting defense spending did not help socialism and in many ways imposed devastating short-run costs on it. Another supporting belief was that unilateral measures would spark a mutual disarmament spiral. But instead, unilateral measures meant to reduce the West's fear of Moscow reduced Eastern Europeans' fear of their own regimes and of those regimes' Russian backers to an even greater extent, leading to a unilateral decommissioning of the Warsaw Pact while NATO remained intact and formidably strong.

It would be difficult to account for the Soviet leadership's dramatic change of direction and for its ability to get its reform policies adopted against conservative resistance, without reference to this apparently misplaced confidence. Had the Gorbachev team had any notion of the effects their policies would have, it is hard to imagine that they would have adopted them in the first place. In short, miscalculations, which can only be known in hindsight, can lead to peace and cooperation.[26] Why wasn't the policy corrected in mid-course? Here, the capriciousness of systems effects comes in. The policy probably appeared to be working quite well until the fall of 1989, when the Soviet system suddenly began to crumble. The feedback from Gorbachev's policies had been mixed (as always), but it had seemed favorable up to that point, especially in foreign policy. (Indeed, the Princeton Conference witnessed a revival of that pre-1989 euphoria. Participants warmed to the recollection of fighting and winning domestic and international battles for superpower cooperation against long odds.)

However, in the summer of 1989 Poland and Hungary began innovative democratizing reforms, as Gorbachev had ardently wished them to do. The mix between those policies and the continued existence of repressive conservative Communist regimes (especially in East Germany) set in motion a series of mutually reinforcing systems-effects that led to the collapse of one Warsaw Pact regime after the next in quick succession. By August, as Sergei Tarasenko reported at the Princeton Conference, Shevardnadze and his aides were sitting on a Black Sea beach contemplating the unraveling of the Soviet empire. The agenda had shifted suddenly from managing the stabilization and reversal of the U.S.-Soviet arms race to keeping up with the rapid pace of events. At the start of 1989, the Soviet diplomatic leadership was confidently refashioning its external security using an innovative package of New Thinking concepts. A year later, Gorbachev and Shevardnadze were desperately making concessions on German unification out of the fear of losing all influence in Europe.[27]

On the American side there are analogous, if less dramatic and consequential, gaps between policy makers' intentions and strategic analyses and the outcome to which those intentions and analyses contributed. The Reagan administration's policies appeared designed at first to rescue America from decline, not to manage the decline of the Soviet Union, which was portrayed as a rising military juggernaut whose geopolitical momentum had to be contained. As the CIA's Lawrence Gershwin and former secretary of defense Frank Carlucci testified at the Princeton Conference, many U.S. officials in the early 1980s thought that the United States was militarily inferior to the Soviet Union in important respects.[28] Arguments raged over whether the United States was strong and secure enough to risk arms negotiations with Moscow. Finally, in the second Reagan term, momentum built behind a policy of seeking "détente under another name" with Gorbachev's Soviet Union. This momentum so alarmed many in the U.S. policy establishment that the incoming Bush administration called a year-long halt in order to conduct a comprehensive strategic review. The review was outdated when complete. The administration then resolved to pin its hopes on a relationship with Gorbachev. That relationship reached full maturity at the December 1990 Malta Summit, which took place as the Soviet Union and Gorbachev were entering the final stage of their decline.

Complexity and unanticipated effects make it harder to assess strategies for ending rivalries on the basis of the experience of ending the Cold War. It is vital not to permit hindsight to obscure the important fact that the decision makers who negotiated the post-1985 improvement in U.S.-Soviet relations had no idea that the bipolar era was coming to an end. They did not think that they were paving the way for a structural transformation of world politics. Indeed, had they thought so they might have acted more circumspectly, or at least differently. Both Moscow and Washington might well have adopted quite different (and less cooperative) strategies had they had a different—more accurate—assessment of Soviet power. What they thought they were doing was stabilizing and regulating the two-superpower world that they had known for the previous four decades. The distinction is important, because most analyses of the Cold War's end conflate the deep détente that emerged before 1989 with the systemic transformation of world politics that got under way in the fall of that year. And the complex relationship between the superpowers' negotiated détente and subsequent revolutionary political change is one of the factors that inhibit comparison.

Incomparability

The problems of uncertainty, immeasurability, and complexity would be less vexing to policy makers and scholars if they could find enough good cases for comparison. For policy makers, the problem boils down to finding useful analogies from the past to use in analyzing the current situation. Analogies do not have to be exact replicas of the current situation; they may well serve as contrasting foils. By comparing or contrasting the current situation with similar episodes from the past, decision makers may reduce their sense of uncertainty, get a better idea of how to measure key variables, and cut through complexity to focus on a few key factors. Of course, analogies can turn out to be devastatingly misleading, as Gorbachev may have discovered about his Roosevelt analogy, and as many leaders before him learned about their favorite lessons from the past.[29]

For scholars, the problem is similar but more heavily theorized. Many social scientists contend that the seemingly intractable problem of complexity is merely the result of looking at causality in the wrong way. In their view, any single major event will always appear impossibly complex. Decision makers' recollections are interesting, they claim, but misleading, since participants will always focus on the unique rather than the generalizable aspects of the events they experience. Political science is about explaining relationships among variables, not explaining single events. The search for causality in a single case, in this view, is metaphysical, unscientific. Causality can be understood only in a correlational sense: that is, causality can be established only by demonstrating covariation between antecedent conditions and outcomes.[30] Thus the end of the Cold War must be seen as an instance of a more general law (or laws) that can be explained scientifically. Ronald Reagan, Mikhail Gorbachev, New Thinking, and the "Reagan doctrine" were just foam on the long waves of world politics. Interesting to contemplate, perhaps, but not the stuff of social science.

A correlational approach to causality is distressing to many historically minded people, but it is understandable in light of the daunting complexity of major historical cases and the indeterminacy of debates on their causes. In international relations, however, the search for knowledge via correlations is hindered by the familiar problem of incomparability: too many variables and too few cases.

Just as decision makers find it hard to locate appropriate analogies, scholars have had trouble finding enough cases within a class of phenomena to isolate causal variables.[31] The problem has dogged the analysis of even such comparatively frequent events as wars and crises.[32] Events such as the end of the Cold War present unique problems.

In order to understand the Cold War's end scientifically, scholars need to know the class of events to which it belongs. The Cuban missile crisis was a crisis. The Korean War was a war. The end of the Cold War was . . . what, exactly? At first brush, it would appear to be an example of the emergence of cooperation between states under anarchy. The universe of cases would include instances in which long-standing rivals became partners or at least attenuated their conflict. Egypt and Israel come to mind, as do Israel and the Palestine Liberation Organization, Britain and the United States, and Britain and France in the first half of the nineteenth century. One could compare cases that ended in war, those that ended when a third power rose, and those few that were brought to an end solely or mainly by the efforts of the two parties.[33] Some intriguing hypotheses might be uncovered and evaluated in this way.

However, as noted above, the complexity of the case makes the end of the Cold War hard to classify. The U.S.-Soviet rivalry was not unambiguously over as of the fall of 1989. It was only undeniably buried by the cataclysmic collapse of Communism in East-Central Europe and Russia. That sudden, almost revolutionary collapse of Communism was functionally equivalent to an exogenous shock to the superpower relationship. After Communism began to collapse, the situation was less and less under the control of policy makers consciously implementing strategies for achieving cooperation. Increasingly, policy makers were reduced to reacting to the storm of events. It was only when the Soviet Union's external and internal situation appeared to be in free fall that Gorbachev and Bush adopted unambiguously cooperative policies. Those who question the utility of the strategies employed by Washington or Moscow for achieving cooperation will put forward the counterfactual speculation that had the Soviet system been more resilient, the late 1980s détente might have yet again slid back into Cold War hostility.

We may be present at the creation of a series of debates rivaling in intensity and inconclusiveness those concerning the onset of the

Cold War. Indeed, the analytical situation may be even more intractable, resembling the one that exists in arguments over the causes
of the decline and fall of Rome. The beginning of the Cold War was
not accompanied by fundamental internal change on either of the
two main sides. It was a much more cleanly international event
than the end of the Cold War, which overlapped and intertwined
with revolutionary upheavals in the Soviet world. Those in the
United States, Europe, and the Soviet Union who understood the
Cold War as a clash of two sociopolitical systems will see the diplomacy of the late 1980s as a sideshow to the real cause of change: the
collapse (or destruction) of the Leninist challenge to liberal capitalism. But others will insist that the New Thinking diplomacy on both
sides was a precondition for the peaceful management of the revolutions of 1989–91. Whether the United States and the Soviet Union
could ever have completely transformed their mutual relationship
while remaining essentially the same societies in approximately the
same international conditions will forever remain an unanswerable
question.

In other words, comparison is hindered by potential disagreement
over the classification of relevant cases. In the case of the Cold War's
end, four individually complex processes intertwine and meld into
one another: the emergence of an unprecedentedly deep détente between the superpowers; the revolutionary implosion of the Soviet
social and economic order in Europe and Russia; the dissolution of
the multinational Soviet state; and the structural transformation of
world politics away from bipolarity. Classifying this as merely an instance of the emergence of cooperation under anarchy will be uncon-
vincing to a great many researchers.

The problems of complexity and incomparability lead many scholars to conclude that the end of the Cold War belongs to a class of
events that simply cannot be studied in a theoretically rigorous way.
According to their view, complex cases, especially those involving
revolutionary change in interdependent systems (in which causality
is hard to establish, and which are inherently difficult to classify and
compare), must lie outside political science's theoretical project.[34]
Though understandable intellectually, this position is unsettling and
possibly deceptive. Complex and revolutionary events may exert a
powerful influence on subsequent periods of relative stability. If so,
excluding them from theoretical analysis may be highly misleading.

It is doubtful that those who lived through the Cold War and took up the study of international politics out of concern for the issues of war and peace that it presented will be satisfied with the conclusion that the end of that epochal conflict is a subject fit only for ad hoc storytelling. They chose to study world politics because of its importance, not its susceptibility to scientific analysis.[35]

Conclusion: Toward a Pragmatic Research Agenda

This analysis suggests two familiar conclusions and a third that is less often noted. First, the end of the Cold War underlines the difficulty of theorizing about international politics. After reading such a litany of problems confronting scholars and policy makers, one naturally asks, why bother to think theoretically and look for causes? The answer is that we have no choice but to do so. To paraphrase Churchill's comment on democracy, explicit theorizing is the worst way to go about understanding international politics, except for all the alternatives. It is better to have one's theory served up explicitly—as pretentious, overstated, or boring as it sometimes can be—than to have it sneaked into the text through the back door. The clear statement of hypotheses and assumptions, and their rigorous empirical evaluation, are not simply faddish practices or reflections of science-envy. They are defenses against the propagation of lies and myths. Recognizing the problems and weaknesses of existing theories is a way of strengthening them, not a reason to give up trying. In other fields, grappling with complexity and uncertainty has led to progress rather than surrender. We are better off even with our weak theories and seemingly endless debates than we would be without them. They generate important empirical research; they sharpen policy debates; they lead to rigorous questioning of the assumptions that underlie policy.

However, the second conclusion is that it is necessary to acknowledge that events such as the end of the Cold War cannot be explained scientifically as instances of the operation of a general law. Failure to recognize this will lead to fruitless debate. The end of the Cold War will hardly be subsumed as a single unit under some General Law of World Politics. The four problems analyzed above interact in particularly vexing ways in such complex events. Yet these events do command our attention, as they set the stage for much of what follows. Explaining events such as the Cold War's end calls for the kind of methodological pragmatism shown even by positivist philosophers of science when they consider analogous explanatory problems.[36] The event needs to be disaggregated, and different generalizations—which may indeed be substantiated by comparison—must be applied to its different parts. In this sense, many of the theories that seem to be competing may in fact be complementary, explaining different pieces of the puzzle. As the pieces are put together, at some stage in the process, it will be necessary to go "beyond correlations," in David Dessler's phrase, and toward "a direct examination of a theory's postulated generative processes."[37] In Alexander George's terminology, such research will involve tracing the process through which the posited cause produced (or influenced) the outcome.[38]

The third and most important conclusion concerns the implications of the convergence between decision makers and scholars for the way we conduct research. Policy makers need to decide how to respond to other states. If they choose the wrong response—if they appease an aggressor or deter a peaceable state—their policies fail, and they and their societies pay costs. Scholars need to know how to measure the behavior of states in order to test theoretical hypotheses. If they fail to measure behaviors accurately, they will classify cases inappropriately and reach fallacious conclusions about the veracity of their theories. Is the end of the Cold War a successful case of containment? Answering that question requires the scholar to meet analytical challenges very similar to those faced by George Shultz and his colleagues as they negotiated with their Soviet counterparts.

Recognition of this convergence reinforces the need for collaboration between the two professions. In their laudable search for a science of politics, many scholars have reinforced the dichotomy between actor and observer. The separation between scientist and subject matter may be useful for some purposes, but if it is carried too far in international relations it obscures the convergence between actor and observer and cuts off fruitful lines of inquiry. There is no better way to assess the basic problems of uncertainty, immeasurability, complexity, and incomparability than to examine how decision makers actually deal with them in real cases.

The Princeton Conference transcripts represent an extraordinary source for this kind of research. Decision makers such as those who gathered at Princeton are, in the final analysis, the subjects of all our theorizing and all our conjectures. States and international systems do not exist. They are necessary analytical constructs. When all is said and done, theories of international relations make empirical statements about the men and women who act on behalf of their nations. It is what they decide to do that is recorded as states' "behavior." It is the results of their negotiations that social scientists call "outcomes." If a force constrains states, it constrained these people. Any good theoretician needs to confront decision makers and their environment to see how postulated causes and influences play out in reality. And the preceding chapters provide a rich opportunity for just such an intellectual dialogue between theory and reality.

Chronology of Soviet-American Relations, 1983–1989   ∴

• 1983

February 15 — Dobrynin meets with Reagan in the White House.

March 8 — Reagan makes his "evil empire" speech.

July 11 — Reagan sends Andropov a letter on improvement of communications.

September 1 — Korean Air Lines flight 007 is shot down by Soviet planes.

September 8 — Shultz and Gromyko meet in Madrid.

September 28 — Andropov makes a policy statement regarding the United States: "Even if someone ever had any illusions about the possible evolution for the better in the policy of the present U.S. administration, the latest developments have dispelled them."[1]

November 2–11 — NATO conducts exercise Able Archer, a secret test of command procedures for employing nuclear weapons.

November 22–23 — West Germany approves U.S. deployments of intermediate-range nuclear missiles; the Soviet Union breaks off the INF talks.

• 1984

January 16 — Reagan's "Ivan and Anya" speech asks for improved relations.

January 18 — Shultz and Gromyko meet in Stockholm.

February 9 — Andropov dies; Chernenko is elected general secretary; Bush attends Andropov's funeral in Moscow.

February 23 — Chernenko's letter to Reagan launches intensive correspondence.

August 13 — Shultz obtains permission from Reagan to proceed with Gromyko's visit to Washington.

September 28 — Gromyko meets Reagan in the White House.

November 6 — Reagan is reelected to a second term.

November 22 — The United States and the Soviet Union agree to a Gromyko-Shultz meeting to work out the resumption of arms talks.

• *1985*

January 7–8 — Shultz and Gromyko agree to nuclear and space talks.

March 10 — Chernenko dies; Gorbachev is elected general secretary; Bush and Shultz attend Chernenko's funeral in Moscow carrying a summit invitation from Reagan.

May 4 — Shultz and Gromyko meet in Vienna.

July 2 — Gromyko is named Soviet president; Shevardnadze, foreign minister. A Reagan-Gorbachev summit meeting is announced for November 19–20 in Geneva.

July 31 — Shultz and Shevardnadze have their initial meeting at Helsinki.

November 5 — Shultz sees Gorbachev during a pre-summit trip to Moscow.

November 19–21 — The Geneva Summit is held.

• *1986*

January 15 — Gorbachev offers a sweeping disarmament plan, calling for the elimination of all nuclear weapons by 2000.

February 25–27 — The Twenty-seventh Party Congress approves basic changes in Soviet doctrines. Gorbachev says that "counterrevolution and imperialism have turned Afghanistan into a bleeding wound" and expresses a desire to withdraw Soviet troops "in stages" as the conflict is "regulated" and Afghanistan is "protected from outside interference."[2]

July 25 — Reagan sends a letter to Gorbachev regarding a space arms offer; Bessmertnykh brings a proposal for a work plan to Washington.

mid-August — At a Crimean dacha, Gorbachev and Chernyaev discuss a plan for a working summit; Gorbachev spells out the rough proposals eventually tabled at Reykjavik.

August 23 — Gennadi Zakharov is arrested in New York.

August 30 — Nicholas Daniloff is arrested in Moscow in retaliation for the Zakharov arrest.

September 18 — Shevardnadze brings a letter to Reagan proposing a quick preliminary meeting in Iceland or Britain.

September 29 — The Soviets drop the charges against Nicholas Daniloff.

September 30 — The United States drops the charges against Gennadi Zakharov; the two sides announce the Reykjavik Summit.

October 11–12 — The Reagan-Gorbachev summit meeting is held in Reykjavik.

October 21 — The United States orders the expulsion of fifty-five Soviet diplomats; the Soviet Union orders the ouster of five U.S. Embassy staff members and the withdrawal of all 260 Soviet employees.

November 5–6 — Shultz and Shevardnadze meet in Vienna.

• *1987*

February 28 — Gorbachev offers to de-link the Intermediate-Range Nuclear Forces Treaty from the Strategic Arms Reduction Treaty and from space arms.

March 30 — Amid charges of spying, the United States replaces all twenty-eight U.S. Marine guards at its Moscow embassy.

April 14 — Gorbachev, in a meeting with Shultz, proposes zero solution on INF.

May 23 — The Soviet Union stops jamming the Voice of America.

May 29 — A West German teenager lands a plane in Red Square; Gorbachev fires Defense Minister Sokolov and other officials.

July 29 — The United States and its allies formally accept the zero solution on INF.

September 15–18 — Shevardnadze visits Washington; Reagan announces an "agreement in principle" to conclude the INF pact at a summit later in 1987.

October 30 — Shevardnadze flies to Washington, sets a date for a summit meeting in December.

November 22–24 — A meeting between Shultz and Shevardnadze in Geneva resolves most remaining INF differences.

December 8–10 — Washington Summit includes the signing of the INF Treaty and negotiations on space issues.

• *1988*

February 8 — Gorbachev announces that all Soviet troops are to leave Afghanistan.

February 21–22 — Shultz visits Moscow for talks.

March 16 — Carlucci and Yazov meet in Bern.

March 22–23 — Shevardnadze visits Washington for talks centering on Afghan issues.

April 14 — Shultz, Shevardnadze, and others sign Afghan accords requiring total Soviet withdrawal by February 15, 1989.

April 21–24 — Shultz visits Soviet Union for talks and a tour of Ukraine and Georgia; Gorbachev complains about Reagan rhetoric.

May 11–12 — Shultz and Shevardnadze hold their final pre-summit talks in Geneva.

May 27 — The Senate votes 93 to 5 to ratify the INF Treaty.

May 29–June 2 — The Moscow Summit of Reagan and Gorbachev takes place.

June 28–July 1 — At the Nineteenth Conference of the Communist Party of the Soviet Union, Gorbachev highlights economic problems; the conference boosts perestroika, glasnost, New Thinking, and democratization.

July — The Soviet General Staff under Akhromeev begins formal analysis of unilateral Soviet reductions of conventional forces.

September 21–23 — Shevardnadze's talks with Shultz in Washington fail to make major headway on START.

September 30 — The CPSU Plenum approves broad reorganization of the Soviet political system and approves limited contested elections.

October 1 — Gorbachev is named Soviet president by the Supreme Soviet.

November 3 — The Politburo approves, in principle, unilateral Soviet reductions in conventional forces.

November 8 — Bush wins the U.S. presidential election.

December 7 — Gorbachev, at the United Nations, announces that five hundred thousand Soviet troops are to be cut; spells out the clearest vision of non-Leninist New Thinking on international politics to date; meets Reagan, Bush, and Shultz at Governor's Island, New York; cuts short his trip after severe earthquake in Armenia.

• *1989*

January 4 — Reagan accepts Vienna conclusion of Conference on Security and Cooperation in Europe, including its provision for a human rights conference in Moscow.

January 17 — Foreign ministers of CSCE member states sign human rights pact.

January 20 — Bush is sworn in as president.

March 26 — In the freest elections in seventy years, the Soviets choose a Congress of People's Deputies.

April 24 — One thousand Soviet tanks pull back from Hungary in the first stage of Soviet unilateral reductions.

May 12 — Bush, speaking at Texas A&M, calls for moving "beyond containment."

August 22 — Gorbachev telephones the Polish Communist leadership, urging participation in the Solidarity-led government.

September 10 — Hungary opens its Austrian border to fleeing East Germans, sparking a massive exodus.

September 21–23 — Shevardnadze visits Jackson Hole for talks with Baker: major progress is made.

October 18 — Honecker is removed as president of East Germany.

November 9 — The Berlin Wall is opened.

December 2–3 — The Malta Summit is held.

∴ Selected Declassified Documents

Documents concerning Soviet Decision Making on Afghanistan

Following are excerpts from classified CPSU Central Committee and Politburo documents, released in 1992 by Russian archivists, concerning the situation in Afghanistan.[1]

Kosygin's Argument against the Introduction of Soviet Troops to Afghanistan, March 29, 1979

Excerpted below is Prime Minister A. N. Kosygin's response to the Afghan request for Soviet military intervention, which Kosygin expressed to Nur Mohammad Taraki, leader of the People's Democratic Party of Afghanistan. The excerpt is from the classified "top secret" memorandum of conversation between Taraki, Kosygin, Foreign Minister Gromyko, Defense Minister Ustinov, and the chief of the CPSU Central Committee's International Department, Boris Ponomarev.

Kosygin: At the present stage we see our task as protecting you against any potential international complications. We will offer you assistance with all possible means: supply arms and ammunition; dispatch people who can be useful to you in securing the leadership of the country's military and economic affairs; and provide specialists for training your military personnel in the use of the most advanced forms of weaponry and military technology, which we will ship to you.

But the introduction of our troops to Afghan territory would immediately incite international public opinion, bringing in its wake sharply negative consequences at many levels. It would essentially be a conflict not only with the imperialist countries but with your own people. Our mutual enemies are just waiting for the moment Soviet troops appear on Afghan territory. That would give them an excuse for the introduction to Afghan territory of military formations hostile to you. I want to underline again that the issue of the introduction of troops has been examined on our side from all angles. We examined thoroughly all aspects of that action and concluded that if we were to introduce our forces the situation in your country would not only not improve but on the contrary would worsen. One cannot help but see that our troops would be compelled to fight not only the foreign aggressor but also against some of your people. And a people never forgives such things.

Central Committee Decree Authorizing the Introduction of Soviet Troops to Afghanistan, December 12, 1979

Seven and one-half months later, on December 12, 1979, Konstantin Chernenko took notes on a meeting of Soviet leaders which affirmed an earlier decision by Brezhnev, Yuri Andropov, Dmitry Ustinov, and Andrei Gromyko to introduce Soviet forces to the Afghan conflict. Chernenko drew up the decree in his own hand, and Brezhnev and the other ten Politburo members in attendance signed it. The document bears out the contention of Princeton Conference participants Bessmertnykh and Chernyaev about the "narrow circle" that made the fateful decision, but it leaves unanswered the question of what had changed, in the period between Kosygin's discussion with Taraki in March and this meeting in early December, to cause the Soviet leadership to change its views on intervention.

Below is a translation of the body of the document.[2]

Top Secret
Chaired by Comrade L. I. Brezhnev   Special File
In attendance: Suslov M. A., Grishin V. V., Kirilenko A. P., Pel'she A. Ya., Ustinov D. F., Chernenko K. U., Andropov Yu. V., Gromyko A. A., Tikhonov N. A., Ponomarev B. N.
Decree of the CC of the CPSU
On the situation in "A"

1. To approve the considerations and measures set forth by comrades Andropov Yu. V., Ustinov D. F., and Gromyko A. A.
To permit them, in the course of implementing these mea-

sures, to make minor adjustments to them.

Issues requiring decisions of the CC are to be raised in a timely fashion with the Politburo.

Implementation of all these measures is assigned to comrades Ustinov D. F. and Gromyko A. A.

2. To instruct comrades Andropov Yu. V., Ustinov D. F., and Gromyko A. A. to keep the Politburo informed about the progress of carrying out the projected measures.

Secretary of the CC L. Brezhnev
[signature]

Andropov's Statements to the Politburo about the Afghan Situation, March 1983

Excerpted below are General Secretary Yuri Andropov's comments on a lengthy report by Foreign Minister Gromyko "on the situation in Afghanistan and additional measures for its improvement." The original document, marked "top secret / sole copy," is a transcript of a Politburo session that addressed the Afghan problem at length. In his report, Gromyko notes the complexity of the situation, the Afghan government's lack of control over the countryside, the growing numbers of the mujaheddin, and the problems with the negotiations with Pakistan. He stresses the need for "political regulation" of the crisis and reports the finding of a special study group recommending a reform plan for the Afghan government and armed forces, coupled with 300 million rubles' worth of assistance from Moscow.

Andropov: You recall the difficulty and circumspection with which we decided the issue of deploying troops to Afghanistan. L. I. Brezhnev insisted on a roll-call vote of Politburo members. The issue was examined at a plenum of the Central Committee.

In resolving the Afghan problem we should proceed on the basis of existing realities. What do you want? It's a feudal country, where the tribal clans always ruled their own territories, and the central government's writ by no means always reached to each village [kishlak]. Pakistan's positions aren't the issue. It's American imperialism that's battling us here, and it knows well that in this zone of international politics it has lost its positions. Therefore, we cannot give up.

There are no miracles in this world. Sometimes we get angry with the Afghans because they act inconsistently and work slowly. But remember our struggle with the *basmachi* rebellion. Almost the entire Red Army was concentrated in Central Asia then, and the struggle with the *basmachi* lasted into the 1930s. So in relations with Afghanistan we need to be both demanding and understanding.

Excerpts from a November 1986 Politburo Meeting on Withdrawal of Forces from Afghanistan

The discussion below is excerpted from another "top secret / sole copy" transcript of a Politburo session, now chaired by Mikhail Gorbachev.[3] In a section entitled "On Further Measures concerning Afghanistan," Gorbachev and Gromyko, now chairman of the USSR Supreme Soviet (or president), consider ways to extract the Soviet Union from the Afghan quagmire. Chief of Staff Akhromeev and the newly appointed chief of the Central Committee's International Department, Anatoly Dobrynin, offer assessments of U.S. intentions.

Gorbachev: Are all comrades acquainted with the contents of the note prepared by cmrds. Chebrikov V. M., Shevardnadze E. A., Sokolov S. L. and Dobrynin A. F.?

Members of the Politburo: Yes.

Gorbachev: Then let's exchange opinions. In my view we must not waste time. Najib needs our support. He assesses the situation objectively, and understands the complexity of the issues. He considers the activation of measures directed toward national reconciliation, the strengthening of the alliance with the peasantry, and the consolidation of the political leadership of the party and country to be the most urgent tasks.

Karmal is twiddling his thumbs.

We've already been fighting in Afghanistan for six years. If we don't change approaches we'll be fighting for another twenty or thirty years. It has cast a shadow on our ability to influence the course of events. We must tell our military as well that they haven't learned well in this war . . . What are we going to do, fight forever, acknowledging that our troops will never be able to deal with the situation? We need an end to this process in the nearest future.

Gromyko: We must set a strategic goal. Not long ago we spoke of sealing Afghanistan's borders with Pakistan and Iran. Experience showed that we could not achieve this due to the complicated local geography and the existence of hundreds of trails in the mountains. Today we must say clearly that the strategic goal consists in leading matters to a conclusion of the war.

Gorbachev: We need to speak in a resolution of the necessity of terminating the war within one year—two years maximum.

Gromyko: Terminating it in such a way that Afghanistan remains a neutral state. Clearly our side did not fully appreciate the difficulties when we gave the Afghan leadership assurance of our military support. Social conditions within Afghanistan rendered impossible a resolution of the problem in a short period of time. We did not receive internal support there.

[Speaks of domestic Afghan developments.]

As far as the Americans are concerned, they're not interested in regulating the situation in Afghanistan. On the contrary, it is advantageous to them if the war is dragged out.

Gorbachev: Right.

[Subsequent discussion reinforces three points made by Gorbachev and Gromyko: (1) the need to end the war while preventing Afghanistan from falling into the sphere of influence of hostile states; (2) the impossibility of ending the war by military victory, though Soviet forces can maintain the situation at its present level; (3) the need to pursue two lines of policy: get rid of those in the Afghan government (Karmal) unwilling or unable to implement new policies of national reconciliation while supporting those (Najib) that do; and work more actively on the diplomatic front to prevent the flow of weaponry to the mujaheddin. Later, Gorbachev sums up:]

At a Politburo session last October we determined a new line on settling the Afghan issue. The goal we set consisted of speeding up the withdrawal of our troops from Afghanistan while at the same time securing a friendly Afghanistan. This was to be achieved by means of a combination of military and political measures. However there is no forward movement in any of those areas. No strengthening of the military positions of the Afghan government has occurred.

National consolidation has not been secured mainly because comrade Karmal continued to expect to sit in Kabul with our aid.

In general, the concept that was outlined previously has been poorly implemented. But the problem is not the concept but rather its implementation. We must move more actively, in particular on two issues. First, in the course of two years complete the withdrawal of our troops from Afghanistan. In 1987 we must withdraw 50 percent of the troops, and in the next year another 50 percent. Second, we must move forward to widen the social base of the regime, bearing in mind the real distribution of political forces. In that connection, we need to meet with Najib and, perhaps, with other members of the Politburo of the CC-PDPA.

We need to begin negotiations with Pakistan. It is most important that the Americans do not get into Afghanistan. But I don't think the U.S.A. will go in militarily.

Akhromeev: They will not go into Afghanistan with military forces.

Dobrynin: It is possible to reach an agreement with the U.S. on that.

Gorbachev: We should instruct comrade Kryuchkov to meet with comrade Najib and convey to him an invitation to visit the Soviet Union with the official visit in December 1986.

It is also vital to tell comrade Najib that he must resolve the key issues himself . . .

Members of the Politburo: Agreed.

Politburo Deliberations on the 1983 KAL 007 Incident

Following is an excerpt from the "working transcript" of the Politburo's meeting on September 2, 1983, chaired by General Secretary Konstantin Chernenko, which considered the downing of Korean Air Lines flight 007 by a Soviet fighter plane.[4] As Don Oberdorfer notes in chapter 3, much of the information that Defense Minister Ustinov provided to the meeting was false.

Chernenko: The measures associated with the incident of the South Korean plane were already discussed by Politburo members yesterday, on an operational basis. As you know, an announcement was published on this matter. You have received more detailed materials, and Yuriy Vladimirovich [Andropov] has expressed a desire for consultations on this complex question at a Politburo session.

The fact is that the American press, and the imperialist press in general, has launched a wide anti-Soviet campaign in connection with this incident. We need a thorough exchange of opinions. The important thing is that the first step has already been taken—an announcement has appeared in our press. Now we must determine our position, map out the necessary steps in the situation that has arisen, and discuss our stance amid the wild orgy of American propaganda that has been launched.

One thing is clear, that we cannot allow foreign planes to overfly our territory freely. No self-respecting state can allow that. But we must define clearly our position and the prospects for further actions.

Gromyko: In the United States, Reagan was quick to speak out on the subject of the incident of the South Korean plane. As usual, his speech was blatantly anti-Soviet and contained a call to "rally the entire international community" against the Soviet Union. The United States is demanding the immediate convocation of the UN Security Council on this question. The Security Council has not yet been convinced, but it will meet, of course, and resolutions very hostile to us will be discussed there. Clearly we will have to use our veto.

Maybe the Americans will go so far as to curtail the grain agreement they signed with us, try to step up certain economic sanctions, and in general do everything possible to whip up international tension and anti-Soviet hysteria.

Among the passengers who died on the plane there were Americans, including Congressman McDonald, Canadians, Australians, Japanese, and Koreans. It was a civilian airliner. The Japanese have stated that they have recordings of our airmen's conversations with the ground services during the period of the shooting down of the South Korean plane. So imperialist propaganda will try to portray our moves as a deliberate attack on a peaceful plane and a violation of all conventions. Various provocations against our own

Aeroflot are very possible. Moves aimed at wrecking the Madrid [CSCE] conference are also possible. That is not, of course, an exhaustive list of the steps our adversary could take. We must define our position and first and foremost state firmly that we acted lawfully, that shots were fired. In this connection we should draw up a weighty representation to the U.S. Government, a resolute protest against Reagan's insinuations.

Ustinov: Only one thing is clear to me, that the Americans will try to take advantage of this affair to divert the world public's attention from the major peace initiatives put forward by the Soviet Union and to undermine our peaceful acts.

I can assure the Politburo that our airmen acted in full accordance with the requirements of military duty, and everything that is set forth in the memorandum that has been submitted is completely true. Our actions were absolutely correct, since a U.S.-made South Korean plane had penetrated 500 km into our territory. It would be extremely difficult to distinguish this plane from a reconnaissance plane by its outline [*po konturam*]. Soviet miliztary airmen are forbidden to fire on passenger aircraft. But in this situation their actions were entirely justified, because, in accordance with international rules, the aircraft was repeatedly instructed to land at one of our airfields.

Gorbachev: The plane was over our territory for a long time.

If it had strayed off course, the Americans would have informed us, but they did not do so.

Ustinov: Our airmen gave them numerous warnings, over Kamchatka and over Sakhalin. The plane was traveling without warning lights. There was no light showing through the plane's windows. Warning shots were fired with tracer shells, as is stipulated in international rules. Then our pilot reported to the ground that it was a combat plane and should be shot down.

My opinion is that in this situation we must show firmness and remain cool. And maybe gradually issue the necessary information through our press. But we should not flinch. If we flinch, it gives all kinds of people the opportunity to overfly our territory. I wish to report that in the region of our Pacific borders there have been 12 violations of this kind recently. As you know, in 1978 in the Murmansk region we had to force a South Korean plane to land on Soviet territory.

I propose that the USSR Defense Ministry, the Foreign Ministry, and the KGB be instructed to form a working group, charged with formulating the necessary measures and submitting proposals in connection with the emerging situation. Comrades N. V. Ogarkov, G. M. Korniyenko, and V. A. Kryuchkov could be in this working group.

Tikhonov: I don't understand what the Seoul pilot was up to. He must have known he was courting certain death. After all, he saw the signals from our planes and their demands to land. In my view that was a planned, deliberate provocation, designed to complicate and excerbate the international situation.

Ustinov: It is hard to say what the South Koreans had in mind.

But it is quite possible that it was a deliberate provocation. The question is how best to report our shots.

Gromyko: We can't deny that our plane fired.

Denychev: They know, of course, that it was a live shot.

Grishin: What did the South Korean pilot say?

Ustinov: We heard nothing.

Vorotnikov: Were the South Korean plane's communications broken?

Ustinov: Nobody can say.

Ogarkov (chief of the USSR General Staff): All the same, we have information that the South Korean plane was talking with the ground.

Chebrikov (KGB chairman): I would like to add a bit to what has been said here. First, it is noteworthy that the American side had very accurate information on the South Korean plane's flight path and was observing it.

Second, the initial reports published by the Japanese are drawn from a single source—information received from the CIA and the U.S. National Security Agency. Therefore the question arises, why were the Americans devoting so much attention to a South Korean plane? Third, the downed plane, according to our information, was not in contact with U.S. aircraft and was in general flying dumb, so to speak. Fourth and last, the American themselves admit that the plane had penetrated deep into Soviet territory and was flying over the Soviet Union's top secret facilities in Kamchatka and Sa-khalin. They also admit that the plane was shot down over our Soviet territory, and went down into the ocean in our waters. In fact it went down in neutral waters. We now have ships and an aircraft in operation there. The Japanese have sent about 20 fishing schooners to the site of the crash. We have picked up a number of objects. The depth of the sea there is about 80–100 meters.

Gromyko: So they could pick up the plane's "black box," or we could.

Chebrikov: They could. As far as we are concerned, should we do that?

Tikhonov: Clearly sooner or later they will come across the wreck-age of the plane.

Dolgikh: And if they do, they will obtain information on how the plane was shot down.

Gorbachev: Did they register the live shot?

Chebrikov: No, they didn't register it. But I want to stress yet again that our actions were completely lawful and clearly stipulated in Soviet Army regulations.

I would like to say specifically that instructions should now be given to our Civil Air Fleet on complying strictly with interna-tional flight paths and corridors. Maybe we should even go so far as to cut certain flights to the east and to the United States. Imperialist forces will undoubtedly provoke demonstrations out-side our embassies and other hostile acts. In this connection KGB and Foreign Ministry organizations must be given appropriate in-structions.

Tikhonov: If we acted correctly, lawfully, then we should state frankly that we shot down that plane.

Gromyko: We should say that shots were fired. We should say so frankly, so as not to allow our adversary to accuse us of being de-ceitful. Our main argument should be that the plane was flying over Soviet territory and had penetrated an exceptionally long way into our territory. Maybe we should even provide a map of the aircraft's flight in the newspapers and on television, so that the readers and viewers can see how grossly the Soviet Union's sovereignty was violated.

Solomentsev: How do things stand as regards compliance with international conventions?

Gromyko: The conventions permit virtually all our actions.

Grishin: First of all, I wish to stress that we should state frankly that the plane was shot down. Maybe this should be done by stages. At the moment we should say that we are investigating the matter, so as to establish the situation precisely. And later we should state that the plane was shot down. At the same time we must take a tough stance against all kinds of anti-Soviet provocations. This must be done today.

Gorbachev: First of all I want to say that I am sure our actions were correct. The plane was over Soviet territory for about two hours, so it can hardly be assumed that this was an unplanned action. We should make it clear in our statements that this was a gross violation of international conventions. It is no use keeping quiet now, we must go on the offensive. While confirming the existing story, we must develop it and say that we are engaged in a serious investigation of the situation that has arisen. At the same time, clearly, eastward flights by our planes should be scaled down to some extent.

Romanov: I support everything that has been said here. Our announcement should, first, point out that it was hard to tell whether the South Korean plane was civil or military. Second, we should emphasize the violation of very important international conventions. Third, we must say that the plane did not respond to any interrogation or signals. After all, under existing laws we are entitled to force a foreign aircraft to land if it is overflying our territory without authorization. Of course, we must determine the timing and procedure for our statments in the press and in the international arena.

Tikhonov: I believe we should take as a basis the announcement we have already published concerning the incident and stress particularly that the plane was in the USSR's airspace for about two hours. We should state frankly that it penetrated nearly 500 km into our territory and stress that the Americans knew about this violation of the Soviet border and could, if necessary, have informed the Soviet side about it.

Ogarkov: It is quite possible that this was a deliberate provocation, since U.S. intelligence is always trying to find out where our air defense forces are located and how they operate. The Defense Ministry now has transcripts of all the conversations that took place in the air on that day. They show that we can certainly stick to the story reported in our press.

Zimyanin: I would like to touch on the propaganda aspect of the problem. First of all, Reagan's rash statement must be refuted. It was gross and reckless. We should make an announcement on this matter on television today, and in the press tomorrow.

Dolgikh: I support the view that we should go on the offensive in tackling this matter. We could, of course, state that we are studying the incident further. But they will certainly raise the plane from the sea bed. Therefore we must speak frankly about the shots fired and actively emphasize that the Americans knew about the plane's flight path and the violation of our border and did not alert us to it.

Korniyenko: We have quite enough material to express the view that this was a deliberate provocation by the CIA. This is indicated by the first Japanese report, citing CIA materials, and a number of other facts. But we must not seek to avoid the fact that shots were fired. Imperialist propaganda could now even go so far as to broadcast on the radio the recordings of our airmen's conversations.

Gromyko: In our statement we must also point out that this provocation is aimed at overshadowing the Soviet peace initiatives put forward recently.

Solomentsev: We have no need to justify ourselves. We should say frankly that the sovereignty of Soviet territory was violated and international conventions were violated. We should go on the offensive, although maybe we could also say that we sympathize with the families of those who died as a result of this deliberate provovation.

Kuznetsov: I support the proposals made here. It seems to me too that this was a well-planned anti-Soviet act, and this must be stated frankly in the press and in our statements, which will reach foreign readers as well as our own. At the same time we should approve directives for our representative on the Security Council, where there will of course be a tough struggle.

Vorotnikov: I would like to support everything the comrades have said here, and to stress once again that we should take a firm stance and that we fired warning shots to the South Korean plane.

Kapitonov: There is no doubt that our airmen acted correctly. Now, rebuffing imperialist propaganda attacks, we must act firmly and circumspectly. The shots must, of course, be admitted, but we must stress that no blame is attached to us here.

Gorbachev: Clearly we should make an official representation to the U.S. government.

Gromyko: And at the same time confidentially brief the leaders of the fraternal socialist countries and certain other states. As for the Americans, they must be given a firm official response. We will prepare today a draft directive for our UN Security Council representative. It is expedient also to say in a TASS statement that we regret the casualties.

Ustinov: We must adhere to a firm line—make an additional announcement mentioning warning shots.

Ryzhkov: I fully support what the comrades propose here, and I think our line should be principled, clear, and flexible.

Chernenko: So, comrades, it is good that we discussed this complex international question collectively here. It is gratifying that we hold a single view, a single stance. We must take an offensive, not defensive, line. Of course, we must be circumspect and cautious and think about the future, but at the same time adopt a resolute and calm stance.

It seems we could adopt the following decision in this connection: First, we approve the measures adopted in connection with the South Korean plane's violation of the USSR's airspace and the announcement on this question that was published in our press.

Second, we should proceed firmly on the basis that this violation constitutes a deliberate provocation by imperialist forces, aimed at distracting the world's public's attention from the major peace initiatives put forward by the Soviet Union. Third, let us note that the USSR Defense Ministry, Foreign Ministry, and KGB are to set up a working group that will speedily formulate the necessary measures and submit proposals to the Politburo in connection with the situation that has arisen. Fourth, I think it would be correct if, in the light of today's discussion, we draw up and publish a TASS statement on this question and a representation to the U.S. Government, and also give instructions for the formulation of a directive for the USSR's Security Council representation. As for briefing the leadership of the fraternal socialist countries and certain other friendly states, this information could be based on our representation to the U.S. Government. Fifth and last, we must agree to respond resolutely to all further anti-Soviet provocations by imperialist forces and to examine at the party Central Committee every official intervention of ours.

I will report the results of today's discussion to Yuriy Vladimirovich Andropov without delay.

Excerpts from "Soviet Capabilities for Strategic Nuclear Conflict, 1982–1992," NIE 11-3/8-82, February 15, 1983

The following excerpts were taken from National Intelligence Estimate 11-3/8-82, which was declassified for the purposes of the Princeton Conference, and which Lawrence Gershwin of the CIA summarized in the second session (chap. 2). The excerpts include the document's summary of recent developments, Soviet strategic priorities and doctrine, and future strategic forces and programs, and the estimate's concluding observations. Blank spaces indicate censored text; ellipses indicate editorial omissions.

Summary

A. Recent Developments

1. The Soviets have made impressive gains in their strategic forces since the 1960s, particularly in land- and sea-based ballistic

missiles. They maintain a vigorous military research, development, and production base and continue to develop, improve, and deploy offensive and defensive weapons of virtually every type. These efforts are continuing, with no evidence in the past year to indicate any letup.

2. In recent offensive force developments:

— The Soviets continued deployment of accurate intercontinental and submarine-launched ballistic missiles (ICBMs and SLBMs) armed with multiple independently targetable reentry vehicles (MIRVs), of the mobile SS-20 intermediate-range ballistic missile (IRBM), and of the Backfire bomber. As of 31 December 1982, we estimate the Soviets had about 7,300 reentry vehicles (RVs) on their more than 2,300 ICBMs and SLBMs.

— In December the Soviets conducted
                                 flight test of their new, MIRVed medium-sized, solid-propellant ICBM to be deployed in silos.

— In February 1983 the Soviets flight-tested a small solid-propellant ICBM.

— The Soviets also probably have in development other new or improved ICBMs and   SLBMs. At least one SLBM and two ICBMs are expected to begin flight-testing later in 1983.

— The USSR maintained a high success rate for flight tests of the SS-NX-20 SLBM; the 1982 tests included   an extended-range launch from the Typhoon nuclear-powered ballistic missile submarine (SSBN). A second Typhoon was launched in 1982, and at least two, probably three, more are under construction.

— The Soviets continued testing of their new intercontinental-range Blackjack A bomber.

— They began operational testing of newly produced Bear aircraft that will probably carry long-range cruise missiles for land attack.

— They continued flight-testing of ground-, air-, and sea-launched (GLCM, ALCM, and SLCM) versions of a long-range (3,000 kilometers) land-attack cruise missile.

3. In strategic defense programs:
— The Soviets continued work on their ballistic missile defenses around Moscow, including the Pushkino radar and 26 new antiballistic missile (ABM) silo launchers (for a total of 64), evidently as part of a plan to upgrade the performance of their defenses and expand them to the ABM Treaty limit of 100 launchers.
— They started deployment of SA-10 surface-to-air missile (SAM) battalions with 12 launchers each; previously deployed SA-10 units have six launchers.
— They are performing at least feasibility tests on three types of high-energy laser weapons for air defense: lasers for point defense of high-value assets on land, ship-based lasers for point defense at sea, and a tactical, land-based mobile system. This year we project Soviet deployment of high-energy lasers for air defense in the period of this Estimate.
— The Soviets continued deployment of the MIG-31 Foxhound A interceptor, which will provide them with an improved capability against low-altitude penetrating targets.
—

4. In supporting systems for strategic forces:
— The Soviets continued efforts to increase the flexibility and survivability of communications available to their national-level commands and to operating elements of their strategic forces.

an extremely-low-frequency (ELF) system for providing communications support to submarines operating at patrol depth.

B. Soviet Strategic Policies and Doctrine

5.   Moscow's concept of its relationship with the United States is fundamentally adversarial. This concept, based on ideological antagonism and geopolitical rivalry, governs Soviet behavior and also shapes Soviet perceptions of U.S. policies toward Moscow. Its most dramatic manifestation is growing Soviet military power and capabilities that form the cutting edge of Moscow's persistent efforts to extend its global presence and influence at the expense of the United States and the West. Soviet leaders view strategic arms policy in the context of a persistent, long-term struggle between two world systems of socialism and capitalism, in which socialism—with Moscow in charge—is destined ultimately to triumph. From their viewpoint, progress in this struggle is measured by favorable shifts in the overall "correlation of forces"—political, ideological, economic, social, and military. They seek through strategic and other military programs to continue shifting the military component of the correlation of forces in favor of the USSR and its allies. They recognize that military power is their principal foreign policy asset and that continued high levels of defense investments are necessary to sustain and expand Moscow's global role.

6.   The Soviets believe that in the present US-Soviet strategic relationship each side possesses strategic nuclear capabilities that could devastate the other after absorbing an attack. Soviet leaders have stated that nuclear war with the United States would be a catastrophe that must be avoided if possible and that they do not regard such a conflict as inevitable. They have been willing to negotiate restraints on force improvements and deployments when it serves their interests. Nevertheless, they regard nuclear war as a continuing possibility and have rejected mutual vulnerability as a desirable or permanent basis for the US-Soviet strategic relationship. They seek superior capabilities to fight and win a nuclear war with the United States, and have been working to improve their chances of prevailing in such a conflict. A tenet in their strategic thinking holds that the better prepared the USSR is to fight in various contingencies, the more likely it is that potential enemies will be deterred from initiating attacks on the Soviet Union and its allies and will be hesitant to counter Soviet political and military actions.

7.   Strategic nuclear forces support Soviet foreign policy aims by

projecting an image of military strength. Soviet leaders appreciate the political importance of world perceptions of military power and have long stressed the contribution of strategic forces to the USSR's superpower status. They view their current strategic position as supporting the conduct of an assertive foreign policy and the expansion of Soviet power and influence abroad.

C. Future Strategic Forces and Programs

8. Our projections of Soviet strategic forces[1] for the next three to five years are based largely on evidence of ongoing programs. During this period—primarily because of the Soviets' military planning and acquistion process—it is unlikely that they would significantly alter planned deployments. Over the longer term, however, we believe they have an expanded number of options in deciding on the size, mix, and characteristics of their strategic nuclear forces and supporting systems. Our projections for five to 10 years from now are based on evidence regarding these options. They also reflect our judgments of the factors that will influence future Soviet forces.

9. Key among these factors are:
— Determination on the part of the Soviets to improve all aspects of their strategic forces and supporting elements.
— Determination to prevent any erosion of the military gains they have made over the past decade.
— The degree of success in Soviet efforts to use arms control negotiations—the strategic arms reduction talks (START) and the talks on intermediate-range nuclear forces (INF)—to protect the USSR's present and planned programs and, probably along with some Soviet concessions, to circumscribe US and NATO modernization options.
— Perceptions of the capabilities of other countries' nuclear forces and key weapon system programs.

Other factors that could potentially influence future Soviet strategic forces are domestic economic difficulties and foreign policy setbacks. In general, however, we do not believe that these latter factors will bear significantly on the size and composition of future Soviet

1. See chapter IV, volume II, for a detailed discussion and rationale for the projections displayed in volume III.

strategic forces because of the high priority the Soviets place on such forces.

10. Fundamental to the options the Soviets have for the composition of their future forces is their vigorous military research and developments (R&D) and production base. They continue to develop a number of weapon systems of virtually every type. We currently are aware of more than 30 new major weapon and support systems for potential strategic application that are in various stages of development. The Soviets' research efforts, coupled with technology acquired from the West, have provided them with sufficient advances in certain military technologies—for example, guidance and navigation, microelectronics and computers, signal processing, and directed energy—to enable them to develop increasingly sophisticated weapons and supporting systems. The pace and the overall quality of the Soviets' future weapons programs will depend to a large degree on their ability to develop and exploit new technolgies, including those acquired from the West . . .

F. Concluding Observations

88. We do not know how the Soviets would assess their prospects for prevailing in a global nuclear conflict. Sizable forces on both sides would survive massive nuclear strikes:

— Soviet offensive forces will not be able to reliably target and destroy patrolling US SSBNs, alert aircraft, aircraft in flight, or land-mobile missiles, particularly those beyond the range of tactical reconnaissance systems. We believe that, in a crisis or conflict, the Soviets would credit undegraded US warning and control systems with the ability to launch ICBMs on tactical warning.

— Soviet mobile missiles and SSBNs patrolling in waters near the USSR are highly survivable, as are most silo-based ICBMs and perhaps dispersed aircraft. We believe the Soviets can launch ICBMs on tactical warning, assuming their warning and control systems are undegraded.

Moreover, the Soviets are well aware of their inability to prevent massive damage to the USSR with their strategic defenses even with the improvements taking place in these forces. They also recognize that US strategic defenses cannot prevent massive damage.

89. We believe that the Soviets' confidence in their capabilities for global conflict probably will be critically dependent on command and control capabilities, and on their prospects for disrupting and destroying the ability of the United States and its Allies to command and to operate their forces. The Soviets continue to make extensive efforts to improve all aspects of their command, control, and communications capabilities. We believe they would launch continuing attacks on US and Allied strategic command, control, and communications to prevent or impair the coordination of retaliatory strikes, thereby easing the burden on Soviet strategic defenses and impairing US and Allied abilities to marshal military and civilian resources to reconstitute forces. We believe that planned US and NATO improvements in command, control, and communications will increase the Soviets' uncertainties about their capability to disrupt enemy force operations.

90. The evidence shows clearly that Soviet leaders are attempting to prepare their military forces for the possibility of having to fight a nuclear war and are training to be able to maintain control over increasingly complex conflict situations. They have seriously addressed many of the problems of conducting military operations in a nuclear war, thereby improving their ability to deal with the many contingencies of such a conflict, and raising the probability of outcomes favorable to the USSR. There is an alternative view that wishes to emphasize that the Soviets have not resolved many of the critical problems bearing on the conduct of nuclear war, such as the nature of the initiation of conflict, escalation within the theater, and protracted nuclear operations. According to this view, the Soviets recognize that nucear war is so destructive, and its course so uncertain, that they could not expect an outcome that was "favorable" in any meaningful sense.[17]

17. The holder of this view is the Director, Bureau of Intelligence and Research, Department of State.

Preface

1. Good examples of reasoned, conservative criticism of Gorbachev's foreign policy are the political memoir of former Soviet first deputy foreign minister Georgiy M. Kornienko and chief of the General Staff Sergei F. Akhromeev, *Glazami marshala i diplomata: Kriticheskii vzgliad na vneshniuiu politiku SSSR do i posle 1985 goda* (Moscow: Mezhdunarodnye Otnosheniia, 1992); and the recollections of Moscow's veteran ambassador to the United States and later advisor to Gorbachev on U.S. policy, Anatoly Dobrynin, *In Confidence* (New York: Random House, 1995), chap. 33. All three men figured prominently in the Princeton discussions.

2. For the argument that the Reagan strategy delayed the Cold War's end and complicated matters for Gorbachev, see R. N. Lebow and Janice Gross Stein, *We All Lost the Cold War* (Princeton: Princeton University Press, 1994); and Raymond L. Garthoff, *The Great Transition: American-Soviet Relations and the End of the Cold War* (Washington, D.C.: Brookings Institution, 1994). More favorable interpretations include Patrick Glynn, *Closing Pandora's Box: Arms Races, Arms Control, and the History of the Cold War* (New York: New Republic Books, 1992), chap 4.; and Fareed Zakharia, "The Reagan Strategy of Containment," *Political Science Quarterly* 105, no. 3 (fall 1990): 373–95.

3. Space constraints also dictated editing out the welcoming remarks of Secretary Shultz and Minister Bessmertnykh. My solution was to provide the relevant quotations from these remarks when discussants referred to them in the regular conference sessions.

Introduction to Part I

1. Don Oberdorfer, *The Turn: From the Cold War to a New Era. The United States and the Soviet Union, 1983–1990* (New York: Poseidon Press, 1991).

2. Following the Princeton Conference, Tarasenko said that Gorbachev had been informed by Marshal Akhromeev immediately after the collapse of the Reykjavik summit that "the Soviet side could have agreed to the American proposal as a fallback." Shevardnadze, who had been present and who later related the conversation to Tarasenko, had reacted angrily to Akhromeev's statement, demanding, "Why didn't you speak up before?" Some American officials also felt in the aftermath of Reykjavik that a U.S. compromise on the SDI issue might have been possible without severely damaging the U.S. program. This suggests that if the leaders had not been so keyed up and tired, the Reykjavik summit could have been further extended and could

have ended in a dramatic success rather than what seemed at the moment to be a failure.

Chapter One: Beginning the Transition

1. The downing of Korean Air Lines flight 007 actually took place in September 1983. Mr Shultz may have had in mind the Zakharov-Daniloff affair, discussed in chap. 3, which occurred in 1986.

2. Here and throughout the conference Chernyaev's comments are translated by Pavel Palazchenko. A thorough review of the videotapes of the conference confirmed the accuracy of Palazchenko's translations in every instance.

3. Bessmertnykh made the following observation in his opening remarks: "Gorbachev immediately understood that the perestroika he planned to implement in his own country was impossible in the Cold War situation. He was serious, sincere, and creative in working out the program that would help to achieve that goal. I was personally with him since 1985, when he developed new approaches to the Soviet-American relations. I participated in preparation and conduct of all the summits with U.S. presidents. Therefore, I can testify to the fact that Gorbachev placed the task of ending the Cold War and of stopping the arms race at the very top of his priority list. As a first step, he removed ideology from foreign policy. And so, to the surprise of everyone, the world suddenly lost its black-and-white dullness and presented itself as multicolored and interconnected."

4. Referring to the famously stormy summit meeting in Vienna in 1961.

5. In his opening remarks, Shultz recalled his introduction of simultaneous rather than sequential translation into U.S.-Soviet meetings, which allowed greater efficiency and a more "human" flow to discussions.

6. After the shooting of Major Nicholson in East Germany by Soviet security forces on March 24, 1985, the U.S. military would not advance contacts with its Soviet counterpart until a formal apology was received. See chap. 3, below.

7. Carlucci here refers to Alexander Bessmertnykh by the diminutive form of his first name, and to the attempted hard-line coup of August 1991.

Chapter Two: Arms Buildups and Arms Reductions

1. See "SDI, Chernobyl Helped End Cold War, Conference Told," *Washington Post*, Feb. 27, 1993, A17; Warren Strobel, "SDI: Lost in Space," *Washington Times*, Mar. 22, 1993, A8; Morton M. Kondracke, "Clinton Is 'Giving Away Store' to Save Yeltsin, Says Shultz," *Roll Call*, Jan. 13, 1994; Peter Schweitzer, "Who Broke the Evil Empire?" *National Review*, May 30, 1994, 46. More dovish interpretations include R. N. Lebow and Janice Gross Stein, *We All Lost the Cold War* (Princeton: Princeton University Press, 1994); and Vladislav Zubok, "The Collapse of the Soviet Union: Leadership, Elites, and Legitimacy," in Geir Lundestad, ed., *The Fall of Great Powers* (New York: Oxford University Press, 1994), 165, and n. 3.

2. "SALT II" refers to the second round of the Strategic Arms Limitation

Talks. The Carter administration negotiated a SALT II treaty with the Soviet Union but withdrew it from Senate consideration after the Soviets invaded Afghanistan in December 1979. Though the treaty was never ratified, both countries abided by its terms.

3. Velikhov was a nuclear physicist and the science advisor to Gorbachev.

4. The reference is to an informal dinner the Reagans hosted for the Shultzes in the White House on February 12, 1983. According to Don Oberdorfer (*The Turn: From the Cold War to a New Era. The United States and the Soviet Union, 1983–1990* [New York: Poseidon Press, 1991], chap. 1), it was on that evening that the president signaled to Shultz his interest in improving relations with Moscow.

5. *Chasti spetsial'nogo naznacheniia*—Soviet "special purpose" units, for behind-the-lines operations in advance of an offensive.

6. The reference is to the U.S. air strike against Libya, conducted on April 14, 1986, which called forth a strong denunciation from Moscow and a swift cancellation of Mr. Shevardnadze's planned visit.

Chapter Three: Managing Crisis Flashpoints

1. Kornienko was referring to Andropov's rapidly declining health. Four further observations appear in Kornienko's memoirs: (1) Gromyko supported coming clean about the incident but would not stand up to Ustinov; (2) Kornienko detected that Andropov seemed to see the wisdom of admitting responsibility for the act, but bowed to Ustinov's wishes; (3) Kornienko himself is convinced that the Soviet pilot and his superiors in the Air Defense Command were sure that they were dealing with a military spy plane; and (4) Kornienko asserts, "that aircraft did not enter USSR airspace by accident." Georgiy M. Kornienko and Sergei F. Akhromeev, *Glazami marshala i diplomata: Kriticheskii vzgliad na vneshniuiu politiku SSSR do i posle 1985 goda* (Moscow: Mezhdunarodnye Otnosheniia, 1992), 48–50.

2. Included in app. B of this volume.

3. For more, see Christopher Andrew and Oleg Gordievsky, *Comrade Kryuchkov's Instructions: Top Secret Files on KGB Foreign Operations, 1975–1985* (Stanford: Stanford University Press, 1993), chap. 4.

4. Mutual and Balanced Force Reduction talks—concerning conventional forces in Europe.

5. Valentin V. Varennikov, deputy defense minister and commander of the ground forces, played a key role in the August coup.

6. On August 24, 1991, Marshal Akhromeev hanged himself in his Kremlin office. This occurred just after the failure of the coup by hardline officials and Boris Yeltsin's political triumph over Mikhail Gorbachev. Akhromeev left a note that read, "Everything I have worked for is being destroyed."

7. Akhromeev writes in his posthumously published memoirs that he and others on the General Staff were convinced by early 1988 that economic stringency dictated the need for unilateral reductions. He describes how the plans were worked out in detail, months in advance of Gorbachev's December announcement. He notes an additional reason for his retirement: appre-

hension about the dissolution of the Warsaw Pact. See Akhromeev and Kornienko, *Glazami marshala i diplomata*, chap. 5, esp. 211–15.

8. Patricia M. (Patt) Derian was assistant secretary of state for human rights in the Carter administration.

9. Just before the U.S. delegation departed for the Geneva Summit, the *New York Times* and the *Washington Post* obtained and published a letter from Secretary of Defense Weinberger to Reagan urging the president to maintain a hard-line stance on SDI and to avoid making any commitment to continue to abide by the terms of SALT II. The leak was interpreted in the press as an effort to hamstring the president in Geneva.

Chapter Four: The Makers of History

1. The reference is to President Reagan's decision to go ahead with a planned visit to a German military cemetery—at the invitation of West German chancellor Helmut Kohl—after it was discovered that Waffen-SS soldiers were among those buried there.

2. The *nomenklatura* was a list of posts in the Soviet Union for which a given Party committee (ranging from District Committees to the Central Committee in Moscow) had the right of confirmation. It became a term designating the Soviet ruling class, or "Partocracy."

3. In a later follow-up discussion, Tarasenko was only able to pin the date of this meeting to August 20–25, 1989. This was when the Solidarity-led government was coming to power in Poland. Tarasenko was at pains to stress that Shevardnadze was particularly sensitive to the issue of imperialism because he was a Georgian.

4. The reference to the "alphabet" means that delegations were seated in alphabetical order according to the French spellings of their countries' names.

Chapter Five: Afghanistan and the Limits of Empire

1. By "other suspicious people" Bessmertnykh probably has in mind the intelligence services of Pakistan, as well as those of China, which at that time was aligning itself closely with the United States in the region.

2. Mohammad Sardar Daoud ruled the country between July 1973—when he organized a coup that ended the forty-year rule of his cousin, King Zahir Shah—and April 1978, when he was overthrown in a coup carried out by the People's Democratic Party of Afghanistan under Taraki.

3. Yury Vladimirovich Gankovsky was the head of the Near Eastern Department of the Institute of Oriental Studies of the USSR Academy of Sciences and the author of dozens of books on Afghanistan, Pakistan, and Central Asia.

4. Anatoly Chernyaev, *Shest' let s Gorbachevym: Po dnevnikovym zapisiam* (Moscow: Progress, 1993); translated into German as *Die letzten Jahre einer Weltmacht: Der Kreml von innen* (Stuttgart: Deutsche Verlag, 1993).

5. The references are to Georgiy Arbatov, founder and head of the Insti-

tute of the United States and Canada; Aleksandr Bovin, the influential *Izves-tiia* commentator; and Nikolai Inozemtsev, head of the Institute of World Economy and International Relations.

6. Arnold Beichman is a senior research fellow at the Hoover Institution, Stanford University, and a columnist for the *Washington Times*.

Chapter Six: The Riddle of Reykjavik

1. Gorbachev was apparently referring to a 1920 article on Lenin by H. G. Wells entitled "The Kremlin Dreamer."

2. Anatoly Dobrynin, formerly Soviet ambassador to Washington and an advisor to Gorbachev, agrees with Bessmertnykh's recollection. He notes that Gorbachev initially shared the view of many of his advisors that it was "time to stop being afraid of SDI"; that is, that the system could be defeated easily and need not be an impediment to arms control in other areas. "But under the influence of our military-industrial complex, Gorbachev gradually began to revert to his insistence on Reagan's withdrawal from SDI as the condition for the success of a new summit on disarmament." Anatoly Do-brynin, *In Confidence: Moscow's Ambassador to America's Six Cold War Presidents, 1962–1986* (New York: Random House, 1995), 667.

Introduction to Part II

1. That, at least, was the assessment of Bush administration officials. See Don Oberdorfer, *The Turn: From the Cold War to a New Era. The United States and the Soviet Union, 1983–1990* (New York: Poseidon Press, 1991), 379.

2. The phrase "enduring rivalry" is from Gary Goertz and Paul F. Diehl, "Enduring Rivalries: Theoretical Constructs and Empirical Patterns," *International Studies Quarterly* 37, no. 2 (June 1993): 147–72. Goertz and Diehl note that most inter-state conflict takes place within the context of such rivalries, but that all such conflicts cannot be captured by a simple "arms race" dynamic. On the rarity of peaceful ends to arms races, see George W. Downs, David M. Rocke, and Randolph Siverson, "Arms Races and Coop-eration," in Kenneth A. Oye, ed., *Cooperation under Anarchy* (Princeton: Princeton University Press, 1985); and the sources cited by Downs, Rocke, and Siverson on p. 119, n. 4.

3. Important contributions to the debate on international theory after the Cold War include Richard Ned Lebow and Thomas Risse-Kappen, eds., *International Relations Theory and the End of the Cold War* (New York: Colum-bia University Press, 1995); Charles W. Kegley Jr., ed., *Controversies in International Relations Theory: Realism and the Neoliberal Challenge* (New York: St. Martin's, 1995); idem, "The Neoidealist Moment in International Studies? Realist Myths and the New International Realities," *International Studies Quarterly* 37, no. 2 (June 1993): 131–47; Michael J. Hogan, ed., *The End of the Cold War: Its Meaning and Implications* (Cambridge: Cambridge University Press, 1992); Hans-Henrik Holm and Georg Sørensen, *Whose*

World Order? Uneven Globalization and the End of the Cold War (Boulder, Colo.: Westview Press, 1995); John Lewis Gaddis, "International Relations Theory and the End of the Cold War," *International Security* 17, no. 3 (winter 1992/93): 5–58; Richard Ned Lebow, "The Long Peace, the End of the Cold War, and the Failure of Realism," *International Organization* 48, no. 2 (spring 1994); and Rey Koslowski and Friedrich Kratochwil, "Understanding Change in International Relations: The Soviet Empire's Demise and the International System," ibid., 48, no. 2 (spring 1994).

4. Robert Jervis, "The Future of International Politics: Will It Resemble the Past?" in Sean M. Lynn-Jones and Steven E. Miller, *The Cold War and After: Prospects for Peace—An International Security Reader* (Cambridge: MIT Press, 1993).

5. Among those who make the case for realism's capability to account for the end of the Cold War are Kenneth Oye, "Explaining the End of the Cold War: Morphological and Behavioral Adaptations to the Nuclear Peace," in Lebow and Risse-Kappen, eds., *International Relations Theory and the End of the Cold War*; William C. Wohlforth, "Realism and the End of the Cold War," in Michael E. Brown, Sean M. Lynn-Jones, and Steven E. Miller, eds., *The Perils of Anarchy: Contemporary Realism and International Security* (Cambridge: MIT Press, 1995); and Kenneth Waltz, "The Emerging Structure of International Politics," in ibid. See also Jervis's contribution to this volume, chap. 8.

6. Oberdorfer, *The Turn*; and George P. Shultz, *Turmoil and Triumph: My Years as Secretary of State* (New York: Scribner's, 1993).

7. Anatoly Dobrynin, *In Confidence: Moscow's Ambassador to America's Six Cold War Presidents, 1962–1986* (New York: Random House, 1995), provides a lively account of the Soviets' efforts to judge whether the Americans were really interested in negotiations.

8. This is stressed in all memoirs by members of the administration. See especially Shultz, *Turmoil and Triumph*; and Robert C. MacFarlane and Zofia Smardz, *Special Trust* (New York: Cadell and Davies, 1994). For secondary analyses confirming that this was the dominant administration view at the time, see Thomas Banchoff, "Official Threat Perceptions in the 1980s: The United States," in Carl-Christoph Schweitzer, ed., *The Changing Western Analysis of the Soviet Threat* (New York: St. Martin Press, 1990); and Michael Jochum, "The United States in the 1980s: Internal Estimates," in ibid.

9. See, e.g., Michael MccGwire, "Deterrence: The Problem—Not the Solution," *SAIS Review* 5 (summer–fall 1985): 105–24.

10. See Stephen F. Cohen, "Soviet Domestic Politics and Foreign Policy," in Fred W. Neal, ed., *Détente or Debacle: Common Sense in U.S.-Soviet Relations* (New York: Norton, 1979).

11. Peter Schweizer, *Victory: The Reagan Administration's Secret Strategy That Hastened the Collapse of the Soviet Union* (New York: Atlantic Monthly Press, 1994); and Patrick Glynn, *Closing Pandora's Box: Arms Races, Arms Control, and the History of the Cold War* (New York: New Republic Books, 1992), make the case for Reagan's policy. R. N. Lebow and Jan-

ice Gross Stein, *We All Lost the Cold War* (Princeton: Princeton University Press, 1994); and Raymond L. Garthoff, *The Great Transition: American-Soviet Relations and the End of the Cold War* (Washington, D.C.: Brookings Institution, 1994), take the opposing view.

12. Jack Snyder, *Myths of Empire: Domestic Politics and International Ambition* (Ithaca: Cornell University Press, 1991), 253–54. See also Charles L. Glaser, "Political Consequences of Military Strategy: Expanding and Refining the Spiral and Deterrence Models," *World Politics* 44, no. 4 (July 1992): 497–538.

13. Kenneth Waltz's *Man, the State, and War: A Theoretical Analysis* (New York: Columbia University Press, 1954), established the "three images" language. See also the later treatment by J. D. Singer, "The Level of Analysis Problem in International Relations," in Klaus Knorr and Sidney Verba, eds., *The International System: Theoretical Essays* (Princeton: Princeton University Press, 1961); and, for an insightful recent treatment, see Barry Buzan, "The Level of Analysis Problem Reconsidered," in Ken Booth and Steve Smith, eds., *International Relations Theory Today* (University Park: Pennsylvania State University Press, 1995).

14. See Otto Hintze, "Military Organization and the Organization of the State," in Felix Gilbert, ed., *The Historical Essays of Otto Hintze* (New York: Oxford University Press, 1975); and Peter Gourevitch, "The Second Image Reversed: The International Sources of Domestic Politics," *International Organization* 32, no. 4 (autumn 1978): 881–911.

15. See, in particular, Robert Jervis, *Perception and Misperception in International Politics* (Princeton: Princeton University Press, 1976), chap. 3; and Alexander George and Richard Smoke, *Deterrence in American Foreign Policy* (New York: Columbia University Press, 1974).

16. Key secondary accounts are cited in subsequent chapters. Informative recollections by participants which are not cited elsewhere in this volume include Georgiy Kh. Shakhnazarov, *Tsena svobody: Reformatsiia Gorbacheva glazami ego pomoshchnikom* (Moscow: Rossika-Zevs, 1993); Vadim A. Medvedev, *V kommande Gorbacheva: Vzgliad izvnutri* (Moscow: Bylina, 1994); Aleksandr N. Yakovlev, *Gor'kaia chasha: Bol'shevizm i reformatsii Rossii* (Yaroslavl': Vernkhne-Volzhskoe, 1994); Pavel Palazchenko, *Interpreting the Whirlwind* (University Park: Pennsylvania State University Press, forthcoming).

17. A very helpful effort to assess various causes is Charles W. Kegley Jr., "How Did the Cold War Die? Principles for an Autopsy," *Mershon International Studies Review* 80, suppl. 1 (Apr. 194): 11–41.

18. Buzan, "Level of Analysis Problem Revisited."

Chapter Seven: Ronald Reagan, Mikhail Gorbachev, and the End of the Cold War

My work on this chapter was supported by grants from the Lynde and Harry Bradley Foundation and the John J. Sherrerd and Oliver Langenberg Funds of the Center of International Studies, Princeton University.

1. Don Oberdorfer, *The Turn: From the Cold War to a New Era. The United States and the Soviet Union, 1983–1990* (New York: Poseidon Press, 1991); Raymond L. Garthoff, *The Great Transition: American-Soviet Relations and the End of the Cold War* (Washington, D.C.: Brookings Institution, 1994). See also Coit D. Blacker, *Hostage to Revolution: Gorbachev and Soviet Security Policy, 1985–1991* (New York: Council on Foreign Relations, 1993). By far the most relevant memoir of the Reagan presidency for present purposes is George P. Shultz, *Turmoil and Triumph: My Years as Secretary of State* (New York: Scribner's, 1993). Other representative works by former Reagan aides include Michael K. Deaver, *Behind the Scenes: In Which the Author Talks about Ronald and Nancy Reagan . . . and Himself* (New York: Morrow, 1987); Donald T. Regan, *For the Record: From Wall Street to Washington* (New York: Harcourt Brace Jovanovich, 1988); Larry Speakes, *Speaking Out: The Reagan Presidency from Inside the White House* (New York: Scribner's Sons, 1988); and David A. Stockman, *The Triumph of Politics: Why the Reagan Revolution Failed* (New York: Harper and Row, 1986). For Reagan's own account see Ronald Reagan, *An American Life* (New York: Simon and Schuster, 1990). See also the memoir of Nancy Reagan, who persistently encouraged her husband to find a modus vivendi with the Soviets: Nancy Reagan with William Novak, *My Turn* (New York: Random House, 1989), 63–64.

2. See Anatoly Chernyaev's comments in chap. 2, above; and Anatoly Dobrynin, *In Confidence: Moscow's Ambassador to America's Six Cold War Presidents, 1962–1986* (New York: Random House, 1995), chaps. 31–33.

3. See in particular Leslie H. Gelb and Richard K. Betts, *The Irony of Vietnam: The System Worked* (Washington, D.C.: Brookings Institution, 1979). See also Daniel Ellsberg, *Papers on the War* (New York: Simon and Schuster, 1972).

4. For an examination of Johnson's actions in February and March 1965 and the context in which he carried them out, see John P. Burke and Fred I. Greenstein, *How Presidents Test Reality: Decisions on Vietnam, 1954 and 1965* (New York: Russell Sage Foundation, 1989). Interestingly, the political actor next in the line of succession to Johnson, Vice President Hubert H. Humphrey, opposed American military intervention in Vietnam at the time that the possibility was being considered in early 1965. In 1954, during the Eisenhower administration's deliberations over military intervention, the president and the vice president also disagreed. In that instance, the vice president (Richard M. Nixon) opposed the president's decision *not* to intervene.

5. In identifying the qualities that a particular leader brought to some action, it is possible to avoid circularity by observing the leader's pattern of action in contexts other than the one under consideration. For a fuller discussion of this and other conceptual and methodological issues, see Fred I. Greenstein, "Can Personality and Politics Be Studied Systematically," *Political Psychology* 13 (1992): 105–28, and the sources cited therein.

6. *Public Papers of the Presidents of the United States: Ronald Reagan,*

1981 (Washington, D.C.: U.S. Government Printing Office, 1982), Jan. 29, 1981; *Public Papers of the Presidents of the United States: Ronald Reagan, 1983* (Washington, D.C.: U.S. Government Printing Office, 1984), Mar. 8, 1983. The crowning provocation, in the Soviet view, may have been the inadvertent transmission of a wisecrack Reagan made while warming up for his August 11, 1984, radio broadcast: "My fellow Americans, I am pleased to tell you that I've signed legislation that will outlaw Russia forever. We begin bombing in five minutes." For an account of Reagan's gaffe and the Soviet reaction to it, see Oberdorfer, *The Turn,* 85–86.

7. Garthoff, *Great Transition,* 75.

8. For the evidence on this point, which comes from a KGB defector, see Oberdorfer, *The Turn,* 66–67. Gorbachev's chief foreign policy advisor, Anatoly Chernyaev, whose perspective was that of a member of the Communist Party Central Committee staff in Moscow, denies that this was a general perception on the part of the Soviet leadership. See his comments in chap. 3, above.

9. Garthoff, *Great Transition,* 168.

10. In 1985, before Gorbachev's public persona had become well known in the United States, the University of Chicago's National Opinion Research Corporation found that only 26 percent of a cross-section of Americans held views of the Soviet Union that were even slightly positive. Four years later, the proportion of positive views had soared to 57 percent. Floris W. Wood, ed., *An American Profile—Opinions and Behavior, 1972–1989: Opinion Results on Three Hundred High-Interest Issues Derived from the General Social Survey Conducted by the National Opinion Research Center* (Detroit: Gale Research, 1990), ix–xii, 1, 145, 428. See also Andrew Kohut and Larry Hugick, "Soviets No Longer Seen as Chief Threat to the U.S.," news release, *Gallup Poll News Service,* Apr. 6, 1989.

11. Oberdorfer, *The Turn,* 299.

12. By the end of the Reagan administration the two foreign secretaries had met thirty times. The negotiations between the two foreign ministers on the release from Soviet captivity of American journalist Nicholas S. Daniloff appear to been an important early stimulus to the cordial relations that developed between them. Shultz later testified to the importance of the replacement of Gromyko with Shevardnadze. "The difference was absolutely dramatic. We could have a real conversation, argue, and actually make headway in resolving contentious issues." Shultz, *Turmoil and Triumph,* 744.

13. Bessmertnykh's discussion of the new working arrangements appears in his and George Shultz's interview with National Public Radio correspondent Daniel Schorr, which is reprinted in this volume.

14. Chernyaev's remarks appear in chap. 4, above. The development of positive personal relations on the part of former adversaries also played an important part in the historic meetings in Oslo which led to the Israeli-Palestinian peace accord of 1993. See in particular Jane Corbin, *The Norway Channel: The Secret Talks That Led to the Middle East Peace Accord* (New York: Atlantic Monthly Press, 1994), esp. 138. For a valuable review of litera-

ture bearing on the circumstances under which former adversaries arrive at rapprochements, see Tony Armstrong, *Breaking the Ice: Rapprochement between East and West Germany, the United States and China, and Israel and Egypt* (Washington, D.C.: United States Institute of Peace Press, 1993), 18–29. Armstrong shows that the literature stresses the importance of trust, but it does not focus on the kinds of personal relationships to which the Princeton discussants attested and which Corbin reports as having been important in the 1993 Israeli-Palestinian discussions.

15. Bessmertnykh's statement was made in the final session of the conference and is quoted at greater length in the epigraph to this essay. For Shultz's statement see chap. 4, above.

16. One is reminded of a crucial exception to the basic finding in the classic studies of obedience to authority by the psychologist Stanley Milgram. Milgram's highly unsettling finding was that a substantial proportion of individuals who were placed in a situation that appeared to call for them to inflict pain on others complied with the experimenter's instructions, even though doing so led many of them to experience intense anxiety. But the more the experimental situation was modified so that the experimental subject was in direct personal contact with the ostensible victim, the more likely it was that the subject would reject the experimenter's instructions and refuse to inflict the painful stimulus. Stanley Milgram, *Obedience to Authority: An Experimental View* (New York: Harper and Row, 1974).

17. For an interview-based account of efforts on the part of various Reagan aides to use an economic strategy to undermine the Soviet Union, see Peter Schweizer's somewhat tendentious *Victory: The Reagan Administration's Secret Strategy That Hastened the Collapse of the Soviet Union* (New York: Atlantic Monthly Press, 1994).

18. Robert C. Tucker, "The Dictator and Totalitarianism," *World Politics* 17 (1965): 55–83; idem, *Political Culture and Leadership in Soviet Russia: From Lenin to Gorbachev* (New York: Norton, 1987); and Jerry Hough, "Gorbachev's Consolidation of Power," *Problems of Communism* 36, no. 4 (July-Aug. 1987): 21–43.

19. The quotation is from George Kennan. For its source, see Oberdorfer, *The Turn*, 108. For representative analyses of Gorbachev, see Robert G. Kaiser, *Why Gorbachev Happened* (New York: Simon and Schuster, 1991); Dusko Doder and Louise Branson, *Gorbachev: Heretic in the Kremlin* (New York: Viking Penguin, 1990); Jerry Hough, *Russia and the West: Gorbachev and the Politics of Reform* (New York: Simon and Schuster, 1988); and Stephen White, *Gorbachev in Power* (Cambridge: Cambridge University Press, 1990).

20. A striking example of Gorbachev's creative opportunism was his use in 1987 of the intrusion into Soviet air space of the West German teenager Mathias Rust, who landed a small plane in Red Square, as the occasion to dismiss Defense Minister Sergei Sokolov. Oberdorfer, *The Turn*, 228–31.

21. For an excellent review of the literature on Franklin D. Roosevelt, see the bibliographical essay appended to Patrick J. Maney, *The Roosevelt Pres-*

ence: A Biography of Franklin Delano Roosevelt (New York: Twain, 1992), 225–44. The assertion that FDR must have been "psychoanalyzed by God" was made by an unnamed early associate of his to John Gunther, who reports it in *Roosevelt in Retrospect: A Profile in History* (New York: Harper, 1950), 33. The remarks of Chernyaev and Bessmertnykh appear in chaps. 4 and 6, above.

22. Lou Cannon, *President Ronald Reagan: The Role of a Lifetime* (New York: Simon and Schuster, 1991).

23. *Report of the President's Special Review Board* (Washington, D.C.: President's Special Review Board, 1987), iv–4. Reprinted as John Tower, Edmund Muskie, and Brent Scowcroft, *The Tower Commission Report: The Full Text of the President's Special Review Board* (New York: Bantam Books and Times Books, 1987). On the question of whether further historical evidence will eventually emerge to reveal that Reagan had indirect or secret control of his administration's operations see Fred I. Greenstein, "Ronald Reagan—Another Hidden-Hand Ike?" *P.S.: Political Science and Politics* 23 (Mar. 1990): 7–13.

24. He had played an active part in collective bargaining negotiations as president of the Screen Actors Guild in Hollywood in the 1940s.

25. Bovin's comment is reported in Oberdorfer, *The Turn*, 438. On Reagan's rhetoric, including the genesis and intellectual underpinnings of the "evil empire" speech, see William Ker Muir Jr., *The Bully Pulpit: The Presidential Leadership of Ronald Reagan* (San Francisco: ICS Press, 1992). On whether it made a difference that Reagan's early rhetoric and policies were threatening to the Soviets, one source that is suggestive is Martin Patchen, "Strategies for Eliciting Cooperation from an Adversary," *Journal of Conflict Resolution* 31, no. 1 (Mar. 1987): 164–85, a review of historical and laboratory studies of strategies for arriving at agreement with adversaries. Patchen concludes that "a strategy that begins with firmness—including the threat or use of coercion—in the early stages of a dispute and then switches to conciliation appears generally to be effective in securing cooperation from an opponent" (182).

26. Reagan appears to have been more like members of the general public than like typical members of the policy community in the very limited extent to which his convictions in one area of his belief system constrained those in others. As Oberdorfer notes, he "saw no contradiction between speaking his mind against godless communists in Moscow and seeking to establish a working relationship with them, or between starting a new high-technology program that would negate the very basis of Soviet power and at the same time seeking to persuade Moscow to make large-scale cuts in its nuclear weapons arsenal." Oberdorfer, *The Turn*, 23. For the classic discussion of the lack of constraint in public belief systems, see Philip E. Converse, "The Nature of Belief Systems in Mass Publics," in David Apter, ed., *Ideology and Discontent* (New York: Free Press, 1964), 202–61. For a later discussion, see Robert C. Luskin, "Measuring Political Sophistication," *American Journal of Political Science* 31 (1987): 856–99.

27. Martin Anderson, *Revolution: The Reagan Legacy,* expanded ed. (Stanford, Calif.: Hoover Institution Press, 1990), 283–92.

28. See the following contemporary reports of Bush's skeptical public utterances: David Hoffman, "Bush Doubts Soviets Have Changed: Vice President Disagrees with Reagan's Assessment at Summit," *Washington Post,* June 8, 1988, A9; and David Broder, "Cold War 'Not Over,' Bush Warns: Slackening Buildup Called a Mistake," ibid., June 29, 1988, A14. On the relations of the Bush administration with the Soviet Union see Oberdorfer, *The Turn,* chaps. 8 and 9; and Michael Beschloss and Strobe Talbott, *At the Highest Levels: The Inside History of the End of the Cold War* (Boston: Little, Brown, 1993).

29. Remarks to Communist Party members of the Soviet Foreign Ministry, Apr. 1990, quoted in Oberdorfer, *The Turn,* 436.

30. The aide in question was Rozanne Ridgway. For her comment, and a general account of Shultz's effort to influence Gorbachev's thinking, see Oberdorfer, *The Turn,* 133, 222–24, 288. Chernyaev's comment appears in chap. 4, above. Chernyaev adds that Shultz had greater influence on Gorbachev than did Shevardnadze.

31. Oberdorfer, *The Turn,* 438–39.

32. Max Weber, "Politics as a Vocation," in H. H. Gerth and C. Wright Mills, eds., *From Max Weber: Essays in Sociology* (New York: Oxford University Press), 128. Weber's essay was originally published in 1919.

Chapter Eight: Perception, Misperception, and the End of the Cold War

1. Kathryn Weathersby, "Soviet Aims in Korea and the Origins of the Korean War, 1945–1950: New Evidence from Russian Archives," working paper no. 8, Woodrow Wilson International Center for Scholars, Cold War International History Project, Nov. 1993; idem, "New Findings on the Korean War," *Cold War International History Project Bulletin,* no. 3 (fall 1993): 1, 14–16; and idem, "Korea, 1949–50: To Attack or Not to Attack? Stalin, Kim Il Sung, and the Prelude to War," ibid., no. 5 (spring 1995): 1–9.

2. Some German documents, presumably incriminating ones, have been destroyed, however: Holger Herwig, "Clio Deceived: Patriotic Self-Censorship in Germany after the Great War," *International Security* 12 (fall 1987): 5–44.

3. The classic statement is Kenneth Waltz, *Theory of International Politics* (Reading, Mass.: Addison-Wesley, 1979). The exact meaning of bipolarity is not entirely clear: see, e.g., Harrison Wagner, "What Was Bipolarity?" *International Organization* 47 (winter 1993): 77–106. Furthermore, although these complications are beyond the scope of this paper, I should note that although the Soviet Union was much weaker after World War II than the United States, the United States could not fight a war against the Soviet Union without bases in Europe.

4. I believe that this phrase was coined by Raymond Aron, but I cannot find the source.

5. Milovan Djilas, *Conversations with Stalin*, trans. Michael B. Petrovich (New York: Harcourt, Brace, and World, 1962), 114.

6. The recent literature is well summarized in Bruce Russett, *Grasping the Democratic Peace* (Princeton: Princeton University Press, 1993).

7. For a related argument, see Stanley Hoffmann, "International Systems and International Law," in Klaus Knorr and Sidney Verba, eds., *The International System* (Princeton: Princeton University Press, 1961), 210–15, 223–33.

8. For Bessmertnykh's remarks on removing ideology from foreign policy, see chap. 1, n. 3, above; for Afghanistan, see chap. 5. Sergei Tarasenko disagreed about the Afghanistan decision: see chap. 5. Also in chap. 5, see Anatoly Chernyaev's remarks on the decision.

9. Mikhail Sergeevich Gorbachev, *Perestroika: New Thinking for Our Country and the World* (New York: Harper and Row, 1987), 144–48; and idem, speech to the United Nations, Dec. 7, 1988, *Pravda*, Dec. 8, 1988, 1–2, reprinted and translated in *Current Digest of the Soviet Press* 40, no. 49 (Jan. 4, 1989), 1–7. Ligachev's views are quoted in Bill Keller, "Gorbachev Deputy Criticizes Soviet Policy Trend," *New York Times*, Aug. 7, 1988.

10. Indeed, an understanding of these dynamics may have been crucial not only for Gorbachev and his civilian colleagues but for Soviet military authorities, who, being charged with safeguarding the Soviet Union, had to be convinced that military cuts could decrease rather than increase the chance of war.

11. Waltz, *Theory of International Politics*, 74–77, 127–28.

12. For discussions of motivated biases, see Irving Janis and Leon Mann, *Decision Making* (New York: Free Press, 1977); Richard Cottam, *Foreign Policy Motivation* (Pittsburgh: University of Pittsburgh Press, 1977); Richard Ned Lebow, *Between Peace and War: The Nature of International Crisis* (Baltimore: Johns Hopkins University Press, 1981); Robert Jervis, Richard Ned Lebow, and Janice Stein, *Psychology and Deterrence* (Baltimore: Johns Hopkins University Press, 1985). The later two books see most sources of motivated bias as stemming from domestic politics, but the basic processes are independent of the source of the needs that drive perceptions.

13. See chap. 3, above.

14. Quoted in Don Oberdorfer, *The Turn: From the Cold War to a New Era. The United States and the Soviet Union, 1983–1990* (New York: Poseidon Press, 1991), 299. Two aspects of Reagan's outlook, documented by Keith Shimko in *Images and Arms Control: Perceptions of the Soviet Union in the Reagan Administration* (Ann Arbor: University of Michigan Press, 1991), esp. 142, 217, 236–38, may have facilitated his openness toward the Soviet Union. First, he was much less pessimistic than many of those in his administration. Although he felt that the United States needed to increase its defense capabilities, he neither believed that the desired goals were out of reach nor shared the belief of many hard-liners that negotiation, especially over arms control, would undermine domestic support for his foreign policy. Second—again unlike many other hard-liners—he attributed the Soviet-American rivalry not only to the ambitions of the Soviet Union but also to

mutual suspicions and incompatible security requirements. Thus, he was more open to the possibility of agreements and better relations than one might think from reading some of his strikingly anti-Soviet pronouncements.

15. "Transcript of Press Interview of President at White House," *New York Times*, Mar. 30, 1983.

16. This also can be true within a state as well. For a striking example, see the account by Greenstein and Immerman of the January 19, 1961, meeting between President Eisenhower and President-elect Kennedy in which three of the participants concluded that Eisenhower was recommending American military intervention in Indochina, one concluded that he was recommending *against* intervention, and two concluded that he was making no recommendation but simply stating contingencies. Fred I. Greenstein and Richard H. Immerman, "What Did Eisenhower Tell Kennedy about Indochina? The Politics of Misperception," *Journal of American History* 79 (Sept. 1992): 568–87.

17. For an account of debates within a nation's foreign policy establishment about what the nation's self-image should be, see Aaron Friedberg, *The Weary Titan: Britain and the Experience of Relative Decline, 1895–1905* (Princeton: Princeton University Press, 1988).

18. Work in marriage counseling has developed protocols to see how accurately each spouse is able to estimate how the other sees him or her. R. D. Laing, H. Phillipson, and A. R. Lee, *Interpersonal Perception: A Theory and a Method of Research* (New York: Harper and Row, 1976).

19. The classic study is Thomas Kuhn, *The Structure of Scientific Revolutions* (Chicago: University of Chicago Press, 1962).

20. James Wirtz, *The Tet Offensive* (Ithaca: Cornell University Press, 1991).

21. Richard Neustadt, *Alliance Politics* (New York: Columbia University Press, 1970).

22. For example, see Greenstein and Immerman, "What Did Eisenhower Tell Kennedy about Indochina?"

23. This conclusion rests on preliminary research I have done on parallel reports of conversations between European diplomats.

24. Much scholarship has similarly moved toward a more orthodox interpretation of the Cold War.

25. Wesley Wark, *The Ultimate Enemy: British Intelligence and Nazi Germany, 1933–1939* (Ithaca: Cornell University Press, 1985).

26. Sarah Mendelson stresses the importance of domestic politics, Douglas Blum sees beliefs as more autonomous, and Jeff Checkel takes a position in-between: Mendelson, "Internal Battles and External Wars: Politics, Learning, and the Soviet Withdrawal from Afghanistan," *World Politics* 45 (Apr. 1993): 327–60; Blum, "The Soviet Foreign Policy Belief System: Beliefs, Politics, and Foreign Policy Outcomes," *International Studies Quarterly* 27 (Dec. 1993): 373–94; Checkel, "Ideas, Institutions, and the Gorbachev Foreign Policy Revolution," *World Politics* 45 (Jan. 1993): 271–300.

27. For discussion of how the Soviets conceptualized some of these questions, see William Wohlforth, *The Elusive Balance: Power and Perceptions during the Cold War* (Ithaca: Cornell University Press, 1993).

28. See chap. 2, above. Also see Wohlforth, *Elusive Balance*, 2–6. The American estimates of future Soviet military strength can be found in National Intelligence Estimate 11-3/8-82, excerpted in app. B, below.

29. The American perceptions at the time are analyzed in Alexander George, "American Policy-Making and the North Korean Aggression," *World Politics* 7 (Jan. 1955): 209–32; see the sources in n. 1 therein for what is revealed by recently released Soviet documents.

30. The Europeans feared this inference as much as the Americans.

31. The general question of the causes of moods of optimism and pessimism is a fascinating one that I cannot even begin to answer.

32. Henry Kissinger, *The Necessity for Choice* (New York: Harper and Brothers, 1960), 1.

33. Jack Snyder, *Myths of Empire* (Ithaca: Cornell University Press, 1991), chap. 6.

34. Eisenhower anticipated this response, however, if only in passing: see his remarks quoted in Marc Trachtenberg, *History and Strategy* (Princeton: Princeton University Press, 1991), 203.

35. I believe that this is the case despite the fact that covert action and invasion plans were well under way: James Herschberg, "Before 'the Missiles of October': Did Kennedy Plan a Military Strike against Cuba?" *Diplomatic History* 14 (spring 1990): 163–98.

36. Quoted in Richard Nixon, *Six Crises* (Garden City, N.Y.: Doubleday, 1962), 62.

37. Quoted in John Spanier, *The Truman-MacArthur Controversy and the Korean War* (New York: Norton, 1965), 97.

38. Eyre Crowe, "Memorandum on the Present State of British Relations with France and Germany," in G. P. Gooch and Harold Temperley, eds., *British Documents on the Origins of the War, 1898–1914*, vol. 3, *The Testing of the Entente, 1904–6* (London: His Majesty's Stationery Office, 1928), 397–431.

39. Patrice Higonnet, "The Origins of the Seven Years' War," *Journal of Modern History* 40 (Mar. 1968): 57–90.

40. Wirtz, *Tet Offensive*. Contrary to common belief, the North Vietnamese did not launch their attack in the hope of altering American public opinion, which is in fact what happened.

41. The failure of the North to win the kind of victory that it had sought is perceptively discussed in Timothy Lomperis, *The War Everyone Lost — and Won: America's Intervention in Vietnam's Twin Struggles* (Baton Rouge: Louisiana State University Press, 1984).

42. Oberdorfer, *The Turn*, 284.

43. This sort of error is quite common: see Robert Jervis, *Perception and Misperception in International Politics* (Princeton: Princeton University Press, 1976), chaps. 8–9.

44. Quoted in Oberdorfer, *The Turn*, 284.

45. See chap. 4, above.

46. See chap. 3, above; the report of the Politburo can be found in app. B of this volume. Similarly, Pavel Palazchenko noted that "in some U.S. statements there was an implication that the plane was shot down knowingly; that they knew that it was a passenger plane, not just deliberately but knowingly. I don't think that there was enough information for the United States to make that statement or even a statement with that implication. And that further aggravated the overall mutual suspicion" (see chap. 3, above).

47. Shultz made this observation in his opening remarks. See also George P. Shultz, *Turmoil and Triumph: My Years as Secretary of State* (New York: Scribner's, 1993), 573. For further commentary on the effects of simultaneous translation, see chap. 1, above.

48. See chaps. 2, 3, and 4, above; Oberdorfer, *The Turn*, 223–24.

49. See chap. 3, above.

50. See chap. 2, above.

51. See chap. 3, above.

52. See chap. 4, above.

Chapter Nine: The Transition in U.S.-Soviet Relations, 1985–1990

I am grateful to the Carnegie Corporation of New York and the MacArthur Foundation for support of some of the research on which this paper is based; and to the Center for Foreign Policy Development, Brown University, for the opportunity to participate in its collaborative project on mutual security with the Institute of the United States and Canada (Moscow), and for permission to draw on the paper that I wrote for that project (see n. 14, below). An earlier version of this chapter appeared under the same title in *Political Psychology* 12, no. 3 (Sept. 1991): 469–86; reprinted here by courtesy of Blackwell Publishers. For useful comments on an earlier draft, I thank Steve Weber.

1. Helpful discussions of Sovietology and the Soviet collapse include Robert C. Tucker, "Sovietology and Russian History," *Post-Soviet Affairs* 8 (July–Sept. 1992): 175–96; George Breslauer, "In Defense of Sovietology," ibid., 8 (July–Sept. 1992): 197–238; Thomas Remington, "Sovietology and System Stability," ibid., 8 (July–Sept. 1992): 239–69; and Peter Rutland, "Sovietology: Notes for a Post-Mortem," *National Interest* 31 (spring 1993): 109–23.

2. For an insightful analysis of Gorbachev as an "event-making" person which deals in a sophisticated and explicit manner with relevant theoretical and methodological issues, see the in-depth study by George W. Breslauer, "Evaluating Gorbachev as Leader," *Soviet Economy* 5, no. 4 (1989): 299–340. Breslauer's analysis focuses mostly on Gorbachev's performance in dealing with domestic issues and deals only very briefly with his initiatives in foreign policy. Janice Gross Stein, "Political Learning by Doing: Gorbachev as Uncommitted Thinker and Motivated Learner," *International Organization*

48, no. 2 (spring 1994): 155–83, is a thoughtful analysis of Gorbachev's individual learning. On the influence of Gorbachev's leadership style on Soviet diplomacy, see James M. Goldgeier, *Leadership Style and Soviet Foreign Policy: Stalin, Khrushchev, Brezhnev, Gorbachev* (Baltimore: Johns Hopkins University Press, 1994).

3. The most influential statement of structural-realist theory is Kenneth N. Waltz, *Theory of International Politics* (Reading, Mass.: Addison-Wesley, 1979). For critical appraisals and Waltz's reply, see Robert O. Keohane, ed., *Neorealism and Its Critics* (New York: Columbia University Press, 1986).

4. In recent years a number of political scientists have addressed the role of learning in foreign policy. George Breslauer and Philip Tetlock organized and directed a major collaborative project on U.S. and Soviet foreign policy learning under the auspices of the National Academy of Science's Committee on the Contributions of the Behavioral and Social Sciences for Prevention of Nuclear War. See Breslauer and Tetlock, eds., *Learning in U.S. and Soviet Foreign Policy* (Boulder, Colo.: Westview Press, 1991). Cf. also Andrew O. Bennett, "Theories of Individual, Organizational, and Government Learning and the Rise and Fall of Soviet Military Interventionism 1973–1983" (Ph.D. diss., Kennedy School of Government, Harvard University, Feb. 1990); Joseph S. Nye Jr., "Nuclear Learning and U.S. Soviet Security Regimes," *International Organization* 41, no. 3 (summer 1987): 371–402. For a critical overview, see Jack S. Levy, "Learning and Foreign Policy: Sweeping a Conceptual Minefield," ibid., 48, no. 2 (spring 1994): 279–312.

5. For a convincing argument that the nature and dynamics of the international system may have an important causal impact on the domestic structure and politics of individual states, see Peter Gourevitch, "The Second Image Reversed: The International Sources of Domestic Politics," *International Organization* 32, no. 4 (autumn 1978): 881–911. However, it should be noted that Gourevitch also acknowledges that domestic structure and politics is a variable that can influence foreign policy. Particularly relevant to the present article are his reference to the "interpenetrated quality of international relations and domestic politics," and his observations that "international politics and domestic structures affect each other" and that they are parts of an "interactive system" (911, 882, 900). Gourevitch's reference to the "second image" is taken from an important distinction that was made among several theoretical orientations to the study of international relations by Kenneth Waltz many years ago in *Man, the State, and War* (New York: Columbia University Press, 1954). See also Robert Jervis's consideration of second and third image causes of the transformation of U.S.-Soviet relations in chap. 8 of this volume.

6. As Foreign Minister Bessmertnykh noted at the Princeton Conference, "when you were talking about SDI and arms control, the economic element of the necessity to go down with the reductions was sometimes, in my view, the number one preoccupation of Gorbachev." See chap. 2, above.

7. See John Herz, "Idealist Internationalism and the Security Dilemma," *World Politics* 2 (Jan. 1950): 157–80; and the more recent analyses by Robert

Jervis in *Perception and Misperception in International Politics* (Princeton: Princeton University Press, 1976); idem, "Cooperation under the Security Dilemma," *World Politics* 30, no. 2 (1978): 167–214; and idem, "Security Regimes," *International Organization* 36, no. 2 (1982): 357–78.

8. The following paragraphs and the next section, "The Impact of Ideology," draw on my "Ideology and International Relations: A Conceptual Analysis," *Jerusalem Journal of International Relations* 9, no. 1 (1987): 1–21.

9. For a well-documented study of how the "bad-faith" model of an opponent operates to bias the policy maker's processing of information, see the classic study by Ole R. Holsti, "Cognitive Dynamics and Images of the Enemy: Dulles and Russia," in F. I. Finlay, O. R. Holsti, and R. R. Fagen, *Enemies in Politics* (Chicago: Rand McNally, 1967).

10. Cited by Jervis, "Cooperation under the Security Dilemma," 169.

11. The lessons drawn by Soviet leaders and the changes of belief that are ascribed to them in the remainder of this chapter were inferred from Soviet writings and conversations with Soviet academicians, and they were checked with similar analyses of Gorbachev's New Thinking prepared by many Western specialists on the Soviet Union. See, especially, Coit D. Blacker, *Hostage to Revolution: Gorbachev and Soviet Security Policy, 1985–1991* (New York: Council on Foreign Relations, 1993); and Stephen Kull, *Burying Lenin: The Revolution in Soviet Ideology and Foreign Policy* (Boulder, Colo.: Westview Press, 1992). They correspond with the picture portrayed by the Soviet participants at the Princeton Conference and by memoirs and other recently published sources.

12. Gorbachev outlined his new approach to international relations most comprehensively in his speech to the UN General Assembly on December 7, 1988. See *Current Digest of the Soviet Press* 40, no. 49 (Jan. 1989): 1–7.

13. See, e.g., A. L. George, "U.S.-Soviet Efforts to Cooperate in Crisis Management and Crisis Avoidance," in A. L. George, P. J. Farley, and A. Dallin, eds., *U.S.-Soviet Security Cooperation: Achievements, Failures, Prospects* (New York: Oxford University Press, 1988), 581–600.

14. This section draws on my chapter "U.S.-Soviet Relations: Evolution and Prospects," in Richard Smoke and Andrei Kortunov, eds., *Mutual Security: A New Approach to Soviet-American Relations* (New York: St. Martin's Press, 1990). That book is the product of a collaborative U.S.-Soviet project sponsored by the Center for Foreign Policy Development, Brown University, and the Institute of the United States and Canada (Moscow). The volume articulates an important and timely new conceptualization of mutual security and a strategy for attaining it.

15. Blacker, *Hostage to Revolution*, documents the connection between economic constraints and change in security policy. See also the comments of Alexander Bessmertnykh and Anatoly Chernyaev in chap. 2, above.

16. For a discussion of Brezhnev's interpretation of the détente of the early 1970s and Soviet expectations of its benefits, see Coit D. Blacker, "The Kremlin and Détente: Soviet Conceptions, Hopes, and Expectations," in A. L. George, ed., *Managing the U.S.-Soviet Rivalry* (Boulder, Colo.: Westview Press, 1983), 119–38. On the Soviets' re-evaluation of the costs and

benefits of superpower "equality," see Blacker, *Hostage to Revolution;* and William Wohlforth, *The Elusive Balance: Power and Perceptions during the Cold War* (Ithaca: Cornell University Press, 1993), chap. 9.

17. *Public Papers of the Presidents of the United States: George Bush, 1989* (Washington, D.C.: U.S. Government Printing Office, 1990), 1:541.

18. For a fuller discussion see George, Farley, and Dallin, *U.S.-Soviet Security Cooperation.*

Chapter Ten: Scholars, Policy Makers, and the End of the Cold War

I am grateful to Richard Anderson for stressing the convergence between the actor's and observer's dilemmas in comments on another paper. My thanks to Alexander George, Fred Greenstein, and Jonathan Mercer for comments on a draft of this chapter.

1. Alexander L. George, *Bridging the Gap: Theory and Practice in Foreign Policy* (Washington, D.C.: United States Institute of Peace, 1993), xviii.

2. Christopher Achen and Duncan Snidal make the point in reference to testing rational-choice theories of deterrence: "The econometric theory of errors in variables demonstrated long ago that, to avoid serious inferential blunders, noisy data like self-reports of international decision-makers must be discounted well beyond what common sense might suggest." Achen and Snidal, "Rational Deterrence Theory and Comparative Case Studies," *World Politics* 41, no. 2 (Jan. 1989): 166 n. 74.

3. Reports in the Soviet and Russian press detail Gorbachev's eager consumption of KGB materials. See John Dunlop, *The Rise of Russia and the Fall of the Soviet Empire* (Princeton: Princeton University Press, 1993).

4. Michael R. Beschloss and Strobe Talbott, *At the Highest Levels* (New York: Little, Brown, 1993), 132.

5. See Robert Jervis, *The Logic of Images in International Relations* (New York: Columbia University Press, 1989), for a general analysis of the problems of signaling when actors face incentives to misrepresent.

6. The notion of "costly signals" is implicit in ibid.; and in Thomas Schelling, *The Strategy of Conflict* (Cambridge: Harvard University Press, 1960). It has received more explicit, formal treatment by game theorists in recent years. See James Morrow, *Game Theory for Political Scientists* (Princeton: Princeton University Press, 1994), for a general analysis. For development of the theory and its application to the problems of deterrence and war, see James D. Fearon, "Threats to Use Force: Costly Signals and Bargaining in International Crises" (Ph.D. diss., University of California, Berkeley, 1992); and idem, "Rationalist Explanations for War," *International Organization* 49, no. 3 (summer 1995): 379–414.

7. For criticisms of the INF Treaty on these grounds, see Jeffrey Record and David B. Rivkin Jr., "Defending Post-INF Europe," *Foreign Affairs* 66, no. 4 (spring 1988): 735–54; William Odom, "Soviet Military Doctrine," ibid., 67, no. 2 (winter 1988–89): 114–34.

8. As ambassador Matlock observed: "If you explained to him [Reagan] that Gorbachev probably had a political problem at home limiting his ability

to do certain things, and that if we could move just this way, we might be able to help him overcome that problem, he would often find this very convincing" (chap. 1, above).

9. See Jervis, Logic of Images, chap. 5, for an analysis of many other incentives for ambiguity in signaling.

10. This is illustrated by Anatoly Chernyaev's account of the November 1988 Politburo meeting at which Gorbachev succeeded in having his unilateral arms reduction initiative adopted. Gorbachev cited economic reform as the main reason for such a dramatic move, but he also deployed the following argument: "We spend two and a half times more than the U.S. on military needs, and not a single country in the world, not to mention the 'less developed' ones we shower with weapons without receiving anything in return, spends more per capita for those purposes than we do. If we bring glasnost to this fact, then our entire New Thinking and our whole new foreign policy will go to the devil." Anatoly Chernyaev, Shest' let s Gorbachevym: Po dnevnikovym zapisiam (Moscow: Progress, 1993), 255. All translations in this chapter are mine unless otherwise noted.

11. An effort to tame this complex subject is Robert D. Putnam, "Diplomacy and Domestic Politics: The Logic of Two-Level Games," International Organization 42, no. 3 (summer 1988): 427–60.

12. Soviet arms negotiators even bragged to their American counterparts about the advantage that this putative information asymmetry conferred upon them. See Leslie H. Gelb, "Keeping an Eye on the Russians," New York Times Magazine, Nov. 29, 1981. Was this a vodka-induced slip or a calculated gambit?

13. Fearon, "Threats to Use Force," utilizes the assumption of unidirectional incentives to misrepresent, though he recognizes the cross-cutting nature of incentives in the real world. In deterrence crises, the subject of Fearon's study, the nature of incentives is much more tractable than in less well defined diplomatic interactions, such as the end of the Cold War.

14. James March, "The Technology of Foolishness," in Decisions and Organizations (New York: Blackwell, 1988), 56.

15. George W. Downs, "The Lessons of Disengagement," in Ariel E. Levite, Bruce W. Jentleson, and Larry Berman, eds., Foreign Military Intervention: The Dynamics of Protracted Conflict (New York: Columbia University Press, 1992).

16. As Rozanne Ridgway noted, "the argument between the hard-liners, or whoever they thought they were, and those who wished to pursue the course the president had chosen never was resolved" (chap. 5, above). Of course, the hard-liners had a different perception of what course the president had chosen.

17. Further discussion and citations may be found in William Wohlforth, The Elusive Balance: Power and Perceptions during the Cold War (Ithaca: Cornell University Press, 1993), chap. 1; and Aaron Friedberg, The Weary Titan: Britain and the Experience of Relative Decline, 1895–1905 (Princeton: Princeton University Press, 1987), chap. 1.

18. Predictive efforts by military intelligence agencies support this contention. Models that distinguish material from nonmaterial sources of victory show that the latter outweigh the former in many instances, sometimes by several orders of magnitude. The German Wehrmacht in World War II is a dramatic example. See Trevor N. Dupuy, *Numbers, Predictions, and War* (Fairfax, Va.: Nova, 1984); specific numbers are included in Sandia National Laboratory, "A Plan for Expanding the Quantified Judgement Model" (n.d.), File 702.2, which I consulted courtesy of Larry Brandt, Lawrence Livermore National Laboratory. Interviews with analysts at Sandia and Lawrence Livermore National Laboratories confirm that most members of the war-modeling and battle-modeling community view battle as inherently difficult to predict reliably. They view their models as tools for identifying trends and generating insights about weapons and doctrines, rather than for prediction.

19. For a fuller analysis, see Richard Herrmann, "Policy-Relevant Theory and the Challenge of Diagnosis: The End of the Cold War as Case Study," *Political Psychology* 15, no. 2 (Mar. 1994): 111–42.

20. A recent example is Judith Goldstein and Robert Keohane, eds., *Ideas and Foreign Policy: Beliefs, Institutions, and Political Change* (Ithaca: Cornell University Press, 1993). See also Robert Keohane, *International Institutions and State Power, Essays in International Relations Theory* (Boulder, Colo.: Westview Press, 1989), chap. 7.

21. See Chernyaev, *Shest' let s Gorbachevym*; Georgiy M. Kornienko and Sergei F. Akhromeev, *Glazami marshala i diplomata: Kriticheskii vzgliad na vneshniuiu politiku SSSR do i posle 1985 goda* (Moscow: Mezhdunarodnye Otnosheniia, 1992); Yegor Ligachev, *Inside Gorbachev's Kremlin*, trans. Catherine A. Fitzpatrick, Michele A. Berdy, and Dorbochna Dyrcz-Freeman (New York: Pantheon, 1993); N. I. Ryzhkov, *Perestroika: Istoriia predatel'stv* (Moscow: Novosti, 1993); Georgiy Arbatov, *The System: An Insider's Life in Soviet Politics* (New York: Random House, 1993); and Valery Boldin, *Ten Years That Shook the World: The Gorbachev Era as Witnessed by His Chief of Staff*, trans. Evelyn Rossiter (New York: Basic Books, 1994).

22. See also Don Oberdorfer, *The Turn: From the Cold War to a New Era. The United States and the Soviet Union, 1983–1990* (New York: Poseidon Press, 1991); and Lou Cannon, *President Reagan: The Role of a Lifetime* (New York: Simon and Schuster, 1991).

23. Robert Jervis, "Systems and Interactions Effects," in Jack Snyder and Robert Jervis, eds., *Coping with Complexity* (Boulder, Colo.: Westview Press, 1993), 26, 41.

24. *Pravda*, Oct. 24, 1989.

25. See Chernyaev, *Shest' let s Gorbachevym*, 255–56; and Akhromeev and Kornienko, *Glazami marshala i diplomata*, chaps. 5 and 6.

26. Of course, to characterize these policies as based on miscalculation requires further counterfactual argumentation that other policies could have better served Gorbachev's ends as he saw them. I think the case would not be hard to make, though there would always be room for disagreement.

27. On late-1989 and early-1990 Soviet decision making on Germany,

see Jeffrey Gedmin, *The Hidden Hand: Gorbachev and the Collapse of East Germany* (Washington, D.C.: AEI Press, 1992); Igor Maximychev, "Possible 'Impossibilities,'" *International Affairs*, no. 6 (June 1993): 108–17; Yuly A. Kvitsinskiy, *Vor dem Sturm: Erinnerungen eines Diplomaten* (Berlin: Siedler, 1993); and Horst Teltschik, *329 Tage: Innenansichten der Einigung* (Berlin: Siedler, 1991).

28. As Frank Carlucci put it: "We saw ourselves as behind quantitatively and slipping behind qualitatively" (see chap. 2, above). See also George P. Shultz, *Turmoil and Triumph: My Years as Secretary of State* (New York: Scribner's, 1993), e.g., 711.

29. For a general analysis, see Robert Jervis, *Perception and Misperception in International Politics* (Princeton: Princeton University Press, 1976), chap. 6. See also Ernest R. May, *"Lessons" of the Past: The Use and Misuse of History in American Foreign Policy* (New York: Oxford University Press, 1973); and Richard E. Neustadt and Ernest R. May, *Thinking in Time: The Uses of History for Decision-Makers* (New York: Free Press, 1986). An excellent case study is Yuen Foong Khong, *Analogies at War: Korea, Munich, Dien Bien Phu, and the Vietnam Decisions of 1965* (Princeton: Princeton University Press, 1992).

30. The classic statement of this "covering law" position is Carl G. Hempel, *Aspects of Scientific Explanation and Other Essays in the Philosophy of Science* (New York: Free Press, 1965), esp. chap. 12. This is the position taken in Gary King, Robert Keohane, and Sidney Verba, *Designing Social Inquiry: Scientific Inference in Qualitative Research* (Princeton: Princeton University Press, 1994). For them, phenomena seem complex only because we do not have good theories to explain them (pp. 9–10). For an illuminating discussion of these issues, see David Dessler, "Beyond Correlations: Toward a Causal Theory of War," *International Studies Quarterly* 35 (1991): 337–55.

31. For a helpful review of two decades' experience with the comparative method in political science which presents relatively optimistic conclusions on the "scientific" status of small-*N* research, see David Collier, "The Comparative Method: Two Decades of Change," in Dankwart A. Rustow and Kenneth Paul Erickson, *Comparative Political Dynamics: Global Research Perspectives* (New York: HarperCollins, 1992).

32. See Dessler, "Beyond Correlations"; and Jack S. Levy, "The Causes of War: A Review of Theories and Evidence," in Philip Tetlock et al., *Behavior, Society, and Nuclear War* (New York: Oxford University Press, 1989), vol. 1, for assessments.

33. On enduring rivalries, see Gary Goertz and Paul F. Diehl, "Enduring Rivalries: Theoretical Constructs and Empirical Patterns," *International Studies Quarterly* 37, no. 2 (June 1993): 147–72. George W. Downs, David M. Rocke, and Randolph Siverson, "Arms Races and Cooperation," in Kenneth A. Oye, ed., *Cooperation under Anarchy* (Princeton: Princeton University Press, 1985), documents the rarity of peaceful ends to arms races; see also the sources that Downs, Rocke, and Randolph cite on 119, n. 4. On the

emergence of cooperation in general see Oye, *Cooperation under Anarchy;* and Arthur A. Stein, *Why Nations Cooperate: Circumstances and Choice in International Relations* (Ithaca: Cornell University Press, 1990).

34. For one explication of this view, see Peter J. Katzenstein, "International Relations Theory and the Analysis of Change," in Ernst-Otto Czempiel and James N. Rosenau, eds., *Global Changes and Theoretical Challenges: Approaches to World Politics for the 1990s* (Lexington, Mass.: Heath, 1989).

35. Two essays by Keohane are relevant here: *International Institutions and State Power,* chaps. 1, 2.

36. As David Dessler has observed, positivist philosophers of science from Hempel to Nagel recognized "the inappropriateness of the covering-law model to the explanation of large-scale historical events." Dessler, "Scientific Realism Is Just Positivism Reconstructed" (paper prepared for delivery at annual meeting of International Studies Association, Washington, D.C., Mar. 28–Apr. 1, 1994). Particularly helpful among the sources cited by Dessler is Ernest Nagel's discussion of explaining "aggregative" or "collective" events in *The Structure of Science: Problems in the Logic of Scientific Explanation* (New York: Harcourt, Brace and World, 1961), chap. 15, esp. 568–75.

37. Dessler, "Beyond Correlations," 349.

38. See Alexander L. George, "Case Studies and Theory Development: The Method of Structured, Focused Comparison," in Paul Gordon Lauren, ed., *Diplomacy: New Approaches in History, Theory, and Policy* (New York: Free Press, 1979); and Alexander L. George and Timothy J. McKeown, "Case Studies and Theories of Organizational Decision Making," in *Advances in Information Processing in Organizations* (Santa Barbara: JAI Press, 1985), vol. 2.

Appendix A: Chronology of Soviet-American Relations, 1983–1989

1. Don Oberdorfer, *The Turn: From the Cold War to a New Era. The United States and the Soviet Union, 1983–1990* (New York: Poseidon Press, 1991), 64.

2. Mikhail S. Gorbachev, *Political Report of the CPSU Central Committee to the Twenty-seventh Congress of the Communist Party of the Soviet Union, February 25, 1986* (Moscow: Novosti, 1986).

Appendix B: Selected Declassified Documents

1. These documents were supplied courtesy of Michael Dobbs, Moscow bureau chief of the *Washington Post.* For his reporting on them, see Michael Dobbs, "Secret Memos Trace Kremlin's March to War," *Washington Post,* Nov. 15, 1992; idem, "Politburo Papers Reveal How Soviets Abandoned War," ibid., Nov. 16, 1992. The second and fourth documents were reprinted among a collection published in the Russian historical journal *Voprosy Istorii,* no. 3 (1993): 3–33.

2. Citation: Tsentr khraneniia sovremennoi dokumentatsii [TsKhSD] fond 89; perechen' 14; dok. 31. See *Voprosy Istorii*, no. 3 (1993): 5. The journal has published further documents confirming the impression conveyed by this one that the decision was taken by Brezhnev, Ustinov, Andropov, and Gromyko.

3. TsKhSD, f. 89, perechen' 14, dok. 42; *Voprosy Istorii*, no. 3 (1993): 22–26.

4. Document published in *Rossiyskie Vesti*, Aug. 25, 1992; text reprinted here as translated in *Foreign Broadcast Information Service — Soviet Union* 92–167 (Aug. 26, 1992): 7–10.

Alexander L. George is Professor Emeritus of Political Science at Stanford University. He has written extensively on international crises and crisis management, the theory and practice of deterrence, and decision making in foreign policy. His works include *Deterrence and American Foreign Policy* (with Richard Smoke; 1974), *Presidential Decision Making in Foreign Policy* (1980), and *Bridging the Gap: Theory and Practice in Foreign Policy* (1993).

Fred I. Greenstein is Professor of Politics and Director of the John Foster Dulles Program for the Study of Leadership in International Affairs at the Woodrow Wilson School of Public and International Affairs, Princeton University. He has contributed to the literatures on American politics, political psychology, leadership studies, and the presidency. He is the author of, among other works, *Personality and Politics: Problems of Evidence, Inference, and Conceptualization* (1987), *The Hidden-Hand Presidency: Eisenhower as Leader* (1982), and *How Presidents Test Reality: Decisions on Vietnam, 1954 and 1965* (with John P. Burke; 1989).

Robert Jervis is Adlai E. Stevenson Professor of International Relations at Columbia University. He specializes in security policy, decision-making, and theories of conflict and cooperation. Among his previous books are *The Logic of Images in International Relations* (1970), *Perception and Misperception in International Politics* (1976), and *The Meaning of Nuclear Revolution* (1989). He is co-editor (with Jack Snyder) of *Dominoes and Bandwagons: Strategic Beliefs and Great Power Competition in the Eurasian Rimland* (1991) and *Coping with Complexity in the International System* (1993).

William C. Wohlforth is Assistant Professor of Politics at Princeton University. His interests include international relations theory, the study of foreign policy decision making, and Russian studies. He is the author of *The Elusive Balance: Power and Perceptions during the Cold War* (1993).

Abramson, Jim, 44, 56, 57
Afghanistan: military secrecy on, 83;
revolution in, 127; U.S. consultation
on, 157; withdrawal from, 7, 138,
141–45, 208, 226
Afghanistan invasion (1979), 6–7, 92,
125–47, 253; Bessmertnykh on, 6,
125–30, 222–23; détente and, 204;
Jervis on, 224; military opposition to,
84, 129; SALT II and, 53
Akhromeev, Sergei: Afghanistan invasion and, 84, 85, 127, 129; arms control issue and, 33; Bessmertnykh on,
81, 82, 168; Carlucci and, 79; Chernyaev on, 86, 87; Krasnoyarsk Radar
Station and, 32; Nitze and, 89, 174,
179; Reykjavik Summit and, 5–6, 88,
165, 179; Ridgway on, 89–90, 172;
SDI issue and, 180
Amin, Hafizullah, 127, 128, 137
Andropov, Yuri, 64, 205; advisers of,
149; Afghanistan invasion and, 7,
126, 128, 129, 137; Gromyko and,
128, 131; KAL incident and, 63; on
Reagan administration, 76
Anti–Ballistic Missile Treaty (1972):
Gershwin on, 25, 28; Krasnoyarsk
Radar Station and, 32; nonwithdrawal proposal on, 169; Reykjavik
Summit and, 165, 179; SDI issue and,
36, 41, 45, 48, 56, 168
arms control, 24–59; Carlucci agenda
and, 21; Gorbachev conception of,
15, 166, 276; human rights issue and,
95, 154; Reagan-Gorbachev commitment to, 108, 150–51, 164; security
dilemma and, 246; Soviet civilian-
military relations and, 80–81

Baker, James, 66–67, 158
Beichman, Arnold, 159
Berlin, 52, 233, 250
Bessmertnykh, Alexander Aleksan-

drovich: on Afghanistan invasion, 6,
125–30, 222–23; on Brezhnev Doctrine, 132; on civilian-military relations, 80–82; on Cold War conclusion, 9, 186–87; on decision making,
148–49, 220; on early Reagan years,
14; on Eastern Europe, 239; on economy, 47; on Gorbachev's UN speech,
92, 94, 97; on human interaction,
161–62, 184, 209, 212–13; on KAL
incident, 62, 66–67; on military
buildup, 31–33; on military-to-
military dialogue, 46; on mutual suspicion, 232; on NATO missile deployment, 74; on Politburo, 70; on
Reagan-Gorbachev relationship, 8–9,
106–8, 199; on Reykjavik Summit,
164–65, 170, 180; Ridgway and, 50,
90, 93; on SDI, 6, 24, 48, 58, 59, 168,
180; on Shevardnadze, 118–19; stag-
nant era and, 51
Bovin, Alexander, 149, 215
Brezhnev, Leonid: Afghanistan invasion and, 6–7; Arbatov and, 149;
"correlation of forces" convictions
of, 251, 253; infirmity of, 7, 126, 131,
205; Nixon and, 110, 250, 252, 258,
263; on U.S. anti-Communism, 205
Brezhnev Doctrine, 132
Britain, 176, 280; German relations
with, 232, 235; INF missile deployment and, 75
Bush, George: on East Germany, 263;
Gorbachev and, 88, 158–60, 280; at
Governor's Island, 86, 158; Greenstein on, 216; Moiseev and, 88; on
Soviet Union, 254; Tarasenko on, 19
Bush administration, 103, 136, 158–59,
175, 278

Carlucci, Frank C., III: early negotiations by, 20–21; on "little green
men" speech, 97; on Moscow Sum-